W9-AKT-568

Glenn D. Shean, PhD

Understanding and Treating Schizophrenia
Contemporary Research, Theory, and Practice

Pre-publication
REVIEWS,
COMMENTARIES,
EVALUATIONS . . .

"This book has been well worth the wait. It offers a refreshing blend of academic scholarship with astute clinical insight. Dr. Shean has thoroughly reviewed the literature, providing us with a wealth of information on causes, symptoms, diagnosis, approaches to treatment and understanding, history, family issues, and social concerns. He explores the controversial and dispels myths and misunderstandings, all the while providing clear and convincing evidence supporting and, at times, bringing into question both old and new approaches. This is an essential reference book for anyone who works with persons with schizophrenia. It is enlightening to the friend or family member, and serves as an outstanding supplementary text for students of abnormal psychology."

Robert Smith, PhD
Licensed Clinical Psychologist,
Southwestern Virginia
Mental Health Institute

"Dr. Glenn Shean has delivered an interesting and provocative book about schizophrenia. Dr. Shean never takes the easy way out by merely championing the currently dominating interpretations of schizophrenia. In the chapter on genetics, for example, he conducts an extensive and evenhanded evaluation of the various competing theories concerning the environmental and genetic factors operating in the etiology of schizophrenia. Dr. Shean leaves it to the reader to decide the merits of the various positions. Each chapter is a comprehensive compendium of the research and conceptual frameworks that attempt to make sense of the heterogenous etiological and pathological processes that characterize the phenomenon of schizophrenia. Serious scholars of schizophrenia will make this book an essential part of their library collection."

Thomas A. Skurky, PhD
Licensed Clinical Psychologist;
Professor of Psychology,
Fort Lewis College, Durango, CO

"**D**r. Shean, an experienced and seasoned clinician, has written a comprehensive, thoughtful, and well-organized book about schizophrenia. It presents a balanced perspective that is a refreshing antidote to the exclusively biological perspective currently in vogue. Readers will find themselves quickly engaged. They will appreciate that difficult and complex data is presented in an accessible manner. The chapter describing delusional thinking is particularly lively and fascinating. However, this book's chief accomplishment may be the much-needed redressing of the balance between biological and psychosocial perspectives. The author is a compassionate teacher and practitioner. His insistence that persons suffering from schizophrenia receive their just portion of respect and fair treatment resonates throughout the book. *Understanding and Treating Schizophrenia* is an important addition to the mental health field."

Suzanne Tignor, LCSW
Private Practitioner,
Rock Landing Psychological Group,
Newport News, VA

∞ ∞ ∞

"**I**t is not often that a literature review of a topic like schizophrenia turns out to be as comprehensive and even-handed as this book. With modesty and economy of expression, Shean evaluates studies and conceptualizations of this sprawling subject in a way that separates the wheat from the chaff and, at the same time, critically evaluates the findings. All attempts to understand this 'convenient abstraction' are covered, ranging from hard-edged neuroscience to phenomenology and family therapy. Shean has immersed himself in this field for several decades and his experience shows; the book would make an excellent introduction for undergraduate or postgraduate students. As a clinician, Shean's sympathies clearly lie with the people who have the diagnostic label of schizophrenia applied to them. He admits that we do not know whether the term refers to a single disorder, and if it does, that we do not know what causes it. His concluding chapter is a sober appraisal of life in the community for people with schizophrenia. This book should help guide future policies."

Richard Hallam, PhD
Visiting Professor of Clinical Psychology,
University of Greenwich,
London, United Kingdom

∞ ∞ ∞

"**D**r. Shean presents a good synopsis and review of the complexity of such a complicated and misunderstood illness, an excellent historical picture, and a balanced view of the enormous amount of literature on schizophrenia throughout time. The author illustrates that much is still unknown about the disease and that there is a tremendous need for better treatment and psychosocial care. Hopefully, future doctors, clinicians, social workers, and advocates will be able to work together to obtain increased funding from policymakers for community-based programs and psychosocial services. The 'revolving door' must stop."

Gayle G. Dhyrkopp
Mother of a son with schizophrenia;
Associate Professor,
Delgado Community College,
New Orleans

Understanding and Treating Schizophrenia

Contemporary Research, Theory, and Practice

HAWORTH Marriage and the Family
Terry S. Trepper, PhD
Executive Editor

Couples Therapy, Second Edition by Linda Berg-Cross

Family Therapy and Mental Health: Innovations in Theory and Practice by Malcolm M. MacFarlane

How to Work with Sex Offenders: A Handbook for Criminal Justice, Human Service, and Mental Health Professionals by Rudy Flora

Marital and Sexual Lifestyles in the United States: Attitudes, Behaviors, and Relationships in Social Context by Linda P. Rouse

Psychotherapy with People in the Arts: Nurturing Creativity by Gerald Schoenewolf

Critical Incidents in Marital and Family Therapy: A Practitioner's Guide by David A. Baptiste Jr.

Clinical and Educational Interventions with Fathers edited by Jay Fagan and Alan J. Hawkins

Family Solutions for Substance Abuse: Clinical and Counseling Approaches by Eric E. McCollum and Terry S. Trepper

The Therapist's Notebook for Families: Solution-Oriented Exercises for Working with Parents, Children, and Adolescents by Bob Bertolino and Gary Schultheis

Between Fathers and Sons: Critical Incident Narratives in the Development of Men's Lives by Robert J. Pellegrini and Theodore R. Sarbin

Women's Stories of Divorce at Childbirth: When the Baby Rocks the Cradle by Hilary Hoge

Treating Marital Stress: Support-Based Approaches by Robert P. Rugel

An Introduction to Marriage and Family Therapy by Lorna L. Hecker and Joseph L. Wetchler

Solution-Focused Brief Therapy: Its Effective Use in Agency Settings by Teri Pichot and Yvonne M. Dolan

Becoming a Solution Detective: Identifying Your Client's Strengths in Practical Brief Therapy by John Sharry, Brendan Madden, and Melissa Darmody

Emotional Cutoff: Bowen Family Systems Theory Perspectives edited by Peter Titelman

Welcome Home! An International and Nontraditional Adoption Reader edited by Lita Linzer Schwartz and Florence W. Kaslow

Creativity in Psychotherapy: Reaching New Heights with Individuals, Couples, and Families by David K. Carson and Kent W. Becker

Understanding and Treating Schizophrenia: Contemporary Research, Theory, and Practice by Glenn D. Shean

Family Involvement in Treating Schizophrenia: Models, Essential Skills, and Process by James A. Marley

Transgender Emergence: Therapeutic Guidelines for Working with Gender-Variant People and Their Families by Arlene Istar Lev

Family Treatment of Personality Disorders: Advances in Clinical Practice edited by Malcolm M. MacFarlane

Understanding and Treating Schizophrenia
Contemporary Research, Theory, and Practice

Glenn D. Shean, PhD

The Haworth Clinical Practice Press
An Imprint of The Haworth Press, Inc.
New York • London • Oxford

Published by

The Haworth Clinical Practice Press, an imprint of The Haworth Press, Inc., 10 Alice Street, Binghamton, NY 13904-1580.

PUBLISHER'S NOTE
Identities and circumstances of individuals discussed in this book have been changed to protect confidentiality.

Cover design by Brooke R. Stiles.

Library of Congress Cataloging-in-Publication Data

Shean, Glenn.
    Understanding and treating schizophrenia : contemporary research, theory, and practice / Glenn D. Shean.
        p. cm.
Includes bibliographical references and index.
    ISBN 0-7890-1887-X (alk. paper)—ISBN 0-7890-1888-8 (pbk. : alk. paper)
    1. Schizophrenia. I. Title.
    RC514 .S484 2003
    616.89'82—dc21
                                                                                2002154814

To my mother, Theresa Emily Sehrt-Shean,
without whom who knows what would have become of me.

ABOUT THE AUTHOR

Glenn D. Shean, PhD, has been Professor of Psychology at the College of William & Mary in Williamsburg, Virginia, since 1976. He has worked in a wide range of clinical contexts, conducting research in The Palo Alto Veterans Administration Hospital in California, The Maudsley Hospital in London, England, and numerous state mental hospitals, private inpatient facilities, and outpatient clinical practices. Dr. Shean has published more than fifty articles in professional journals, edited *Perspectives in Abnormal Psychology* and *The Study of Abnormal Behavior,* and authored *Schizophrenia: An Introduction to Research and Theory.*

CONTENTS

Preface xiii

SECTION I: THE DEVELOPMENT, EVOLUTION, EPIDEMIOLOGY, AND SUBSYNDROMES OF SCHIZOPHRENIA 1

Chapter 1. History of the Concept of Schizophrenia 3

The Premodern Period 4
The Nineteenth Century 6
Origins of the Concept of Schizophrenia 8
Emil Kraepelin 8
Adolph Meyer 13
Eugen Bleuler 14
Summary 22

Chapter 2. Evolving Diagnostic Criteria 23

Diagnosing Schizophrenia 23
DSM-I 24
DSM-II 24
Problems with Diagnostic Reliability 26
European Diagnostic Efforts 27
Research Definitions 30
DSM-III 32
DSM-IV 33
Reliability and Validity 36
Summary 37

Chapter 3. Epidemiology, Course, and Outcome 39

Prevalence and Incidence 39
Phases of Schizophrenia 43
Long-Term Outcome 46
Positive and Negative Symptoms 50
Symptoms and Premorbid Predictors of Outcome 52

Schizophrenia and Comorbid Substance Use 52
The Role of Culture in Outcome: The WHO International
    Pilot Study of Schizophrenia (IPSS) 53
Summary 55

Chapter 4. Language, Thought, and Syndromes
of Schizophrenia **57**

Delusions 58
Categories of Symptoms 63
Summary 74

SECTION II: INTEGRATIVE MODELS AND LEVELS
OF ANALYSIS **77**

Chapter 5. Vulnerability-Stress Models **79**

A "Two-Hit" Biological Model of Diathesis Stress 81
Vulnerability 83
Stress 85
Summary 91

Chapter 6. Epistemology, General Systems Theory,
and Schizophrenia **93**

General Systems Theory 95
Summary 96

SECTION III: BIOLOGICAL PERSPECTIVES **99**

Chapter 7. Genetics and Schizophrenia **101**

Genetic Models 101
The Nature of Genetic Influence 103
Concordance Research 104
Basic Genetic Research 116
Summary 119

Chapter 8. Neurobiological Models and Research **123**

Studies of Specific Brain Abnormalities 126
Neurobiological Modular Systems and Clusters
    of Schizophrenia Symptoms 128

Cognitive Dysmetria   130
Modular Disjunction   132
Dysfunctions in Interrelated Systems and Symptom
    Clusters   134
Summary   137

**Chapter 9. Antipsychotic Medications and Neurochemical
Theories   139**

Efficacy of Typical Antipsychotics   140
The Dopamine Hypothesis   142
Atypical Antipsychotics   144
The Hyperdopaminergic Hypothesis and Glutamate   147
Schizophrenia: A Neurotransmitter Imbalance Syndrome?   148
Summary   150

**SECTION IV: COGNITIVE-BEHAVIORAL,
NEUROCOGNITIVE, AND NEURO-
DEVELOPMENTAL RESEARCH   153**

**Chapter 10. Neurocognitive and Neurodevelopmental
Research   155**

Neurocognitive Indicators of Vulnerability   155
Neurodevelopmental Precursors to Clinical Symptoms   158
Therapies for Neurocognitive Deficits   160
Summary   162

**Chapter 11. Cognitive-Behavioral Approaches
and Therapies   165**

Applied Behavioral Analysis   166
The Cognitive-Behavioral Approach   168
Broad-Spectrum Cognitive Therapy   169
Symptom-Focused Cognitive Interventions   173
Social Cognition and Schizophrenia   175
Cognitive-Behavioral Intervention Programs Tailored
    to Symptom Phase   177
Personal Therapy (PT): A Disorder-Relevant Therapy   191
Summary   195

SECTION V: PSYCHODYNAMIC, PHENOMENOLOGICAL, AND FAMILY-BASED THEORIES 197

Chapter 12. Psychodynamic Theories: The Role of Early Experience 199

Background 200
Sullivan's Interpersonal Theory 202
The Kleinian School 205
Margaret Mahler 216
Object Relations and Delusions 218
Robbins' Hierarchical Systems/Psychoanalytical Model 221
Contemporary Psychodynamic Therapies 229
Summary 231

Chapter 13. Phenomenology and Schizophrenia 233

Delusions and the Relationship to the Outer World 236
The Process of Delusion Formation 236
Schizophrenic and Nonschizophrenic Delusions 238
Daseinsanalysis 238
Summary 242

Chapter 14. Schizophrenia and the Family 243

Murray Bowen and the Washington Group 245
Theodore Lidz and the Yale Group 247
Y. O. Alanen and Finnish Family Research 251
The Palo Alto Group—Jackson, Bateson, Haley,
    Weakland, Satir, and Watzlawick 253
Experimental Family Studies—Mishler and Waxler 256
The Rochester Research Group—Wynne and Singer 257
Nonreactive Family Research 260
Summary 263

SECTION VI: LIFE IN THE COMMUNITY 265

Chapter 15. Schizophrenia and Life in the Community 267

Community Support and Recovery 268
Model Programs 271

The Importance of Work   280
The Community Needs of the Severely Mentally Ill   281
Summary   284

Chapter 16. Conclusion   **287**

References   **293**

Index   **329**

Preface

I wrote this book because I care about people who have been diagnosed with schizophrenia. It is an attempt to present a reasonably balanced and critical overview of the research and theoretical perspectives that are most influential at this time. As with any review written on a subject as complex as schizophrenia, only a fraction of the research and theory published on the topic is covered. I apologize to those dedicated scholars and clinicians who were overlooked.

Attempts to explain schizophrenia on the basis of a single level of analysis, whether genetics, biochemistry, brain structure, intrapsychic processes, family relations, or sociocultural influences, inevitably confront a dilemma similar to that faced by the proverbial five blind men who set out to "describe an elephant." Each man described the elephant from the point of view of the particular part he was able to experience from the position he assumed. One attempted to describe the elephant's long nose, another attempted to reach around its tree-trunk-like rear leg, one felt its huge fanlike ears, a fourth stroked its huge flanks, and the fifth stroked its long ivory tusks. All were correct in what they described, but each was able to describe only part of the elephant.

Like the five blind men, researchers often report on very different groups of patients, all diagnosed as schizophrenic. In addition, those with the same diagnosis are often studied during different and unspecified intervals in the course of the disorder(s). Promising results are often not replicated in follow-up studies. The bias in scientific literature toward publishing only significant findings leads us to overlook these inconsistencies and, along with our zeal for a particular point of view, to conclude that we have fully described the elephant. Today researchers who do chromosomal analyses, MRIs and PET scans, and experimental research have the greatest prestige and credibility, but it is unlikely that any one level of focus will be sufficient to describe schizophrenia. In fact, we are not presently sure whether we are looking at a single beast, a group of loosely related creatures, or many different animals.

This book is about the efforts of many dedicated clinicians and clinical researchers who are doing their very best to describe, explain, and more effectively treat schizophrenia. This book is an attempt to summarize what each group involved in the study and treatment of schizophrenia has to say. Some views may be mistaken; others may prove to be correct. One cannot say which ideas will turn out to be most accurate fifty years from now. Some approaches are based on empirical research, others on clinical descriptions and narrative histories. Each may have its place. We do not have any final answers, but over the years we have learned a great deal about schizophrenia.

The book is divided into sections based on theoretical groupings and levels of analysis. Section I is an introductory section that covers history, the evolution of diagnostic criteria, epidemiological studies, and descriptive case examples. Chapter 1 presents the history of the origins of the concept of schizophrenia. The writings of Kraepelin and Bleuler are covered in detail because the ideas of these men have a great deal to do with the controversies about schizophrenia that continue to this day. Chapter 2 traces the changes in diagnostic guidelines that have occurred during the past fifty years and summarizes available epidemiological research. Chapter 3 presents epidemiological, cause, and outcome data. Chapter 4 considers the associated language, thoughts, and syndromes of schizophrenia.

Section II includes summaries of stress-vulnerability and diathesis-stress models and advocates for the adoption of a general systems theory perspective to understanding schizophrenia. Section III provides chapters on genetic, biological, neurochemical, and pharmacological research and theory. Section IV includes chapters on cognitive-behavioral, neurodevelopmental, and neurocognitive models of schizophrenia. Section V includes chapters on psychodynamic and family-based theory and research. Finally, Section VI addresses schizophrenia and the community.

The truth is we do not know what causes schizophrenia or whether the term refers to a single disorder. Readers who are interested in understanding different points of view, and who can accept that there are currently more questions than answers related to this topic, will learn by reading and understanding the material in this book. Those who believe they already know what schizophrenia is and what causes it may not. I hope that reading this book will help motivate some individuals to become involved in the care of and search for improved understanding of our friends, relatives, and neighbors who have or may someday suffer with the symptoms and consequences of this debilitating disorder.

SECTION I:
THE DEVELOPMENT, EVOLUTION, EPIDEMIOLOGY, AND SUBSYNDROMES OF SCHIZOPHRENIA

The four chapters included in this section cover a wide range of topics. Chapter 1 provides a detailed historical account of Kraepelin's development of the concept of schizophrenia and Bleuler's revisions. Chapter 2 traces the different diagnostic definitions and criteria that have been introduced since the first attempt at standardization of American usage in DSM-I. Chapter 3 summarizes a great deal of research on epidemiology, course of symptoms, and outcome of schizophrenia, and Chapter 4 provides extensive illustrations of three syndromal patterns that hold promise for improved descriptions of symptoms. Reading this summary of a large and often confusing body of literature can at times be tedious, but it is a necessary first step if the reader is to understand the basis for the many controversies and opinions described later in the book.

Chapter 1

History of the Concept
of Schizophrenia

A review of the terms used to refer to people who speak strangely or act out of control gives some indication of the level of cultural preoccupation associated with such actions. Common terms that are applied, such as insanity, unsoundness of mind, abnormality, and derangement, have prefixes (in-, un-, ab-, de-) that indicate negative contrasts: not, without, away from, absence of, removal from. Insanity, a legal term, is derived from the Latin *insanitas* which literally means not *(in)* healthy *(sanitas)*.

The colloquial terms that are commonly used to refer to insanity are also revealing. The term *crazy,* for example, is a derivative of the middle English word *crazen* which meant "to break into pieces." The implication is that madness is associated with thought that is broken and derailed (Wrobel, 1990). Other colloquial terms imply derisive meanings, such as bats in the belfry, cracked, unhinged, gone off the rocker, run off the trolley tracks, loose bolts in the head, and nutty as a fruitcake. The diversity of this language suggests that madness is and has been a matter of considerable concern and interest to English speakers for a long time. People do not develop so many descriptors for phenomena that are of marginal interest.

We sometimes hear people speak of someone having a complete "nervous breakdown," a generic term that refers to nearly all serious mental problems. Insanity and mental incompetence are terms that have legal implications. The term *psychosis* is a clinical rather than a legal term that refers to the most serious forms of mental and behavioral disturbances. Psychosis implies something about both the level of seriousness of the mental disturbance and the fact that the disturbance is global, involving cognitive, behavioral, emotional, and interpersonal disturbances. Emotional disturbances may involve a mixture of anxieties and depression or substance abuse, as well as problems with anger and affect modulation. Psychotic individuals fail to meet most criteria for normality: they lack adequate emotional control and capacity for self-direction, and they typically evidence persistent patterns of maladaptive behaviors. In addition, the term psychosis implies that the patient has lost reality contact. That is, there is some form of distur-

3

bance or peculiarity in cognitive processes having to do with how the individual views reality. This aspect of cognition has nothing directly to do with intelligence or objective knowledge. Psychotic patients may be very intelligent or mentally retarded; intelligence and objective knowledge are not necessarily related to loss of reality contact.

Psychotic individuals are by definition no longer in touch with the reality of people and situations around them, or with the reality of who they are, in a way that is believable or "makes sense." Delusions and hallucinations, feelings of being unreal, disorganized speech, bizarre ideas, and tangentiality are examples of the cognitive aspects of psychological functioning that distinguish psychosis from other groupings. Extremes of emotionality and bizarre and eccentric behaviors may also be associated with these cognitive characteristics. Psychotic conditions can result from a wide variety of causes, including infections, vitamin and nutritional deficiencies, head injuries, arsenic or lead poisoning, hyperinsulinism, Alzheimer's disease, the interactions of prescribed medications, and the effects of vulnerabilities and life stresses.

The degree range of disturbance or loss of reality contact in psychosis is quite broad. The majority of acutely disturbed psychotics benefit from an interval of institutionalization, for their protection and the protection of others. Other "subacute" psychotics may not require hospitalization, and many "residual" psychotics who have been discharged as "improved" can function with varying degrees of independence outside of an institution, although they may continue to evidence mild or moderate symptoms.

The term *functional psychosis* implies that the disorder is not currently known to be caused by any lesion in the nervous system or specific biochemical or endocrine disturbances of the body. Functional does not necessarily mean that the disorder is caused by psychological or social factors; it simply means "etiology unknown." The functional psychoses are divided into two broad groups: (1) *affective psychoses* in which the emotional disturbance is primary and the cognitive disturbance is derivative and (2) *schizophrenic disorders* in which the cognitive disturbance is primary and the emotional and behavioral disturbances appear to be derivative. Affective psychoses include bipolar disorder, with psychotic features, and major depressive disorder, with psychotic features. Functional psychoses characterized by primary cognitive dysfunction are called schizophrenic disorders.

THE PREMODERN PERIOD

Mental disorders have afflicted humanity throughout history. Written accounts of systematic attempts to classify and understand several mental disorders extend back several thousand years. Hippocrates (*ca* 460-377 B.C.) was among the first to provide systematic descriptions of the characteristics of disorders such as mania, melancholia, hysteria, and delirium. He viewed systematic description as a necessary first step in the development of a naturalistic understanding of these problems. Hippocrates believed that brain function was affected by the balance of hypothetical body humors (blood, phlegm, black bile, and yellow bile).

Five hundred years later the Greek physician Galen (129-*ca* 216) integrated Hippocratic medicine with the belief that a spiritual force united mind and body. Galen made observations on the cranial nerves, provided detailed descriptions of disorders such as mania and melancholia, and argued that these disorders were the result of disturbances in the brain. Although similarities exist between ancient and modern descriptions of mania and melancholia, no descriptions of a separate mental disorder that resembles modern definitions of schizophrenia are available prior to the nineteenth century (Gottesman, 1991).

The rational-empiricist orientation of the Greek philosophers was eventually replaced by religious dogma in Western Europe. After the fourth century A.D., when Christianity was established as the official religion of the Roman Empire, the study of the Greek philosophers and attempts at naturalistic understanding of human problems were suppressed. For the next 1,000-plus years superstition and religious doctrine determined how events were to be understood. Fortunately, Islamic philosopher-physicians, such as Avicenna (980-1037), preserved and continued the rationalist traditions of the Greek philosophers. Avicenna helped to create asylums for the mentally disturbed based on humanitarian ideology and rationalist assumptions about physical causes derived from Greek thought (Palha and Esteves, 1997). Some monasteries in Europe also provided shelter and humanitarian care for mentally disturbed individuals during the Middle Ages, but most individuals were simply driven from the towns and left to wander the countryside. There were, however, some exceptions to the neglect of the mentally ill that prevailed in the Middle Ages, such as the colony based in Gheel, Belgium, the asylums in southern Spain that were under Arab influence, and the asylum established in London by Saint Mary of Bethlem in 1247.

With the reintroduction of Greek thought during the early Renaissance in the thirteenth century it became acceptable to attempt to understand the universe through empirical and deductive methods. Gradually, new scientific discoveries and technological advances improved people's lives, and with time even the taboo against the scientific study of the human body and mind was overcome. During the seventeenth and eighteenth centuries attempts at scientific understanding of mental disorders truly took hold. The Copernican revolution, as extended by Harvey with his research on the circulation of blood, Galvani's study of nerve impulses, and Descartes in philosophy, contributed to a climate that was increasingly receptive to naturalistic explanations of mental phenomena. Nevertheless, incarceration, neglect, and punishment were the predominant ways of dealing with madness well into the eighteenth century. Psychotics were generally viewed as subhuman animal-like degenerates, the objects of fear and loathing, well beyond the period of the French Revolution.

Political and social reforms of the eighteenth century coincided with an increased focus on the provision of asylums for the insane and eventually a renewed interest in the classification of mental disorders. Of those who contributed to the acceptance of rational and empirical approaches to classification and understanding of mental disorders during this period, Phillipe Pinel (1745-1826) is among the most prominent. Pinel was instrumental in reintroducing the notion that mental disorders were the result of natural causes, and he provided detailed descriptions of cases of melancholia, manias with and without delirium, and dementia. Pinel attempted to improve the treatment of mental patients and is renowned for his courage in requesting that the feared Robespierre allow him to unchain the insane. He asserted that the insane were not subhuman animals but men and women who were suffering from a combination of moral failures and brain disorders. Pinel emphasized the importance of providing healthy diet, hygienic conditions, kindness, understanding, and moral rehabilitation; advocated the segregation of the insane from other prisoners; and was among the first to use the term *asylum* to refer to places designated to house only the insane.

THE NINETEENTH CENTURY

The first half of the nineteenth century was characterized by an increased emphasis on the role of emotions in human life. This emphasis was in part a reaction against what was perceived to be an overemphasis on the primacy of reason by eighteenth-century philosophers. John Etienne Esquirol (1772-1840) emphasized the dominance of emotions over reason and studied the role of precipitating life events in the origins of symptoms such as hallucinations. Johann Christian August Heinroth (1773-1843) argued that mental disorders were caused by demoralization and emphasized the role of immorality as a cause of emotional distress and conflict.

Pasteur's subsequent discoveries regarding the role of bacteria in illness and infection and Darwin's publication of *On the Origin of Species* profoundly affected mid-nineteenth-century thought and fostered a renewed emphasis on biological explanations. The revolutionary ideas associated with Darwin's theory of evolution and scientific successes in the understanding of infectious diseases provided a foundation for the establishment of asylums as places of medical treatment and placed a renewed emphasis on the importance of the delineation of disorders based on standardized diagnosis.

As understanding of human anatomy increased it became more plausible to assume that genetic inheritance and/or infections of the brain caused mental disorders. The delineation of the asylum as a place of confinement solely for the mentally disturbed and the successes of internal medicine in identifying the causes of several infectious diseases during the nineteenth century contributed to the adoption of policies that madness is a brain-based illness; therefore, only medically trained individuals should be appointed to be asylum directors. These individuals naturally assumed that the first step in developing a scientific understanding of the disorders was to formulate a comprehensive diagnostic system. Pinel's student Esquirol continued his emphasis on precise descriptions of syndromes and symptoms. This descriptive work laid the foundation for attempts by German psychiatrists during the latter half of the nineteenth century to develop a more complete diagnostic system (Spitzer, Williams, and Skodel, 1983).

Wilhelm Griesinger (1817-1868) was an influential German physician who wrote about psychotic mental disorders during the first half of the nineteenth century. He assumed all mental disorders were the result of brain diseases and denied the role of psychological concepts in the treatment or understanding of these disorders. Griesinger moved away from an emphasis on defining separate symptom syndromes and emphasized the unitary nature of all major mental disorders. He maintained that there is only one fundamental disease process. Melancholia, mania, delusional insanity, and dementia were assumed to be successive stages of the same underlying psychotic process. Griesinger argued that differences in symptoms of patients could be attributed to the particular stage of the underlying unitary process of psychotic disintegration that was observed. In 1868 Griesinger reemphasized his belief that all of the "functional" psychoses were expressions of a single disease referred to as *Einheitspsychose*. He grouped persistent psychotic states together with transient psychotic episodes and did not emphasize differences in either course or symptoms as the basis for separating out different disease categories.

Despite Griesinger's dominance during the mid-nineteenth century, many asylum directors continued to strive to develop a diagnostic system that established separate syndromes or categories of psychotic disorders. At the same time neurologists were developing a taxonomy of clinical neurological syndromes based on symptom comparisons.

ORIGINS OF THE CONCEPT OF SCHIZOPHRENIA

In 1852 the Belgian physician Benedict Morel (1809-1873) described the case of a young adolescent boy who had been a cheerful, outgoing individual and good student, but who gradually became melancholy and withdrawn and appeared to progressively lose his cognitive abilities. Morel believed that the deterioration was the result of an arrest in brain development which he attributed to hereditary causes. He considered such cases to be irremediable and named the disorder *demence precoce* to refer to his observations that the degenerative processes began early in life and progressed rapidly to dementia.

Morel wrote in French; however, most French-speaking physicians in the late nineteenth century were influenced by Jean Martin Charcot (1825-1893) and Pierre Janet (1859-1947). Consequently, the French were more interested in hypnosis and the study and classification of hysteria than in psychotic disorders. German psychiatrists were the primary contributors to the development of systems for the classification of psychotic disorders during the latter part of the nineteenth century. Griesinger's view of a unitary psychotic process was challenged as physicians increasingly emphasized the importance of separate symptom syndromes.

Karl Ludwig Kahlbaum (1828-1899) was among the first to study the course of psychoses over time and categorize the symptoms. He published descriptions of two patterns of psychotic symptoms: "hebetic paraphrenia," marked by hallucinations, delusions, and bizarre behavior that began in adolescence and progressed to severe deterioration, and "katatonia," marked by extreme disturbances in motility and dementia. Kahlbaum used the term *catatonia* (katatonia) to describe the characteristics of patients who developed an impairment in "self-will," sat or stood physically immobile, and displayed no reactivity to external stimuli. Hecker independently confirmed Kahlbaum's observations and proposed the diagnostic term *hebephrenia* to replace Kahlbaum's term hebetic paraphrenia. Ewald Hecker also elaborated on Kahlbaum's work and described hebephrenia as a disorder that began in adolescence with a succession of erratic mood states followed by a rapid and irreversible decline in all mental functions. Catatonia and hebephrenia were viewed as separate disorders by both Kahlbaum and Hecker. During the same period Jean Pierre Falret (1794-1870) revived the tradition of separating mania from other psychotic disorders (Kringlen, 1994).

EMIL KRAEPELIN

Emil Kraepelin (1856-1926) studied under the psychologist Wilhelm Wundt at Leipzig and was trained in the methods of experimental psychology. He applied his scientific training in psychology to his work as a diagnostician and systematically recorded hundreds of case observations of patients. Kraepelin believed there were important underlying similarities in the many variations he observed among patients. He synthesized the works of Morel, Kahlbaum, Hecker, and others and organized his own integrative diagnostic system.

In 1896 Kraepelin published the fifth edition of his textbook on psychiatry in which he introduced a new nosological system. Kraepelin broadened Morel's demence precoce, incorporated Griesinger's notions of a predisposing diffuse cerebral pathology, included Kahlbaum's catatonia and Hecker's hebephrenia, added the category dementia paranoides, and concluded that all were actually subtypes of a single disorder he called *dementia praecox*. Kraepelin based his diagnostic grouping on what he believed to be a common course of the symptoms of dementia praecox. He argued that all patients who evidenced symptoms of catatonia, hebephrenia, and dementia paranoides evidenced a common pattern of early deterioration and inexorable mental decline. Kraepelin assumed that catatonia, hebephrenia, and dementia paranoia were the result of a common underlying disease process.

Kraepelin integrated two seemingly opposite viewpoints. He incorporated Griesinger's views on the commonality of psychotic disorders with Kahlbaum's emphasis on the importance of the time course of symptoms and his descriptions of catatonia, hebephrenia, and paranoia hallucinatoria into the unifying concept of dementia praecox. Kraepelin also reintroduced the distinction between dementia praecox and manic-depressive psychosis as variants of "endogenous" psychoses. He used the term *endogenous* to refer to psychoses that were not caused by a demonstrable anatomic lesion, by toxic agents, or by traceable metabolic or hormonal disturbances but, he believed, were biologically caused.

Kraepelin divided Griesinger's unitary psychosis into two major categories: dementia praecox, which resulted in progressive, persistent weakening of mental faculties, and manic-depressive psychosis, an episodic disorder characterized by extremes of melancholia and excitement with normal mental function between episodes. The defining characteristics central to the assumption that dementia praecox was a single disorder with various subtypes were early onset and progressive mental deterioration to dementia.

In the sixth edition of his textbook (1899), Kraepelin provided more detailed descriptions of the three subtypes of dementia praecox: hebephrenic, catatonic, and paranoia (including paranoid dementia and paranoia) and stated that the three clinical forms could occur over time in the same patient. The common underlying symptoms in the clinical picture included thought blocking, negativism, impaired judgment, decreased psychological productivity, motor impairment, lack of energy, and affective disturbance.

Kraepelin was criticized for including paranoia among the clinical types of dementia praecox and later introduced the new grouping *paraphrenia* to classify individuals who evidenced primarily symptoms of either system-atized (i.e., organized) or nonsystematic (i.e., fantastic, expansive) delu-sions.

Kraepelin brought order to psychiatric classification of psychotic disor-ders by first lumping several syndromes together and then by differentiating dementia praecox with poor outcome from manic-depressive illness with a more favorable course. Kraepelin noted that the "disease picture appears so varied that upon superficial observation the fundamental symptoms are not recognized" (Defendorf, 1902, p. 154). Nevertheless, he believed several basic symptoms, such as lack of motivation, pleasure deficit, flat affect, and attentional impairment, tended to co-occur and were signs of an underlying fundamental abnormality (Andreasen, 1997). Kraepelin focused on two broad deficits in his attempts to capture the descriptive unity of the disorder: (1) weakening of the "mainsprings of volition," or what today we refer to as negative symptoms, and (2) the presence of bizarre, disorganized thought and behaviors:

> There are apparently two principal groups of disorders that character-ize the malady. On the one hand we observe a weakening to those emotional activities which permanently form the mainsprings of voli-tion. Mental activity and instinct for occupation become mute. The re-sult of this highly morbid process is emotional dullness, failure of mental activities, loss of mastery over volition, of endeavor, and abil-ity for independent action. The second group of disorders consists in the loss of the inner unity of activities of intellect, emotion, and voli-tion in themselves and among one another. The near connection between thinking and feeling, between deliberation and emotional activity on the one hand, and practical work on the other is more or less lost. Emotions do not correspond to ideas. (Kraepelin, 1919, pp. 74-75)

Kraepelin attempted to provide a logic for his view that dementia praecox represented a single disease and was more than just another grouping of symptoms. He based his argument on three points (Reider, 1974). First, he emphasized that the subtypes of dementia praecox have many symptoms in common, such as hallucinations, impaired judgment, delusions, withdrawal, impulsiveness, shifting attention and interests, disturbances of emotion and volition, and loss of inner unity of activities of intellect, emotion, and voli-tion. Second, he provided a rationale for grouping these subtypes beyond their symptomatic similarities by emphasizing that they begin early in life and lead to progressive decline to a similar "demented" end state. Third,

Kraepelin argued that all forms of dementia praecox must be the result of a single underlying cerebral disease process:

> The nature of the disease process in dementia praecox is not known, but it seems probable, judging from the clinical course, and especially in those cases where there has been rapid deterioration, that there is a definite disease process in the brain, involving cortical neurons. (Kraepelin, 1907, p. 221)

Because Kraepelin put these ideas forth at the same time—common clinical symptoms, common downhill course, and common etiology—the ideas have since been associated with one another and with implicit assumptions about the disorder (Reider, 1974). Embedded in the concept of dementia praecox is the assumption that there is a close correlation between etiology, physiopathology, and symptoms. Kraepelin believed that all patients with similar symptoms and a deteriorating course must suffer from a common underlying cerebral disease process or deficit and eventually have a similar outcome. He drew on the model of internal medicine to justify this assumption:

> Judging from our experience in internal medicine it is a fair assumption that similar disease processes will produce identical symptom pictures, identical anatomy, and an identical etiology. Cases of mental disease originating in the same causes must also present the same symptoms, and the same pathological findings. In accordance with this principle, it follows that a clinical grouping of psychoses must be founded equally upon all three of these factors, to which should be added the experience derived from the observation of the course, outcome, and treatment of the disease. (Kraepelin, 1907, p. 117)

Kraepelin maintained that although the course of dementia praecox varied, even in the most favorable cases the inevitable outcome is a state of severe and permanent mental impairment. He was convinced that premorbid levels of functioning could never be fully recovered in dementia praecox. Kraepelin described the prodromal signs of the disorder as typically beginning gradually with disturbances in sleep and appetite, sensory disturbances, loss of affective control, irritability, withdrawal or bursts of energy, confusion, giddiness, or preoccupation with cosmological beliefs. Hallucinations, especially auditory experiences of abuse, threats, demands, and whispers are common during stages of acute exacerbation along with exaggerated hypochondriacal concerns, suspiciousness, and uncanny sensory and perceptual experiences. He believed these disturbances inevitably progress to a condition evidenced by a kaleidoscope of bizarre delusions and eccentric behaviors. Kraepelin noted that as delusional ideas are formed, signs of affective disturbance diminish and signs of dementia become more prominent. This process of deterioration may be interrupted by unpredictable acute episodes in which outbursts of florid excitement, hallucinations, delusions, and bizarre behaviors may reoccur, intermittent with a return to varying degrees of dementia.

The thread that tied the diverse patterns together, in Kraepelin's view, was that patients progress into dementia. He believed that this "high-grade" state of dementia was evident in loss of the ability to comprehend and develop new ideas, to connect experiences and ideas in such a way that new concepts, coherent conclusions, and rational judgments are possible. He recognized that impairment differed from and was more subtle than other forms of dementia observed in neurological disorders and struggled to provide an adequate description of the essence of this unusual pattern of deterioration.

> Some patients may still achieve a certain standard of rote learning, while others may take days to master a few words or proverbs. They are always, however, completely incapable of comprehending and developing new ideas. Individual components of experience are no longer connected; there is no interaction between them; they lead to no concepts, judgments or conclusions. In spite of the good memory retention, therefore, there is still an inevitable and progressive mental deterioration, the most striking features of which are the patient's inexplicable lack of judgment and the incoherence of all his thinking. (Kraepelin, 1883, pp. 426-427)

Later in his career Kraepelin (1919) referred to the fundamental dysfunction in dementia praecox as the destruction of the "inner harmony of the psychic personality" (p. 221). In later attempts to clarify his thoughts he wrote that the essence of dementia praecox was observable in the destruction of conscious volition which is expressed as a loss of interests, energy, and drive, and in disjointed volitional behaviors, impulsive instinctual activity, and lack of planned reflection or suppression of impulses. Kraepelin concluded that the disease must affect the brain's frontal lobes. He speculated that involvement of the frontal lobes explained the loss of will and inner harmony of psychic functions, and temporal lobe involvement accounted for the peculiar speech and auditory hallucinations common in dementia praecox patients.

In summary, Emil Kraepelin founded the discipline of diagnosis as it is now applied to mental disorders. He believed in the linear unfolding of cause, onset, course, and outcome and argued that dementia praecox patients suffer from a single underlying disease. He believed that the basic underlying disease process was manifested in a unique form of progressive and irreversible dementia. Among the signs that Kraepelin considered central in addition to course were discrepancies between thought and emotion, negativistic and stereotyped behaviors, unconnected ideas, hallucinations, delusions, and general deterioration that was evidenced in the form of a global loss of "will" or "psychic integration." Kraepelin provided detailed case descriptions to clarify the diagnosis of this disorder and its various subtypes. Kraepelin's legacy is a concept of dementia praecox as a progressive brain disorder from which there is no possibility of full recovery and for which psychosocial factors are of minimal etiological concern.

Challenges to Kraepelin's Views

Kraepelin's concept of dementia praecox encompassed a bewildering variety of clinical presentations. In addition, the symptom pictures he described did not always match with the assumption that progressive deterioration must be evidenced by all patients. Some patients with symptoms of dementia praecox evidenced the course described by Kraepelin, but some stabilized, some evidenced periods of recovery between episodes, and others made good recoveries. Diagnostic disputes arose over whether patients who did not deteriorate should be diagnosed with dementia praecox or some other disorder. Kraepelin struggled with this issue and in 1919 narrowed the concept of dementia praecox to exclude both catatonic and paranoid (paraphrenia) cases that started in middle adulthood and did not show a progression to dullness and indifference. In later editions of his textbook Kraepelin referred to these conditions as "bordering on dementia praecox." In addition, his emphasis on dementia and the total absence of any attempt to understand aspects of the disorder in the context of psychosocial influences did not sit well with some professionals who noted the relationships between the content of some symptoms and life history and situational factors.

ADOLPH MEYER

In 1906 Adolph Meyer (1866-1950) introduced the term *psychobiology* to emphasize the point that people are integrated at both mental and neurobiological levels and that activities at one level could affect processes at all other levels. Although trained as an anatomical pathologist, Meyer argued that dementia praecox was not a disease in the traditional sense but a loose grouping of behavioral and psychological reactions to the interaction of biological vulnerabilities and environmental stressors. He argued that the symptoms of the disorder were fully understandable in terms of the patient's constitutional makeup and life experiences and were the result of the accumulation of "faulty habits of reaction." His environmentalist views were compatible with the values of the United States, a "melting pot" of diverse ethnic groups that emphasized the merits of individual initiative and hard work rather than inherited social station.

Meyer believed that the symptoms of dementia praecox were not the result of structural changes in the brain, but were "habit deteriorations which resulted from failed attempts to avoid or cope with life difficulties" (1912, p. 98). Meyer argued that habit deteriorations may be reflected in changes at the neurobiological level, but that does not necessarily mean the neurobiological correlates are primary or causal.

Meyer emphasized the interactive nature of problems, including psychotic disorders, and their development. He emphasized the reactive aspects of symptoms and the role of external environmental factors in shaping the individual's adaptation and placed emphasis on understanding the process of becoming psychotic rather than speculating about the structure of the underlying biological deficits. Meyer's psychobiological views gained wide acceptance in the United States during the early twentieth century and were reflected in the DSM-I, published in 1952.

EUGEN BLEULER

Eugen Bleuler (1857-1939) introduced the term *schizophrenia* in 1911 as an alternative to Kraepelin's concept of dementia praecox. Bleuler was the physician in charge of a clinic in Zurich, Switzerland, for many years. His chief assistant during the early 1900s was psychoanalyst Carl Jung. Jung introduced Bleuler to Freud's writings on dream theory and symptom formation and influenced his thinking about the role of unconscious emotional influences in the formation of symptoms.

Bleuler supported the assumption that schizophrenia had an organic cause but recognized that the psychological aspects of the disorder should be understood and studied. He collaborated with Jung to study the unconscious symbolic aspects of schizophrenic thought. In 1903 Bleuler wrote, "Twenty years of experience has taught me to delineate the disease in the same manner as Kraepelin has done" (p. 113), but "dementia is not always an accompaniment of the disease, nor is the disease always praecox" (p. 120).

Later, in his monograph *Dementia Praecox or the Group of Schizophrenias* published in 1911, Bleuler described his reasons for introducing the alternative term: (1) The term dementia praecox describes the disease but not the person afflicted. (2) The term leads to a misconception that the disease must begin during adolescence and end in a state of dementia. This is not always the case. (3) The proposed substitute name schizophrenia (from the Greek roots *schizo* [split] and *phrenos* [mind]) is descriptive of important characteristics of the disorder and does not imply either early onset or progressive dementia. Bleuler concluded: "As the disease need not progress as far as dementia and does not always appear praecociter [i.e., during puberty or soon after], I prefer the name schizophrenia" (1924, p. 373).

Bleuler also argued that the course of the disorder could not be predicted from the symptoms, since "it may come to a standstill at any stage and many symptoms may clear up very much or altogether; but if it progresses, it leads to dementia of a definite character" (1924, p. 373). He objected in particular to Kraepelin's assumption of a common course of progressive dementia since he observed that many patients showed good recoveries.

Bleuler placed greater emphasis on the relevance of symptom content rather than course and introduced a different set of diagnostic criteria than those described by Kraepelin. He believed that there is more than one type of schizophrenia, but all subtypes share a common unifying characteristic, that is, a split between affect and intellect. Bleuler was ambivalent about whether schizophrenia was a single disorder or a group of disorders but most often used the singular because he believed all schizophrenic patients evidenced "a specific kind of alteration of thinking, feeling, and of the relations with the outer world that occur nowhere else" (1924, p. 373).

Bleuler divided the symptoms of schizophrenia into two broad categories: fundamental and accessory symptoms. He believed that the fundamental symptoms were present in all patients with schizophrenia and were unique to this disorder. The accessory symptoms were not diagnostic and could occur in a variety of different disorders. Bleuler was not always consistent over the years and used different terminology at different times to identify between four and six fundamental symptoms of schizophrenia, depending on how one interprets his writings. The fundamental symptoms of schizophrenia that should be used to definitively diagnose the disorder were associational disturbance, affective disturbance, ambivalence, autism, loss of volition, and attentional disturbance (Andreasen, 1997).

> Certain symptoms of schizophrenia are present in every case and in every period of the illness even though, as with every other disease symptom, they must have attained a certain degree of intensity before they can be recognized with any certainty. . . . Besides the specific permanent or fundamental symptoms, we can find a host of other, more accessory manifestations such as delusions, hallucinations, or catatonic symptoms. As far as we know, the fundamental symptoms are

characteristic of schizophrenia, while the accessory symptoms may also appear in other types of illness. (Bleuler, [1911] 1950, p. 13)

Fundamental Symptoms and the "Simple" Mental Functions

Bleuler believed that the unique and peculiar essence of schizophrenia was due to splitting in what he referred to as the three *simple* mental functions: association, affectivity, and ambivalence. In his view the other simple functions—sensation, perception, orientation, memory, consciousness, and motility—were unaffected in schizophrenia. The only *compound* function uniformly present in schizophrenia was autism, or a split in the person's relation to reality. The three simple functions and autism formed Bleuler's "four As," which he believed were fundamental to schizophrenia.

Among the alterations of simple mental functions that he believed were fundamental symptoms of schizophrenia, Bleuler viewed disturbances ofassociation as especially important. According to Bleuler, what gives schizophrenic thought its peculiar and unique quality is, "the normal associative connections suffer in strength so that the links of association following one another in sequence may lack all relation to one another so that thinking becomes disconnected" (1924, p. 373). Disturbance of associations was the sine qua non of the diagnosis, the most important and fundamental symptom in Bleuler's model. Bleuler understood associational disturbance in the context of the prevailing psychology of the time and introduced the term schizophrenia to emphasize this fundamental and defining feature of the disorder. He believed that a biologically based weakness of the associations allowed affects to dominate over the train of thought, so that individuals could not organize the elements of ideas into meaningful sequences. Wishes, intrusions, and fears rather than logic controlled thought so that speech is confused. Dereistic (fantasy-driven) thinking predominates in schizophrenia, and delusions are formed as the associational disturbance leads to a turning away from reality and reliance on Freud's psychological mechanisms to create fantasies and substitute sources of gratification. Pressured speech, incoherent deteriorated thought, perseveration of ideas, and poverty of thought were all examples of the secondary consequences of the basic underlying disturbance of association that Bleuler believed to be at the core of schizophrenic disturbance.

Bleuler described affective disturbances in schizophrenia as ranging from profound indifference to labile reactions that lack depth. He emphasized the diagnostic importance of signs of a split or discontinuity between emotions and the rest of the patient's mental life. In severe cases Bleuler believed that this splitting process leads patients to become indifferent to all stimulation. In less severe cases affective expressions remain, but they are circumscribed. For example, moodiness and irritability may be exaggerated but all other affects are absent. Even in cases where livelier affects are present, there is an indifference regarding important matters. Bleuler observed that patients often appear indifferent to their vital interests, their own future, and their family, while simple events such as a present may trigger exaggerated euphoria. Absence of the capacity to modulate affects was also characteristic of many schizophrenic patients according to Bleuler. An additional characteristic was what Bleuler referred to as a loss of unity to affects. He described a patient who had murdered her child, which she loved but also hated as the child of her estranged husband. Afterward, she wept in desperation with her eyes and laughed with her mouth. The range of affective disturbances in schizophrenia was so varied that Bleuler could describe only the various manifestations of this disturbance. Lack of emotional rapport or the ability of patients to react appropriately to others' affects, as well as lack of the ability to modulate affects, appear to be the most characteristic aspects of this fundamental schizophrenic disturbance.

Bleuler referred to a third fundamental symptom of schizophrenia as ambivalence. He believed that the schizophrenic disturbance of associations allowed contrasts that otherwise would be mutually exclusive. Ambivalence could be expressed in the affects, such as feelings of love and hatred toward the same person, or the will, in the form of wanting to eat and not to eat. Intellectual ambivalence is expressed in coexisting contradictory beliefs such as "I am a supernatural being" and "I am a person just like you." Finally, ambivalence of will is evident when the patient shows incompatible motives.

Bleuler referred to a fourth complex function as the fundamental symptom of autism, or the tendency of patients to withdraw from contact with reality and to live in a world of fantasy. "This detachment from reality, together with the relative and absolute predominance of the inner life, we term autism" ([1911] 1950, p. 63).

It is difficult to ascertain Bleuler's intent in distinguishing between the four *fundamental* symptoms (disturbances of association, affect, ambivalence, and autism) and his descriptions of three *basic* or *primary* symptoms. In his early writing Bleuler ([1911] 1950) emphasized the diagnostic importance of the four fundamental symptoms. Later Bleuler (1923) switched terminology and focused on the diagnostic importance of primary symptoms (association, affect, and ambivalence) that he believed were direct manifestations of brain disease. Bleuler completely omitted any reference to the fundamental symptom autism in his 1923 textbook.

In Bleuler's opinion, other basic mental functions such as sensation, memory, orientation, and motility were not directly disturbed in schizophrenia. He attributed incorrect and nonsensical responses to questions given by patients to negativism, delusions, and lack of interest or motivation. Perceptions and orientation could also be indirectly falsified by hallucinations and illusions that altered the patients' orientation to their own situation. Bleuler believed that patients could recall their experiences as well as normal persons, but attention may be impaired by schizophrenic tendency toward distraction or emotional complexes. He did not think that patients evidenced impairments in motility, in terms of either strength or coordination. Thus, Bleuler did not view schizophrenia as the direct results of impairments in other basic mental processes such as attention, perception, or motor control.

The Accessory Symptoms

Bleuler believed that *accessory symptoms,* such as delusions and hallucinations, complicate the fundamental symptom picture of schizophrenia, in some cases permanently and in other cases in transient appearances. Hallucinations are more frequent during the acute stage of the disorder and tend to be more rare or fragmentary during chronic or residual phases. Bodily hallucinations tend to be bizarre. Patients may believe that they have been burned to a crisp, their lungs sucked out, their hearts removed, or sexual organs mechanized, or that they have been the victim of countless sexual indecencies. They may experience themselves as controlled by external forces or their thoughts, actions, and feelings influenced by external forces. Bleuler believed that schizophrenic delusions typically begin with delusions of reference in which everything that happens has some direct reference to the patient. He noted that over time patients "transfer themselves into another world, into a separated part of the ego, which is decidedly cut off from reality" (Bleuler, 1923, p. 389). With time most schizophrenic patients adjust themselves to their hallucinations; however, some continue to react with excitement, threats, and violence even after many years. These changes, Bleuler believed, were different from what is observed in true dementia.

Revisions to Bleuler's Views

If, as Bleuler assumed, schizophrenia is caused by brain disorder then the content of a patient's behavior and experience becomes of secondary importance to its form. Symptoms become understood as markers of brain dysfunctions, and the content and context associated with them are of little relevance to understanding their etiology or treatment. For many reasons, concrete facts have more standing in medicine than phenomenology and narrative. Bleuler placed himself at the center of two divergent approaches to the understanding of mental disorders. One, associated with Kraepelin, was widely recognized and influential; the other, of which Freud was the chief proponent, was novel and highly controversial. Bleuler paid tribute to both Freud and Kraepelin in the foreword to his 1911 monograph. He described Kraepelin's delineation of the categories of psychosis as the first and decisive step in the establishment of a scientific psychiatry. At the same time Bleuler applied psychoanalytic insights to the understanding of psychoses. He was initially convinced that unconscious emotional influences could play a role in the formation and content of accessory symptoms, borrowing from Freud's theory to explain how certain wishes and conflicts, particularly powerful affective energies associated with "sexual complexes," could result in the seemingly bizarre accessory symptoms observed in schizophrenic patients. He focused on how unconscious complexes could overpower and distort basic language functions. Bleuler believed that life experiences had a strong influence on both symptomatology and the course of the disorder and believed that the psychoanalytic view of schizophrenic symptoms brought meaning to what had seemed to be a mixture of incomprehensible, bizarre, and deranged behaviors (Stierlin, 1967).

Bleuler's attempts to give credibility to the views of Freud were extremely controversial within the profession. He came under intense criticism for his views and over the years began to backpedal from his espousal of Freud's concepts. Bleuler's initial genius was to formulate a metamodel that could incorporate two seemingly contradictory perspectives, Freud's psychoanalytic theory with Kraepelin's physiological assumptions (Stierlin, 1967). Bleuler adapted Richard Wolfgang Semon's associationistic theory of psychic engrams and their links in order to integrate Freud's psychological concepts with Kraepelin's biological assumptions. According to Semon, associations are formed on the basis our experiences. They are formed into clusters and megaclusters in order to facilitate cognition and cognitive development. Associative clusters with the greatest affective charge are brought to bear in any given situation. If there is a weakness or defect in the switches that control and coordinate clusters of associations and their hierarchical arrangements, there will be a loosening of associations and a loss of goal-directed cognition. Bleuler emphasized the importance of a weakness of the *Schaltspannung* or *Assoziationsspannung,* that is, of the force that keeps the associations organized and coordinated, as the basic underlying defect in schizophrenia. This concept was used by Bleuler to mediate between Kraepelinian assumptions and psychoanalytic constructs (Stierlin, 1967). The key biological weakness in schizophrenia, according to Bleuler, was "a decrease in Shaltspannung, which corresponds to the nature of the illness, namely one which is not functional but which is the direct consequence of a direct chemical or anatomical or molecular brain alteration" (1920, p. 12).

Bleuler believed that loosening of the associations was the underlying cause and allowed for the expression of unconscious complexes that were observed in schizophrenia. In other words, psychological influences could be useful in understanding the nature and content of accessory symptoms, but in Bleuler's view, these influences had nothing to do with the root cause of the disorder. He believed that psychosocial factors played a role only in a secondary manner after the primary biological defect was expressed in associational disturbance:

> [P]sychic experiences—usually of an unpleasant nature—can undoubtedly affect the schizophrenic symptoms. However, it is highly improbable that the disease itself is really produced by such factors. Psychic events and experiences may release the symptoms but not the disease. (1920, pp. 345-346)

From 1913 on, Bleuler attempted to minimize and move away from his earlier endorsements of the usefulness of Freudian psychology. Bleuler deemphasized Freud's contributions and reasserted his basic agreement with Kraepelin. With each edition of his textbook Bleuler became more insistent in his emphasis on the hereditary nature of the disorder and its underlying biological cause.

Bleuler's Legacy

Bleuler attempted to clarify diagnostic practice by identifying those symptoms that were definitive for the diagnosis of schizophrenia. He described four fundamental symptoms that he believed should be the primary criteria for the diagnosis of schizophrenia, stating "once the schizophrenic affective disturbance or the schizophrenic anamolies of association have been proven, the diagnosis is assured" ([1911] 1950, p. 283). However, Bleuler's model of schizophrenia resulted in several unanticipated consequences (Stierlin, 1967). First, the reshuffling of the diagnostic criteria that resulted from the distinction between fundamental and accessory symptoms ran counter to common usage. This change implied that schizophrenia was no longer necessarily limited to individuals who displayed only extreme, bizarre, and highly deviant behaviors. Bleuler believed the fundamental symptoms that were truly diagnostic were often subtle and could be difficult to differentiate from normal behaviors and patterns of thought. In this way he placed schizophrenic disturbance closer to the realm of normal human experience:

Even normal persons, show a number of schizophrenic symptoms when they are emotionally preoccupied, particularly inattentive, or when their attention is concentrated on a single subject. Among these symptoms are peculiar associations, incomplete concepts and ideas, displacements, logical blunders, and stereotypes. ([1911] 1950, p. 253)

Bleuler not only humanized schizophrenia but also widened the concept. He maintained that the latent form of schizophrenia was the most frequent form of the disorder. Paradoxically, Bleuler, who attempted to provide the definitive criteria for the diagnosis of schizophrenia, provided the basis for a significant widening of the concept. By emphasizing the similarities between exaggerated normal and schizophrenic experiences and the ubiquity of latent forms of the disorder, as well as the potential usefulness of psychodynamic understandings, Bleuler contributed to undermining the objective diagnostic approach that he had set out to strengthen. In many ways Bleuler's diagnostic views were more consistent with the Meyerian view that schizophrenia is not a disease in the traditional sense, but a loose grouping of psychological reactions to varying combinations of biological vulnerabilities and psychosocial stressors. Yet Bleuler believed he was clarifying the definition of schizophrenia and providing a set of diagnostic criteria that would improve the reliability of diagnosis.

Several problems followed from Bleuler's redefinition of the diagnostic criteria for the disorder (Reider, 1974). First, it is difficult to precisely define and recognize the fundamental symptoms that he chose to emphasize. Bleuler picked as fundamental symptoms behaviors and experiences that are not always present, are not easily ascertainable when they are present, and are often observable in normals. Second, Bleuler confounded his definition with his assumptions about etiology. He rejected Kraepelin's ideas about progressive deterioration but assumed that some cerebral disease process must ultimately be the criterion for the diagnosis of the illness and, like Kraepelin, believed that he was developing a classification that grouped people suffering from a common etiological agent. Bleuler assumed that the etiological agent or underlying pathophysiological disease process would be present even when the symptoms are in remission. Finally, Bleuler titled his book *Dementia Praecox or the Group of Schizophrenias* and is often credited with the idea that schizophrenia could be several different diseases that share certain phenomenological similarities. This contradicts the view that schizophrenic symptoms correspond to a single common etiology. Bleuler was also inconsistent in his writing about whether schizophrenia is a single disease or a symptom syndrome. For example, in one section at the beginning of his textbook he wrote, "it is apparent that the group includes several diseases" ([1911] 1950, p. 8). Later in another section of the same book

Bleuler wrote that "psychic experiences—usually of an unpleasant nature—can undoubtedly affect the schizophrenic symptoms. However, it is highly improbable that the disease itself is really produced by such factors" ([1911] 1950, p. 345).

Bleuler's diagnostic concepts were widely accepted, especially by American practitioners, in part because of the great influence of Freud's psychoanalytic theory on this side of the Atlantic. Eventually, however, researchers began to recognize that interclinician diagnosis based on Bleuler's fundamental symptoms was not adequately reliable, and alternative diagnostic systems were proposed.

SUMMARY

Kraepelin emphasized the diagnostic importance of early fragmentation of mental functions and of progressive and enduring mental deficits as diagnostic of dementia praecox. Bleuler emphasized the diagnostic importance of the fundamental symptoms, especially looseness of associations. He considered many of the diagnostic signs included in Kraepelin's system to be accessory or transient symptoms that were not unique to or diagnostic of schizophrenia. Bleuler broadened the concept of schizophrenia, in part because his diagnostic symptoms were not easy to reliably observe.

Bleuler's diagnostic concepts fostered a climate in which many practitioners developed idiosyncratic interpretations of the symptoms of schizophrenia. It became increasingly apparent during the following decades that new, more concrete and criterion-driven approaches to diagnosis were needed. An additional impetus was provided by the success of newer pharmacological interventions, introduced since the late 1950s, in treating signs of acute disturbance. The effects of the new neuroleptic medications reinforced the conviction that schizophrenia was a biological syndrome with clear boundaries and could be diagnosed reliably given objective guidelines.

Despite improvements in diagnostic reliability that are associated with recent revisions to the American Psychiatric Association's *Diagnostic and Statistical Manual of Mental Disorders,* Fourth Edition (DSM-IV), it is important to remember that schizophrenia was originally and remains a *provisional construct.* Each definition and redefinition of the disorder changes its boundaries.

Chapter 2

Evolving Diagnostic Criteria

DIAGNOSING SCHIZOPHRENIA

Different descriptions of schizophrenia have been suggested since Bleuler's original proposal. Schizophrenia has been diagnosed using definitions that range from narrow to broad. Different definitions and criteria have a significant impact on estimates of the incidence and prevalence of the diagnosis. Variance in diagnostic practice results from differences between clinicians in their preferred theoretical models. Lack of uniformity of diagnostic criteria and vague wording of descriptions have resulted in a great deal of confusion and inconsistency in the professional and scientific literature. Clinicians and researchers may be talking about quite different populations if they are not using the same diagnostic criteria. Even with uniform criteria the problem of heterogeneity can be significant when one is studying such a broad descriptive syndrome as schizophrenia.

The impact of using different criteria for schizophrenia on diagnostic rates was illustrated by Gottesman and Shields (1972). The authors used 120 case histories of schizophrenic patients as case material to be reviewed by one highly experienced clinician using several different diagnostic systems and by several experienced clinicians of varying diagnostic persuasions. Results indicated an average of eleven different diagnostic opinions assigned to each patient. Using the narrowest interpretation based on Present State Exam criteria only seventeen of the 120 cases were diagnosed as schizophrenics. Application of another widely used system increased the number to fifty-two of the 120 cases. The use of broad diagnostic criteria yielded 4.5 times more schizophrenic diagnoses than the narrowest system. With reference to differences among clinicians, one diagnostician identified thirty-four of 120 cases of schizophrenia, a six-judge consensus panel identified sixty-nine cases, and one clinician identified seventy-nine cases.

Berner, Katschnig, and Lenz (1986) conducted a study in which seven different widely used diagnostic systems were employed to diagnose a sample of 200 first admissions. The authors reported the following results: 121

patients were diagnosed as schizophrenic because they evidenced at least one of Schneider's first-rank symptoms; ninety-one evidenced at least one of Bleuler's fundamental symptoms; eighty met DSM-III criteria for either schizophrenia or schizophreniform disorder; fifty-three were diagnosed on the basis of evidencing two of Bleuler's fundamental symptoms; and twenty-two evidenced at least three of Bleuler's four primary symptoms. Endicott and colleagues (1982, 1986) reported a comparative study of diagnostic systems in which several hundred hospitalized patients were diagnosed according to seven different standardized diagnostic systems. Results indicated that there was an eightfold variation among the systems in the rates of diagnosis of schizophrenia. Efforts to standardize diagnostic practice in the United States formally began with the introduction of the DSM-I.

DSM-I

By the middle of the twentieth century the need for standardization of diagnostic practice in the United States was evident. In response to this need, the American Psychiatric Association published the first official diagnostic manual in 1952. Psychoanalytic theory was dominant among American psychiatrists at that time. Since psychoanalytic theory does not lead to an emphasis on the importance of categorical diagnostic groupings, the description of schizophrenia published in DSM-I was written in very general terms.

The term *schizophrenic reactions* was used in DSM-I to emphasize the assumed role of psychosocial factors in the origins of the disorder. Schizophrenic reactions were listed under the heading Disorders of Psychogenic Origin or Without Clearly Defined Physical Cause or Structural Change in the Brain. *Schizophrenia* was defined as a group of psychotic reactions associated with disturbed relationships to reality and concepts, as well as behavioral, emotional, and intellectual disorders. Tendencies toward withdrawal, social deterioration, and regression were also associated with the diagnosis. Subtypal classifications were based on predominant symptoms and included simple, hebephrenic, catatonic, paranoid, acute undifferentiated, chronic undifferentiated, schizoaffective, childhood, and residual types.

DSM-II

In 1968 the second edition of the American Psychiatric Association's diagnostic manual was published (DSM-II). The goal that guided the formulation of the revision was to rewrite the manual so that the format and content was consistent with the mental disorders section of the International Classification of Diseases (ICD-8) that was approved by the World Health Organization in 1966. A second goal was to reduce the ambiguity of diagnoses. Schizophrenia in DSM-II was listed under the heading Psychoses Not Attributed to Physical Conditions Listed Previously. Despite the stated goal of reducing the ambiguity of diagnosis, the disorder was described in narrative terms without clear inclusion or exclusion criteria. Bleuler's broad conceptualization of schizophrenia continued to dominate diagnostic practice as dictated by the description provided in DSM-II. Schizophrenia was described simply as a group of disorders manifested by disturbances of thought and concept formation that often lead to reality distortions, delusions, and hallucinations. Schizophrenic behaviors were described as tending to be highly deviant and regressive, and the capacity for empathy with others is generally impaired. Subtypal classifications included simple, hebephrenic, catatonic (excited or withdrawn), paranoid, acute, latent, residual, schizoaffective (excited or depressed), chronic undifferentiated, and other types.

Although the DSM-II description was once again written in general terms without specific criteria, the revised definition did provide more descriptive detail than DSM-I. Consistent with the prevailing Bleulerian approach, the definition of schizophrenia included in DSM-II implied that symptoms such as delusions and hallucinations have psychological functions. The manual did attempt to more clearly distinguish between schizophrenia, major affective disorders, and paranoid states. In addition, Bleuler's "latent" subtype and the "other" subtype were added. As was the case with DSM-I, the description provided in DSM-II allowed for considerable variation in the interpretation and application of the diagnosis of schizophrenia. By the 1970s it was evident that the DSM-II description of schizophrenia did not significantly improve reliability of diagnosis.

The widespread use of neuroleptic medications during the 1960s that decreased the intensity of the symptoms of schizophrenia eventually had a profound effect on diagnostic practice. One effect was to undermine the credibility of psychodynamic explanations of schizophrenia and of Bleuler's diagnostic concepts.The declining influence of psychodynamic psychiatrists and the rapidly growing popularity of a biological perspective contributed to growing emphasis on the need to develop more reliable diagnostic systems, since now specific medications appeared to be appropriate for specific disorders. However, reaching a consensus on a more precise definition of schizophrenia proved difficult, since there are no objective criteria on which to base choices.

PROBLEMS WITH DIAGNOSTIC RELIABILITY

The US/UK Diagnostic Project conducted during the 1970s (Cooper et al., 1972) reported that of 250 consecutive admissions American psychiatrists in Brooklyn diagnosed 163 as schizophrenic, compared to eighty-five patients given this diagnosis in the United Kingdom. This research indicated that American psychiatrists diagnosed schizophrenia at approximately four times the rate of their British counterparts (Kendell et al., 1971). It was further demonstrated that the difference in diagnostic rates was a function of differences in the definition of schizophrenia rather than national differences in the incidence of the disorder. Additional applications of diagnostic systems to this cohort of patients indicated that a computer program based largely on Schneider's first-rank symptoms placed fifty-five patients within the schizophrenia category. Application of the Research Diagnostic Criteria identified only twenty-eight patients as schizophrenic, and similar to DSM-III criteria reduced the number of diagnosed schizophrenic patients to nineteen. In other words, the number of patients diagnosed as schizophrenic by American psychiatrists changed from 163 to nineteen between 1970 and 1981, yet the same diagnostic grouping was used to refer to these groups.

It was clear after the results of the US/UK Diagnostic Study were published that research on the causes of schizophrenia could not be based on a concept that was so varied in its application. In addition, the challenges of "antipsychiatrists" such as R. D. Laing (1967) and Thomas Szasz (1957), who argued that mental disorders were metaphorical illnesses that disguise underlying social ills, challenged the validity of psychiatric diagnosis. These critics stimulated a biological countermovement in the discipline that was determined to prove that mental disorders were "real" and could be reliably identified. Advances in neuroscience and technology during the 1970s also allowed for increasingly sophisticated approaches to the study of brain and biochemical abnormalities that promised to identify the underlying brain dysfunctions that cause diagnostic groupings. It was assumed these techniques would be more likely to identify abnormalities in the brains of schizophrenics if the populations studied were more narrowly defined and homogenous. As a consequence, narrower and more specific criteria for the diagnosis of schizophrenia were needed, both to bolster the reliability of diagnosis and to enhance the scientific credibility of the concept of schizophrenia as a single disorder. Clinicians and researchers increasingly turned to definitions of schizophrenia that resembled the original concept proposed by Kraepelin. This led to a corollary decline in the influence of Bleuler.

EUROPEAN DIAGNOSTIC EFFORTS

The inherent difficulties in reaching diagnostic consensus based on DSM-I, DSM-II, or Bleuler's diagnostic criteria were increasingly clear by the middle of the twentieth century. Study after study indicated that different clinicians, and clinicians at different sites, used idiosyncratic definitions of the disorder in arriving at a diagnosis of schizophrenia. European psychiatrists were never as accepting of broad definitions of schizophrenia such as those proposed by Bleuler. As a consequence, several prominent clinicians developed what they thought to be more objective diagnostic systems. The definitions developed by Gabriel Langfeldt (1939) and Kurt Schneider (1959) were among the most influential of these systems and heavily influenced the committee that decided on the new criteria published in the third edition of the *Diagnostic and Statistical Manual* of the American Psychiatric Association (DSM-III), issued in 1980.

Langfeldt's Criteria

Gabriel Langfeldt rejected Bleuler's diagnostic criteria and redefined schizophrenia in a manner that was more consistent with Kraepelin's original ideas. He, like Kraepelin, focused on the importance of a deteriorating course. Langfeldt (1939, 1956) tried to improve on Kraepelin's ideas in order to meet some of Bleuler's original objections. He assumed that the essential characteristics of schizophrenia included poor outcome and a chronic deteriorating course, but Langfeldt also observed that some patients who evidenced symptoms similar to schizophrenia improved rather than deteriorated. Like Kraepelin, Langfeldt concluded that those patients who improved were not "true" schizophrenics. He referred to patients who improved as having "schizophreniform" disorder. This disorder, although similar in symptomatology to schizophrenia, could not be schizophrenia because these patients evidenced a nondeteriorating course. The term *schizophreniform* implies that the symptoms of these patients took the form of schizophrenia but could not be schizophrenia since the patients improved. Thus, embedded in the concept of schizophrenia since the time of Kraepelin and revived by Langfeldt is the assumption that schizophrenic patients do not ever completely recover. The 1980 edition of the *Diagnostic and Statistical Manual* (DSM-III) incorporated this distinction and included the new criterion of six months of continuous symptoms as necessary for the diagnosis of schizophrenia. The purpose of this decision was to define schizophrenia as a chronic disorder.

Langfeldt believed that he was describing a disease and that a one-to-one correlation between symptoms, etiology, and outcome would eventually be found. He set out to identify a group of symptoms that were uniquely associated with chronic deterioration, or "true" schizophrenia. He believed that he had determined the symptoms that were associated with poor outcome and the "basic disorder" or underlying biological defect. Langfeldt (1956) listed the following symptoms as indicators of true schizophrenia:

1. depersonalization,
2. derealization,
3. a break up in the development of personality (apathy, flat affect, and peculiar repetitive behaviors typical of hebephrenic patients),
4. catatonic stupor or excitement, and
5. primary delusions as seen in paranoid patients (incomprehensible, seemingly unmotivated persecutory delusions).

He did not, however, provide clear criteria or descriptions of what he meant by the first two symptoms. Langfeldt attempted to differentiate depersonalization and derealization as observed in schizophrenia from similar processes observed in other conditions in terms of qualitative, experiential differences:

> The terms depersonalization and derealization are here given special meaning. The principal differentiating signs are that the schizophrenic patient has no insight into his own condition and that he always experiences the disturbances as originating outside himself. I cannot here describe in detail the symptoms characteristic of the depersonalization and derealization states, but to be sure of the diagnosis of true schizophrenia it is not enough that the patient talks about being influenced by forces outside himself or that his surroundings are changed; he must also experience these influences and changes. (1960, p. 1050)

Langfeldt's definition of schizophrenia resembled Kraepelin's. He stated that patients with the symptoms of true schizophrenia inevitably had a poor outcome, but he published no data to support his assertions. Research has not supported Langfeldt's assertions regarding the prognostic value of his diagnostic system (Carpenter, Strauss, and Bartko, 1974).

Schneider's First-Rank Symptoms

It had become apparent by the 1950s that Bleuler's system for diagnosing schizophrenia did not lend itself to adequate levels of diagnostic reliability. The influential German psychiatrist Kurt Schneider (1959) set out to provide clear descriptions of what he referred to as the first-rank symptoms of schizophrenia. Although Schneider believed that his system was different and more objective than Bleuler's, he emphasized the importance of the patient's current mental state rather than the course of the disorder. Like Bleuler, Schneider believed that he had identified the first-rank symptoms that were fundamental to the disorder. First-rank symptoms, Schneider argued, had no analogues in normal life. He observed that a fundamental aspect of schizophrenia was an inability to find and maintain the boundaries between self and not-self and a loss of a sense of personal autonomy. These observations led him to identify certain first-rank symptoms that he believed were indicators of the unique characteristics of the schizophrenic loss of autonomy and boundaries.

Schneider was also strongly influenced by the philosopher-psychiatrist Karl Jaspers and his phenomenological approach. As a consequence, he was interested in the subjective experiences of patients. Schneider, who set out to make the diagnosis of schizophrenia more objective, viewed the core of the disorder as present not literally in the first-rank symptoms themselves but in the internal mental states that they indicated. He believed that diagnosis must be based on florid, psychotic, presenting symptoms such as delusions and hallucinations, not on the course of the disorder. Yet he was emphatic in expressing his views that schizophrenia was caused by an as yet unknown physical disease process.

Schneider's system was rapidly accepted in the United States as an alternative and potentially more reliable approach to diagnosing schizophrenia. According to Schneider, schizophrenia should be diagnosed if a patient exhibits any one of the following first-rank symptoms:

1. Voices speak the patient's thoughts aloud.
2. Two or more voices (hallucinated) discuss the patient in the third person.
3. Voices describe the patient's actions as they happen.
4. Bodily sensations are imposed by an external force.
5. Thoughts stop and the patient feels the thoughts are extracted by an external force.
6. Thoughts not "really" the patient's own but are inserted among his or her own.
7. Thoughts are broadcast into the outside world and heard by all.
8. Alien feelings are imposed by an external force.
9. "Volitional" actions are imposed by an external force.
10. Perceptions are delusional and not understandable.

Schneider believed that diagnosis must be based on the presenting situation; therefore, he argued there could be no latent forms of schizophrenia—one either has the symptoms or one does not. His rationale for selecting the first-rank symptoms was that he believed these symptoms have no analogues either in normal psychic life, neurotic problems, or personality disorders. Bleuler focused his concept of schizophrenia on what he believed to be the characteristic formal properties of schizophrenic thought. Schneider made the content of certain types of delusions and hallucinations the cornerstone of his diagnostic system, thus his first-rank symptoms would be accessory symptoms in Bleuler's model.

Schneider believed that in the first-rank symptoms he had discovered those unique characteristics that allowed for the differentiation of schizophrenia from all other disorders. Subsequent research indicated that Schneider's first-rank signs are observed in many patients who would not be considered schizophrenic (Carpenter, Strauss, and Bartko, 1973; Wing and Nixon, 1975). A second problem with Schneider's diagnostic system is that his first-order symptoms involve private experiences that require the willingness of the patient to describe his or her experiences. This obviously complicates the requirement of interobserver agreement that Schneider set out to resolve. Nevertheless, ultimately Schneider exerted a greater influence on revisions of DSM since 1980 than Bleuler did.

RESEARCH DEFINITIONS

Problems with diagnostic reliability and inconsistencies in the definition of schizophrenia prompted several research groups to also develop alternatives to the vague and theory-driven DSM-II criteria. These investigators attempted to develop clear inclusion and exclusion criteria and rating systems to improve interrater reliability. They included rating scales and scoring criteria for a list of explicit symptoms, and the rating systems quickly became the standard for participant selection in research. Unfortunately, different research groups often used different criteria to diagnose schizophrenia.

The Research Diagnostic Criteria (RDC)

In 1972 a St. Louis research group published a set of criteria (Research Diagnostic Criteria, or RDC) for diagnosing major mental disorders (Feighner et al., 1972). In order to diagnose schizophrenia using this system, three sets of criteria A through C must be met. Under the A criteria both of the following were required: (1) a chronic disorder with at least six months of symptoms prior to evaluation without return to premorbid level of psychosocial adjustment and (2) absence of a period of depressive or manic symptoms sufficient to qualify for diagnosis of affective disorder. B criteria included at least one of the following: (1) delusions or hallucinations without significant perplexity or disorientation or (2) verbal production that makes communication difficult or lacks understandable organization. Criteria listed under C included at least three of the following for a diagnosis of "definite" schizophrenia:

1. single,
2. poor premorbid social adjustment or work history,
3. family history of schizophrenia,
4. absence of alcoholism or drug abuse within one year of onset of psychosis, and
5. onset of illness prior to age forty.

The RDC criteria (Spitzer, Endicott, and Robins, 1978) incorporated Kraepelin's assumptions about course, along with several assumptions about age of onset, psychosocial adjustment, family history, and substance use. During the 1970s many researchers used RDC criteria rather than DSM-II-based diagnoses in order to improve diagnostic reliability.

The Flexible Diagnostic System

The flexible system for the diagnosis of schizophrenia developed by Carpenter, Strauss, and Bartko (1973) was among several alternative systems that were introduced as an attempt to improve the reliability of the diagnosis of schizophrenia. The flexible system consisted of a checklist of symptoms previously developed and published as the Present State Exam (PSE) by Wing, Cooper, and Satorius (1974). The PSE uses a semistandardized clinical interview which includes a set of standard questions designed to detect the presence and determine the severity of symptoms. A modified version of the eighth edition of the PSE was included in the International Pilot Study on Schizophrenia conducted by the World Health Organization (Wing, Cooper, and Satorius, 1974). The PSE is convenient for research purposes because scores from the eighth edition on can be entered into a computer algorithm (Wing, Cooper, and Satorius, 1974) that together with a brief etiological questionnaire yields both a diagnosis of schizophrenia and an index of severity.

Research groups at different centers used different objective diagnostic systems during the 1970s. They achieved adequate reliability within diagnostic systems, but comparisons among groups remained problematic.

DSM-III

The DSM-III criteria for schizophrenia were published in 1980 as an attempt to improve reliability by combining the positive aspects of several research-based diagnostic systems. The impetus to develop more specific diagnostic criteria and a more limited definition of schizophrenia was the outgrowth of several factors. First, the U.S./U.K. study (Kendell et al., 1971) indicated that the American concept of schizophrenia was much broader that the European one. This evidence indicated a need to narrow the definition of schizophrenia in the United States. Second, evidence of the effectiveness of various psychoactive medications led to an increased emphasis on the importance of differential diagnosis, particularly between affective disorders and schizophrenia. As a consequence, several important changes were introduced in DSM-III. First, diagnosis was based on specific, operational inclusion and exclusion criteria. In the case of schizophrenia DSM-III adopted a hybrid system that incorporated the RDC criteria which included Bleuler's syndromal diagnostic approach along with specific inclusion criteria based on Schneider's first-rank symptoms. DSM-III included only one of Bleuler's fundamental symptoms in the listing of diagnostic criteria and that was on a conditional basis. In addition, DSM-III criteria added Langfeldt's requirement of six-month symptom duration. This addition was an endorsement of a narrow concept of the disorder as a chronic condition.

One result of the new DSM-III criteria was that several syndromes previously diagnosed as schizophrenia were separated out as different disorders. These disorders were differentiated on the basis of the duration of symptoms and level of deterioration evidenced by the patient and included, at a minimum, delusional paranoid disorder, schizophreniform disorder, brief reactive psychosis, and psychotic disorder not elsewhere specified.

Prior to DSM-III, variance among research applications of criteria for diagnosing schizophrenia was common. The disorder seemed to shrink or expand, overlap or not overlap depending on which definition was used. Stephens and colleagues (1982) studied 283 hospitalized patients previously diagnosed as schizophrenic using eight widely used diagnostic systems. The authors reported that quite different groups of schizophrenics were identified by the different systems. They concluded that the restrictiveness of DSM-III criteria may be desirable for research purposes; however, clinicians may have difficulty with a system in which 53 percent of the cases not diagnosed schizophrenic by DSM-III are diagnosed schizophrenic by at least four of the other eight systems.

The DSM-III committee introduced alternative diagnostic categories placed at the same hierarchical level in diagnostic decision trees to cover the

51 percent of all patients previously diagnosed as schizophrenic using DSM-II who were no longer classified as schizophrenic after 1980 (Winters, Weintraub, and Neale, 1981; Harrow, Carone, and Westermeyer, 1985). The revision to DSM-III, published in 1987 (DSM-III-R), did not substantially change the DSM-III criteria for schizophrenia other than to increase emphasis on several negative symptoms and delete the criterion of symptom onset before age forty-five.

DSM-IV

The fourth edition of DSM, published in 1994, and its revision in 2000, the DSM-IV-TR, introduced several changes in diagnostic practice. First, by adopting a hierarchical approach to assigning subtype designations they acknowledged that patients may evidence symptoms of more than one subtype. Second, the diagnosis of schizoaffective disorder, previously discouraged in DSM-III, was given unequivocal subtypal status in DSM-IV and DSM-IV-TR. The primary difference between DSM-III and DSM-IV has to do with the duration of symptoms. DSM-IV introduced the criterion of at least a one-month duration of A criteria symptoms rather than the one-week duration specified in DSM-III-R. This change is reflective of the trend in diagnostic practice since 1980 to narrow the range of patients to be included in the diagnostic grouping. DSM-IV and DSM-IV-TR criteria for the diagnosis of schizophrenia are summarized here.

1. *Characteristic symptoms:* Either one or more of the following:

   - bizarre delusions (clearly implausible and nonunderstandable delusions, including delusions of control over mind or body)
   - hallucinations in the form of voices commenting or conversing

   Or two or more of the following:

   - other delusions
   - other hallucinations occurring in a clear sensorium
   - disorganized speech
   - grossly disorganized or catatonic behavior
   - negative symptoms (i.e., affective flattening, alogia, avolition)

The characteristic symptoms must be present for a significant proportion of time throughout a one-month period, or less if successfully treated. The period during which the required characteristic symptoms are present is referred to as the active phase. In addition, there might be prodromal or residual phases during which there are either negative symptoms alone or at least two attenuated characteristic symptoms.

2. *Social/occupational dysfunction:* For a significant proportion of the time since the onset of disturbance, at least one major area of functioning such as work, interpersonal relations, or self-care is markedly below that achieved before the onset, or there has been failure to achieve the expected level of interpersonal, academic, or occupational achievement in cases with onset during childhood or adolescence.

3. *Six-month duration:* Continuous signs of disturbance for at least six months, including an active phase of at least one month (or less if successfully treated).

4. *Exclusion of affective or schizoaffective psychosis:* Any episodes of mood disorder accompanying the active phase of characteristic symptoms must be brief in relation to the total duration of active and residual symptoms.

5. *Exclusion of toxic substances or a general medical condition:* The disturbance is not due to the direct physiological effects of a substance (drug abuse or medication) or a general medical condition.

6. *Relationship to pervasive developmental disorder:* If there is a history of pervasive developmental disorder such as autistic disorder, schizophrenia can be diagnosed only if prominent delusions or hallucinations are present for at least one month (or less if successfully treated).

Subtypes

Since DSM-III the simple subtype has been eliminated, the hebephrenic subtype is now referred to as disorganized, and the undifferentiated subtype was added in DSM-IV. Since many patients evidence mixed symptom pictures and symptom patterns often change over time, little evidence seems to support the continued use of these subtypes other than tradition. There is reasonable evidence, however, that the paranoid (with systematized delusions), nonparanoid (Magaro, 1980), and positive-negative symptom distinctions (Andreasen et al., 1995) have some empirical support. Whether these groupings refer to actual categorical subtypes or symptom dimensions remains a topic of debate.

Is Schizophrenia a Spectrum of Disorders?

DSM-III and DSM-IV narrowed the concept of schizophrenia. This narrowing has resulted in a more homogenous population of individuals diagnosed as schizophrenic. However, several large adoption studies, such as the Danish-American adoption study (Kety, Rosenthal, Wender, and Schulsinger, 1968), did not find evidence of increased concordance rates among biological relatives using narrow diagnostic definitions of schizophrenia. As a consequence, most genetic concordance statistics are based on the concept of a schizophrenia spectrum rather than standard DSM diagnoses of schizophrenia. Rosenthal and Kety introduced the term *schizophrenia spectrum disorder* in their Danish-American adoption studies. They used this concept to refer to nonpsychotic relatives of schizophrenic probands. The grouping encompassed relatives who were eccentric, detached, and presented features of perceptual, cognitive, and interpersonal problems that resembled schizophrenic symptoms. Their research demonstrated an apparent genetic link between these features and chronic schizophrenia.

Family studies have provided additional support for the notion of a spectrum of schizophrenia-related disorders, particularly one which includes features of schizotypal and paranoid personality disorders. Studies have confirmed a higher prevalence of both patterns in first-degree relatives of schizophrenic probands versus normal controls (Kendler and Gruenberg, 1984; Baron et al., 1985). Additional support linking schizotypal personality traits with first-degree relatives of schizophrenic patients has come from laboratory studies using measures such as smooth-pursuit eye movements (Siever, 1991).

The concept of a spectrum of schizophrenia-related disorders goes back to Paul Meehl's concept of schizotaxia or a genetic vulnerability to schizophrenia and related disorders that is expressed in the form of certain personality traits (e.g., anhedonia, cognitive slippage). It is not clear which disorders belong in this spectrum and represent the phenotypic expression of this assumed constitutional vulnerability. How the spectrum is defined is a matter of common practice and ad hoc speculation, but definite membership is generally granted to schizophrenia, delusional disorders, and schizotypal personality disorder. Probable categories include schizophreniform disorder, schizoaffective disorder, paranoid personality disorder, schizoid personality disorder, borderline personality disorder, affective disorder with mood incongruent delusions, brief reactive psychoses, avoidant personality disorder, compulsive personality disorder, Asperger's disorder, and possibly childhood-onset pervasive developmental disorder (McGlashan, 1991).

Adopting the notion that a spectrum of disorders may be genetically related to vulnerability for schizophrenia generates higher concordance rates between proband and biological relatives but adds to confusion about the classification and boundaries of schizophrenia. Nevertheless, genetic researchers now routinely incorporate the concept of a schizophrenia "spectrum of disorders" that includes groupings such as paranoid delusional disorder and schizotypal, borderline, and schizoid personality, as part of the schizophrenia spectrum concept. On the other hand, researchers looking for brain-based neuropathological differences tend to study a narrowly defined group of patients that evidence "core" symptoms or deficit symptoms of schizophrenia, which makes it a relatively rare disorder.

RELIABILITY AND VALIDITY

The revisions of the DSM since 1980 have been driven by the quest for clearer boundaries between diagnostic groupings and improved reliability of diagnosis. Reliability is an important first step in the accumulation of scientific knowledge; however, reliability in identifying and naming a syndrome is different from validity. One can formulate nonsensical diagnostic constructs based on criteria that will allow these groupings to be identified with great reliability. It is not reliability, however, but judgments based on social values and cultural expectations that enable us to differentiate between plausible groupings of patterns of problematic emotions and behaviors that people evidence and nonsensical groupings. Once social consensus is reached about plausible groupings, criteria are established to define the disorder and to differentiate it from other disorders. Since 1980 and the introduction of DSM-III, the diagnosis of schizophrenia has become potentially more reliable, but marked narrowing of the concept renders the relevance of pre-1980 research questionable. Harrow, Carone, and Westermeyer (1985), for example, studied a group of DSM-II-diagnosed schizophrenic patients who were later rediagnosed using DSM-III criteria. Only 41 percent of the DSM-II schizophrenic patients were diagnosed with schizophrenia using DSM-III criteria.

In order for the validity of a particular disorder to be demonstrated the category must correlate with other phenomena that are deemed causally relevant according to some conceptual framework or theory. For example, evidence of a unique response to a particular class of drugs, common life history variables, or common underlying physiochemical or structural brain abnormalities could be interpreted as evidence for the validity of a diagnostic construct.

Criticisms of the Concept

Critics maintain that something must be wrong with the concept of schizophrenia, a concept that has proved so unstable in its usage (Brockington et al., 1991). Brockington and colleagues note that the American Psychiatric Association, through the DSM, has attempted to establish an orthodoxy of diagnostic rules decreed by a professional hierarchy in order to ensure the equivalence of patient groups studied in different contexts. These efforts may potentially improve reliability but do not address the possibility that there could be fundamental flaws in the diagnostic groupings themselves. Perhaps we have failed to reach agreement on the diagnosis of schizophrenia because schizophrenia is an idea without a single underlying defining principle.

Brockington et al. (1991) point out that Kraepelin's original idea of dementia praecox was that all subtypes shared a common course ending in a defect state, as evidenced in "a peculiar destruction of the internal connections of the psyche" (Kraepelin, 1919, p. 37). Later Kraepelin introduced a second defining principle he believed was common to all subtypes of dementia praecox. He referred to this unifying principle as a "psychic fission" expressed as a "schism within the individual psyche" in which the will is eroded by competing thoughts or impulses. Schneider's first-rank symptoms are generally consistent with this second grouping. However, symptoms such as systematized delusions cannot be related to either the defect state or the nuclear schism, and long-term symptom course is not clearly related to either grouping. To further complicate matters, delusions are ubiquitous in all forms of psychotic disorders. Brockington (1992) argues the richness of the psychopathology of schizophrenia, described by Kraepelin and Bleuler, is the source of the weakness of the construct. He cites evidence which indicates that the symptoms of schizophrenia—verbal hallucinosis, passivity, delusions, defect symptoms, and deterioration—are continuously distributed within the population of psychotic patients, including those with affective disorders (Brockington et al., 1991). This suggests that schizophrenia may be a conceptual artifact that does not correspond to any natural co-occurrence or grouping of patients and their problems, since schizophrenic patients evidence different levels of symptom patterns and many of these patterns lie on continua with other psychotic disorders on a variety of interforms.

SUMMARY

The operational approach to diagnosis fosters improved reliability (Guze et al., 1983). However, reliability of diagnosis of a disorder is not the same as validity. Reification of the DSM-IV diagnosis can foster the impression that we know what schizophrenia is, what causes it, and how best to treat it, when in fact we do not. A false complacency can be fostered by our ability to reliably name what we observe. We can be misled into believing that naming a patient's experience and behavior means that we have causal knowledge and understanding of what we have named.

Review of the available evidence suggests that one should remain agnostic about the validity of the concept of a single brain-based disorder called schizophrenia. Schizophrenia is a descriptive term, one that may represent a single disease entity, a group of disorders, or a heterogenous grouping of symptoms that share or do not share certain features at a descriptive level. The pathways to this disorder or group of symptoms are not known, but evidence suggests the symptoms most likely represent the outcomes of the interactive effects of a wide variety of contributing factors.

DSM-IV categories should be recognized as the provisional consensus agreements that they are. The symptom focus of DSM-IV has contributed improved reliability at the expense of decreased interest in the value of understanding individual patients based on extensive history taking, phenomenological understanding, exploration of the possible contributions of contextual factors, and sensitivity to the life context and unique qualities of individual patients. There is no alternative to using the term, but it should be considered a construct that remains open to substantial revision.

Reification of the concept of schizophrenia has also discouraged exploration of alternative ways to think about grouping psychotic disorders. There are currently few if any widely accepted and viable social or scientific alternatives to the idea that a single brain disorder called schizophrenia exists. It is important to recognize that more valid alternative ways of grouping the problems currently subsumed under this term may potentially be developed.

The term *schizophrenia* refers to a descriptive syndrome or group of behaviors and experiences that are judged by others to be dysfunctional and disturbing. Whether it will eventually be replaced by other constructs remains an open question.

Chapter 3

Epidemiology, Course, and Outcome

PREVALENCE AND INCIDENCE

The diagnosis of schizophrenia is based on clinical judgment; thus, it should come as no surprise that there are wide variations in reports of the incidence and prevalence of the disorder. Different definitions and variations in application of the diagnostic criteria result in varying estimates of occurrence. Broad definitions of schizophrenia yield prevalence rates up to five times greater than do narrow definitions (Warner, 1994).

Prevalence is the total number of cases of a disorder, new and old, known to exist. Point prevalence refers to the total number of cases known to exist during a given interval, such as one year. Prevalence figures also vary widely because they can be affected by factors such as differences in incidence rates, in life span/death in rates, and in rates of recovery, as well as in economic and political factors. Cross-study comparisons are compromised by methodological differences between studies, such as differences in selection criteria, diagnostic criteria, and practice. Despite these limitations, overall prevalence figures suggest that schizophrenia may be less frequent and have better outcomes in developing countries than in industrialized countries (Warner, 1994).

Comparisons of point prevalence figures indicate wide geographic variations in the frequency of schizophrenia which seem to involve more than error variance. Reports of unusually high prevalence rates have been published for areas in the north of Sweden (Book, 1953), the north of Russia (Gainullin, Shmaonova, and Trubnikov, 1986), the west of Ireland (Eaton, 1991; Torrey et al., 1984), and the coast of Croatia (Crocetti et al., 1971). In contrast, low prevalence rates have been reported in island groups in the South Pacific (Torrey, Torrey, and Burton-Bradley, 1974; Dohan et al., 1983) and the coastal area of British Columbia (Bates and van Dam, 1984). Estimates of the prevalence of schizophrenia in the United States vary from 0.3 to 4.7 per 1,000, in Europe from 1.8 to 17.0 per 1,000, and from 0.4 to 7.0 per 1,000 in developing countries, depending on the design and methodology of the studies (Warner, 1994). The reasons for these variations in prevalence rates are not clear, although several psychosocial and cultural explanations have been offered (Warner, 1994; Jablensky, 1988).

The *incidence* of a disorder is the rate at which new cases occur in a given period of time, such as one year. Data on incidence are typically gathered by counting the number of referrals to treatment agencies. Estimates of incidence are likely to be contaminated by factors such as the availability and social acceptability of treatment resources. Incidence figures are obviously difficult if not impossible to obtain in areas where access to services is not readily available. The U.S. annual incidence rate for schizophrenia is estimated to be 0.5 per 1,000 of the general population. This figure is reasonably close to incidence rates reported for most industrialized countries (Jablensky, 1986).

In contrast to regional variations in prevalence rates, other evidence suggests that the incidence of schizophrenia occurs at roughly the same rate around the world, about one to four cases per 10,000 population at risk per annum (Jablensky, 1988). This assertion is based on the findings of one large-scale study conducted by the World Health Organization (WHO) (Satorius, Jablensky, and Korten, 1986). In the WHO study annual incidence rates based on first lifetime contact were determined for seven research centers. The seven centers studied were located in widely different cultures in both developed and developing nations around the world. Each was selected because it provided complete or nearly complete coverage of the catchment area that was included in the study sample. Incidence rates were calculated separately for cases meeting a "broad" definition of schizophrenia and cases meeting criteria for narrow or "core" schizophrenia. For the broad definition, differences in incidence figures between centers were significant, such as from 1.5/10,000 in Aarhus, Denmark, to 4.2/10,000 in Chandigarh, India. However, use of restrictive diagnostic criteria resulted in the disappearance of significant differences among the seven centers. Since incidence rates did not differ significantly among the seven study centers for the narrow definition of schizophrenia, the researchers concluded that schizophrenia must occur at the same rate around the world. However, etiological interpretations of the incidence figures of the WHO study, in terms of a unitary underlying cause for the disorder, are questionable since the authors stated at the outset that the study was not designed to be an epidemiological study or to recruit representative sample groups of patients (Satorius, Jablensky, and Shapiro, 1978).

Some authors believe that schizophrenia was extremely rare prior to the industrial revolution and that schizophrenia continues to be rare to nonexistent in nonindustrialized societies (Torrey, 1980). The WHO investigation was designed in part to address this issue. Results indicated that ratings of patients could be reliably completed in twelve countries around the globe using a diagnostic system derived from the Present State Exam. Although no single symptom of schizophrenia was invariably present in every patient, reports of symptoms such as thought stopping, thought insertion, and thought broadcasting were reported by participants as varied as peasants in rain forest communities and educated city dwellers. The authors of the WHO study concluded that the symptoms of schizophrenia are culture independent. Counterarguments point out that there are bound to be similarities in the symptoms of such a severe disorder as schizophrenia, since all humans share the same basic neuroanatomy that limits the possibilities for cognitive confusion and other forms of expression of extreme distress.

Socioeconomic Class

Lower socioeconomic classes in industrialized countries have higher prevalence rates for schizophrenia than do the middle and upper classes (Hollingshead and Redlich, 1954; Silverton and Mednick, 1984).There are several ways to interpret this finding. One is that schizophrenic patients tend to "drift" down the socioeconomic stratum as a result of dysfunctions that are present before their symptoms become overt. Evidence for this downward drift hypothesis was observed after comparing the social status and mobility of schizophrenic males and their fathers, uncles, brothers, and grandfathers (Kohn, 1975). Schizophrenic sons were disproportionately represented in the lowest socioeconomic class in comparison to their male relatives. Twenty-nine percent of the fathers were in the upper two socioeconomic classes compared to the status of only 4 percent of the patients, assessed immediately prior to admission. It makes sense that individuals who have difficulties adapting to the demands of adult life prior to a schizophrenic episode would not do well in the job market. Therefore, a higher percentage of schizophrenic patients would be expected to be found in the lower rung of economic success. However, evidence relevant to the drift hypothesis is not entirely consistent. Other studies indicate that fathers of schizophrenics tend to more often come from lower socioeconomic groups (Turner and Wagenfeld, 1967).

Kohn (1975) reviewed the literature and concluded that the evidence on schizophrenia and socioeconomic class does not support a drift hypothesis but does indicate that lower-class families produce a disproportionate number of patients with schizophrenia. Kohn's interpretation is consistent with what is referred to as the "breeder" hypothesis. This explanation suggests that the cumulative effects of stressful conditions associated with a life of poverty, such as increased risk for poor diet, poor education, crime, decreased access to health care, and higher rates of abuse and neglect among the lower socioeconomic classes "breed" increased risk for schizophrenia.

Research also indicates that patients with schizophrenia are more likely to have been born in cities than in rural areas (Astrup and Odegaard, 1961; Castle, Scott, and Wessely, 1993). This finding has been interpreted as evidence that many patients with schizophrenia developed the disorder consequent upon environmental factors related to the stressful life circumstances associated with poverty in crowded urban areas. Environmental factors such as life stress associated with poverty and the long-term impact of increased risk resulting from damage to the developing brain that is a consequence of a higher incidence of intrauterine infections, poor prenatal care, or obstetric complications are proposed as explanations for the increased incidence of schizophrenia among individuals from poor, inner-city areas (Lewis and Murray, 1987). Most poor people who live in urban areas do not develop schizophrenic symptoms, however, so other factors must also be involved. The relationship between the stresses associated with a life of poverty and schizophrenia suggests that these social conditions contribute to increased risk for schizophrenia along with other factors, perhaps primarily in those who are somehow predisposed and more vulnerable.

Some economically and socially alienated rural subpopulations (e.g., Eskimos, Australian Aborigines, Tamils in South India) are reported to have high prevalence rates for schizophrenia, as are areas in which there is a high incidence of rural unemployment and a long history of economic and political oppression (e.g., the southwest of Ireland). In contrast, prevalence data indicate that groups enjoying stable employment and clear role expectations and social structures, such as the Amish and Hutterite Bretheren in the United States, evidence low prevalence rates. This evidence suggests that any viable comprehensive explanatory theory of schizophrenia must incorporate broad social contributors, such as social, political, and economic factors, class status, and social structure, as well as biological and psychological factors, in order to present a coherent summary of the evidence.

Gender

There is a *gender effect* that has been consistently reported in the schizophrenia literature. Despite a similar total cumulative risk of developing schizophrenia for males and females, the mean age of onset for women in industrialized societies appears to be higher than for males by five years (Lewine, 1988). In the United States median age of onset for males is twenty-one years versus twenty-seven years for females. In Greece the mean age of onset is twenty-three years for men and 26.6 years for women (Beratis, Gabriel, and Hoidas, 1994). The gender effect does not seem to be a function of differences in role expectation or help-seeking behavior (Castle and Murray, 1991), since the effect is present in societies that vary considerably in terms of gender roles (Warner, 1994). Cognitive impairment, poor premorbid adjustment, and negative symptoms are also reported to occur earlier and to be more severe in male than in female patients (Flor-Henry, 1990; Goldstein and Tsuang, 1990; Gur et al., 1988; Haas et al., 1990). Females also have better outcomes than males (Angermeyer, Kuhn, and Goldstein, 1990). Late-onset schizophrenic disorders after age forty rarely occur in men, but women show a secondary peak of onset of mainly paranoid schizophrenia during their late forties (Beratis, Gabriel, and Hoidas, 1994).

The implications of gender differences in understanding the causes of schizophrenia remain unclear. It could be that higher incidence rates for a variety of neurological disorders and other risk factors among males are related to these findings. Differences in age at which the brain matures, endocrine levels (testosterone/estrogen), gender-role expectations, and the social threat implicit in the symptoms of male patients may be related to these puzzling variations in onset, symptom pattern, and course.

Season of Birth

Evidence indicates that schizophrenic patients are 5 to 10 percent more likely than the general population to be born during the winter or early spring (Bradbury and Miller, 1985). This effect has been attributed to the effects of a seasonal pathogen such as a flu virus that may act on the developing fetus. Bradbury and Miller (1985) reported a correlation between rates of flu during times mothers were in their second trimester of pregnancy and rates of subsequent births of schizophrenic patients. This evidence indicates that maternal viral infection may play a role in risk for schizophrenia, but since most mothers who have a viral infection during the second trimester do not have children who are at increased risk for schizophrenia, viral infections appear to be only one of many possible contributing risk factors. Evidence in support of the viral risk factor will be reviewed in greater detail in Chapter 8.

PHASES OF SCHIZOPHRENIA

A study by Hafner and colleagues (1995) indicates that the first signs of the *prodromal phase* of schizophrenia often begin with a wide variety of nonspecific signs, including mixtures of anxiety, tension, irritability, restlessness, aggression, depression, difficulty concentrating, sleep problems, low energy, withdrawal, odd behavior, religious preoccupation, deteriorating work performance, reduced communication, beliefs of being laughed at or talked about, and growing distrust of others. These problems may continue and gradually increase in intensity for as long as several years before clear symptoms of psychosis become evident. Disorganized and undifferentiated symptoms of schizophrenia tend to have a gradual and early onset during adolescence and are associated with poor premorbid psychosocial adjustment and poor outcome (Fenton and McGlashan, 1991a). Paranoid patients with systematized delusions tend to have a later and more rapid onset, experience a better outcome, and evidence less cognitive deterioration.

During the *acute phase* the most frequent positive symptoms are delusions and hallucinations. The most common negative symptoms are avolition (lack of motivation) and anhedonia (pleasure deficit). Positive symptoms tend to dominate the clinical picture on admission, but about six months after admission negative symptoms tend to become more prominent (Hafner et al., 1995). Symptoms of disorganization, formal thought disorder, and bizarre behavior are relatively rare in new admissions and occur in extreme form in only about 10 percent of admissions (Andreasen and Flaum, 1991). Most symptoms decrease during hospitalization, but at least 70 percent of all patients suffer a relapse of acute symptoms within five years (Wiersma et al., 1998). Over time, positive and disorganized symptoms decrease more than negative symptoms. Signs of self-neglect, withdrawal, and anhedonia remain prominent even during the *residual phase* of the disorder (Arndt et al., 1995).

The clinical course and outcome of schizophrenia has been the subject of numerous studies and reports throughout the twentieth century. Outcome statistics have varied considerably over the years as a function of at least two factors: (1) how schizophrenia is defined (narrow or broad definitions) and (2) access to treatments.

Kraepelin (1899) maintained that schizophrenia (dementia praecox) was a chronic illness characterized by a progressive deteriorative course. He reported limited improvement at follow-up in only 17 percent of his cases. Hegarty and colleagues (1994) conducted a meta-analysis of 320 studies in the schizophrenia outcome literature from the previous 100 years. The results indicated the proportion of patients who were rated as improved at long-term outcome increased significantly after the middle of the twentieth century (48.5 percent versus 35.4 percent). However, during the late 1980s to mid-1990s, the average rate of favorable outcome declined to 36.4 percent. The authors attribute the changes in outcome rates to several factors. First, during the 1950s changes in the conceptualization of schizophrenia introduced by Eugen Bleuler significantly broadened inclusion criteria from the narrow definition advocated by Kraepelin. Clinicians in the United States using broad Bleulerian criteria during the 1960s and 1970s diagnosed schizophrenia at much higher rates than in other countries (Kendell et al., 1971). The reintroduction of a duration of illness requirement and a narrow definition with DSM-III effectively reoperationalized neo-Kraepelinian criteria and resulted in a self-fulfilling prophecy in terms of declining outcome figures. Outcome figures are significantly better when patients are diagnosed by using broad Bleulerian/Schneiderian cross-sectional criteria (46.5 percent) and worse when duration and neo-Kraepelinian criteria are used (27.3 percent) (Hegarty et al., 1994).

Studies of the long-range outcome of schizophrenia have been limited by methodological difficulties, not the least of which has been the lack of stable agreement about how to define the boundaries of schizophrenia (Hoffman, 1985). Attempts to differentiate schizophrenia from conditions such as schizophreniform disorder have not been extensively evaluated in terms of differences in long-term outcome. Available evidence suggests that these distinctions do not permit accurate predictions of long-term course and outcome (Valiant, 1978). The use of different definitions of schizophrenia in outcome studies led Strauss and Carpenter (1978) to conclude that none of the widely used cross-sectional diagnostic definitions used prior to DSM-III defined a group of schizophrenics with homogeneously poor outcome, and no system was superior in terms of predicting prognosis. Genetic loading in terms of a family history of schizophrenia does not appear to accurately predict poor prognosis (Bleuler, 1978).

The WHO International Pilot Study of Schizophrenia (Jablensky, 1988) suggests that mode of onset, defined in terms of time between the first appearance of a psychotic manifestation and onset of a full syndrome, may be a predictor of subsequent course of the disorder. In the WHO study this relationship was bimodal in nature and held for both developed and developing countries. Acute onset was associated with briefer psychotic episodes and gradual onset with more long-term psychotic symptoms. The acute versus gradual onset groups could not be distinguished on the basis of symptoms or background factors.

Choice of appropriate outcome criteria presents another problem in assessing outcome. Assessment of symptoms, readmissions, and duration of hospital stay are too narrow to serve as valid outcome criteria and can be contaminated by extraneous influences. Strauss and Carpenter (1978) suggest that long-term outcome studies should include at a minimum ratings of symptoms, hospitalizations, quality of social relationships, and ability to work. However, these indices are not highly correlated, and may have separate determinants (Bland and Orn, 1979). McGlashan (1994) recommends that outcome dimensions should include (1) clinical signs and symptoms, including hospitalizations, medication, and types and amount of aftercare utilization; (2) social functioning indicators such as frequency of interpersonal contacts, closeness of these contacts, and degree of involvement in a meaningful social network; (3) instrumental functioning including the ability to learn and work, amount of initiative, drive, and frustration tolerance; and (4) humanitarian concerns such as adequate food, shelter, clothing, and living situations appropriate to the level of functioning of the individual. Clearly outcome is complex and difficult to assess adequately and objectively.

The demographic characteristics of the sample of patients studied as well as economic conditions and cultural and social contexts can have an effect on course and outcome. For example, hospitalization rates decline during times of national emergencies such as war and increase during economic recessions (Beck, 1978). In addition, political and economic factors play a role in the context and quality of the treatment that patients receive, which in turn affects outcome. During the first half of the twentieth century nearly two-thirds of all schizophrenic patients admitted to mental hospitals remained in the hospital for over two years (Strauss and Carpenter, 1978), and more than one-third never left the hospital (Rennie, 1939). By the late 1960s only 9 percent of schizophrenics remained in hospital more than five years. Obviously, factors such as policies, funding priorities, access to disability pensions, access to medications, and the quality of outpatient community support have a greater impact on outcome than does the nature of the symptoms of the disorder.

LONG-TERM OUTCOME

From the very beginning, schizophrenia has been assumed to be a chronic deteriorating condition. If good recovery occurs some clinicians believe the patient must have been misdiagnosed. This assumption has been contradicted by the results of several studies. These studies indicate that schizophrenic patients are heterogenous with regard to long-term course.

Long-term follow-up research conducted in developed countries demonstrated that about 20 to 35 percent of schizophrenic patients improve rapidly with treatment with little deficit; a similar proportion evidence serious long-term social impairment; and about 50 to 60 percent evidence a fluctuating long-term course. These outcome statistics have not changed with changes in policies, treatment philosophies, or the introduction of more effective antipsychotic medications.

Ciompi and Muller (1976) traced the course of the disorder for 228 schizophrenics, all over sixty-five years of age, back to the time of their initial diagnosis. The lives of the patients were charted over a minimum period of thirty-seven years from first admission to reexamination; in some cases the histories extended back more than fifty years. The authors reported that onset of symptoms was acute (less than six months from first signs to clear

TABLE 3.1. Summary of Patterns of Course in Schizophrenia

Pattern	Onset	Type of Episodes	Improvement Later in Life
1	Gradual	Chronic	Fair to good
2	Gradual	Chronic	Poor to absent
3	Gradual	Episodic	Fair to good
4	Gradual	Episodic	Poor to absent
5	Rapid	Chronic	Fair to good
6	Rapid	Chronic	Poor to absent
7	Rapid	Episodic	Fair to good
8	Rapid	Episodic	Poor to absent

Source: Adapted from Ciompi (1980) and Carpenter, Kirkpatrick, and Buchanan (1990).

psychosis) in about half the patients and gradual in the other half. The course of schizophrenic symptoms was episodic (acute episodes mixed with intervals of partial to complete recovery) in about one-half of the cases. Signs of continuous impairment but with a decrease in severity after several years were observed in the other half of the sample.

Ciompi (1981) described eight different variations in long-term course that were observed in his sample (Table 3.1). His results indicate that about 45 percent of the patients in the study achieved a favorable outcome (complete remission or minor residual symptoms), 24 percent achieved an intermediate outcome, and 22 percent continued to evidence severe symptoms. The remaining 9 percent were rated in the uncertain or unstable category. Comparisons of condition at follow-up with first admission notes revealed that about two-thirds of the cases were completely or partially improved.

In a study of outcome and course, conducted at the Burgholzli Hospital in Zurich, Switzerland, Manfred Bleuler (1978) followed up on 208 schizophrenic patients that he had personally worked with for a period of over twenty years. Bleuler reported that about 25 percent of the patients recovered and remained recovered, about 65 percent alternated between phases of improvement and acute episodes, and about 10 percent remained psychotic and in need of continuous hospital care. Bleuler collected additional data from sites in Basel, Switzerland, and New York. Altogether this sample comprised 1,158 patients and an additional 950 patients from three other teams of investigators. He arrived at several summary observations based on the data from these samples:

1. On average, after five years' duration the psychosis does not progress any further but instead tends to improve.
2. At least 25 percent of all schizophrenics recover entirely and remain recovered, even when the criteria for recovery include lack of psychotic signs, a normal social integration, and the ability to work. On the other hand, Bleuler observed that many improved schizophrenics remain underactive, lack initiative, and have somewhat apathetic, colorless personalities. He compared this impoverishment in personality to the effects observed in other mental hospitals that force an uneventful, unstimulating life on a person.
3. About 10 percent of schizophrenics remain permanently severe psychotics who require hospitalization.
4. The number of recovered patients at any given moment after the onset of the disorder reaches close to 50 percent; some, however, will have acute relapses.
5. Of the 25 percent of patients who had attained a long-lasting favorable outcome, not one was under long-term neuroleptic treatment. Of the patients admitted before 1950, Bleuler concluded that the factor that contributed most to improvement was progress in social and environmental therapies provided in the hospital. The lack of relationship between long-term outcome and ongoing pharmacological treatment was subsequently confirmed by Vailant (1978).

Bleuler's study has been criticized on methodological grounds, but a more rigorous longitudinal study conducted in Vermont reached similar conclusions (Harding et al., 1987). In the Vermont study chronic patients released from an early-model rehab-deinstitutionalization program between 1955 and 1960 were followed. On average these were medication refractory, lower-class, middle-aged patients, with an average of six consecutive years in a hospital and sixteen years since their original admission. A retrospective assessment of these patients was completed twenty-five years later. Seventy percent of the original sample was alive and could be located at follow-up. Of that group 68 percent evidenced no schizophrenic symptoms, 60 percent scored in the normal range on the Global Assessment Scale, and 45 percent showed no psychotic symptoms at all. Eighty-four percent remained on antipsychotic medication, and only 40 percent of those of working age had held a job during the previous year. Many of the patients in the "middle range of outcome" reported continued delusions and auditory hallucinations but stated that they had learned not to talk about these experiences.

Harding and colleagues (1987) included a recalibration of the original diagnosis of each patient using the DSM-III restrictive definition. Despite rediagnosis using a narrow definition, 62 to 68 percent of the chronic patients showed no signs of schizophrenia at follow-up. The authors compared the Vermont outcome figures with a matched control group of patients from Maine who received traditional psychiatric treatment but had not received any psychosocial rehabilitation or systematic outpatient follow-up psychosocial involvement other than medications, maintenance, and stabilization. The controls had a 48 percent recovery rate. This evidence suggests programs that offer more comprehensive psychosocial aftercare interventions to improve self-sufficiency and social integration result in better long-term outcome rates.

In contrast to the encouraging results reported by Ciompi, Bleuler, and the Vermont study group, other researchers have reported more pessimistic outcome figures. It is difficult to determine whether these differences are the result of truly different outcomes, differences in samples or type of care provided, or a different perspective through which ostensibly similar outcome criteria were viewed. McGlashan (1984) followed up fifteen years later on 163 upper-middle-class schizophrenic patients who were admitted to Chestnut Lodge and received three to four years of psychotherapy there. Results indicated that two-thirds remained chronically disturbed and only one-third showed improvement. A smaller study published by Breier and colleagues (1991) of fifty-eight young schizophrenics followed up between two and twelve years indicated that 75 percent had been rehospitalized at least once. Carone, Harrow, and Westermeyer (1991) followed seventy-nine young schizophrenic patients for a period of five years. Only 15 percent of the outcomes were rated as positive at five-year follow-up. Ram and colleagues (1992) noted a relapse rate of 60 percent within two years for a group of first-admission patients.

A meta-analysis published by Harding, Zubin, and Strauss (1992), of over 1,300 patients from five different studies that were followed for at least twenty years, indicated that fully one-half to two-thirds of the patients studied achieved "recovery or significant improvement" by the end of the observation interval. Hegarty and colleagues (1994) conducted an analysis of worldwide long-term outcomes. The social recovery rate they reported was 40.2 percent for the period 1895 through 1991. There was no significant difference between contemporary outcome results (1986-1991) and the years with the most stable plateau (1926-1955). Social recovery rates increased to 50 percent after 1955 but went back to around 40 percent after 1975. The authors attributed this drop in outcome to the implementation of more stringent diagnostic criteria around that time.

It seems clear that the course of schizophrenia is highly varied. Most schizophrenic patients have several relapses, especially during the first six to ten years after the initial episode. Patients continue to deteriorate, remit, or have a fluctuating course before reaching a stable state. Medications and access to quality psychosocial rehabilitation and community support programs obviously play an important role in determining outcome, more so than family history or symptom picture on admission.

Clearly, different researchers are using different criteria as the basis for their ratings of categories such as "recovered," "improved," and "disturbed." Recall that Bleuler rated many patients as "improved" who remained underactive, lacked initiative, and had apathetic, colorless personalities. Other researchers might rate these "residual" symptoms as evidence of marginal to poor functioning. An additional factor that complicates outcome research is that indicators of outcome, such as symptom severity, work adjustment, and psychosocial functioning, do not correlate (Strauss and Carpenter, 1978).

POSITIVE AND NEGATIVE SYMPTOMS

The concepts of positive and negative symptoms were first used to describe cases of epilepsy. He described negative symptoms as the result of a negation of "vital properties." Positive symptoms were, in contrast, the result of the excess of vital properties. Hughlings Jackson later adapted this distinction to his hierarchical model of the nervous system. Jackson (1932) explained positive and negative symptoms in terms of four assumptions: (1) negative symptoms result from impairment that affects a given level of neurological function, (2) impairment of a higher center results in the functional release of a lower center, (3) the now uninhibited lower center produces exaggerations or new forms of behavior termed positive symptoms, and (4) positive symptoms occur only in the context of negative symptoms. Jackson's concepts have been applied to the symptoms of schizophrenia. Positive symptoms refer to an increase or excess of certain symptomatic behaviors and experiences, and negative symptoms refer to a deficit or decrease.

Crow (1985) included delusions, hallucinations, disturbed affect, and thought disorder as positive symptoms, and flat affect and poverty of speech as negative symptoms. He distinguished two syndromes of schizophrenia. Type I is equivalent to acute schizophrenia and is characterized by a preponderance of positive symptoms. Crow's Type I schizophrenia is hypothesized to relate to disturbances in dopaminergic transmission. Type II schizophrenia, associated with negative symptoms, is thought to be associated with cognitive impairment and structural brain abnormalities.

Kay and Singh (1989) also viewed schizophrenia in terms of at least two different subsyndromes: (1) a neuroleptic medication resistant pattern expressed mostly in negative symptoms and (2) a neuroleptic responsive component associated with positive symptoms. They reported evidence that the negative syndrome is associated with a family history of psychosis, lower levels of occupational, educational, and economic attainment, and cognitive deficits. The authors noted that the phase during which negative symptoms are most pronounced, rather than the simple presence or absence of negative symptoms, is related to outcome. If negative symptoms occur during an acute break in association with depressive symptoms and the absence of a family history of psychosis the outcome is more likely to be favorable. Kay and Singh reported that positive symptoms are related to briefer but more frequent hospitalizations and higher doses of antipsychotic medications.

Andreasen and Grove (1986) view negative symptoms as variations of Bleuler's fundamental symptoms and provide a broader definition than Crow, one that includes symptoms such as alogia (language deficit), avolition, apathy, flat affect, anhedonia, asociality, and attention impairment. Andreasen did not adopt the assumptions of Jackson's neurological model that positive symptoms cannot occur without negative symptoms. Recent studies (Arndt et al., 1995) suggest that positive and negative symptoms can be divided into at least three subtypes, with positive symptoms divided into two subtypes: disorganization and a psychotic syndrome labeled psychoticism.

Buchanan and colleagues (1990) have further differentiated these groupings by distinguishing between negative and defect symptoms. The authors believe that negative and defect symptoms overlap but are not coextensive. They propose that negative symptoms are descriptive but do not have clear implications concerning cause, stability, or duration. They use the term *deficit symptoms* to refer specifically to those negative symptoms that appear to be enduring traits which are not secondary to environmental factors such as drug side effects or prolonged institutionalization. Deficit symptoms are selected negative symptoms (restricted affect, diminished emotional range, poverty of speech, diminished interest, curiosity, sense of purpose, and social drive) that endure for more than one year and cannot be explained by depression, anxiety, drug effects, or environmental deprivation. Deficit syndrome patients evidence a preponderance of negative symptoms with early onset of disorder and a chronic course and tend to show a variety of neurocognitive deficits (Buchanan et al., 1990). Lifetime prevalence of the deficit syndrome within a population of schizophrenics is estimated to be 16 percent. Risk for schizophrenia is 1.75 times higher in families of deficit compared to nondeficit probands.

It is difficult to assess the literature on outcome and symptom patterns due to variability in research design and the scales used to assess symptoms. However, contrary to the implications of Crow's model, negative symptoms do not appear to be irreversible, but they are stable in about one-fifth of all patients at two-year follow-up and one-third of all patients at four-year follow-up (Pogue-Geile and Harrow, 1984). Evidence also indicates that most positive-symptom patients show increasing signs of negative symptoms at follow-up. At present the long-term stability and prognostic value of the positive-negative symptom distinction remains unclear, and the validity of the negative-deficit symptom distinction as a predictor of outcome remains to be reliably demonstrated.

Despite the absence of consistent evidence to support Crow's distinction between the two types of schizophrenia, his speculative model has been influential, and early and consistent negative symptoms are widely viewed as poor prognostic signs. Until the introduction of the newer atypical antipsychotic medications that have fewer side effects, it was widely assumed that antipsychotic medications were not effective in treating negative symptoms. Newer atypical antipsychotic medications have been reported to be somewhat more effective in reducing the severity of negative symptoms.

SYMPTOMS AND PREMORBID PREDICTORS OF OUTCOME

A predominance of negative symptoms that appear early in the psychotic process is generally associated with the likelihood of longer hospitalizations, reduced social contacts, and partial remissions (Fenton and McGlashan, 1991). Acute, late-onset, good premorbid functioning, and paranoid symptoms, in contrast, are associated with shorter first and subsequent acute psychotic episodes (Wiersma et al., 1998). Nevertheless, attempts to predict outcome based on symptoms or even premorbid history must be qualified since these indices ignore the influence of concurrent contextual life factors. For example, the continuity and adequacy of aftercare for most discharged schizophrenic patients is largely limited to medication management in most communities. Therefore, it is not surprising that outcome statistics are disappointing (Stein, 1992).

The fact that the readmission rate in the United States for schizophrenic patients after two years is about 70 percent (Wasylenki et al., 1985) can as readily be attributed to deficient planning, lack of access to adequate housing and vocational and recreational services, and provision of fragmented and haphazard therapy and case management services as to patient symptom characteristics.

SCHIZOPHRENIA AND COMORBID SUBSTANCE USE

The rising incidence of comorbid substance-use disorders, especially in young-adult patients, has complicated estimates of long-term course and has become a serious obstacle to effective treatment for many individuals with schizophrenia. The percentage of schizophrenic patients with comorbid drug or alcohol use disorder is currently about 47 percent of all individuals with a lifetime diagnosis of schizophrenia or schizophreniform disorder (Regier et al., 1993). Dual-diagnosis patients are likely to be among the most active participants in the "revolving door" of hospitalization, release, and rehospitalization. These individuals also have great difficulty managing the practical aspects of their lives and are prone to homelessness and unstable living arrangements (Belcher, 1989).

Dual-diagnosis patients are more likely to be noncompliant with medication and all other treatment recommendations (Kashner et al., 1991). Problems with intoxication and drug use interfere with relationships with service providers and exacerbate the effects of mental illness. As a result, this population is difficult to treat, poorly served, and has a course characterized by repeated hospitalizations. Since both substance-use disorders and schizophrenia are characterized by high rates of relapse and poor treatment retention, integrated programs have been developed that concurrently focus on the problems associated with each disorder (Dixon and Rebori, 1995). Adequate long-term follow-up studies have not been conducted to evaluate the effectiveness of these programs.

THE ROLE OF CULTURE IN OUTCOME: THE WHO INTERNATIONAL PILOT STUDY OF SCHIZOPHRENIA (IPSS)

The initial IPSS included 1,202 patients in nine countries: China, Colombia, Czechoslovakia, Denmark, India, Nigeria, the Soviet Union, the United Kingdom, and the United States (Satorius et al., 1972). Two- and five-year follow-up studies were conducted to evaluate the long-term outcome of the patients (Satorius et al., 1987). The same rating scales and diagnostic criteria were used in all countries. The results of the follow-up studies were similar. Patients with an initial diagnosis of schizophrenia in developing countries (e.g., Colombia, Nigeria, India) had a more favorable course and outcome than did their counterparts in developed countries (Czechoslovakia, Denmark, Soviet Union, United Kingdom, United States). These results held for all measures, including percentage of time spent in psychotic episodes, course of the disorder, measures of social functioning (self-care, occupational adjustment, sexual adjustment, interpersonal functioning in the community), and a global rating of social functioning.

Over one-quarter of the patients in developing countries had one single episode followed by full remission, compared to only 8 percent of patients in the developed countries. Fifty percent of patients in developing countries had full remission between episodes compared to 17 percent of the patients in developed countries. Fourteen percent of the patients in developing countries and 24 percent in developed countries had a continuing episode of illness over the five-year follow-up period. A similar pattern was observed in social functioning. Patients in developing countries evidenced no or mild impairment in social functioning in 65 percent of the cases, compared to 43 percent in developed countries.

Taken together, of the 226 patients followed for five years in the developing countries, 73 percent showed the "best" pattern of course, while 13 percent evidenced a "worst" pattern. Comparable figures for developed centers were 52 percent (best) and 24 percent (worst). Fully one-half of the patients in the developing countries showed a pattern characterized by periods of complete remission punctuated by episodic relapses; only 17 percent of patients in developed countries evidenced this pattern. The most frequent pattern in the developed countries was a chronic residual state punctuated by recurring acute psychotic episodes. The most frequent course in developing countries was a full remission after the first episode with no further episodes during the five-year follow-up period. These differences in outcome between developed and developing countries held even when other predictors, such as sex, marital status, premorbid personality, and type of onset, were included in the regression model.

Expenditures were substantially higher and access to the latest antipsychotic drugs and case managers was more available to patients in the developed countries. Why do the patients in developing countries do so much better? Warner (1994) suggests several possible answers: (1) there is less social stigma associated with having a serious mental illness in rural third world areas; (2) patients return to an intact social structure consisting of the extended family or tribal social structure in developing countries, in contrast to their plight in developed countries; and (3) it is easier to return to meaningful and productive social and occupational roles in developing countries with largely agricultural economies than in industrialized countries. The substantial implications of these findings for funding priorities and development and implementation of truly innovative models of aftercare services unfortunately have not resulted in the substantial changes in the services provided in most developed countries that one might expect. It is much simpler, less controversial, and in the short term less expensive in the minds of most policymakers to rely on medications and custodial living to manage the severely mentally ill.

SUMMARY

We know generally what the incidence of schizophrenia is in industrialized countries. We also know that prevalence rates vary widely between rich and poor, rural and urban, economically oppressed and privileged, and socially intact and disrupted subcultures. Contrary to widespread opinion, schizophrenia, although sometimes a chronic and debilitating condition, need not be viewed as a life sentence for most patients. The course of schizophrenia is highly varied, and we are not able to predict either course or outcome on the basis of severity or type of symptoms. We do not know to what degree the course of the disorder is a function of endogenous biological factors versus premorbid history or to what degree the quality of aftercare provided can significantly impact overall outcome rates. In all likelihood, both factors play an important role, but the WHO study indicates that industrialized countries have sorely neglected the psychosocial aspects of providing care. Warner (1994) maintains that cultural differences in prevalence, course, and outcome rates between developing and developed countries are the result of factors such as differences in opportunities for patients to assume meaningful social roles and to engage in social participation and social integration. To the extent that patients are reintegrated into an extended and supportive social context and are able to gradually assume meaningful and productive social roles, the long-term outcome for schizophrenic patients appears to be much better than much of the literature implies.

Chapter 4

Language, Thought, and Syndromes of Schizophrenia

In 1973 the Harvard social psychologist Roger Brown decided to attempt a "total immersion" in the topic of schizophrenia for several weeks in order to better prepare to lecture on the topic in his introductory psychology classes. Brown (1973) noted that after many years of reading research articles that contrast schizophrenics with other groups, he had developed a preconception that schizophrenics were a homogenous population, bearing the mark of "schizophrenicity." What he soon discovered, after numerous conversations with patients in various contexts, is that persons called schizophrenic are "as diverse as the rest of us." Brown searched in vain for common examples of odd behaviors, disorientation, and schizophrenic speech during his many interactions with patients and former patients. In time all of his hunches and generalizations failed, except one. He observed that however normal the patient was in talking about most subjects, eventually he would find an area of delusion. When he encountered such an area, Brown's unequivocal reaction was something like, "I have followed you perfectly well thus far, but now you are saying things I cannot agree with."

Conversations with most unremitted schizophrenic patients will eventually trigger a similar response. Some patients are difficult to understand or follow; others express bizarre and sometimes uncensored thoughts. Many patients have little interest in conversation and tend to repeat a few unusual ideas over and over. Others seem normal in nearly every respect except that at some point in the conversation hints at delusional ideas are expressed.

Schizophrenic language does not necessarily differ from normal speech in terms of the formal rules of grammar or prosody (Maher and Spitzer, 1993). The content of what is expressed rather than its form is what guided Brown's reactions and judgments. Brown noted that the basis for his identification of a belief as deluded is a judgment that *reality testing,* as we know it in this society at this time in history, is insufficient to justify the beliefs or risks attendant upon the actions contemplated. He suggests that research efforts to make the notions of rationality on which we operate more explicit, including efforts to describe psychological implication, affective consistency, attribution, and common fallacies of logic and evidence, evaluation eventually might make more clear the rules we use to judge propositions to be delusional.

Brown assumes that schizophrenic delusions might have something to do with the factors that lead other people to break with their society's ideas about reality and rationality and to develop idiosyncratic ways of communicating and understanding their world. He suggests that delusions may not be so unique or qualitatively different in origin from other idiosyncratic beliefs that people form about politics, religion, paranormal phenomena, or other ethnic groups. In fact, it may help clarify our thinking if we recognize that delusional beliefs exist on a continuum with ordinary beliefs and attitudes. Strauss (1969) studied psychotic patients' accounts of their symptoms and argued that delusions and ordinary beliefs could be classified along four dimensions: the strength of the individual's conviction in the objective reality of the experience or belief; the extent to which the experience seems to be independent of stimuli or mainstream cultural determinants; the individual's level of preoccupation with the belief; and its implausibility. Bentall (1990) has developed a psychological model of how beliefs are formed that can be applied to delusional as well as normal beliefs.

DELUSIONS

Delusions are firmly held and formative beliefs of varying degrees of organization and cognitive complexity that strongly influence emotions and behavior and are directly or indirectly communicated to others. The term can refer to a wide range of quite different phenomena that range from fragmented utterances to highly organized and consistent beliefs about reality.

Bleuler (1950) believed that delusions resulted from disturbances of association and could be grouped into two classes: basic and elaborative. *Basic delusions* are themes or beliefs that developed as a result of strong affective influences. Once a basic delusion is established (e.g., delusions of persecution or grandiosity), it spreads in influence across many domains in the form of *delusional elaborations.* He assumed that delusions are the result of the interaction of thought disorder and disturbances of affect. Bleuler viewed the sequence that leads to the formation of schizophrenic delusions as beginning with an associational disturbance that leads to increased affective disturbance which in turn leads to weakening of logical reasoning that leads to the formation of delusions. Other theorists also posit that delusions are based on the experience of biologically based primary perceptual anomalies that the individual seeks to explain using normal cognitive mechanisms (Maher, 1966).

The assumption that an underlying biological anomaly is the cause of schizophrenic delusions was adopted by the phenomenological psychiatrist Karl Jaspers (1963). Jaspers distinguished between *primary and secondary delusions* in a manner that resembled aspects of Bleuler's model. Primary delusions, Jaspers assumed, result from biological causes that completely overwhelm the capacities of the individual and have no link to the subject's psychological history. Primary delusions begin with the experience of "uncanny" changes in experience and affect-laden perceptions that things and events suddenly seem to have special meaning. Jaspers argued that these experiences are not explainable in terms of life history, trauma, defenses, or conflicts, and thus he referred to them as primary. Primary delusions are indicators of transformations of the structure of experiencing that result from the effects of biological diatheses. The content of delusions were of interest to Jaspers because they tell us something about the "new order of being" that emerges from the diathesis (Bovet and Parnas, 1993).

Psychodynamic and interpersonal theorists, in contrast, emphasize the relationship between delusions and life history. Their focus is on the role of current and past relationships, underlying conflicts, and defensive structures in understanding the origins and meaning of delusions (Lansky, 1977). But what possibly could lead to such idiosyncratic ways of thinking and organizing one's experience as we observe in delusional thinking?

Wrobel (1990) suggests that the language and thought of schizophrenic patients is confusing because they have undergone such a profound transformation that their experiences are no longer commensurate with those of normals. Wrobel believes the origins of delusions can be traced to transformative experiences as times in which emotional functions are subject to incessant, abrupt oscillations. These oscillations are experienced as catastrophic and outside of voluntary control, resulting in feelings of terror and a profound sense of uncanniness.

Wrobel (1990) emphasizes the key role of a transformation of experience in schizophrenia. He refers to the acute symptom stage as the "illumination" period, a time in which emotional arousal causes every aspect of experience and one's surroundings to increase in meaning, and the sense of fear and uncanniness about what is happening intensifies. Once delusional ideas appear, it is as if a curtain has been removed and the essence of everything that has been happening is revealed. Events no longer appear to be random and happenstance but filled with a deep meaning and purpose. Descriptions of acute prepsychotic crises are similar to descriptions of mystic experiences, in that linear time ceases to exist and the experience results in basic transformations in perceptions, thoughts, and feelings about the world. This transformation of experience, Wrobel believes, is the kernel that forms the basis of schizophrenic delusions.

Schizophrenia is viewed as primarily a *semiotic disorder* by Wrobel (1990), because the conceptual world that allows for a common language that relates signifier and referent, and orders our experience undermines the psychotic experience of illumination. Schizophrenic illumination results in a transformation in cognition and experience in which ordinary associational conventions, meanings, and life patterns are disrupted. Wrobel, writing from a psychodynamic perspective, believes that fears, impulses, fantasies, and feelings which were unconscious before the onset of the disorder are now, through the transformations in cognition and experience that occur during acute episodes, consciously experienced.

Delusion and Myth

There are many ways of thinking about and understanding schizophrenic delusions, including subjective approaches. Gruszecka (1923) and Storch (1924) suggest that the transformations in experience, thought, and language observed in schizophrenic patients have parallels in mythology. Gruszecka believes that schizophrenic delusions result from the patients' inability to express what they are experiencing using ordinary logical categories and linguistic rules. As a consequence, schizophrenic thought has similarities to primitive myths, since both are based on forms of experience that cannot be accommodated and expressed through the ordinary rules of language and logic. Gruszecka (1923) identified the common elements of myths and delusions are as follows:

1. *wishful thinking;*
2. *projection of feelings;*
3. *complex thinking,* characterized by multiple, disparate concepts being attached to the same word or symbol;
4. *pictorial-sensory thinking,* where thoughts and feelings are expressed in concrete images;
5. *belief in the omnipotence of thought,* as in magic and sorcery there is a lack of distinction between imagination and the outside world; and
6. *lack of distinct separation between self and external environment,* so that thoughts cause events and external events and forces influence or control thoughts and feelings.

This approach draws upon the work of anthropologist Levi-Strauss (1969, 1973) who believed that primitive myths are as meaningful and comprehensible as ordinary logic. The difference between myth and ordinary logic, according to Levi-Strauss, is that myths are ways of organizing experience that are not based on external reality or natural occurrence but according to categories that derive from structures which are internal to the mind. Gruzecka argues that delusions, like myths, may appear bizarre and outlandish to the outsider yet reflect an inner reality that serves as a form of psychological defense. Many delusions have to do with important emotional and developmental issues that may be universal.

Delusions are also thought to be expressions that reflect what has been dissociated, hidden, and overlooked in life (Searles, 1960; Siirala, 1963; Sullivan, 1952). Psychodynamic theorists argue that biological vulnerabilities may have played an important role in the developmental process that led to this outcome, but they are not sufficient to explain the end result. From this perspective the knowledge references of delusions that appear ridiculous to the outsider can hold importance for the self whose psychological foundation revolves around the delusional beliefs.

Delusions As Signs of Cognitive Defects

Maher and Spitzer (1993) grouped theories of delusion formation into three broad categories:

1. There is a fundamental cognitive defect that impairs the capacity to draw valid conclusions from evidence. This defect is posited to be caused by an underlying neurobiological defect.
2. There is a pattern of deviant motivation, such that an otherwise intact cognitive system is distorted in the service of motives.
3. There is no cognitive defect present. Delusions arise from the operation of normal cognitive processes directed at explaining abnormal experiences, which may be either internal or attributable to genuinely anomalous experiences.

Maher (1990) developed a model of delusion formation which emphasizes the role of neuropsychological defect-caused anomalous experiences as the basis for delusional thinking in schizophrenia. This model differs from psychodynamic explanations in terms of two points: (1) it assumes a biological rather than mixed diathesis-psychosocial stress etiology for schizophrenic delusions and (2) the propositions describing the process of delusion formation subsequent to the anomalous experiences are consistent with psychodynamic descriptions but more systematically described. The basic propositions of Maher's model are as follows:

1. Delusional thinking is not in itself cognitively aberrant; the cognitive processes by which delusions are formed are not different from those by which normal beliefs are formed.
2. Delusions are similar to scientific theories in that they serve the purpose of providing order and meaning for empirical observations.
3. As in normal theorizing, the need for a theory arises when observations are discrepant with expectations.
4. When unpredicted events occur, they attract attention and trigger a feeling of significance and tension.
5. This tension motivates a search for explanation. The longer the search continues, the greater the tension.
6. Explanations bring relief, even if the explanation is not fully adequate to the situation.
7. Once the explanation is established, dissonant new data are disturbing and tend to be ignored or reinterpreted to fit the explanation. Data consistent with the explanation give relief and therefore are sought after.
8. The content of delusional explanations is likely to come from the experience and preoccupations of the individual. Thus, a person who feels guilty and ashamed of some act may develop the belief that he or she is being punished by God.
9. Theories are judged delusional by others if
   • they are based on observations made by the patient that are unavailable to others;
   • the data are available to others but do not appear to be anomalous to them; and
   • the feeling of discrepancy and puzzlement is activated neuropathologically when there is no actual discrepancy in the sequence of external events.

Maher notes that the coherence and quality of delusional beliefs are likely to be influenced by the intelligence and educational level of the patient, as well as the cultural context. Evidence that delusional beliefs involving thought broadcasting, thought insertion, thought withdrawal, and delusions of control or, influence and impulses occur with a frequency up to 70 percent in all schizophrenic patients across different cultures (Murray, 1986) is explained by Maher's concept of anomalous experiences as triggers. Evidence suggests that during acute schizophrenic episodes patients' experiences of internal and external reality are changed dramatically. Maher and Spitzer (1993) posit that these frightening and discrepant subjective experiences result from basic neuropsychological defects unique to schizophrenia. These frightening anomalous experiences, possibly along with perceptual disturbances, prompt the patient to seek explanations. These explanations, rather than descriptions of changes in experience, are delusions.

CATEGORIES OF SYMPTOMS

Multivariate analyses of ratings of positive and negative symptoms of schizophrenic patients have consistently derived three or four clusters of symptoms. These studies indicate that about 70 percent of shared variances in positive and negative symptom ratings can be accounted for by three symptom dimensions (Liddle, 1987, 1995; Cuesta and Peralta, 1995; Lenzenweger and Wetheringon, 1991). The three-factor structure has been confirmed in studies of long-term and recently admitted patients (Arndt, Alliger, and Andreasen, 1991). These dimensions hold promise as a way of reducing heterogeneity.

Andreasen and colleagues (1995) describe the three-symptom grouping as (1) negative symptoms (avolition, anhedonia, and affective flattening), (2) disorganization (inappropriate affect, thought disorder, and bizarre behavior), and (3) psychoticism (delusions and hallucinations). These different syndromes are often evident in the language and thoughts of schizophrenic patients. Delusions are included as a symptom of an active or psychoticism pattern in the three-factor model, but thought disturbance (e.g., tangential speech, thought derailment, bizarre thoughts) associated with symptoms of disorganization is also expressed in language. Negative symptoms tend to be associated with limited, unsystematized bizarre beliefs rather than systematized delusional content.

Tamminga (1999) described three similar patterns based on observations of unmedicated patients. Tamminga's active syndrome is similar to psychoticism and includes positive features of overactivity; pressured speech; manic, grandiose, and paranoid ideas; exaggerated or inappropriate labile affect; and affective delusions. A withdrawn syndrome consists of negative symptoms including social and emotional withdrawal, motor retardation, blunted affect, and poverty of speech. An unreality syndrome consists of Schneider's first-rank symptoms coexisting with symptoms of the other two syndromes.

Positive psychotic and disorganized syndromes are easier to illustrate than the negative syndrome, since thought disorder, delusions, and hallucinatory experiences are expressed in large part in language content and style. Negative symptoms, on the other hand, are primarily based on behavioral rather than thought and language deficits, therefore these narrative samples are briefer and less rich in content. The interviews that constitute the remainder of this chapter are presented as monologues, although in every case there originally was an interviewer present. The content has been substantially modified so that all personal or identifying information has been deleted or changed, but the basic structure of each patient's beliefs is retained. In each case the interview began with questions about how the patient ended up in the hospital.

Symptoms of Disorganization

Disorganization symptoms are often associated with severe levels of social, emotional, and cognitive impairment. Predominantly disorganized patients constitute no more than 10 or 15 percent of the population of patients.

Emma

Emma was appropriate in her behavior throughout the interview and was truly appreciative of the opportunity to have someone listen to her without being judgmental or giving advice. She had been frequently volatile and unpredictable during her lengthy hospitalization. The interview material clearly illustrates what is meant by tangentiality, thought derailment, illogicality, bizarre ideation, and delusional perception.

I'm in the hospital because I got tired of them pulling my teeth and them pulling babies out of me, things like that. The staff stole everything I worked for. They wouldn't let me stand, wouldn't let me sit down, nothing.

My father was an Indian. He flew planes, but he was mean to me. He didn't like me. He beat me. He had a bad disposition. I grew up everywhere, in cars, trucks, cars.

My memory is dying from being in a mean disposition. I got no teeth, everything is hurting, and there is nothing but lying. But you know you can't have them. They can walk out in the street every day and night. What do they want to treat me like that for? I had a lot of sickness from drinking and smoking and lying. I'm dying in here. Men drinking, smoking, pulling on me. They spray stuff on me. It feels like animals around here, lots of bees and snakes everywhere.

The staff poisons me with urine. They put medicine in my vagina and rectum every day. They are trying to get rid of me. They spray stuff on my cigarettes to make me sick. They talk about me like I was a dog. They say the old girl has spots all over her. They better not come around me—I'll kill them. Every time they give me something they poison me. They either give me urine or some kind of concentrate in pills. They cut on my vagina and rectum. They are trying to get rid of me because they want what is mine. They stabbed a man and burned him up, and I don't know how to deal with it. They talk to me like I am a dog.

Sometimes I can't go to sleep at night—these young girls excite me. Then the voices start to say do this, do that, don't do that or they might poison you, they might take your stuff. All day long, all night long, the voices concentrate on my mind. What bothers me is my mind. I think I got a tumor somewhere inside my brain. They are all my enemies trying to poison me, always asking for something out of my hand. I can't take it anymore.

Betsy

Well, an old man put his hands on my neck and I shot him. He kept trying to sneak around and peek in the windows, and I shot him right through the butt [laughs]. And then I shot him again. I had to have my breast operated on. There was blood in them, and I had to nurse my babies. Then he knocked me in the head with a stick and tried to kill me. My father wrote and told him that I couldn't hold food in my stomach and I was throwing up all the time. And I was taking care of my mother because my sister was mistreating her, so I beat the hell out of her.

First time I came here was twenty-eight years ago, and I been home a bunch of times.

I make bombs here out of dynamite. I have a big machine set up, and I use the energy from the sun to run it. It is a hard job, and I don't ever take any vacations. I had a boyfriend, but the Japanese came around and my baby was killed. They had my baby murdered. They did that in here. She was murdered, and they proved that from the blood-type analysis.

All my children are doctors. I been trying to get my daddy out from China. My daddy was an American man, but he was in China. But the Chinese tried to rape me one night, and I pushed him so he fell and broke his neck. I bombed the hell out of China.

I went to Washington, and I shot them, I shot them, I shot them all. I shot a whole lot of them. Because my son had to go to China and Vietnam too. Only son I had, and he beat me the whole time he was over there. I told him I wrote a book on my life and I wanted that book sold so he could make something out of himself. I'm afraid that people will steal my secrets and sell them. Then they will bomb Germany. I am a marine nurse, MD, that goes around to sing and dance. I love to dance, but my husband was too damned jealous. He put big tires on my little car so I could get killed. But I fooled him. I told the doctor that I couldn't nurse my son because I was all bloody and didn't have any milk in my breasts because I had a tumor.

Dora

I been so prayerful that I know you can tell that I was kin to myself or something. I know you can tell me what was going on. Oh, I am so glad to have weather like this and that they let me come down here. I just love every boy and man [laughs loudly]. No, I didn't, I declare I can do it in the bathtub [laughs loud and long].

I don't know why I'm doing talking about these things at all. I must be talented or something. It is dangerous to get near it, you know. What I'm getting is a whole bunch of voices, but it's not too bad. They might be eating you up, you know. I got slits inside of me. I can't choose what to do anymore. I'm not afraid of nothing.

They say we don't love our mother, but we do. They say a lot of things, we know we are not afraid of it. I'm more afraid of it, but daddy was tough. I shouldn't love my brother too much either. I'm going home to become a virgin again and go out.

I'm not a very nice person. I'm trying, although I'm not a very nice person and I'm not supposed to be a very nice person.

I love my aunt for eating me up. Honey, I am brazen just like her. And it's not broken, but it might break now. She is always ready willing and able and available. And he is not better than my father, is not better than my father.

I hated it there—she is so mean, she is a witch. You can be him and you could be dead too. I'm trying to find out what I'm doing this for. I don't want you to be too close because I could be dangerous to you. If I start messing with you or something. If you really were him I could be very dangerous to you. It sounds bad that I am dangerous, but he got beat up way before me. It must have been the devil that made me do that because I was trying to make him jealous.

Who does the soul belong to anyway?

I'm nice, nicer, and nicest and better, best, and better best. And I'll be a hands-on girl and I'll be nice today. It's this place that is confusing. If they put me in mean places like this I'll stay very much or too much, or go to jail or prison, or the doctor's office, and take the medicine. The personality is nothing. We'll be safe at the drinking party. My personality was good, but then the rules went all wrong. You have to live, you know, but not right is all wrong.

That stuff they give you could blind you.

You could be famous and I could be famous. They helped me again, the Lord and the devil. Lord [shrieks], my eyes are on fire. I hated my daddy. He said, "Who do you think you are, thinking you are so pretty?" He took advantage of me is what he did. I am swamped with his damned tongue. I'm a full woman. I didn't hit you or take off my clothes. Somebody shoved a cylinder into my chest, because they didn't like my type. And you see those star types that got out of the operator because the show must go on. They do it in the grave.

Symptoms of Psychoticism

Most patients characterized by symptoms of psychoticism remain cognitively intact to a greater degree than other groups. Their delusions tend to be systematized and coherent, but the content can be bizarre. Symptoms are most likely to be episodic; they may remit, remain fixed, or be replaced by a predominance of negative symptoms over time, but delusions tend to become fixed. These beliefs may preoccupy the patient during active phases of the disorder and diminish somewhat during remission. The systematized delusions of paranoid patients seem particularly refractory.

Juanita

I have been debriefed and computerized. When I was operated on they also treated me with a laser. While they were putting the electrodes in my lungs, my brain, and the vagina, down in the intestinal tract, all over they were also seating electrodes. Once they got the electrodes in they began to debrief me and divested me of all of my information.

My brain is working via transmit and receive. The laser is hooked up to a computer that makes a little figure up of you, and the laser works on that figure at the same time that it is working on you. It is something like a mechanical man—you work on the mechanical man and it works on you. Now the question is why was I computerized?

I was computerized by the medical research people. When I was in there to be diagnosed the research people told me that there is going to be a revolution between black and white. They said, "Why do you want to be black?" I said, "I don't want to be black, I just want to be me." They said that I have to choose, they wanted me to be either a whore or a spy. I said, "No, whore or spy" so they decided that they would have to computerize me because they couldn't have someone with my high quality going around as a black person.

If you talk to the FBI they will know what I am talking about. I've been to the FBI twice to be debugged. It is easy for them to throw an extra bug on you when you are being debriefed. I went by FBI headquarters in Washington, and they took it out for me.

What do you think it means when you hear on the televisions things like, "Ladies of the evening are meeting in the church to vie for political plums?" That is how far this thing has gone—now call girls are vying for political favors and they are announcing it on the television. I don't know if the research institute is outside of us or inside of us. They could be fascists as communists.

A piece of the computer works with me at all times. It covers each area of my past life, my likes, knowledge, thoughts, opinions, feelings—it is endless. Of course they couldn't get it all, that would have required that they have everything there when they debriefed me. They took my knowledge with the laser, but they can put some of it back in me. They can do that with the laser and mesa. That is why I went to the research institute to get my computer part, and when I got upset they put me in here.

Suzy

Suzy is a shy, quiet, anxious person. She is helpful to the staff and industrious. Her appearance seems slightly eccentric in that she wears a head scarf indoors even in the warmest weather; otherwise her behavior is unremarkable. One could have a lengthy conversation with Suzy and never learn of her voices. She would simply appear to be a somewhat shy, mildly anxious, distracted individual.

I hear voices, and sometimes I think that people around me have microphones in the walls so they can hear everything that I think. I can't sleep at night because I hear those awful voices every day. I get afraid because I think criminals are coming to get me—especially at night. Sometimes I think the hospital has been taken over by new people overnight, and they are out to get me. I think they are spying on me and I can't get away.

If I put something in my hair like a comb or a scarf over my head, that helps the voices go away. It makes me feel more secure. I don't want them to know what is in my head. I feel like people are just in the air and in the walls. It's like you are thinking something to yourself, and the walls hear you and they repeat it, and then the people hear what the walls say. I don't have any privacy at all! And the wall will say things like, "We know that you are a homosexual, you can't deny that at all." And I have to say, "No, I am not a homosexual." Then the walls repeat it again and again and it just repeats and repeats.

And nobody acts like they hear it. I know that they do hear it, but they don't show any emotion or act like they hear it. I get so tense when I go through it. I get upset and I suffer so much. I am usually calm in the mornings. Then the voices start up in the afternoon, and they can be terrible at night after supper. I don't know where they come from or why they like to torture me so.

Annette

In my estimation a psychosexual, homicidal, sadistic personality is giving abnormal suggestions to seduce me. She gives other signs in the form of frustrations, abnormal sex, anything that produces an emotional reaction, eventually producing cruelty to the point that the psychosexual, homicidal, sadistic personality has tried to prove that its daughter is guilty.

She, no it, had me put in here. Since the psychosexual, homicidal, sadistic personality has claimed possession of me I am considered to be part of the black community, but I am not. I am of French-Polynesian extraction.

I have always realized that her mental vibrations were contrary to my way of thinking. I have always been completely immune to her vibrations. The psychosexual, homicidal, sadistic personality sticks her head into my personal sexual matters mentally. This same psychosexual, homicidal, sadistic personality killed my father who was a French-Polynesian priest. She killed him because of a metaphysical love.

The psychosexual personality saw such a profound epitome of metaphysical love that she decided to kill the idea in order to please herself, and this she did. Now she is trying to destroy me.

Thelma

I've had spiritual experiences. It is interesting because it is hard to distinguish between spiritual experiences and sickness. Now I am questioning the value of spiritual experiences because there isn't much point in devoting my life to spirituality, is there?

I was convinced that there is order in these experiences and that they mean something. I am very pure now. I have no sexual desires anymore. And I am really a masturbator. I know what real sexual desire is like. I know these spiritual experiences have freed me from desire, or as John put it, "I can perform evil no more." It's not that sex is evil. It's not only sexual desire, it's that you have no desire, period.

You don't really know what is going on after this though. I hate to say it, but I think that it is the penis. I think the penis is the foundation of intelligence. And I don't even like the penis. It really doesn't do much for most women.

I am impressed that God seems very limited in what he can do. Like I am not sure what miracles he can perform. People are sick and I am sick. I don't think I would be in this state if I hadn't had spiritual experiences. I think they opened me up. Spirituality is a double-edged sword. I am also convinced that Jesus made some mistakes, based on my own spiritual experiences.

My experiences have taught me what civilization is about. But I am not sure it is worth committing my life to. I used to hear voices. I've reached out to a spiritual master. But my spirituality is really a hobby.

My voices talk about the CIA, about drugs, and all the time are talking about sex. I think I've got a homosexual spirit that has possessed me. I am convinced that it is a spirit and not myself. It was always the voice of the same guy. He would pretend to be other people. Sometimes he would pretend to be a psychiatrist.

I think this voice, this spirit may still influence me subconsciously. I am very suspicious of the voice. He hates me, he wants to kill me. He told me that. I had a car crash one time because he blinded me. He will burn through my skin, through my leg, and like he is supposed to be a fabric of my imagination? You are not supposed to exist, but I know that you do exist, you stupid spirit!

He makes my heart race and feel really painful. He is trying to terrify me. He doesn't command me now, but he does try to terrify me. If he can block my vision, what else can he do? He told me he was going to make my eye wander around by loosening the muscles. I couldn't close my eyes or go to sleep. Finally something lured him away. Maybe God finally did something for once.

William

William's delusions of grandeur and persecution are prominent. Why do we assume that some underlying brain dysfunction is causing William to think this way, yet the same attribution is not made about other individuals with deviant spiritual beliefs?

Insanity is caused by eating seed, human sperm. It gets lodged in the brain and causes a shift so you get lost in time and acquire the personality of other people. That is what causes people to remain in the hospital.

Others were trying to learn how to reclaim my form of seed. Because each seed can receive radio messages from God's brain. They thought they could get all the stored seed and give them different personalities. It wouldn't work though, because you cannot separate the individual from the knowledge that they thought they were going to get.

They wanted people to swallow seed to get educated. But people get educated by God's brain putting out messages, specifically by the universe which is the highest thinking cell in my brain.

The universe is the highest thinking cell in my brain. There is only one of them, and it is two billion years old. And it is in my brain. It announced itself to me by a message from God to me that stimulated my whole brain. Everything around me began to disintegrate by radio waves, except for my speaking voice me and I was the only thing left. This happened to me when I was in my bed resting. It was like a dream. It was an escape into my subconscious, into the universe which is my subconscious. It happened that way to show me that I was the universe. There is another concept of the universe too, as the whole of everything. One is the highest thinking cell in my brain, and the other is the whole of everything, all of matter, all of space that ever existed, expanding forever.

The world had to disintegrate in order to show me that I have the universe inside my brain. Only the God family can have the highest thinking cell. The God family has seven individuals—my mother and father, me, my wife, and our three children. They are waiting in orbit above the earth in a stationary orbit, waiting to come down when the time is right, to pick me up and bring me back to heaven. It will take a million years to get there.

I am here on Earth to kill all the people who persecuted me when I was a child, with my radio brain, and to protect all of the good people who never swallowed seed. Those who never swallowed seed and didn't have to go crazy. Those who have swallowed seed will be in abject pain when they die. Everything must come to an end on Earth in order to perfect the universe. Everything on Earth will move to heaven with me or will expire peacefully if they never swallowed seed or had antagonism toward the God family. Everyone that swallowed seeds killed themselves off because of the way the seed operate. They cause you to feel air and space and punishment and pain forever, expanding for a million years.

For years the family persecuted me as an infant and throughout my whole life span. But they have been countered since I was born again with the universe taking over everything. They tried to kill me because they wanted to kill God. They beheaded me, tortured me, mutilated me. That is why I want to get even with them, and I can do it with my radio brain. All I have to do is think it and they will be destroyed, but first they will have to feel intense pain and their bodies will twist and wither.

I am here to set an example for all people who haven't turned to darkness and swallowed seed. They will be able to join me up in heaven. When I leave for heaven I will be changed into my perfect self and will have no hair on my body, my eyes will be blue, and my skin will be olive, and my hair will be golden the way it was when I was born. My body will be sealed. I will have no penis and no anus. I will only eat perfect food, and I will never have to worry about excreting.

They thought it was necessary to kill God so they could continue to exist as they like to with all the sexual perversity they wanted. Sexual perversion was the whole cause why everything went crazy. They were paid to get rid of me. And I was dead but receiving more and more punishment. They beheaded me, carved me up, burned me, hung me. They did every conceivable thing to punish me. That is why I am here to get even with them. And I could do it easily with my radio brain, without giving them a scratch or scar that can be detected by anyone. My mere presence causes them to feel pain—the same pain they caused me to feel, intense pain for five years. They would experience this for a million years in just two seconds time.

It takes just one signal to your consciousness in order to die out. When everything comes to an end on earth everything will fold right up. There will be nothing left on earth at all. Nothing at all except for the good people who I will take to heaven. The good people will expire perfectly on earth in two milliseconds and will experience everything that the God family could have experienced. It took me a million years to put it together. I came here filled up with a message and enough information to have made it possible for every living soul on earth to have expired without feeling pain and to have ascended into heaven. But, because of the things that happened to me after I arrived on earth, it became impossible for people to expire without feeling the pain and agony that they caused me to feel.

I was born perfectly in heaven. I could have stayed perfect and grown out to full height and lived on in heaven apart from real people. But I elected to come down, to take a million-year voyage when I was an infant down to earth to straighten things out. To make it perfect for as many people who wanted to make it that way for themselves and who preserved themselves by not swallowing seeds.

William Fifteen Years Later

That depends on what you mean by age. I believe that I am two billion years old, since I am one with the universe. If you mean date of birth then I am one million years old, born through my mother in heaven a million years ago. If you mean date of my arrival on earth, I arrived on Earth forty-three years ago. If you mean age in terms of resurrection, after years of being murdered and tortured I was born again thirty-six years ago. So for legal purposes and the purposes of this hospital I'm forty-three years old.

I was tortured and murdered because the people tried to destroy God's plan to judge and perfect the Earth. I was murdered, tortured, bled to death, and then shot with guns and stabbed repeatedly with knives and eventually cremated, burned up. But my soul escaped from my body and made myself over again in the household for the family that murdered me.

This was all revealed to me along with my true identity and my plan for the Earth, as the true Son of God.

I have been in this hospital five times. The first time was right after I graduated from college. In this lifetime I've never been married. I have a wife waiting for me and three infants in heaven.

I'm in multiple locations. I can be anywhere, anytime that I want to be. I am an infant now—an infant Jesus in a heavenly dream. I believe I'm an infant now, dreaming, so I can be anywhere I want to be at anytime. This hospital is just one place I am. I'm many places at many different times. My imagination is real because my dreams are real.

This hospital and heaven are the only places that I'm aware of right now. But during the last decade I was president of every country in the world. And knowledgeable to every individual who had been judged.

In my subconscious mind there are many channels—that part is the God of the universe. The God part is separate from the man. I am both, man and God.

The God part is infinite, the man part is just as ordinary as you are except that it is the guide, the controller of my subconscious mind which is infinite.

I was in heaven for two billion years plus one million in the head of my father thinking about what was to come to pass in the cosmos, including what each individual would do on an individual basis. It took me two seconds to plan a human life span, and I was thinking a plan for each individual on an individual basis.

I was placed in here because of a conspiracy of people at this hospital. Those people discovered my consuming flesh and became frightened. In the seed of flesh is the messages of the subconscious of individuals. Those people consume infancy. They discovered that I would be born on Earth, and they brought me here as an infant first in an institution of elementary school, then in this mental institution, then in college at the college level. They thought they could acquire all my knowledge by consuming my flesh. And they thought I was related to the X family because I had been living with and raised by that family.

They wanted me placed in institutions in order to consume my unborn children to discover the truth of the universe. Then they plan to destroy me and have my children enslaved in their heads forever—the way God made the planets and the stars.

I'm safe here because I have in my brain God watching me. I was not safe in my community because they wanted to destroy me. They stopped me on the road in my car and commanded me to give them instructions to operate the X rays in my car. They thought I had destroyed me as well as taken the X ray over and that they could use it to get to go to the cosmos. They thought that they would be able to do that. These were people from the hospital, all in conspiracy to destroy me. They were afraid because they knew God gave me final judgment for starting total destruction in hell which is the final act in creation. God and I have capacity to use any mechanism that is to be imagined to protect my thoughts. My father announced, God announced that to the world.

I taught vicariously from projections from my mind in universities throughout the world. That was televised to every real person through the channels of God's mind.

The doctors would say that I hear voices because I hear radio messages from God, but they're not voices. They're telepathic messages that come through waves which can be modulated and turned on and off.

Negative Symptoms

Negative symptoms are evidenced in the absence of social behaviors, interpersonal involvement, and goals. These symptoms are minimally evident in language, since alogia (the absence of dialogue) is an important marker of this pattern. Many long-term patients evidence negative symptoms, but this does not necessarily mean that they are mentally inactive.

George

There ain't nothing that caused me to come into the hospital. They killed my family, and the woman who killed my family does what ever she wants to do. She lies, steals, and murders. She killed my brother and told them that I was him. My brother was killed in 1946, and the court keeps saying that I am my brother.

She was in New York on the assembly line, and the barber said to put him in jail because he is a Russian right. Her son went to my grandfather—he was a Chili-Creole. He was part Indian and part white who bred with a black woman. She was a Denmark-Cuban.

I am taking medicine against my will. It affects me bad. I feel like I am going blind, my head hurts, my tongue gets like it's made of rubber so I can't speak. She keeps me here so she can get my money and because I am being punished by the government because of discrimination. Discriminations like from the Black Panthers, the Ku Klux Klan, and others. You see all the staff is either Black Panthers, Ku Klux Klan, or African Congo people, and they are working for the woman and the judge to keep me from my money.

Freida

The evil people keep putting me back in here. I don't know why. I suppose it's the red, white, and blue. People in my past have caught up with me. The Bible, it's in the Bible. In the Bible it says it was a Christian for the red, white, and blue. I should have married them and gotten straightened out. Then God's kingdom would have come to Earth.

Maybe it's not the communists, maybe it is the devil and God. The Chinese or anybody could be on the devil's side, and they are. I am on the Lord's side. See you've got to have somebody to keep that sun down. Sunshine in my eyes makes me blue. Makes me cry.

If people had caught up with me before all this happened, but they waited until the last minute. I don't know whether it is the communists or, well, the communists represent the devil, don't they? They don't want me to keep America free—that's why they put me in here.

Larry

Well, they treat me but so good and it's not bad in here, but not that they can't. It's like it's not too bad and not too good. This is my place. It's kind of like a place I want to be in and that I never want to leave. It is comfortable to sleep in. It usually is unless some reason happens you know. There's some reason sometime and things that happen.

Sometimes I wonder about that nuclear war that is coming up. I do know who is pushing the button. I don't know the exact person. Not that I know the truth about who or what would do it for real. It's close if somebody does something. I've possessed nuclear rockets. I could have done it a few times myself too.

Erika

Well, you draw light from the sun in the sky. Then you draw lightning into a big thing like a ball—it comes out and it makes a bomb. I made the first airplane one time when I was only five years old. Now I'm getting old. I made it like this. A pelvis here and a tail line there. They threw it on China.

I was worried about my son. He is a doctor in Korea. Now the war is over. The United States couldn't never get along with anybody. They always make fusses with other countries.

I found out and I am getting praise from God too. And the plane hit the sound barrier. Now it's just lightning and the plane will burn up. The Germans are smart people. The doctor here is a German, smart, smart.

The Germans plant flowers like this. You put your flowers down in the dirt, pull a tray over them, pour water all around them, and then they take the seeds from the flowers and make perfume. I saw them do it. I saw my daddy do it too.

I saw Jesus one night in the sky. That's when my body started getting better. But I couldn't speak none. I choked.

SUMMARY

The interviews presented in this chapter provide a sampling of the variety of types of delusional thinking that is characteristic of schizophrenic patients. The range of thoughts expressed by these individuals illustrates the difficulties of describing the common underlying features that are "pathognomic" of delusional thinking in schizophrenia. Given the fact that delusions occur in a number of disorders, it is unlikely that any one explanatory model will explain the etiology of delusions in general. It is possible that delusional beliefs, even among schizophrenic patients, have very different etiologies.

Some researchers argue that we should discard the assumption that schizophrenia is a unitary disorder and analyze patients' difficulties in terms of individual dysfunctions in functional areas such as attention, memory, problem solving, and information processing (Bentall, Jackson, and Pilgrim, 1988). Brockington (1992) proposes that the notion of schizophrenia as a single disorder should be discarded and replaced by alternative descriptive models that will foster new energy, freedom of inquiry, and ultimately more complex and appropriate models for understanding the origins of symptoms and functional deficits. He suggests that the systematized delusions of many positive-symptom patients may require complex explanatory models that incorporate the influence of many factors, including the formative role of affects, conflicts, self-esteem issues, and biological and cultural influences, as well as the role of symptom-maintaining factors such as inertia, the need for self-justification, social isolation, hypervigilance for confirmatory cues from others, and restricted interests and experiences. The defects and symptoms of disorganization, on the other hand, may be based on a more limited range of biological and psychosocial dysfunctions.

These arguments have not had much impact on the mainstream literature on schizophrenia; however, it is apparent, even in these brief excerpts, that schizophrenic patients are a heterogenous group. The question is this: "Is there an underlying biological etiology common to this diagnosis?"

SECTION II:
INTEGRATIVE MODELS
AND LEVELS OF ANALYSIS

Section II presents several integrative approaches that help to move beyond single-cause models of thinking about schizophrenia. Stress-vulnerability or diathesis-stress models foster thinking about schizophrenia in terms of multiple contributing causes. In some cases stress is used by researchers to refer only to environmentally caused biological dysfunctions, and in other cases the term is used in the more typical manner to refer to psychological or life stress. In either case, it is evident to most researchers that causal models of schizophrenia formulated in terms of only one level of analysis are unlikely to be valid. Most professionals espouse some form of stress-vulnerability explanatory model, although what this means varies enormously between researchers of different theoretical orientations. General systems theory, described briefly in Chapter 6, seems so eminently sensible that most professionals agree with the concept, but no one has yet been able to formulate an actual systems model or description of schizophrenia. These chapters will provide a framework in which to think about the single-level analysis models that are summarized in Chapters 7 through 14.

Chapter 5

Vulnerability-Stress Models

Many writers espouse some variation of a stress-vulnerability or diathesis-stress model of schizophrenia. These models attempt to bridge the gap between genetic and environmental contributing factors and emphasize the role of feedback loops and chance events in the development of schizophrenia. Vulnerability-stress or diathesis-stress models can integrate a complex array of factors that potentially contribute to the risk, course, and outcome of schizophrenia.

A *diathesis* is commonly thought of as a biological predisposition to develop a disease or morbid condition (Campbell, 1989), although there is no reason to assume that experiences could not also result in diathetic vulnerability or predisposition. Most biological models assume that the diathesis for schizophrenia is some polygenetic defect that is beyond the confines of normal variability. The diathesis for schizophrenia is also assumed to be some adverse event during prenatal development that results in brain dysfunction. Diathetic (vulnerable) individuals are assumed to be predisposed to respond with abnormal reactions to the ordinary stresses of life.

Diathesis-stress models vary with regard to their assumptions about whether diathesis and stress are understood to be necessary, sufficient, or contributing causes. Theorists also differ on the issue of whether the genetic diathesis for schizophrenia is monogenetic or polygenetic in nature. Polygenetic theorists assume some form of an additive model of diathesis-stress interaction, in which multiple genetic factors and stressors contribute additively to a liability threshold. The role of environmental factors is thought to be a function of the magnitude of genetic liability (Gottesman and Shields, 1982). Persons genetically above the threshold require little or no stress to develop schizophrenia, those just below the threshold will develop the disorder under most circumstances, those moderately below the threshold require severe stress to develop the disorder, and those far below the threshold are unlikely to develop brief psychotic reactions even under conditions of extreme stress (Fowles, 1992).

Many theorists assume that the genetic diathesis for schizophrenia is quite restricted in the general population (Guze, 1989). Consequently, life stress is viewed as a relatively trivial element in the etiology of schizophrenia. Other theorists assume that the polygenetic influences that contribute to risk for schizophrenia are widely distributed in the normal population, and they emphasize the additional importance of life stressors. Since no one has been able to identify a genetic marker for schizophrenia, the nature and necessity of a genetic diathesis for vulnerability to schizophrenia remains a matter of speculation.

There are several neurological diseases where a genetic diathesis alone is sufficient to produce the disorder. This cannot be the case with schizophrenia, since monozygotic twins do not usually both manifest the disorder. Therefore, most theorists assume that vulnerability to schizophrenia is polygenetic in nature. The diathesis-stress model implies that additional influences in the form of stressors must be present to activate the potential for schizophrenia. Most assume that the diathesis must be expressed in the form of behavioral or biological characteristics that are present regardless of the clinical state of the individual (Nuechterlein et al., 1992). Although no vulnerability marker has been reliably established that is present in all persons prior to onset, or after diagnosis in most schizophrenic patients and their biological relatives, there are several strong candidates, including soft neurological signs detectable in early childhood that have probable fetal or perinatal origins (Lyon et al., 1989), maternal viral infections during pregnancy (Lyon et al., 1989), and obstetrical complications (Cannon, 1998). It may be, as many contemporary versions of diathesis-stress models suggest, that these environmental influences result in brain-based impairments that contribute to schizophrenic outcomes among only those genetically predisposed to the disorder.

Other researchers have attempted to identify vulnerability markers in the form of various neurointegrative deficits that are present more often in schizophrenic patients and their first-degree relatives than in controls. Eye-tracking deficits are among the top candidates (Iacono, 1993). Eye tracking is the ability to follow a moving target with the eyes. Many schizophrenic patients are unable to track a visual stimulus moving horizontally across the visual field with smooth eye motions. This deficit is observed in about only 8 to 15 percent of the normal population. When following the target, some schizophrenic patients' eyes tend repeatedly to fall back and catch up with a jerky movement. Eye-tracking deficits have been reported to occur in somewhere between 20 to 80 percent of schizophrenic patients and to occur with higher incidence among first-degree relatives of schizophrenic patients than in the normal population (Iacono, 1993). Thus, theorists propose that impairments in eye-tracking ability may be indicative of an underlying neurointegrative deficit that is a marker for vulnerability to schizophrenia. Since not all or even most schizophrenic patients evidence this deficit, it may turn out to be a vulnerability marker for only a certain subset of patients with this diagnosis.

Some theorists propose that *schizotypal* personality predispositions or traits, such as anhedonia, tendencies to dissociative experiences, and superstitious beliefs, are expressions of a genetic diathesis for schizophrenia (Chapman, Chapman, and Fowles, 1993).

A "TWO-HIT" BIOLOGICAL MODEL OF DIATHESIS STRESS

Mednick and colleagues (1998) propose a "two-hit" model to explain the basis for schizophrenia. The model includes the following assumptions:

1. The *first hit* stems from a genetic liability for schizophrenia, which results from a preprogrammed disruption of fetal neural development during a critical period of gestation.
2. This disruption can be partially mimicked by teratogenic factors (e.g., maternal influenza infection in the second trimester) that coincide with the critical neural development period for schizophrenia.
3. The genetic disruption is more serious and extensive than the effect of an adventitious teratogen.
4. The first hit (genetic or teratogenic) creates a vulnerability for schizophrenic decompensation. If the individual's perinatal and childhood experiences are free of severe stress, he or she will exhibit adult behavior that approximates DSM-IV schizotypal or paranoid personality disorder.
5. The *second hit* can take the form of delivery complications or nonoptimal early child rearing. The nature of the second hit helps determine the course of the illness.
6. For those made vulnerable by the first hit, delivery complications may damage periventricular brain regions (associated with autonomic nervous system excitatory responding) and contribute to severe reductions in emotional expression and responding.
7. Those made vulnerable by the first hit who do not experience delivery complications may decompensate if they encounter severe stresses during early childhood. Those individuals with responsive autonomic nervous systems may decompensate with predominantly positive symptoms.

8. Those with delivery complications that lead to periventricular damage will have increased risk for predominantly negative symptoms, regardless of the presence or absence of childhood stressors.

Evidence in support of the two-hit model was obtained in a longitudinal study of a cohort of high-risk offspring and controls over a period of approximately twenty years. Brain scans indicated significant linear increases in sulcal enlargement of the cerebral cortex as a function of level of genetic risk. In addition, high-risk individuals who developed schizophrenia, especially those with negative symptoms, evidenced more sulcal enlargement than all other groups.

Additional evidence in support of the two-hit model includes research conducted in Helsinki, Finland, which indicated that mothers of schizophrenic patients were significantly more likely to have been treated for an upper respiratory infection during the second trimester of pregnancy than those exposed during the first or third trimesters. Second-trimester patients were significantly elevated on paranoid symptoms. Comparisons of sulcal and ventricular cerebrospinal fluid (CSF) brain volume ratios for the right and left hemispheres among viral (nineteen patients) and control schizophrenics (sixty-six patients) indicated that the viral schizophrenia patients showed a significant increase in sulcal CSF-brain ratio in the left hemisphere. There were no differences between these groups in ventricular CSF-brain ratio.

These data are interpreted by Mednick and colleagues (1998) as indicating that maternal influenza infection during the second trimester acts as a teratogenic disturbance that disrupts the development of the fetal brain. The second trimester is thought to be critical because it is a period of rapid development of specific brain regions. Periods of rapid development are periods of special vulnerability for brain areas. A teratogen or genetically based disruption of development during this vulnerable period will have significant effects on areas undergoing rapid growth. For example, the prefrontal cortex and thalamus are developing rapidly during this period and may be at heightened risk. Mednick and colleagues (1998) suggest that maternal influenza infection may disrupt fetal neural migration, positioning, connecting, and pruning. Failures in these processes result in cognitive deficits that are evident during infancy and early childhood.

To test this prediction, measures of infant habituation of visual attention were obtained in samples of six-month-old children. Measures of habituation of attention in infants are good predictors of later school readiness and intellectual development. Rapid habituation is indicative of a well-developed central nervous system. Infants with mothers who were diagnosed with a second-trimester influenza infection evidenced greater deficits in habituation of visual attention than those whose mothers had no infection or whose infection occurred during the first trimester.

Comparisons of Chinese nineteen-year-olds exposed to a severe earthquake while in utero in the third and sixth months with controls born one year later (not earthquake exposed) were consistent with findings of habituation in six-month-old infants exposed to influenza in the sixth month of gestation. The nineteen-year-olds exposed during the sixth month of gestation scored significantly lower on the Raven Progressive Matrices than the other two groups. Mednick et al. (1998) believe this evidence indicates that cognitive deficits evident during infancy are likely indicators of vulnerability to later schizophrenia and are associated with a disruption of development caused by second-trimester maternal exposure to influenza infection or severe stress associated with an earthquake. The authors speculate that severe prenatal stress experienced by the parent may cause vasoconstriction of the placenta, which, in turn, results in damaging effects on the fetus's developing brain structures.

The idea of a viral infection during fetal development compromising the way the genetic code unfolds in the development of the brain, that in turn results in a range of possible vulnerabilities that have a significant impact on the developmental process is plausible. However as Sanislow and Carson (2001) indicate, lack of a clear theoretical model of the way these neurological insults affects developmental processes and their relationship to identifiable pathophysiological processes and eventually to behavioral symptoms renders these findings just among many that have been catalogued.

VULNERABILITY

Vulnerability refers to the phenotypic or trait expression of the magnitude of a person's diathesis, in other words, his or her relatively enduring proclivity toward developing the symptoms of a disorder. In this sense, vulnerability is generally thought of as a stable trait that is independent of nonenduring clinical symptoms so that its phenotypic features should be present premorbidly, at onset, during acute symptom stages, and in remission. Vulnerability should not be thought of as fixed but as shaped during each developmental stage by transactions with the environment (McGlashan, 1994). Aspects of vulnerability can be genetic; acquired biologically through intrauterine, birth, and postnatal complications; or psychosocial in origin. The list of postulated vulnerabilities is extensive.

Vulnerability models are not tied to a particular theoretical perspective and have the advantage of being able to integrate etiological concepts and interventions based on multiple perspectives. The vulnerability-risk perspective is sometimes associated with the assumption that risk for or vulnerability to schizophrenia is normally distributed in the population and that vulnerability markers are independent of stage of the disorder. Eysenck (1992), for example, cites evidence that genetic risk for schizophrenia is normally rather than bimodally distributed in the population (Eysenck, 1992).

Zubin and Spring (1977) proposed an early and somewhat unique risk-vulnerability model. In this model each person is assumed to be endowed with a degree of vulnerability that under suitable circumstances can express itself in an episode of schizophrenic illness. Vulnerability is more than the result of genetic inheritance; the term also refers to acquired characteristics and propensities. Inborn vulnerability is genetic and is evidenced in the neurophysiology and biology of the person. Acquired vulnerability may result from trauma, perinatal complications, diseases, family influences, adolescent peer interactions, and other life stresses that have an effect on the likelihood of development of the disorder.

Zubin and Spring maintain that vulnerability to schizophrenia is a complex function of the influence of genetic and acquired characteristics, and as such is one aspect of the range of human variability as evidenced in diverse characteristics such as competence, intelligence, achievement, and other aspects of functioning. They maintain that no one is entirely immune from the possibility of a schizophrenic episode. Individuals with a high genetic loading are more likely to "break down" in response to relatively mild stress or hassles and to have repeated, severe, and long-lasting schizophrenic episodes. Less vulnerable individuals, with low genetic loadings and/or acquired vulnerabilities, can manage significant stressors without experiencing a schizophrenic episode or are more likely to have one brief episode with good recovery. Each person is assumed to have a threshold of vulnerability, and the level of stress required to precipitate a schizophrenic episode is a function of one's level of vulnerability. Zubin and Spring (1977) maintain that vulnerability is normally distributed in the population and is not necessarily genetic in origin.

A second departure from orthodoxy implied in the risk-vulnerability model proposed by Zubin and Spring (1977) is that schizophrenia is not viewed as a steady state or chronic deteriorating condition but as a permanent vulnerability to develop episodes of the disorder. The authors distinguish between vulnerability to schizophrenia, which they regard as an enduring trait, and episodes of the disorder that tend to wax and wane. They reviewed the evidence regarding chronicity of schizophrenia and concluded that in most cases schizophrenia has a course much like an episodic disorder, such as depression or allergies, rather than a chronic process of deterioration. Therefore, Zubin and Spring argue that in most cases schizophrenic patients are capable of eventually returning to relatively normal levels of functioning.

Stress has a dual role in the stress-vulnerability model; it has both a formative influence, when childhood experiences increase vulnerability, and a precipitating influence, when current stressors trigger symptoms. Negative symptoms are not necessarily viewed as intrinsic to the disorder but can be understood as the result of being labeled, medicated, institutionalized, and treated as schizophrenic. Chronicity and poor outcome are thought to be the result of how the disorder is treated rather than an inevitable aspect of schizophrenia. Zubin and Spring maintain that outcome is largely determined by the appropriateness of the ecological niche and social context to which the patient is returned, rather than innate biological deficiencies.

STRESS

"Stress" is a generic term that can mean many different things depending on the theoretical perspective of the writer. Stress is often used to refer to proximal life events that appear to contribute to or provoke the appearance of symptoms. Understanding the role of stress in schizophrenia is complicated by the reciprocal influences between distal and proximal life stressors, personality traits and propensities, possible neurological deficits, and symptoms (Norman and Malla, 1993). A child that is emotionally labile, aggressive, inattentive, impulsive, immature, and/or moody and difficult to console is likely to provoke harsh discipline, frustration, and rejection from parents, teachers, and peers. A shy, anxious, inhibited, passive, and withdrawn child with or without mild cognitive deficits, on the other hand, is likely to elicit overprotectiveness, enmeshment, and confused boundaries from parents and rejection or indifference from peers. The nature of stress that is experienced is associated with reciprocal influence processes between parent, child, and others and cannot be defined independent of context.

Biological theorists tend to refer to factors such as prenatal infections or delivery complications when they introduce the term *stress* in their formulations. Psychosocial theorists, in contrast, mean something related to current and past life events of an interpersonal nature.

The role of different stressors in the risk for and etiology of schizophrenia remains largely undetermined, but once an episode of schizophrenia has occurred ample evidence is available to indicate that stress is associated with changes in symptoms (Norman and Malla, 1993). Many schizophrenic patients are highly vulnerable to even minor hassles (Norman and Malla, 1993). Even after patients are stabilized on medication, stressors can be critical factors in relapse (Nuechterlein et al., 1992). Studies show that a pattern of high *expressed emotion* (EE) in families of schizophrenic patients is associated with increased risk for relapse of patients sent home after medication and hospitalization (Vaughan and Leff, 1976). Research on EE has demonstrated the effects of family members' criticism, anger, guilt inducement, and overinvolvement on the likelihood of patient relapse; it is not however, related to the risk for onset of the disorder (Valone et al., 1983).

Day (1986) suggests that at least four classes of environmental settings are particularly stressful for individuals with a vulnerability to schizophrenia: (1) *cognitively confusing environments,* such as those associated with family communication disturbances; (2) *emotionally critical or intrusive environments,* such as those identified in EE studies; (3) *overly demanding environments* that place demands on the patient which are beyond his or her capabilities, and (4) *threatening or demoralizing environments.* These stressors appear to play a role in the risk for schizophrenia, as well as the risk for relapse (Kuipers, 1979; Leff et al., 1982).

The term *stress* is used in contemporary biological diathesis-stress models to refer to factors such as prenatal infections, complications during delivery, and exposure to infectious agents or toxins (McGuffin et al., 1994). Day (1986) suggests that researchers should move away from a focus on single sources of stress (e.g., life events, expressed emotion) and include the more comprehensive concept of "toxic environments" that include multiple, interacting sources of stress.

Meehl (1993) is one of the few prominent diathesis-stress theorists that allows for a role for family factors as potentiators for schizophrenia. He suggests that a commonsense interpretation of EE research indicates some of these attitudes must have been present to influence the child long before the onset of symptoms. There are only a few well-designed prospective studies of the role of childhood experiences, parenting, and family communication in schizophrenia, but the available evidence supports the view that family influences play a role in the etiology of schizophrenia (Goldstein and Doane, 1982; Tienari et al., 1987).

A second vulnerability-stress model was proposed by Nuechterlein and Dawson (1984) and revised by Nuechterlein (1987). The model is consistent with the formulations of Zubin and Spring but focuses more on the psychological processes that appear to be related to the stress-vulnerability interaction. Four vulnerability characteristics (reduced information capacity, impaired coping skills and self-efficacy, impaired family problem solving, and a family environment high in the expression of negative emotions) are identified as socioenvironmental stressors that increase vulnerability to prodromal symptoms of schizophrenia.

Vulnerability models such as the one described by Nuechterlein and Dawson have stimulated the search for early vulnerability markers, based on the assumption that schizophrenia is the result of a lifelong predisposition that is activated by life stress and situational factors. Indices of vulnerability that have research support include hyporeactivity of the electrodermal skin response (finger sweat gland activity) in response to novel stimuli (Zahn, 1986), abnormalities in smooth-pursuit eye tracking (Zahn, 1986), and impaired cognitive performance on measures of attention (Cornblatt and Erlenmeyer-Kimling, 1985). There is an impressive literature available on neurocognitive indicators of risk for schizophrenia (David and Cutting, 1994). The list includes impaired processing of complex information, deficits in maintaining a steady attentional focus, problems distinguishing relevant from irrelevant stimuli and forming consistent abstractions, deficits in sensory inhibition and autonomic responsivity, impairments in processing interpersonal information, and deficits in coping skills (Nuechterlein and Dawson, 1984).

Diathesis Stress

In the 1950s the psychoanalyst Sandor Rado (1956) hypothesized that most cases of schizophrenia involve an inherited disposition or genotype that interacts with environmental influences to produce a schizophrenic phenotype or pattern of personality traits called the *schizotype*. Rado believed that a central schizotypal trait is *anhedonia,* or an inherent incapacity to experience pleasure. This defect, Rado believed, impairs development of initiative and contributes to adaptations such as compensatory overdependence on others and development of cognitive processes devoid of affect, along with weak emotional ties to others that lead to attenuated relationships. In severe cases, schizotypal individuals are prone to develop bizarre beliefs and behaviors and to become impaired or incapable of adaptation (McGlashan, 1991). Rado believed the nature and severity of the schizotypal adaptation depends on the degree of genetic loading and the degree of familial and environmental stress.

In the 1960s the research psychologist Paul Meehl expanded on Rado's model. Meehl (1962) posits a single dominant "schizogene" which produces a *schizotaxic* defect that is the biological diathesis for schizophrenia. The assumption of a diathetic dominant schizogene contrasts with the views of most other theorists who interpret risk figures from family aggregation and twin studies to be more consistent with a multilocus or polygenetic mode of transmission, in which susceptibility is the result of the joint action of multiple genes (Risch, 1990). Meehl nevertheless allows for the role of other genetically based traits as sources of nonspecific potentiating or protective traits that function to either increase risk or contribute to resilience.

Meehl assumes that a genetically based schizotaxic neural integrative defect is the basic pathophysiology of schizophrenia. He refers to this neural defect as *hypokrisia,* which possibly involves a slight quantitative aberration in the synaptic control of the spiking of neurons. Meehl maintains that the genetically based neural defect (hypokrisia) results in a diathesis (schizotaxia) which takes the form of a dysfunction that prevents the cortical integration of input signals. He posits that this genetic diathesis is a sufficient cause for the development of schizotypic personality characteristics in that, given the schizotaxic defect, all social reinforcement schedules will lead to development of a *schizotypal personality* organization. The most prominent characteristics of *schizotypy* in Meehl's model are cognitive slippage, ambivalence, anhedonia, and social anxiety.

Stress in the form of environmental influences is the major factor that determines whether a schizotype eventually develops schizophrenia. The characteristics of the schizotypal personality function to increase risk for schizophrenia in two ways. First, these characteristics directly contribute to vulnerability and predisposition to the disorder. Second, schizotypal features complicate interpersonal processes and trigger negative reciprocal influence processes that in turn result in increased stress and risk for the disorder.

Meehl's initial model proposed a direct line of causation between the schizogene, the schizotaxic neural deficit, and schizotypal personality characteristics. Whether or not one develops schizophrenia, Meehl argued, is a function of exposure to "deviant reinforcement schedules" during childhood (Meehl, 1972).

Meehl later expanded the list of features of the schizotypal personality to include characteristics such as interpersonal alienation, ambivalence, dereism, autism, anhedonia, cognitive slippage, social anxiety, and aversive drift (Meehl, 1972). There does not have to be anything particularly stressful or dysfunctional in the background of the schizotaxic individual to produce schizotypal personality characteristics. Meehl estimates that the majority of schizotypes (90 percent) do not go on to develop schizophrenia. Instead, most schizotypes evidence subclinical personality patterns that include varying degrees of unusual thought, eccentric thinking, and social ineptitude, but they do not develop schizophrenia unless a combination of additional factors are added to the equation. He estimates that only about 10 percent of all schizotypes go on to develop schizophrenia. Those who are likely to develop schizophrenia are at increased risk because of the influence of two additional factors: (1) the inheritance of other polygenes associated with predisposing trait patterns (e.g., anxiety proneness, submissiveness, extreme introversion, and hypohedonia) that potentiate the schizotypal maladaptive tendencies and further compromise coping ability and (2) "bad luck" in the form of adverse developmental life experiences and precipitating factors.

In 1989 Meehl expanded the list of polygenetic heritable traits to about a dozen. The traits are potentiators which increase the probability or protectors which decrease the probability of occurrence of schizophrenia in a schizotype. Potentiating polygenes are normally distributed in the general population and are different from the schizotaxic genetic diathesis that is hypothesized to be specific for the etiology of schizophrenia. The list of polygenetic potentiators includes low capacity for pleasure, low energy level, low or high aggression and sex drive, and high introversion and anxiety proneness. Protectors include high IQ, good looks, and special talents. Meehl argues that the genetic influences underlying these traits are independent of the specific etiology for schizophrenia but function to potentiate or protect persons with varying degrees of genetic susceptibility.

Meehl (1990) refers to the potentiating polygenetic traits as the SHAITU syndrome, an acronym formed from the initial letters of the terms: *submissive, hypohedonic, anxious, introverted, traumatized,* and *unlucky.* Meehl views the SHAI components of the acronym (submissive, hypohedonic, anxious, and introverted) as polygenetically based personality trait extremes. The TU components (frequent minor or major trauma and unlucky events in adult life) are environmental events that increase risk for schizophrenia. He postulates that major trauma during childhood, repeated minor stresses or hassles, or "unlucky" events can trigger a schizophrenic episode in a vulnerable individual, whereas these events might have little lasting effect on normal individuals. As a consequence, Meehl argues that retrospective studies of life events are not likely to reveal consistent differences in the life histories and backgrounds of schizophrenic patients and controls.

In 1990 Meehl revised his earlier assumption that all schizophrenics must carry the schizogene. He concluded that the combination of potentiating influences (SHAITU) can in some cases produce schizophrenia in individuals who do not carry the schizogene. Meehl estimated that approximately 85 to 90 percent of all patients are cases of "true" schizophrenia (schizotaxic), whereas only 10 to 15 percent are what he refers to as genophenocopies (SHAITU, plus life stress and aversive developmental factors) that do not carry the schizogene. He suggests that patients without the schizogene are more likely to evidence disturbances in the content of thought rather than in the form of thought (derailment, tangentiality, disorganization).

Many biological theorists do not share Meehl's view of the potential etiological role of disturbances in family functioning. They argue there is no reliable evidence that measurable differences exist between schizophrenics and nonschizophrenics in terms of gross indices of childhood stressors such as loss of a parent or divorce (Neill, 1990). Biological theorists tend to recognize the etiological role of only two sources of "stress." The first has to do with events that occur prenatally or perinatally, such as obstetric complications or viral infections, which can act jointly with the genetic substrate to increase risk for schizophrenia (Torrey, 1980). The second refers to the cumulative effects of nonspecific psychological and somatic events over the life course that interact with genetic influences to increase susceptibility (Gottesman and Shields, 1982).

High-Risk Studies

Studies of the offspring of schizophrenic patients and adult relatives have shifted away from attempts to identify traits predictive of future schizophrenic pathology toward a search for phenotypic markers of the genes themselves. Trait anomalies that have been reported to occur with increased frequency among high-risk offspring and relatives include attentional, cognitive, and neuromotor difficulties beginning in childhood, impaired event-related P300 brain wave potentials, impaired eye tracking, anhedonia, and social incompetence (Erlenmeyer-Kimling, 1996). These developmental markers appear to function as risk factors that in interaction with myriad other variables increase risk for schizophrenia. Schizophrenic patients evidence performance deficits on nearly every behavioral or psychometric measure, but the relationships between groups of marker traits, deficits, and symptoms have not been established.

Personality and Vulnerability

Zuckerman (1999) maintains that diathesis-stress models do not adequately distinguish between genetic and biological aspects of schizophrenia. These models assume genetic influences result in brain-based structural or neurochemical abnormalities that in turn result in increased risk for schizophrenia, but he points out that increased risk can also result from the subtle effects of brain damage which is caused by environmental factors such as prolonged labor-induced anoxia, trauma, poor diet, and disease during developmental periods when the brain is most susceptible. Zuckerman argues that most diathesis-stress models arbitrarily limit the meaning of stress to external sources rather than to internal reactions and do not distinguish between distal and proximal stressors. In particular, he argues that the ongoing and compounding influence of distal stressors that occur during childhood have been overlooked.

Zuckerman (1999) proposes that the concept of a diathesis should be thought of as quasicontinuous rather than dichotomous. He argues that a quasicontinuous view of the diathesis for schizophrenia is more compatible with polygenetic additive models and differentiates between independent diatheses and the stress that results from the diathesis itself. Thus, a diathesis toward anxiety may trigger excessive concern or rejection on the part of one or both parents that in turn compounds the diathesis and influences the development of a later disorder. In similar fashion, proximal stressors such as marital conflict or job stress may interact with the person's ways of coping and existing personality, which were developed from the interaction of polygenetic influences and distal stressors, to influence the particular form of disorder that develops.

Zuckerman proposes a quasicontinuous multiple-pathway model of schizophrenia which assumes that in some cases aspects of personality development may be a function of a diathesis that increases risk for the disorder. In other cases the diathesis may be based on a completely different set of genetic and biological factors than those that influence personality development. Thus, in any given case of schizophrenia some polygenetic factors may contribute to a disorder-specific additive vulnerability factor, while other polygenetic influences may affect brain systems related to the development of normally distributed personality traits. It is the interaction of these separate risk factors with distal family and environmental influences and proximal life stressors that determines the nature of the clinical disorder that is developed. The equation that best describes the interactions of contributing factors that culminate in schizophrenia will vary considerably among individuals, even among those who evidence similar symptoms.

SUMMARY

There is little understanding of how to conceptualize the complex relationships that characterize the interplay of biological and psychosocial influences on development. The evidence is strong that schizophrenia tends to run in families and that genetically based biological factors increase or result in vulnerability to developing the disorder. Evidence also suggests that a variety of environmental influences, ranging from viral infections during gestation to disturbed family communication patterns, can play a role in increasing vulnerability, but the manner in which these influences unfold and influence one another is unclear and may vary from individual to individual. This likelihood led Meehl to add the element of "bad luck" to his model, suggesting that varying sequences of unspecified and idiosyncratic events probably play an important role in vulnerability to the disorder.

Diathesis-stress models provide a useful framework for thinking about etiology if not understood in terms of simple additive models. There are three general approaches to understanding the role of stress in the diathesis-stress framework. The first, a strong genetic predisposition model, holds that life events trigger something in the vulnerable individual which was bound to become manifest sooner or later anyway (Rabkin, 1980). Stress, from this perspective, is neither a necessary nor sufficient cause for the appearance of schizophrenic symptoms. It simply hastens onset. The second position, articulated by Zubin and Spring (1977), proposes that stressful life events are necessary to "trigger" episodes of schizophrenia in individuals of varying degrees of vulnerability. Life events are conceptualized as necessary but not sufficient causes of a schizophrenic episode. The third position, articulated by Dohrenwend and Egri (1981), maintains that stressful life events can act to precipitate schizophrenic episodes in vulnerable individuals and play a role in the etiology of schizophrenia. One need not be genetically vulnerable or predisposed to develop schizophrenic symptoms. These theorists tend to focus on the etiological importance of social influences and developmental life events in the context of the family (Lidz and Lidz, 1949). Today the mainstream emphasis in the literature is on the primary role of genetic and brain-based diatheses. During the decades between 1930 and 1970 emphasis was on the importance of family and early childhood experience as predisposing factors. Despite lack of agreement on the diathesis-stress model that best fits the available data, the general framework of these concepts can foster the integration of evidence for the role of biological and psychosocial influences into more comprehensive explanatory models.

Chapter 6

Epistemology, General Systems Theory, and Schizophrenia

Research and theory in science tend to focus on a single level of analysis. Psychodynamic theorists focus on intrapsychic constructs, interpersonal theorists on interactions, cognitive therapists on thoughts, behaviorists on the behavioral responses to environmental reinforcing effects, biological theorists on genetics, neurochemistry, and brain function, and so on. Many factors contribute to individual preferences for a particular level of analysis. Personality traits, family background, training, career opportunities, and the selective awareness that increases with specialization all play roles in determining individual commitment to a particular point of view. Most clinicians and researchers have preferences for levels of analysis and types of explanations offered to explain mental disorders and find one point of view or level of analysis more plausible than others, but the concepts and assumptions associated with each level of analysis provide conceptual filters that are both useful and limiting. They allow us to perceive, to think, and to theorize at only one particular level of analysis. Like each of the blind men who set out to "look at" and describe the elephant, each can describe and explain only one facet of a multifaceted reality.

Theories clarify and explain, but they also install blinders that foster a tendency to think in terms of only one point of view. Many differences in theoretical perspective are based on different ideas and preferences about what science should be and of what scientific data should consist. It is unlikely that most mental disorders can be understood adequately from one point of view. The idea that a single theoretical perspective or level of analysis is sufficient or has priority in the study of human beings has been discredited among most philosophers of science but not among many clinical scientists and practitioners. The contemporary literature on schizophrenia favors reductionistic thinking that is associated with a hierarchy of values in which "higher" psychosocial levels of analysis are assumed to become dispensable once "lower" more quantifiable explanatory concepts are available.

Diathesis-stress models seem to integrate both biological and psychological factors (Engel, 1980; Meehl, 1962; Gottesman and Shields, 1982), but most models give little more than lip service recognition of the importance of psychological processes. Few if any prominent diathesis-stress models of schizophrenia attempt even superficial understanding of the potential importance of the context of individual lives, of formative developmental issues, prebreakdown sources of interpersonal or intrapsychic stress, or phenomenology (Robbins, 1993). Biology is assumed to provide the foundation for understanding schizophrenia, and psychological and social dimensions are typically treated as secondary or surface layers to be stripped away to get at the infrastructural, i.e., biological, or neurocognitive base (Kleinman, 1988). Theories that propose concepts of upward and downward causation in which forces at one level (e.g., the neuron or neurotransmitter) act to cause changes at another level (e.g., thoughts and feelings) or vice versa are often simply variations of monistic thinking.

Reliable diagnostic categories are of varying importance to practitioners of different theoretical persuasions. Psychodynamic theorists are more interested in the unconscious meanings and developmental roots of current symptoms than they are in precise classification. They do not assume that a direct relationship necessarily exists between symptoms and underlying causes. Biological theorists assume that schizophrenic symptoms are associated with unique patterns of underlying neurochemical and structural brain abnormalities. Therefore, schizophrenia must be defined as reliably and precisely as possible given current knowledge, so that the unique underlying causes can be identified. Diagnostic categories and criteria are both descriptive and theory driven. How we view and classify what we observe is a function of our assumptions.

Whether a disorder that can definitively be labeled schizophrenia exists, beyond a broad description of a range of problematic behaviors and experiences, remains to be determined. There is research on the occurrence of marker characteristics, such as aberrant eye tracking, impaired information processing, and an elevated frequency of occurrence of Axis I and Axis II mental disorders among first- and second-degree relatives of schizophrenic patients, which supports the assumption that there is a biological disorder called schizophrenia. On the other hand, the diversity of symptoms, backgrounds, abilities, outcomes, and course of patients with this diagnosis suggests that this grouping is far too broad to represent a single brain-based disorder. To many practitioners who emphasize the role of psychosocial factors, it seems implausible that causation must always be in one direction, i.e., from brain to behavior, or that any one biological deficit or neuromodular dysfunction could result in such diverse symptoms.

GENERAL SYSTEMS THEORY

Von Bertanlanffy asserts that the human sciences cannot progress beyond the dilemma of developing more and more information about less and less if the analytic procedures of classical science are followed exclusively (1952, 1967, 1968). In particular, the classical scientific assumption of linear causality connecting two variables as the basic paradigm is insufficient. He argues that organized wholes of many variables are more similar to the nature of what is studied in the human sciences. Understanding at this level requires new categories of interaction that cannot be understood as the outcome of a series of cause-and-effect sequences.

Von Bertanlanffy postulates that this process of reorganization to hierarchically higher levels which is characteristic of living systems cannot be accounted for by summing the parts. General systems theory asserts that the levels of organization of living systems, ranging from the individual cell to social systems, must be recognized as discontinuous but related dynamic systems which are characterized by the property of emergence. Lower levels are essential to the emergence of higher levels but are not sufficient to account for phenomena at that level and vice versa. New and unique principles are characteristic of each level of a system hierarchy.

The terms *higher* and *lower levels* denote differences in perspective, not validity. Different sciences afford different conceptual lenses through which we are able to think about different aspects or properties of the same phenomena. Disciplines such as neurochemistry, neuroanatomy, neuropsychology, cognitive psychology, psychoanalysis, family systems, sociology, and cultural anthropology apply unique and potentially valuable levels of focus that cannot be analyzed at lower levels or synthesized at higher levels without the loss of important information. It is natural for individuals to focus on only one of these levels. In so doing, however, it is important to bear in mind that the information and knowledge obtained is one dimensional and limited.

Systems theory suggests that psychopathology does not *exist* at any single level and no single level of analysis has greater a priori theoretical relevance or explanatory value. Observations across levels can be weighted in terms of their relevance to etiological theories only if clear causal relationships are established among observations at different levels.

The relevance of hierarchical systems theory to the field of psychopathology is to provide a conceptual framework in which to relate and eventually integrate scientific knowledge derived from different levels. It is likely that contributory factors at one level interact with contributory factors at other levels in complex ways to increase risk long before symptoms of psychopathology are observed. Thus, our early experiences may alter neurochemistry and brain functioning just as genetics influence temperament and brain function. If one accepts this fact, then a model of schizophrenia which allows for the conceptualization of multiple interacting systems over the life span must be developed.

Robbins (1993) points out that several genotypes may predispose a person to schizophrenia. At-risk individuals must successfully complete the same developmental tasks and manage all of the interpersonal and social challenges as the rest of us, but the nature of their resolution, meaning, and life impact may differ substantially because of inherited risk factors. General systems theory would attempt to specify how constitutional and temperament differences interact with developmental experiences and qualities of parents. This perspective suggests that constitutional vulnerabilities increase the likelihood for developing a particular disorder in the context of certain patterns and levels of developmental problems and interpersonal failures. Particular styles of parenting may activate, compound, protect from, or fail to compensate for certain inborn vulnerabilities. These experiences can in turn modify the brain in ways that increase risk and vulnerability. Constitutionally vulnerable children may grow up to be normal given adequately supportive and appropriate parenting and socialization opportunities. Likewise, Robbins argues, it is possible that children without any identifiable constitutional vulnerabilities may grow up to develop psychotic disorders, including schizophrenia, given sufficient dysfunction in their life histories.

The various perspectives applied to understand the origins and symptoms of schizophrenia must eventually be either discarded or integrated into a comprehensive model of schizophrenia. At this point we have several interesting but limited models that attempt to integrate biological vulnerabilities, dispositional characteristics, and life stress into viable "biopsychosocial" models.

SUMMARY

General systems theory is based on the view that events at one system level cannot be fully described or understood in terms of cause and effect descriptions of events within a system which is conceptualized at another level. Concepts at one level of analysis should be consistent with those of a lower level, but attempts to specify explanatory cause and effect relationships across levels in either direction (up or down) inevitably transform the nature of what is studied. One cannot account for or adequately explain the meaning and content of delusions of persecution, for example, in terms of alterations of dopamine activity in the forebrain any more than one can adequately explain aberrations in dopamine activity in terms of delusional thinking. It may be that dopamine hypersensitivity and disturbances in neuromodular function combine to increase vulnerability to life stressors throughout the life span and contribute to the interpersonal and emotional stressors which culminate in episodes of acute psychotic symptoms. It may be equally true that life stressors throughout the life span generate or enhance neurochemical and neuromodular brain dysfunctions that increase vulnerability. The concept and diagnosis of schizophrenia has evolved since the turn of the twentieth century largely in response to changes in the dominance of one or another theoretical model. Today brain-based and neurocognitive models dominate the literature, but it is unlikely that these models will provide adequate understanding of even such a severe form of mental and behavioral disturbance as schizophrenia.

SECTION III:
BIOLOGICAL PERSPECTIVES

The remainder of this book is organized in a way that fosters an illusion. Discussions of purported biological and psychosocial factors in schizophrenia are treated as though they contribute to the disorder independently or in some additive fashion, as suggested by simplistic interpretations of the diathesis-stress model. This is unlikely to be the case for several reasons. First, the role of different biological and psychosocial contributing factors is likely to be highly idiosyncratic, even in cases that share a common symptom picture. Second, contributing factors are most likely not additive or even orthogonal or independent in their effects but continuously impact one another throughout development. Thus, genetic contributors are influenced by environmental factors, and environmental factors are influenced by genes in ways that impact both psychosocial and biological development in a continuous pattern of complex interactions. By organizing chapters according to level of focus, the illusion of relative independence of these influences is maintained. Unfortunately and despite the recognized need for application of a systems perspective, this author is unable to construct a better alternative format. Therefore, the illusion that contributes to much misunderstanding is reflected in the organization of this book.

In Section III, Chapter 7 summarizes a large body of literature on genetic research and describes the controversies that are associated with this evidence. Chapter 8 summarizes brain-based research and models of schizophrenia. Finally, neurochemical theories and their relationship to what is known about the operation of antipsychotic medications are reviewed in Chapter 9.

Chapter 7

Genetics and Schizophrenia

Evidence indicates that genetics play an important role in determining risk for schizophrenia. Estimates of the role of genetic inheritance range from 50 to 80 percent of the total risk variance for schizophrenia. However, there is considerable disagreement about the form of genetic transmission and the degree to which genes play a role in determining risk and vulnerability. Biological theorists assume that schizophrenia is a single brain-based disorder and that genetic predisposition along with perinatal and prenatal physical problems are the causes. Psychosocial theorists more often view schizophrenia as a loose descriptive grouping or final common pathway of symptoms that can result from a multitude of contributing factors and that the weighting of these factors, can vary from individual to individual. Genes are but one, albeit often an important one, of these factors.

GENETIC MODELS

One can make several assumptions about the role of genetic factors in schizophrenia. Genetic factors may be thought of as necessary, sufficient, or contributing causes of the disorder. If schizophrenia is assumed to be a heterogenous grouping, then it seems likely that there may be different weightings and combinations of genetic factors which are related to risk for different syndromes. McGuffin (1991) maintains that the relative contribution of genetic factors which is relevant in any given case is a function of the severity and type of symptoms and age of onset. Thus, risk for early-onset highly regressed forms of schizophrenia, such as disorganized and hebephrenic patterns, may be largely genetic in origin, while environmental factors play a much larger role in the origins of positive psychotic symptoms and late-onset paranoid patterns.

Kringlen (1967) regards genes as contributing factors that play a role in the etiology of most cases of schizophrenia. However, the genetic diathesis may simply be a weakly inherited, nonspecific tendency or an additive group of traits or tendencies (e.g., anxiety proneness, introversion, irritability, and negative affect) which must be precipitated and enhanced by significant socioenvironmental stressors to result in schizophrenia. Torrey (1988), in contrast, denies any contributory role for psychosocial stressors in the etiology of schizophrenia and views the disorder as entirely genetic and viral in origin.

Meehl (1993) advocates a monogenetic or single dominant-gene model to account for most cases of schizophrenia but allows for the etiological role of polygenetic personality traits that may interact with other social environmental potentiators to result in schizophrenia without a genetic diathesis in a minority of cases. Gottesman (1991, 1993) argues that evidence from twin and family studies does not fit a single major gene model for schizophrenia. He proposes a multifactorial genetic model that combines several approaches. First, a small number of cases may be characterized by specific physiological deficits that result from single (monogenetic) Mendelian-type genes. In most cases Gottesman maintains that a vulnerability-stress model best fits the data, one in which additive polygenetic combinations of a large number of genes produce an inborn vulnerability that must interact with environmental stressors to result in schizophrenia. Thus, the more polygenes the individual harbors, the greater the vulnerability to schizophrenia. Gottesman recognizes that common genes, linked to widely distributed traits, may also play a role in schizophrenia when they are potentiated by a combination of specific polygenetic influences and environmental stressors. Polygenetic theories, such as the one proposed by Gottesman, allow for greater flexibility in accounting for the wide variations in the phenomenology of schizophrenic disorders, since variations can be explained by differences in the quantities and types of genes that combine to form the diathesis.

Kety and colleagues (1968) adopted a diagnostic model of a "spectrum of schizophrenic disorders" based on the rationale of a polygenetic model to guide the influential Danish-American studies of genetic concordance in schizophrenia. The authors proposed that a core polygenetic diathesis is the basis for a schizophrenia spectrum of disorders that includes diverse phenotypic groupings.

Polygenetic theories are widely accepted because they can more readily account for the paradox of the maintenance of a diathesis for schizophrenia in the population when the fertility rate of diagnosed schizophrenic patients is relatively low. Prevalence rates are thought to remain relatively constant because the polygenes that may additively combine to exceed the threshold for a diathesis for schizophrenia may be normal variants circulating widely in the population.

A large body of literature is available to convincingly document the role of genetic factors in schizophrenia. However, changes in diagnostic practice, sampling errors, and inconsistencies in methodology have also been identified as sources of error in much of this research. Tienari (1968) noted that ratings of concordance for schizophrenia vary between 6 and 36 percent based on which set of diagnostic criteria is applied. Concordance rates in twin studies vary from 6 to 73 percent for monozygotic (MZ) twins and 2 to 13 percent for dizygotic (DZ) twins (Tienari, 1968). Many textbooks report only average concordance rates derived from multiple studies, assuming that averages will eliminate or adequately take into account variations in sampling, diagnostic practice, and other sources of methodological error, but this procedure is based on the assumption that methodological errors are normally distributed.

THE NATURE OF GENETIC INFLUENCE

Since genes rarely directly determine phenotypic expression, there can be a range of possible phenotypic expressions of most genetic influences. Environmental factors interacting with the same genotype will also result in different phenotypes. Psychosocial events interact with the genotype to actively shape and influence the phenotypic expression of genetic potential. Genetic and experiential influences interact from the very beginning and are impossible to separate completely. Since most researchers believe the evidence indicates that schizophrenia does not derive from a single gene, there may also be many normal variations of personality traits that play a role in the diathesis for schizophrenia.

No phenotypic personality traits have been reliably associated with risk for schizophrenia. Nor have any genetic markers or specific chromosomal abnormalities been determined to be the mechanisms for transmission of the disorder. The nature of the phenotypic expressions of the genotypes and the modes of transmission of schizophrenia remain obscure (Cancro, 1985). Although we do not know very much about those traits that are associated with genetic risk for schizophrenia, some evidence indicates that vulnerability to the schizophrenia spectrum of disorders is transmitted genetically.

Estimates of penetrance of genetic factors in schizophrenia also vary widely. Fisher (1973) reported that monozygotic twins discordant for schizophrenia had the same incidence of the disorder (16 percent) among their offspring, suggesting a penetrance of 32 percent. Karlsson (1988) estimated penetrance of 25 percent, and Slater and Cowie (1972) reported a rate of 20 percent. Others report estimates of heritability as high as 90 percent (McGuffin et al., 1994). The reasons for these varying estimates are unclear but probably have to do with different samples, as well as differences in diagnostic practice and methodological rigor.

Whatever the nature of the schizophrenia genotype, it is not clearly expressed phenotypically. Research on the interaction of genotypes and life events, including variables known to increase risk such as viral infections, birth complications, substance abuse, and family communication among others, are needed to clarify the factors influencing penetrance.

CONCORDANCE RESEARCH

Until recently most genetic research on schizophrenia was directed at trying to prove that there is a genetic component to the risk for schizophrenia rather than attempting to understand the nature of the genetic action. Three approaches characterize this body of literature.

Family Consanguinity Studies

The family consanguinity approach is based on the assumption that if genes are involved in the transmission of schizophrenia, then the disorder will be more prevalent in the relatives of an index case (diagnosed patient) than in the general population. Familial studies support this prediction in that they consistently indicate the closer the individual is genetically to the index case, the higher the prevalence of the disorder (Gottesman, 1991). The magnitude of increased risk varies with the amount of gene sharing. For example, averaged figures indicate that identical twins and offspring of dual schizophrenic matings have higher risks (about 45 percent) than first-degree relatives (parents 6 percent, dizygotic twins 17 percent, children 9 percent, siblings 9 percent), who in turn have higher risks than second-degree relatives (uncles and aunts 2 percent, nephews and nieces 4 percent, half siblings 6 percent) and third-degree relatives (first cousins 2 percent; Gottesman, 1991). Knowledge of family history can provide important information even though 89 percent of all schizophrenic patients do not have a schizophrenic parent, and 81 percent have neither a schizophrenic parent nor a schizophrenic sibling. Conclusions based on family consanguinity studies must be qualified by the fact that common environmental influences are also likely to be more prevalent among close relatives (Gottesman, 1991).

Consanguinity studies are generally regarded as suggestive but not highly persuasive indicators of the role of genetic factors (Rosenthal, 1970). As stated previously, 89 percent of schizophrenic patients had two parents that were not schizophrenic, and 65 percent of all schizophrenic patients do not have any first-degree or second-degree relatives with the diagnosis (Gottesman, 1991). An alternative to family consanguinity research is to identify some reasonably reliable neuropsychological marker of schizophrenia and then study the frequency of occurrence of this marker in biological relatives. Several trait markers for vulnerability to schizophrenia have been proposed. Among these markers, deficits in sensory gating or suppression of event-related potentials (EEG activity indicated by the second P50 wave; Cadenhead et al., 2000), abnormalities in saccadic eye movements during smooth-pursuit eye tracking (O'Driscoll, Lenzenweger, and Holzman, 1998), working memory deficits (Tallent and Gooding, 1999), and attentional problems (Mirsky et al., 1992) appear to be promising. These markers are found to occur with higher frequency in schizophrenic patients than in controls, although there is considerable variation in the frequency with which the markers are reported to occur in patients and controls in different studies, and not all patients evidence the markers. However, consanguinity studies generally indicate that schizophrenic patients and their first-degree relatives show greater deficits on each of these trait measures than matched controls.

Mirsky and colleagues (1992) reported that deficits in attention occur with greater frequency in persons from families of patients with schizophrenia, as well as being features of the disorder itself. They argue that deficits in these measures may be trait markers of schizophrenia that are inherited along with other aspects of the schizophrenic diathesis. Kendler and associates (1995) conducted a large-scale study of schizotypal personality disorder symptoms in relatives of schizophrenic probands in Ireland. The authors examined twenty-five schizotypal signs and symptoms, assessed by structured personal interviews, in 1,544 first-degree relatives (without chronic psychosis or mental retardation) of five proband groups: schizophrenia, other nonaffective psychoses, psychotic affective illness, nonpsychotic affective illness, and matched, unscreened controls (Kendler et al., 1995). The authors reported that factor analysis of schizotypal symptom ratings resulted in seven orthogonal schizotypal factors: negative schizotypy, positive schizotypy borderline symptoms, social dysfunction, avoidant symptoms, odd speech, and suspicious behavior. All of the factors except borderline symptoms significantly discriminated relatives of schizophrenic probands from relatives of controls. In descending order of odds ratios, the factors that discriminated relatives of controls and schizophrenic probands were odd speech, social dysfunction, suspicious behavior, negative schizotypy, avoidant symptoms, and positive schizotypy. Additional analyses, in which each factor's unique relationship to familial vulnerability to schizophrenia was examined, indicated that four of the factors remained predictive: negative schizotypy, social dysfunction, avoidant symptoms, and odd speech. Three of the schizotypal factors also discriminated relatives of probands with other nonaffective psychoses from relatives of controls: negative schizotypy, social dysfunction, and odd speech. Thus, only one of the four factors that reflected familial liability to schizophrenia was specific to relatives of schizophrenic probands (avoidant symptoms). These results do not support the hypothesis that schizotypal traits are specific indicators of vulnerability to schizophrenia; rather they appear to be indicators of vulnerability to psychosis. However, the study does indicate that relatives of psychotic probands are significantly more likely than controls to evidence signs and symptoms of schizotypy, but these schizotypal signs and symptoms are indicators of vulnerability to nonaffective psychosis rather than specific indicators of vulnerability to schizophrenia. Social class of the relative also predicted several of the schizotypal factors, although results did not substantially change when social class was statistically controlled in the analyses.

Twin Studies

The equal environment assumption is the foundation of twin studies (Gottesman, 1991; Kendler et al., 1994). It is assumed that MZ twins and DZ twins of the same gender experience the same set of family circumstances; therefore, any differences in concordance rates between these groups must be the result of genetic influence. This assumption is rejected by those who assume that environmental factors play a role in etiology (Bleuler, 1978; Jackson, 1960; Joseph, 1998). These researchers cite several reasons for rejecting this assumption. First, MZ twins are peculiar in several ways and are at increased risk for a number of disorders. This increased risk or idiopathic general susceptibility may impact vulnerability in several ways; therefore, comparisons between MZ and DZ twins might not be the best design. The assumption that each identical twin experiences exactly the same environmental effects in utero is also called into question by the evidence that identical twins typically have different birth weights. Methodological flaws in the determination of zygosity and biased, nonblind diagnoses are problems in some twin studies, especially those published during the first half of the twentieth century. These methodological flaws appear to be one reason that research published since the 1960s has generally reported lower MZ-DZ twin concordance rate differences than earlier studies. A second source of variation is related to the fact that concordance is reported differently in different studies. Concordance can be reported on a pairwise or probandwise basis. The same data set can yield different concordance rates depending on which method is used. For *pairwise concordance,* a pair of schizophrenic twins is counted as one pair in the numerator and denominator. Thus, if forty pairs of twins are concordant for schizophrenia and sixty pairs are discordant in a sample of 100 pairs, the pairwise concordance is 40 percent. For *probandwise concordance,* concordant twins, for reasons that escape this author, are counted as two pairs in the numerator and denominator only when both twins are schizophrenic. This method will obviously result in a higher concordance estimate than the alternative method. Probandwise concordance, for example, would be estimated by dividing the total number of concordant individuals in the sample (N = 80, or 40 concordant twin pairs + 40 concordant twin pairs) by the total number diagnosed with schizophrenia, including both concordant and discordant pairs (100 + 40). Probandwise concordance will obviously give a higher concordance rate than pairwise.

Probandwise rates are generally reported in the literature because it is argued that they are the only rates which are directly comparable to population risk figures (Gottesman, 1991), but they also serve to inflate the impression of actual pairwise concordance. Differences between MZ and DZ twin probandwise concordance rates are variable but impressive. Differences in sample characteristics undoubtedly account for some of the between-study variance. Kringlen (1967) reported an overall identical twin probandwise concordance rate for schizophrenia of 45 percent for MZ twins and 15 percent for DZ twins, based on a Norwegian sample. He reported an identical twin concordance rate of 60 percent for the most severely disturbed patients and 25 percent for the least disturbed. Fisher (1973) reported a Danish MZ twin probandwise concordance rate of 56 percent compared to 27 percent for DZ twins. Kendler and Robinette (1983) reported on male twins in the United States based on a "broad" definition of schizophrenia. The probandwise rates were 31 percent for MZ pairs and 6 percent for DZ pairs. Gottesman and Shields (1982) reported on a British sample for concordance rates of "schizophrenia-like" psychoses. The probandwise concordance rates were 58 percent for MZ pairs and 12 percent for DZ pairs. These results indicate that the identical twin of a schizophrenic patient is more likely to develop schizophrenia or schizophrenia-like symptoms than is the fraternal twin. Despite differences in how schizophrenia is defined and the type of concordance rates reported, twin studies do appear to provide impressive evidence that genetic factors play a role in determining risk for schizophrenia.

Critics of the twin method have raised several additional issues with regard to the validity of this body of research (Cassou, Schiff, and Stewart, 1980; Jackson, 1960; Joseph, 1998; Lewontin, Rose, and Kamin, 1984; Pam et al., 1996). First, potential bias in the diagnosis of schizophrenia, including wide inconsistencies in how the diagnosis is defined, and questions about the classification of zygosity may have resulted in inflated MZ concordance rates in some studies. Second, comparisons of MZ and DZ twins are inevitably confounded by environmental factors, since the "equal environment" assumption that is the basis for twin studies is questionable. Thus, twin and family consanguinity studies provide strong but not unequivocal evidence that genetic inheritance plays a role in determining risk for schizophrenia.

Schneider and Deldin (2001) have pointed out that an orthodoxy has developed in the literature about the heritability of schizophrenia based on twin studies. It begins with statements that twin studies have demonstrated a concordance for schizophrenia among monozygotic twins of slightly more than 50 percent (probandwise) compared to a rate of about 15 percent for dizygotic twins. This leads to calculations of heritability of schizophrenia of around 50 percent. The authors point out that such logic ignores the fact that behind these averages there is great variability. Torrey (1992) summarized eight studies that reported monozygotic concordance rates ranging from 26 to 68 percent and a range for dizygotic twins from 4 to 18 percent. If evidence from the three reasonably well-designed studies is examined, according to Torrey (1992), the concordance rate for monozygotic twins using pairwise statistics is 28 percent and for dizygotic twins 6 percent. When one adds in methodological concerns about likely environmental effects that confound these figures, the orthodoxy of averaged evidence from twin studies supporting an estimated 50 percent heritability factor for schizophrenia is questionable.

Adoption Studies

Adoption studies were initiated during the 1960s as an alternative approach to settling the question of the role of genetic inheritance in the etiology of schizophrenia. Conceptually, adoption studies were thought to control for the potential confound in twin studies: twins reared together are likely to share environmental influences. The problem of locating sufficient numbers of adopted offspring of schizophrenic parents was solved by conducting the studies in Scandinavian countries which have less mobile populations than does the United States and maintain nationwide health utilization records. By using a population of all children adopted at an early age, large samples can be identified and control groups can be established. Adoption studies are generally viewed as providing the strongest available evidence for the role of genetic factors in the risk for schizophrenia.

Several variations of adoption research strategies are used. The first approach begins with the identification of adult adoptees who have been diagnosed as schizophrenic and studies the past and present psychiatric status of their biological and adoptive relatives. This approach is referred to as the *adoptee as proband method*. Typically, a matched control group of nonschizophrenic adoptees is also identified, and their relatives are evaluated for comparison.

Kety and colleagues (1968; Kety, 1988) published the first of the Danish studies using the adoptee as proband design. Identification of those adoptees who were diagnosed as schizophrenic as adults and controls who were not is the starting point of this approach. The next step is to compare their biological and adoptive relatives for incidence of mental disorders. Kety and colleagues reported that 6.4 percent of the biological relatives of schizophrenic adoptees were diagnosed as schizophrenic compared to 1.4 percent for the controls. For ratings of schizophrenia spectrum disorders, 21.4 percent of the biological relatives were diagnosed compared to 5.4 percent of the adoptive relatives.

In summary, results of the Danish-American adoptee as proband study indicate that the occurrence rates of schizophrenia and schizophrenia spectrum disorders were higher. This suggests that genetic traits rather than family environmental factors play a role in the origins of schizophrenia spectrum disorders.

A second approach to genetic research compares adults who were given up for adoption as children by birth parents who were diagnosed as schizophrenic. This approach is referred to as the *parent as proband method*. The first of the adoptee studies was conducted by Heston (1966). Heston interviewed the adult offspring of forty-seven women who had been diagnosed as schizophrenic in the 1930s. The children, as required by law at the time, were placed either in orphanages or with nonmaternal relatives within three days of birth. A control group of children was selected whose mothers had no record of mental illness but were placed in foster homes due to parental death or desertion. Fifty control and forty-seven "index" adoptees were matched for gender and placement type and followed up until at least age thirty-six. Results indicated that five of the forty-seven index cases were diagnosed as schizophrenic at follow-up versus none of the fifty controls. Heston concluded that biological factors rather than family environment are contributors to risk for schizophrenia.

Data from the Danish-American adoption research were also published using the parents as proband method (Kety et al., 1968). This research compared the incidence of schizophrenia in a group of adopted-away offspring of schizophrenic parents (mothers and some fathers) with incidence in a comparison group of adopted-away offspring of parents who had never been diagnosed as schizophrenic. The median age of separation from the mother was 5.9 months for the schizophrenic offspring and 5.8 months for the controls, although some children were adopted as late as four and one half years of age. The researchers found only one diagnosed schizophrenic adoptee from a schizophrenic parent. However, when the proband adoptees, now adults, were rated by a blind rater using the schizophrenia spectrum diagnosis, thirteen of thirty-nine index cases were diagnosed with spectrum disorders versus seven of forty-seven controls. This difference was statistically significant. A subsequent paper published by Rosenthal in 1971, with an increased sample size, reported thirty-four of seventy-six index cases with spectrum diagnoses versus twelve of sixty-seven controls. Thus evidence from the Danish-American parents as proband studies demonstrated a role for genetic inheritance in schizophrenia spectrum disorders. However, the validity of the concept of a schizophrenia spectrum of disorders as indicator of risk for schizophrenia remains a point of controversy (Joseph, 1999b). Critics argue that adoption of the spectrum concept by the Danish-American research team was a post hoc change in procedure which was adopted only after evidence indicated that concordance using diagnoses of schizophrenia did not confirm its assumptions. A second criticism of this research which has not been refuted is that evidence suggests diagnostic ratings were not blind (Lewontin, Rose, and Kamin, 1984).

A third design, called the *cross-fostering method,* starts with the children of normal biological parents (without psychiatric records) who were adopted into homes where an adoptive parent was later diagnosed as schizophrenic. Research using this methodology was published by the Danish-American research group (Wender et al., 1974). Cases of cross-fostering occurred twenty-eight times among the 5,500 adoptees in the greater Copenhagen sample. After the sample was restricted to parents who were not deviant in other ways before adoption (had syphilis or a psychiatric diagnosis other than schizophrenia), the sample was reduced to twenty-one. The rate of spectrum diagnoses was 4.8 percent for normal children cross-fostered to disturbed parents, compared to 18.8 percent reported for children of schizophrenic parents adopted into the homes of normals. On the basis of this evidence, the authors concluded that "schizophrenic parenting" is not a powerful factor in the etiology of schizophrenia spectrum disorders, but genetic inheritance is.

Criticisms of the Danish-American Adoption Studies

The Danish-American studies have been widely cited as providing convincing evidence of the heritability of schizophrenia (Gottesman, 1991; Neale and Oltmanns, 1980; Snyder, 1976), yet several informed and detailed critiques of these studies have been published, three of which impugn the scientific integrity of the researchers. After reviewing the diagnostic data Lidz, Blatt, and Cook (1981) pointed out that manic-depressive patients were inappropriately included in the schizophrenia spectrum group in the Rosenthal and colleagues (1968) study, and inclusion of these patients made the difference in terms of finding significant results.

Benjamin (1976) questioned how the researchers could arrive at their conclusions when statistical significance came from the biological schizophrenia spectrum relatives who were paternal half siblings. He pointed out that this finding violates the principle that genetic effects increase with consanguinity, since it indicates that second-degree relatives had higher concordance rates than first-degree relatives.

Cassou, Schiff, and Stewart (1980) pointed out that most of the adoptees were raised by their mothers for at least the first six months of their lives and should more accurately be referred to as "throwaway" or abandoned children. The authors also argue that the Danish-American research team's claims of "blind" diagnoses are not supported by the way in which records indicate that cases were assigned and reassigned to different diagnostic groupings and statistics juggled to assure a finding of genetic heritability. Lewontin, Rose, and Kamin (1984) also described evidence of selective adoptive placement in the Danish sample. They point out that a quarter of the adopting families of schizophrenic adoptees had at least one parent that had been a patient in a mental hospital, whereas not one adoptive parent of a control adoptee had. The authors argue that when this fact is taken into account the Danish adoption studies actually provide evidence of the role of environmental factors in the etiology of schizophrenia, since selective placements mean that adoptees who originate from dysfunctional biological parents are more likely to be placed with dysfunctional adoptive families. Lewontin, Rose, and Kamin (1984) also point out the findings of the Danish studies indicate no schizophrenic parents produced schizophrenic children. Correspondence between Rose, Kamin, and Lewontin (1984) and one of the Danish-American investigators revealed that in cases when the relatives were unavailable the psychiatrist prepared a "pseudo-interview" based on a review of hospital records only. This pseudo-interview was then rated by diagnosticians. In some cases these diagnoses changed from one phase of the study to another and differed from hospital diagnoses. These issues have never been adequately addressed by the authors of this research and appear to compromise the validity of the results of the Danish-American studies.

One subcomponent of the Danish-American adoption study focused on the role of family environment in risk for schizophrenia and appears to contradict the conclusions of the primary Danish-American research group. A team of prominent family researchers (Wynne et al., 1975) analyzed parental communication patterns in verbatim records transcribed from structured interviews of adoptive parents. Results indicated that using blind ratings based solely on interview transcripts, the researchers were able to differentiate the adoptive parents who had reared schizophrenic offspring from adoptive parents of nonschizophrenics with complete accuracy. Furthermore, the mean frequency of communication deviances was equal in the adoptive schizophrenic and biologic schizophrenic parent groups, both being more than twice that found with the adoptive normal parents. The authors concluded that findings strongly suggest characteristics of adolescent and young adult schizophrenic patients are linked by both genetic factors and nongenetic psychosocial processes related to the communication deviances of the parents. The authors also pointed out that even if one assumes that the patterns of communication deviances of the parents were secondarily induced by the illness of the offspring, the assumption itself gives recognition to the significance of psychosocial processes.

Joseph (1999a,b) has also challenged the validity of published adoption studies. He argues the following points:

1. Researchers have failed to seriously consider evidence of selective placement of adoptees in their samples.
2. They have arbitrarily expanded the definition of schizophrenia to include a schizophrenia spectrum of disorders, due to the lack of chronic schizophrenia cases among those under study.
3. The researchers have ignored the fact that the rate of schizophrenia among index biological relatives must be significantly higher than the expected rate in the general population (it was not) in order to demonstrate that genes have anything to do with schizophrenia (Boyle, 1990).
4. The researchers never provided an adequate or consistent definition of either schizophrenia or schizophrenia spectrum disorders. Heston, for example, conducted nonblind ratings of his adoptees based on what he referred to as "generally accepted standards," and the Danish-American diagnoses were made using what was described as the "global" diagnostic method.
5. First-degree and second-degree relatives were counted equally in statistical analyses comparing index and control biological relatives.
6. The researchers have never provided an adequate number of case histories in their publications so that reviewers can determine the symptoms of the adoptees and their relatives and the conditions they were raised under.

On the basis of these and other criticisms Lidz, Blatt, and Cook (1981) suggested that the Danish-American investigators confused axiom with hypothesis. They transformed a hypothesis and limited data based on questionable methodology into what is now viewed as an axiom.

It may be that some of these questions raised about the methodology and design of the Danish-American studies can be satisfactorily answered. Open disclosure and public access to the data files are the answer to resolution of a number of the issues and questions raised by critics, but access to this publicly funded research data has reportedly been denied to critics by the researchers (Joseph, 1999b).

The Finnish Prospective Adoption Study

A limitation of most adoption studies is that they are retrospective in nature. An alternative prospective design was adopted by Finnish researchers. The project is designed to examine the adopted-away children of schizophrenic parents and their adoptive parents both *prospectively* and *longitudinally.* This research is still under way, although a series of interim reports has been published. The project has been ongoing for over two decades and incorporates important improvements over the design of the Danish-American studies. Most important, the Finnish study includes a careful evaluation of the family environments of adoptees (Tienari et al., 1994). The goal of the Finnish research is to assess the roles of both genetic contributions and the adoptive-family rearing environment in the etiology of schizophrenia.

The authors initially identified 19,447 women who had been diagnosed schizophrenic in Finland between 1960 and 1980. From this sample a total of 184 adopted-away offspring of 171 schizophrenic mothers were identified and accessible. The maximum time that any of the 171 adoptees lived with the biological parent was four years and eleven months. A control group was identified by independent researchers and matched with probands on the basis of gender, age at placement, age of adoptive parents (within ten years), and social status. Detailed taped interviews were completed with all families together and with the adoptive parents only. A battery of psychological tests was administered to adoptive parents and adoptees. Interviewers and testers were blind to the status of the families.

The Finnish research is unique in several ways. First, it is the first adoption study to use operationalized diagnostic criteria, adopted from DSM-III-R. Second, it is the first to adequately rate the functioning of the families in the study prospectively, before the potential onset of schizophrenia in the offspring. However, the researchers also adopted the schizophrenia spectrum grouping when comparing index and control groups. This grouping included delusional disorders, schizophreniform psychosis, schizoaffective disorder, psychosis not otherwise specified (NOS), and schizotypal personality disorder.

In 1987 Tienari and colleagues reported that of 112 index cases (offspring of a mother who had been diagnosed schizophrenic) for which follow-up data were available, eight individuals (7 percent) were diagnosed as psychotic, ten individuals (9 percent) were diagnosed as borderline, and sixteen (14 percent) were diagnosed as evidencing severe personality disorder, yielding an overall spectrum rate of 30 percent among index cases. Among the 112 matched controls (offspring of a mother who had never been diagnosed schizophrenic) two individuals (1.5 percent) were diagnosed psychotic, eight (6 percent) as borderline, and ten (7.4 percent) as having a personality disorder, yielding an overall spectrum rate of 15 percent among control cases. The authors concluded that these data support the hypothesis of a genetic contribution to the spectrum of serious mental illness. There was no statistical difference between the numbers of index and control adoptees receiving no psychiatric diagnosis.

Of the 43 offspring reared in adoptive families that were rated as "seriously disturbed" based on previous interviews, 16 percent *(n = 7)* of the adoptees were rated as psychotic, 37 percent were rated as either psychotic or borderline *(n = 16)*, and 65 percent (*n* = 28) were rated with at least one diagnosis. In contrast, there were no psychotic or borderline adoptees and only three offspring (6 percent) with personality disorders among the adoptees raised in the forty-nine healthy or mildly disturbed families (Tienari et al., 1987). In other words, 37 percent of the forty-three offspring of schizophrenic mothers who were reared in a severely disturbed adoptive-family developed either schizophrenic or borderline disorders, while none of the offspring of schizophrenic mothers raised in a healthy adoptive-family environment were diagnosed as either schizophrenic or borderline. Tienari and colleagues (1994) conclude that genetically transmitted vulnerability appears to be a precondition for schizophrenia, but a disturbed and disturbing rearing environment appears to be necessary to transform vulnerability into clinical schizophrenia. However, a strict interpretation of the data indicates that the individual psychopathology of the adoptive parents can be used as a predictor variable for all subjects, both index and control (Tienari et al., 1994).

Limitations of the Finnish Study

The prospective study conducted by Tienari and colleagues (1994) is widely acknowledged to be the most comprehensive and well-planned schizophrenia adoption study yet conducted. Expectations have been high that this project will provide answers to questions about the relative contributions of nature versus nurture in schizophrenia, but this project is not without flaws. Joseph (1999b) described several problems in the design of the Finnish study that limit the interpretation of the results. First, the Finnish research team concluded that both genetics and family environment are predictor variables for schizophrenia, but they have not explained why 85 percent of the adoptees experiencing both genetic loading and disturbed family environments did not become psychotic. Even in families rated as severely disturbed, proband adoptees were found to be psychotic only 10 to 15 percent of the time. This leaves 85 percent of the prediction variability as outcome unknown. Given exposure to two major theorized predictor variables of schizophrenia, genetic inheritance and disturbed family environment, Joseph argues one would expect a higher incidence rate. Second, Joseph argues it is likely that adoptees were selectively rather than randomly placed in adoptive homes. Tienari and colleages (1994) indicated, for example, that in approximately one-third of the cases the diagnosis of the mother was most likely known to the adoption officials prior to the adoption. Joseph suggests that this knowledge likely resulted in the children being considered "hereditary taint-carriers" (a concept widely accepted by Scandiavian adoption agency personnel) which led to placement of index children in families with a family history of or biological relative with a psychiatric diagnosis. Evidence consistent with this argument was published by Tienari and colleagues in 1985. In this report the authors indicated that twice as many index as control adoptees were placed in "severely disturbed" families (index 18 percent, control 9 percent), and conversely, twice as many control as index adoptees were placed in "healthy" families (control 11 percent, index 5.7 percent). Joseph suggests that selective placement of index adoptees into less functional adoptive families, not the adoptees' genetic makeup, may be responsible for the higher rate of psychiatric diagnoses found in the index groups of the Finnish and other adoption studies. Lewontin, Rose, and Kamin (1984) pointed out similar evidence of an implicit placement bias in the Danish-American adoption studies and the study published by Heston.

An additional limitation of the Finnish study has to do with the age of the children at the time of adoption or abandonment. Some adoptees lived with their biological parent until the age of four years and eleven months. Although adoptee mental health ratings were not associated with age of transfer (Tienari et al., 1985), many theorists would argue the fact that a number of adoptees lived with their biological parents for several years is a problem in any study attempting to discriminate between the relative contributions of genetics and environment. Finally, Tienari and colleagues (1994) adopted the schizophrenia spectrum concept introduced by the Danish-American researchers. Although Tienari's index adoptees were more likely to be diagnosed schizophrenic than controls using strict DSM-III-R criteria, they did not contain significantly more cases of schizophrenia than the population rate expectation. Finally, when all but the cases of chronic schizophrenia are eliminated from the results of the Finnish study, the rate of schizophrenia in index adoptees is not significantly greater than that expected for the general population.

BASIC GENETIC RESEARCH

Genetic material is stored in a double helix of DNA strands. Each strand is assembled into twenty-three chromosomes and contains around 3 billion nucleotide base pairs. A gene is a location on the DNA strand that is made up of a sequence of these nucleotide bases. The sequences contain instructions that enable cells to make proteins essential to life. Humans have about 100,000 genes that come in different versions, or alleles. These alleles or gene variations govern the ways proteins essential to life and cell reproduction are synthesized and produced in the body. Basic genetic research on schizophrenia is designed to search for those alleles that contribute to risk for schizophrenia. Since the diathesis for schizophrenia is widely thought to be polygenetic, researchers are looking for several alleles that contribute to characteristics which increase risk for the disorder. It would be easier to determine the role of genetic influences in the etiology of schizophrenia if the disorder was caused by a single dominant gene, but schizophrenia does not seem to fit a single-gene pattern (Barondes et al., 1997). Geneticists believe that risk for schizophrenia results from the influence of several genes working together, but the number of susceptibility loci and the degree of interaction between suspected loci remain unknown (Bray and Owen, 2001).

It is possible that what we call schizophrenia is actually several different disorders, each having its own separate and distinct method of transmission. Negative symptoms could be caused by one set of interacting genetic influences, positive symptoms by another, and disorganization by yet another. Or one set of influences could be related to specific deficits correlated with the diagnosis, such as cognitive impairments, anxiety proneness, attentional and other information processing problems, eye tracking deficits, hypohedonia, and dereism but not found in those patients who do not evidence these characteristics. Of course, environmental influences, such as maternal viral infections during critical periods of pregnancy, birth complications, low birth weight, and developmental experiences that overtax the coping capacity of the child, may also interact with and compound any phenotypic expressions of genotypic risk markers to increase risk during adolescence and young adulthood.

In spite of the inherent difficulties in identifying the role of particular genes, molecular geneticists have attempted to develop strategies to further progress in this area. Three strategies are used in basic genetic research on schizophrenia: linkage studies, cytogenetic approaches, and association studies (Bray and Owen, 2001).

Linkage studies attempt to identify chromosomal regions containing susceptibility loci by studying the segregation of a given disorder with alleles of polymorphic genetic markers in multiply affected families (Bray and Owen, 2001). The logic of linkage studies is that if a marker allele is observed in affected family members then the schizophrenia-relevant genes must be nearby. Linkage studies search for a region of the DNA strands in which there is a reasonable likelihood of knowing where on a chromosome to look for an allele. These strategies are particularly useful if a small number of genes are involved in a disorder and genetic heterogeneity is minimal. Early optimism about the promise of linkage studies has abated. The disadvantage of this approach is that the gene or genes contributing to risk for the disorder in a particular kindred group may not have general applicability. Claims of the location of a gene for schizophrenia on various chromosomes have not been replicated. Reported findings have not been replicated and when valid appear to be specific to the small subpopulations studied (Pulver, 2000).

To date, no genes associated with any major aspect of schizophrenia have been found, suggesting that highly penetrant mutations causing schizophrenia must be extremely rare if not nonexistent. In every case in which positive findings were initially reported, an equal or greater number of negative findings has also been reported. In summary, linkage studies have indicated broad chromosomal regions of interest but have not yet been able to narrow them down (Bray and Owen, 2001), but with data on the human genome sequence now available researchers have started to identify a few loci that are plausibly involved in schizophrenia.

One recently published series of linkage studies holds promise for the identification of at least one susceptibility allele. An Irish-American team studied the multipoint linkage of 270 high-density schizophrenia pedigree Irish families compared to 1,425 genotyped individuals (Straub et al., 1995; Straub, Jiang, et al., 2002; Straub, MacLean, et al., 2002). Results suggest that a schizophrenia susceptibility gene may be located in region 6p24-21. The 6p24-21 gene, known as dysbindin, lies on the sixth of 23 pairs of human chromosomes. Dysbindin is also considered to be a plausible candidate for a susceptibility allele since it plays a role in synaptic signaling and plasticity, and evidence shows that synaptic changes are associated with the diagnosis of schizophrenia. The research team worked by analyzing small runs of DNA markers along the genome (total DNA) of each subject. They used statistical methods to identify markers associated with diagnosed schizophrenic patients but not present in their unaffected relatives or controls. The pattern of linkage disequilibrium observed to be significantly more common in schizophrenic patients is also consistent with the presence of more than one susceptibility allele. The authors acknowledge the possibility that their findings could represent yet another false-positive result but are reassured by the internal consistency and strength of their findings. Future linkage research will undoubtedly focus on dysbindin as a potential genetic marker site for schizophrenia. It will be some years before results are determined to be reliable by other scientists working with different populations to independently confirm these results.

Cytogenetic studies search for chromosomal abnormalities in affected individuals as potential clues to the location of susceptibility genes. These abnormalities can function to implicate a gene or region by disruption of the function of a gene directly, by having a positional effect on gene expression, or by showing linking with a susceptibility variant (Bray and Owen, 2001). Thus far cytogenetic studies have not yielded any substantiated findings. The problem with this approach is the great diversity that exists among individuals with schizophrenia; a single incidence of a cytogenetic abnormality or even a few abnormalities is not sufficient to demonstrate causality.

Association studies attempt to determine what contribution individual genes make to susceptibility. These studies begin with a particular suspect gene. Groups of unrelated individuals with the diagnosis are compared to controls to identify a DNA marker that is in or close to the hypothesized genetic susceptibility locus. Gene variants are evaluated on the basis of their relative distribution within unrelated groups of affected and nonaffected individuals. Most association studies are guided by neurochemical models of schizophrenia, focusing on genetic influences on specific neurotransmitter receptors and metabolizing enzymes. These studies typically focus on genetic influences that are related to certain neurotransmitters thought to be of importance for a particular disorder, such as dopamine and schizophrenia. The challenge of this approach is daunting because it is likely that multiple genes are involved in the production of any neurotransmitter and its receptor sites, and we are not certain at present precisely which neurotransmitters are actually relevant to the etiology of schizophrenia. Most association studies thus far have yielded negative results, and no consistent pattern of replication of the few positive results reported has emerged (Bray and Owen, 2001). The hope is that as the human genome is mapped successfully, association studies will bear more fruit.

It is also possible that clinical schizophrenia is too narrow a grouping to yield reliable evidence from association studies. Since only about 10 percent of the offspring of schizophrenic parents are likely to develop schizophrenia, it may be that not all schizophrenic patients share a particular allele. It may be necessary to adopt broader groupings based on dysfunctions observed to occur somewhat more frequently in samples of schizophrenic patients and their biological relatives, such as abnormal eye tracking, impaired sensory gating, or other markers of cognitive deficits, in order to increase the sample sizes included in association studies. Freedman and colleagues (2002) cite evidence that an attentional deficit, indicated by a decrease in the normal inhibition of the P50 auditory-evoked response to the second of paired stimuli, is associated with attentional disturbances in schizophrenic patients and in many of their nonschizophrenic relatives. Thus, the P50 evoked auditory response deficit can be used as a possible phenotypic trait marker of genetic susceptibility to schizophrenia. The authors reason that a nicotinic cholinergic receptor could be related to some of the sensory processing deficits observed in schizophrenic patients. However, the significance of this evidence must be qualified until the mutations responsible for the linkage between this response deficit and nicotinic receptors are identified and replicated and their neurobiological effects in the brain are understood. Larger samples based on empirically based risk indices would increase the likelihood of identifying groups of alleles that could be correlated with these groupings. To date, however, large-scale genetic association studies based on this approach have not been published.

SUMMARY

The study of the genetics of schizophrenia is a complex and difficult undertaking. Despite considerable progress, we are still far from understanding either the genetic contributors for schizophrenia or how genetic factors might lead to clinical features. Hypotheses that seem promising have yielded inconclusive results. The accumulated evidence from published family consanguinity, twin, and adoption studies indicates that genes are contributors to risk for schizophrenia spectrum disorders. However, the precise role of genetic risk factors and how genetic influences translate into increased risk remain to be determined. It seems whatever is genetically transmitted that increases risk for schizophrenia lacks specificity and seems to relate to some general form of compromise in overall functioning. Given the complexities and design issues regarding this body of research, it would seem prudent to remain cautious about reaching conclusions about the precise role of genes in determining vulnerability.

The bulk of the available evidence indicates that genetic inheritance increases risk for schizophrenia. The nature of how these genotypic factors are expressed phenotypically or otherwise function to increase risk remains unknown. Promising leads have been provided, but the reliability of these findings remains to be established. Obviously, genetics cannot account for all of the variance in determining the risk for schizophrenia. Research indicates that environmental factors including maternal viral infections during pregnancy, birth complications, learning problems, low socioeconomic status, and family communication disturbances also appear to play a role in increasing risk. The particular combination of influences may vary considerably within the population of diagnosed schizophrenic patients, making the search for a general schizogene an extremely difficult task at best.

The preponderance of available evidence is compatible with a graduated model of genetic transmission that is loosely correlated with adequacy of premorbid adjustment and symptom severity (McGuffin, 1991). Family, twin, and adoption studies have taken us about as far as this methodology can, and future progress in this area must await advances in basic genetic research. Genetic researchers have turned to molecular genetics as the format in which to search for the inherited sources of schizophrenia (Green, 1998). Most geneticists now believe that the genetic risk factor for schizophrenia is caused in part by a combination of several genes, but the number of susceptibility loci, the risk conferred by each locus, and the interaction among loci remain unknown (Bray and Owen, 2001). In addition, it is widely recognized that these polygenetic influences in most cases probably must interact with idiosyncratic environmental experiences to result in schizophrenia (Moldin and Gottesman, 1997).

Possibly the assumption that schizophrenia is a homogenous grouping is mistaken and the DSM-IV diagnosis may not be adequate for refined genetic research. Many biological researchers suspect that the syndrome may encompass several disorders, characterized by different genetic vulnerability profiles (Thaker, 2000). It has been suggested that schizophrenia can be thought of as a disorder similar to diabetes (Gurling, Read, and Potter, 1991). One subtype of diabetes is caused by a single point mutation in the insulin gene; another type has a strong genetic component and has a late age onset. A third type is less strongly genetic in origin, has an early age onset, and is thought to be associated with genes that affect immunological susceptibility (Green et al., 1985). Risk for schizophrenia may also be related to different genetic and biological subtypes, with both dominant and recessive modes of transmission present. The responsible genes may encode for neurotransmitter receptors, enzymes, neuromodulators, brain development, or all of these. Studies of genetic linkage markers in large samples of patients and their biological relatives will be required to resolve the problems that derive from the likelihood that schizophrenia may be related to both complex etiologies and genetic heterogeneity (Ott, 1986). An alternative strategy that has been suggested is to group patients using a combination of phenotypic symptoms (e.g., deficit symptoms) and physiological anomalies that often accompany the diagnosis and are also observed with higher frequency in the biological relatives of patients. Measures such as eye movement dysfunction (jerky eye tracking movements) or abnormal P50 responses to paired auditory stimuli (e.g., lack of normal inhibition of the second P50 wave in patients and relatives) in combination with phenotypic symptoms may allow for greater homogeneity of subject groupings that will facilitate the search for the genetic factors involved in a diathesis for schizophrenia.

At present some form of diathesis-stress model seems to be best supported by the available evidence. This is evident in data that the concordance rate for monozygotic twins is somewhere around 28 to 50 percent, and in families known to be at genetic risk for schizophrenia only a small proportion of family members actually develop the disorder. On the other hand, exposure to environmental risk factors, including communication deviance (Tienari et al., 1994) and viral infections (Barr, Mednick, and Munk-Jorgensen, 1990), results in only a small minority who develop the disorder. Many questions remain unresolved regarding the relationship between symptoms, outcome, and the relative contributions of genetic, biological, and psychosocial factors. Whatever genetic mechanisms are inherited that contribute to risk for schizophrenia, evidence suggests that in most cases genes do not guarantee the development of schizophrenia but contribute to varying degrees of predisposition to the disorder.

Given the consensus that the heritability of schizophrenia is a polygenetic phenomenon of low penetrance, it seems unlikely at present that researchers will find a gene that codes directly for most forms of schizophrenia or even a particular subtype. Neuroimaging and neurodevelopmental studies suggest instead that genetic factors contribute to a defect or combination of defects in the control of neurodevelopment which in turn produces brain-based changes that predispose to later risk for schizophrenia (Jones and Murray, 1991), but brain development is also subject to many mutations and environmental influences. So many factors can potentially contribute to aberrations in neurodevelopment it seems likely that schizophrenia is etiologically heterogenous, the result of the interaction of multiple contributory genes and sources of adversity (Murray, Lewis, and Reveley, 1985; Risch, 1990). Schneider and Deldin (2001) suggest that two models can account for the contribution of both environmental effects and genetics to schizophrenia. One approach suggests that at least two separate and distinct disorders happen to share a number of symptoms. One disorder is a familial type that exhibits genetic transmission; a second disorder is a sporadic type, caused largely by environmental stressors. This model leads to an emphasis on efforts to identify symptoms (e.g., psychoticism, deficit, disorganized) that could be used to distinguish the disorders. An alternative to the separate disease model is the diathesis-stress approach which assumes that schizophrenia is a single disorder, one that is the result of varying degrees of genetic predisposition which interact with environmental stressors. Researchers are actively working to develop evidence in support of both models, and it will be some time before conclusive evidence is available.

Chapter 8

Neurobiological Models and Research

Schizophrenia is a devastating disorder or group of disorders that typically begins in late adolescence or young adulthood. In most cases there is no apparent developmental history of serious psychological dysfunction prior to onset of the disorder. Given the severe level of dysfunction and tendency to chronicity observed in many patients, it is not surprising that a primary role for neurobiological causes is assumed by a majority of clinicians. It is unlikely, however, that any one brain area would produce the many symptoms of schizophrenia. The diversity of schizophrenic symptoms suggests both heterogeneity of causal pathways among diagnosed patients and the likely involvement of multiple interacting systems or areas of the brain rather than one or more localized lesions. Recent structural and functional brain imaging and postmortem studies have generally confirmed this view. The connections between behavioral symptoms and brain areas are neither direct nor simple, however, and no alterations of the morphology of particular brain systems have been reliably associated with any group or subtype of schizophrenic symptoms. Most studies that report abnormalities in biological parameters indicate that only a minority of schizophrenic patients have abnormal indicators when compared to controls (Goldberg and Weinberger, 1988). That is, in most cases the distribution of neurobiological measurements of schizophrenic patients overlaps considerably with that of the controls. This fact is generally interpreted as evidence that the identified dysfunction is most likely a marker for an etiologically distinct subtype, although alternative interpretations have been offered (Daniel and Weinberger, 1991). These authors argue that overlap between schizophrenic cases and controls on indices of brain dysfunction can be understood as the result of nonspecific variability in brain morphology and physiology.

Many researchers believe that the symptoms of schizophrenia can be adequately explained in terms of disruptions in normal brain functions. Others believe that symptoms such as hearing voices result from some abnormality in brain systems. Despite the widespread conviction that symptoms are caused by brain dysfunctions, we are not able to explain a single sign or symptom of schizophrenia on the basis of neural mechanisms. Expert opinions about the future promise of identifying neuroanatomical abnormalities range from positive (Andreasen and Carpenter, 1993) to skeptical (Levy, 1996). Reliable relationships between the symptoms of schizophrenics and specific patterns of altered brain morphology may eventually be discovered, but for now the evidence is not conclusive. Research is rendered more difficult because seemingly different symptoms may result from the same causes, and similar symptoms may arise from different causes. To attempt to trace a process from effect (symptom) to cause (brain dysfunction) is extremely difficult and is a problem that faces most researchers. New findings of abnormalities in the brains of schizophrenic patients are reported in the literature with such remarkable and bewildering regularity that it is difficult to make sense of the available evidence, especially because there is so little evidence or theory available that ties changes in brain structure and function to psychological and behavioral processes.

There is a more fundamental problem with this area of research: It is still not clear that schizophrenia is a single disorder. Buchanan and Carpenter (1997) maintain that the failure to identify the neuroanatomical substrates of schizophrenia is related to a failure to address the heterogeneity of schizophrenia. There are additional design issues in etiological studies, including the complexity of influences on symptoms. For example, even when separate symptom domains are used to group patients, questions of whether the symptoms are *primary* (a direct manifestation of the pathophysiology) or *secondary* (e.g., the result of some comorbid disorder, lifestyle, or treatment) are often not clear. Negative symptoms can result from antipsychotic drug side effects, depression, the effects of prolonged institutionalization, or brain pathology. In order to separate cause from effect, information that allows for accurate distinctions between primary and secondary symptoms must be included to supplement symptom-based groupings (Kirkpatrick et al., 1996).

The difference between *trait* and *state* phenomena is another potentially important distinction (Buchanan and Carpenter, 1997). Anatomical studies of brain pathology are based on the assumption that symptoms of schizophrenia are permanent traitlike differences, yet most researchers use cross-sectional assessments of symptoms to classify patients and ignore the historical course of the expression of the symptom. However, symptoms frequently undergo episodic changes in form and severity. If, for example, research focuses on the study of abnormalities in the temporal lobe that could be associated with vulnerability to auditory hallucinations, the study should contrast closely matched patients with and without a history of auditory hallucinations, including those currently in remission, in order to reduce state-dependent artifacts. The problem with studies based on cross-sectional symptom group comparisons is that expression of trait vulnerability may vary with the state of the participant or the phase of the disorder. Thus, this design cannot establish that differences obtained are stable and will be found at a later date even in the same sample. Longitudinal studies also suggest that the course of schizophrenic symptoms can be divided into three phases (Carpenter and Kirkpatrick, 1988). In the late phase, symptoms such as delusions, hallucinations, and disorganized behaviors tend to decrease in severity and frequency and may remit in many patients. Failure to evaluate the patient in the context of a longitudinal history could result in mistaken false-positive placements (state-related symptoms mistaken as temporary or fixed traits) or false negatives (trait characteristics overlooked during periods of remission due to cross-sectional classification). Questions about the degree of isomorphism between behavioral patterns and brain structure are also a matter of concern. Inferences about the causes of symptoms based on methods for assessing brain structure and function are based on assumptions that are often uncertain. Finally, with regard to symptom domains, there is the question of whether symptom dimensions should be studied as categorical domains rather than continuous or dimensional variables in neuroanatomical studies. Positive and negative symptoms, for example, are dimensional rather than categorical in occurrence.

Brain imaging studies are generally reported for groups of schizophrenic patients and controls, but rarely are the patients grouped according to the parameters that are most likely to be important in studying the relationship between diagnosis and brain function and structure (e.g., symptom syndromes, specific symptoms, or neurocognitive deficits). Controls are also rarely selected that match the patient groups on key variables such as length of hospitalization or socioeconomic status.

In summary, problems in conducting research on the defining etiological characteristics of schizophrenic patients include difficulties separating causes from effects of institutionalization, drug treatment, and lifestyle. It is also nearly impossible to identify control groups that differ from the schizophrenic group only in that they have not been diagnosed as schizophrenic. There are problems with the diagnostic construct itself, since patients vary widely in types of symptoms, background, and many other factors, and there is no agreement on the kind of patient that is a "true" schizophrenic. Most neurobiological research is conducted on small samples of patients, described only in terms of their diagnosis. Issues of generalizability of results and participant selection bias are rarely addressed. Finally, reported statistically significant group differences are typically observed in only a minority of the patient sample, with considerable overlap between patients and controls. Given these limitations, one should view current neuroanatomical evidence as promising but not conclusive.

STUDIES OF SPECIFIC BRAIN ABNORMALITIES

Initially, new brain imaging technologies were used to look for deficits in specific areas of the brains of schizophrenic patients. Studies reported evidence of diverse areas of dysfunction. Computerized tomography (CT scan) and magnetic resonance imaging (MRI) studies demonstrated abnormalities in the ventricular system in about 25 percent of chronic schizophrenic patients. Enlarged ventricles reflect one or more specific brain abnormalities, since ventricle size increases with brain tissue atrophy. Additional structural abnormalities have been reported for areas of the temporal lobe, the amygdala, nucleus accumbens, and hippocampus (DeLisi, Hoff, and Schwartz, 1991; Pakkenberg, 1993; Suddath et al., 1990).

O'Donnell and Grace (1998) suggest that abnormalities in the nucleus accumbens in particular may play an important role in schizophrenic symptoms, since the accumbens is a brain area in which cortical regions implicated in schizophrenia interact with dopaminergic pathways. The nucleus accumbens has unique afferent connections from nearly every brain area that has been implicated in schizophrenia, including the hippocampus, amygdala, and prefrontal cortex, and has one of the densest dopaminergic innervations in the brain (dopamine has long been thought to be the neurotransmitter most directly implicated in schizophrenia). Studies also indicate that some schizophrenic patients show alterations of cytoarchitecture of the dorsolateral prefrontal cortex (Daviss and Lewis, 1995), as well as loss of glutamate binding and a decrease in dopamine fibers (Akil and Lewis, 1996). These abnormalities are consistent with models which postulate that schizophrenia results from altered connections between the prefrontal cortex and limbic or anterior cingulate circuitry (Bogerts, 1993). Other studies report abnormal enlargement of nuclei in the basal ganglia (Bogerts, 1993).

Given the diverse symptoms and course of schizophrenia, several researchers have attempted to formulate models that relate specific symptom patterns to different underlying brain abnormalities. Studies have demonstrated an association between negative symptoms and decreased blood flow and metabolic activity in the prefrontal cortex (Liddle et al., 1992; Wolkin et al., 1992), as well as abnormalities in dorsolateral prefrontal cortical circuitry (Buchanan, Breier, and Kirkpatrick, 1993). Weinberger (1987) proposed a neurodevelopmental theory that integrates neurochemical and neuroanatomical evidence to explain positive symptoms in terms of hyperdopaminergic limbic pathophysiology and negative symptoms in terms of hypodopaminergic dorsolateral prefrontal aberrations.

There is a growing consensus that schizophrenia must be a disorder of functional brain systems involving failures of integration between brain regulatory regions or modules rather than the result of specific localized deficits. One area, the nucleus accumbens, appears to be critically involved in many of these proposed dysfunctional modules (O'Donnell and Grace, 1998). The activity of the accumbens is controlled by several limbic inputs that provide contextual and spatial information from the hippocampus and emotion-relevant information from the amygdala. The information coming from these sources interacts with afferents from the prefrontal cortex. Thus, activity levels of nucleus accumbens neurons must influence the level of thalamic-prefrontal cortical activity. Tracts also radiate from the accumbens core to aspects of the reticular thalamic nucleus that contributes to the filtering of sensory activity. Thus, the medial prefrontal cortex is both a primary source of input to the accumbens and strongly influenced by circuits connected to the nucleus accumbens. The role of dopamine in accumbens activity is not well understood, but this neurotransmitter appears to be involved in the timing and coordination of neural ensembles in the accumbens, ensembles that influence the activity of prefrontal cortical neurons.

Csernansky and Bardgett (1998) maintain that an anatomical circuit linking the functioning of the nucleus accumbens with the hippocampus and other limbic-cortical structures is most likely involved in schizophrenia, since this is where abnormalities have often been found in patients. Animal research also indicates that lesions of limbic-cortical neurons cause decreases in glutamatergic input to the nucleus accumbens that are associated with decreases in presynaptic dopamine release and increases in the density of dopamine-like receptors. The authors suggest that schizophrenic symptoms may result from an abnormal dopaminergic state that develops secondary to a primary limbic-cortical lesion and deficits in glutamatergic input to the nucleus accumbens. They speculate that negative symptoms result from the abnormal functioning of frontal lobe structures which receive extensive connections from limbic structures. Sudden reversals of negative symptoms, in the form of episodes of excitement and increased sensitivity to stimulation, occur with stress-induced increased dopamine release that is combined with increased sensitivity of postsynaptic dopamine receptors.

Stevens (1997) compared evidence from anatomical studies of schizophrenia with research on epilepsy, to develop a neurodevelopmental model of the positive and negative symptoms of schizophrenia. In epilepsy, axonal sprouting in the dendate gyrus represents an aberrant response of glutamatergic cells to brain insult. This sprouting can result in seizure patterns. Stevens suggests that schizophrenia represents a genetically determined compensatory proliferative response of axons, dendrites, or receptors in nonglutamate systems in response to brain insults from any number of sources. He cites evidence from studies of the effects of neuroleptic agents and the psychotogenic properties of excitatory antagonists such as amphetamines and phencyclidine which indicate, rather than an excess of excitatory elements or decrease in inhibition as in epilepsy, in schizophrenia the brain responds to injury or precipitating events with excessive elaboration of cerebral inhibitory networks. The specific type of brain response depends on multiple factors such as the nature of the precipitant, age of occurrence, and genetic factors that regulate neuronal processes.

Twin studies indicate that in some cases brain abnormalities may be the result of environmental factors, with a history of prenatal and perinatal problems associated with ventricular enlargement in particular (Lewis and Murray, 1987; Casanova et al., 1990). In most cases, however, it is believed that the brain abnormality associated with risk for schizophrenia must be genetic in origin and becomes manifest clinically during the normal course of maturation of the brain. The idea of schizophrenia as a neurodevelopmental disorder is supported by studies which indicate that most schizophrenic patients do not show evidence of brain degeneration as indicated by gliosis (Roberts and Bruton, 1990). This suggests that associated impairments are not the consequence of environmentally induced degenerative processes.

NEUROBIOLOGICAL MODULAR SYSTEMS
AND CLUSTERS OF SCHIZOPHRENIA SYMPTOMS

Neuroimaging studies suggest that certain brain areas are dysfunctional in many schizophrenic patients. However, the symptoms of schizophrenia are not indicative of damage to a particular area as is typical in neurological disorders. As a consequence, investigators have shifted their focus from searching for deficits in a single area of the brain to searching for networks or connections between regions of the brain that may be abnormal. Andreasen, Paradiso, and O'Leary (1998), describe the history of study of the neural mechanisms of schizophrenia as having passed through three stages in the past several decades. During the first phase, efforts were focused on using computerized tomography (CT) to demonstrate that schizophrenic patients had diffuse nonspecific abnormalities in the brain, such as ventricular enlargement. The second phase attempted to localize anatomical abnormalities and relate them to specific manifestations and symptoms using the enhanced resolution of magnetic resonance imaging (MRI). Specific relationships were hypothesized, and limited evidence verified these relationships, for example, between prefrontal cortical dysfunction and negative symptoms (Andreasen, 1997) and between temporal lobe dysfunction and auditory hallucinations (McCarley, Shenton, and O'Donnell, 1993). The third and current phase draws on models of distributed parallel processing from cognitive psychology and the study of neural circuitry in the brain.

This approach does not focus on the relationship between symptoms and regions but attempts to understand schizophrenia as a unitary disorder, the result of abnormalities in basic cognitive processes and related neural circuits. Rather than studying brain abnormalities related to specific symptoms, Andreasen (1997) attempts to determine those cognitive disturbances and abnormalities in neural circuits that explain the symptoms.

O'Donnell and Grace (1998) published an integrative model which links altered functions in subcortical systems that influence higher cortical functions in schizophrenia. The authors propose that different patterns of disturbances in regions such as the nucleus accumbens of the ventral striatum, prefrontal cortex, hippocampus, and dopamine systems may be correlated with clusters of schizophrenic symptoms. Positive symptoms are correlated with increased cerebral blood flow in the medial temporal lobe and ventral striatum. Patients with predominantly positive symptoms also show abnormal temporal lobe functions (Liddle et al., 1992; Wible et al., 1995). O'Donnell and Grace (1998) further speculate that the striatal region which is involved in the interaction between cortical and dopaminergic systems is the accumbens shell, since clinically active dopamine antagonists (e.g., antipsychotic medications) are generally effective against positive symptoms and modify activity within this region. Thus, positive symptoms may involve some neurochemical or lesion-based dysfunction in this circuit.

Negative symptoms are associated with hypofrontality, particularly in the dorsolateral prefrontal cortex, which could be associated with a dopamine deficiency (Liddle et al., 1992; Wolkin et al., 1992). O'Donnell and Grace (1998) suggest that hypofrontality results in a decrease in tonic, glutamate-dependent dopamine release within the integrative regions of the striatum that are involved in motor planning and volition. As a result, the striatal neurons receive less excitatory influence from the cortex, which results in less cortical control over behavior and in a tendency toward perseveration and negative symptoms. The disorganization syndrome may result from decreased activity within the core region of the nucleus accumbens that indirectly interferes with the ability of the reticular thalamic nucleus to selectively suppress incoming information. The model proposed by O'Donnell and Grace to integrate research evidence with symptom dimensions and knowledge of aberrations in functional neuroanatomy and neurochemistry provides a promising framework to guide future research.

Frith (1992) proposed an alternative cognitive approach to explaining symptom heterogeneity. He argues that the three symptom dimensions of schizophrenia are special cases of a more general underlying disorder of consciousness or self-awareness which impairs the ability to think with "meta representations" or higher order abstract concepts that are representations of mental states. Frith divides the symptoms of schizophrenia into three broad groups that parallel the groupings referred to by O'Donnell and Grace (1998) and others but with a cognitive emphasis. The first grouping is referred to as *disorders of willed action* as evidenced in negative symptoms of alogia and avolition. The second grouping includes *disorders of self-monitoring,* evidenced in positive symptoms such as auditory hallucinations and delusions of control. The third grouping is called *disorders in monitoring the intentions of others,* which lead to formal thought disorder and delusions of persecution, described as disorganization.

Frith provided an alternative framework for the relationship between brain dysfunctions and specific symptom patterns. He maintains that each symptom pattern is associated with a specific set of cognitive deficits, although all patterns share the underlying characteristic of an impairment of self-awareness which in turn impairs the ability to think effectively with "meta representations." Disorders of willed action are attributed to relative decreases in frontal lobe activity and increases in temporal regions in comparison to normals. Research on blood flow in frontal and temporal regions generally supports the notion that the relationship between these areas is impaired in many negative-symptom patients (McGuire and Frith, 1998). Symptoms such as hallucinations are thought to result from erroneous attributions of inner speech to other persons, due to a defect in self-monitoring. Evidence for this hypothesis comes from comparisons of hallucinators to nonhallucinators, indicating that hallucinators have decreased blood flow in areas associated with monitoring of speech, such as the left, middle temporal gyrus, and supplementary motor area (McGuire and Frith, 1998). Recordings made while patients were experiencing hallucinations indicated activations in subcortical (thalamus and striatum), limbic and paralimbic regions (anterior cingulate and parahippocampal gyrus), and the cerebellum (McGuire et al., 1996). The authors speculate that subcortical activity may moderate hallucinations, with the content (auditory, visual, olfactory, or tactile) determined by the neocortical regions that are activated (Silbersweig et al., 1995). Defects in monitoring the intentions of others are associated with increased blood flow to the left medial frontal gyrus and posterior cingulate.

COGNITIVE DYSMETRIA

"Cognitive dysmetria" is the term Andreasen, Paradiso, and O'Leary (1998) use to refer to the cognitive and motor coordination (dysmetria) deficits observed in schizophrenia. Evidence suggests that cognitive dysmetria involves not only the "executive" system but also functions such as memory, attention, emotion, and motor activity. This suggests that the underlying neurobiological deficit in schizophrenia must be widely distributed rather than localized. Andreasen, Paradiso, and O'Leary (1998) have drawn upon a large body of research to develop a neurobiological model in which the symptoms of schizophrenia reflect abnormalities in connectivity in the circuitry of functional brain modules. The origin, i.e., the developmental injuries, can occur anytime between conception and early adulthood. Variations in the severity of disruption in connectivity at different levels are thought to explain the diversity of symptoms and outcome observed in schizophrenia.

The term *cognitive dysmetria* refers to poor coordination of mental activities. The result of cognitive dysmetria is that a person with schizophrenia has a fundamental deficit in taking measure of time and space and in making inferences about interrelationships between self and others or among past, present, and future. Andreasen (1997) postulates that patients with cognitive dysmetria cannot accurately time input and output, and therefore they cannot coordinate perception, prioritization, retrieval, and expression of experiences and ideas.

Support for the model comes from a broad range of studies using MRI, photon emission tomography (PET), and single photon emission computed tomography (SPECT) imaging. PET studies have revealed abnormalities in frontal-thalamic-cerebellar circuitry of schizophrenic patients across a broad range of cognitive tasks (Andreasen, 1997). Neuropathological studies have indicated abnormalities in frontal, thalamic, and pontine regions of the brain—regions that are implicated in cognitive activities (Bogerts, 1993). Abnormalities in this circuit are consistent with hypotheses about disturbances in neurotransmitter systems, since these systems are concentrated in midline regions (Carlsson and Carlsson, 1990). Andreasen (1997) believes the common thread which ties diverse observations of brain dysfunction in schizophrenia is that the disorder reflects a disruption in a fundamental cognitive process which is based on the integrity of specific brain circuits.

Nodes of Dysfunction in the Cognitive Dysmetria Network

Node 1, the *prefrontal cortex,* is essential for higher executive functions and has long been thought to play a key role in the origins of schizophrenic symptoms. This area is much larger in humans than in other primates and contains areas that are present only in the human brain. The prefrontal cortex is associated with functions such as language and speech. It is diffusely connected to other areas of the brain and has been demonstrated to play a key role in complex executive and decision-making functions. Despite extensive study of this region, the findings of impairment in prefrontal areas of schizophrenic patients have not been consistent. This may be the case because many sources of variance in brain imaging studies can confound neuroanatomical research and contribute to inconsistent results. Differences in intelligence, educational level, socioeconomic class, diet, medication effects, measurement techniques, small sample sizes, and the cognitive tasks used during imaging studies can all lead to nonreplications of results. Overall, the available evidence indicates that varying levels of hypofrontality (decreased prefrontal lobe function) are observed in many schizophrenic patients. This deficit is associated with abnormalities in "willed action" (Frith, 1992).

Node 2, the *thalamus,* is a nucleus of relay junctions that is thought to have both "gating" and "generating" functions. Relay nuclei project to sensory and motor cortical regions and receive projections from these areas, which allows the thalamus to modulate sensory and motor inputs. Diffuse projections from the thalamus throughout the brain play a role in governing arousal. MRI and PET studies suggest that thalamic abnormalities in schizophrenic patients may be associated with deficits in the sensory filtering role of the thalamus (Andreasen et al., 1986, 1994; Buschbaum et al., 1996).

Node 3, the *cerebellum,* is of interest because, like the cerebral cortex, it is one-third larger in human beings than in nonhuman primates and has substantial connections with the prefrontal cortex. This anatomical evidence suggests that it could play an important role in cognitive as well as motor functions. Gross cognitive deficits have not been observed in patients with cerebellar lesions, although more subtle effects on speech and cognition have been reported (Andreasen et al., 1995, 1996). Studies indicate that many schizophrenic patients show a lack of normal activation of the entire fronto-thalamic-cerebellar circuit during performance of a cognitive task (Andreasen et al., 1996).

Andreasen and colleagues (1996) maintain that neuroanatomic disruption of the fronto-thalamic-cerebellar circuit results in the clinical abnormality called "cognitive dysmetria" or "poor mental coordination."

MODULAR DISJUNCTION

Cleghorn and Albert (1990) suggest an alternative model of the underlying neuroanatomical deficit in schizophrenia. Examination of patients typically reveals several characteristics, including impaired attention, reduced self-awareness and self-monitoring, incomplete recall of spatial and verbal information, and impaired planning and goal-directed behaviors. In addition, emotional responsiveness is reduced, continuity in time is altered, and self-other distinctions and self-cohesion are impaired. Many patients also have difficulty maintaining a shared focus of attention, respond in socially inappropriate ways, and have difficulties screening out distracting information. These characteristics suggest a lack of modulation of communication systems in the brain rather than permanent structural impairments.

In the normal brain, messages are sent to modular parts of the brain that are specialized for the required functions, and other parts of the brain are in turn inactivated or activated appropriately. Cleghorn and Albert argue that this level of modular coordination does not occur in schizophrenia. The authors note that individual modules of simple attentional, language, and motor functions have been found to be intact in schizophrenic patients. They conclude that abnormalities must emerge when the patient is required to integrate these basic functions into more complex expressions which include combinations of affect and meaning. At this point, it is hypothesized that individual modular activities and outputs are inappropriately relayed to parts of the brain not specialized for the information. As a result, neural networks that form the substrate for cognitive and emotional modules are activated and inactivated in disorganized or inappropriate temporal sequences.

Cleghorn and Albert (1990) argue that the diverse symptoms of schizophrenia reflect asynchronous activation and disjunction of functional units in the brain. The results are incongruities between thought and affect, odd and incoherent communications, and faulty attributions of meaning. In the case of delusions, for example, early in the psychotic process strong emotions may trigger a delusional perception. This perception is commonly experienced as a sudden insight that a perception or set of events has special significance for the person. This "insight" or "uncanny" experience is in effect a mismatch of the sense of significance of an event which has not been correctly checked with an expectancy based on personal memory. In the case of the symptom of thought insertion, there is an experience of part of oneself as alien, a form of disjunction of the sense of ownership of the thought. The patient, it is thought, attributes part of the self to the nonself because of the disjunction of functional brain activities.

Cleghorn and Albert argue that much of the behavior and experience of schizophrenic patients is consistent with the idea that cognitive modules, although individually functionally intact, are not integrated with one another in a normal manner. They maintain that modular disjunction provides evidence of dysfunctional information processing in schizophrenia and that brain imaging studies of schizophrenic patients provide support for their proposal. For example, evidence shows that many schizophrenic patients show activation of cerebral blood flow or glucose metabolism in parts of the brain which are inappropriate to a particular experimental task. The authors believe that several additional sources of data support their concept of modular disjunction: (1) the various brain structures implicated in schizophrenia are connected to widely distributed anatomical systems, e.g., prefrontal, temporolimbic, parietal, thalamic, and striatal; and (2) pharmacological studies indicate that tuning mechanisms in animal brains are regulated by norepinephrine and switching mechanisms are subserved by dopamine, both neurotransmitters implicated in schizophrenia.

Cleghorn and Albert maintain that schizophrenic symptoms result from disturbances in the selection, activation, sequencing, and switching of compartmentalized motor and cognitive programs which produce errors in communication between modules.

DYSFUNCTIONS IN INTERRELATED SYSTEMS AND SYMPTOM CLUSTERS

Other researchers have presented evidence that the brain regions most consistently implicated in schizophrenia interact as complex systems; in particular, the system that includes the ventral striatum, prefrontal cortex, hippocampus, and dopamine systems is thought to be involved in schizophrenia (O'Donnell and Grace, 1998). The authors have attempted to link dysfunctions in these brain regions with each of the three symptom clusters of schizophrenia (disorganization, negative symptoms, and psychotic symptoms). O'Donnell and Grace hypothesize that the symptoms of schizophrenia arise as a result of aberrant information processing in subcortical structures, which results in abnormal regulation of cortical activity.

Disturbances in the prefrontal cortex have often been reported in schizophrenic patients. This evidence includes MRI studies that indicate decreases in prefrontal cortical (PFC) volume (Andreasen et al., 1994), loss of glutamic receptor binding (Ulas and Cotman, 1993), and a decrease in dopaminergic fibers in the prefrontal cortex (Akil and Lewis, 1996). Researchers have also reported reduced hippocampi in schizophrenic patients (Bogerts et al., 1993; Suddath et al., 1990) along with other regions of the neocortex and paleocortex. The nucleus accumbens is of particular interest to schizophrenia researchers because it has a unique set of input connections from virtually every area of the brain that has been implicated in schizophrenia, including the prefrontal cortex (PFC), hippocampus, and amygdala, and it is one of the densest dopaminergic innervations in the brain (O'Donnell and Grace, 1998).

Dopamine (DA) is the neurotransmitter that has been most associated with research on the neurochemistry of schizophrenia, since all neuroleptic and atypical antipsychotic drugs are to varying degrees D_2 antagonists (block DA receptors), and the clinical efficacy of neuroleptics correlates with their affinity for these receptors (Seeman, 1987).

Activation of accumbens neurons reportedly disinhibits thalamocortical projections to the PFC and thus alters the modulation of PFC through the accumbens. These PFC units receive feedback through this circuit in conjunction with the context established by hippocampal afferents to the accumbens. The flow of cortical information through the nucleus accumbens appears to impact thalamocortical activity through a complex system of interactions. These interactions include circuits in which accumbens neurons activated by hippocampal/PFC inputs send inhibitory projections which indirectly disinhibit neurons in the mediodorsal thalamic nucleus. This thalamic nucleus is involved in filtering the flow of sensory information in thalamocortical systems. Hippocampal inputs to the accumbens activate those units that are appropriate to a given situation and allow the appropriate areas of the PFC to be reinforced via thalamic afferents. DA agonists (drugs that increase DA effects) reduce the response of accumbens neurons to PFC and hippocampal inputs (O'Donnell and Grace, 1994; Pennartz et al., 1992).

A link has also been proposed by O'Donnell and Grace (1998) between DA activity in the basal ganglia and neocortical disturbances of perception. Several areas of the basal ganglia project to neocortical areas. The accumbens also has pathways that project to a thalamic nucleus that plays an important role in the regulation and filtering of thalamocortical activity and coordinates interactions between cortical regions. Dopamine-related inhibition of the reticular thalamic nucleus would disrupt the individual's ability to selectively activate circuits and coordinate cortical activity. The results of dysfunctions in this parallel system would most likely be disruptions in the flow of thought and the inability to selectively focus on stimuli.

Finally, hippocampal disturbances result in difficulties with context dependency in processing information, a deficit reported in many schizophrenic patients (Spitzer, 1993). These disturbances affect the interactions between the PFC and hippocampal inputs to the nucleus accumbens so that there is reduced gating of cortical throughput in the nucleus accumbens, which would lead to inhibition of thalamocortical activity. The result is a form of functional hypofrontality and a lack of activation of circuits that are congruent with what the context requires.

O'Donnell and Grace (1998) present explanations based on their concepts of how dysfunctions in different neurobiological systems may underlie the symptom clusters of schizophrenia symptoms. Positive symptoms such as hallucinations are related to an increase in DA levels or activity, since DA agonists such as amphetamines can induce positive but not negative symptoms. The accumbens shell appears to be involved in the interaction between cortical and dopaminergic systems that is associated with positive symptoms. O'Donnell and Grace (1998) believe this is the case because drugs that are generally most effective against positive symptoms over time appear to modify activity in this area (O'Donnell and Grace, 1995). Increases in phasic release of DA in the accumbens shell would inhibit the cells in this area. As a consequence, the normal flow of information would be impaired, since most of the input from the prefrontal cortex would be ineffective in exciting neurons in the nucleus accumbens. Only very strong glutamatergic input would overcome this inhibitory state and stimulate activation of small but inappropriate areas of the accumbens. The authors speculate that input which would overcome the inhibition of accumbens cells would be likely to stimulate inappropriate cells and result in the activation of inappropriate cortical areas. The inhibitory effects of increased DA on the flow of cortical information through the nucleus accumbens would also induce a decrease in accumbens neuron activity. The combined effects of activation of inappropriate subsets of neurons in this loop and abnormally low levels of mediodorsal thalamic-PFC activity could be the basis for hallucinations. Thus, O'Donnell and Grace (1998) propose that positive symptoms involve the DA-related, abnormal flow of cortical information through the nucleus accumbens.

Negative symptoms are thought to be associated with hypofrontality, particularly in the dorsolateral PFC. A decrease in DA system activity related to the frontal lobes is also more pronounced in patients that meet criteria for the deficit syndrome (Rao and Moller, 1994). One consequence of hypofrontality is likely to be a decrease in tonic, glutamate-dependent DA release within the integrative areas of the brain involved in motor activity planning and motivation. This in turn could result in a decrease in cortical control over planned behavior. The result could be a cycle of PFC inhibition that maintains PFC hypofrontality.

Symptoms of disorganization suggest a loss of coordination and regulation of activity among cortical circuits. O'Donnell and Grace (1998) hypothesize that decreased activity within the core region of the nucleus accumbens results in impaired ability of the reticular thalamic nucleus (RTN) to selectively suppress incoming information. Since one consequence of this impairment is that input coming into the dorsal thalamus would not be regulated, patients are not able to focus or maintain a coherent train of thought.

To summarize, O'Donnell and Grace believe that disruptions of cortical functions in schizophrenia are caused by dysfunctions in subcortical systems which are involved in the regulation of thalamocortical activity. Their model specifies that the interaction of basal ganglia systems with the cortex via the thalamus is supported by reports of reduced thalamic volume in schizophrenic patients (Andreasen et al., 1994).

SUMMARY

Access to new technologies has contributed to an explosion of research on the role of brain abnormalities in the etiology of schizophrenia. There is general agreement among neurobiologists that neuropathological changes of a developmental nature must precede the onset of the active phase of schizophrenia and that these changes are associated with disturbances in prenatal or postnatal neurodevelopment (Bloom, 1993; Bray and Owen, 2001). However, no single brain abnormality has been shown to be present in all or even most schizophrenic patients, and not all or even most people who evidence these differences develop schizophrenia. The available research tends to indicate the heterogeneity of schizophrenic patients, a characteristic that complicates the task of identifying underlying causes. Recent research on monozygotic twin pairs discordant for schizophrenia suggests, however, that two abnormalities reported in schizophrenic patients—anatomical deviations and metabolic hypoactivity in the frontal lobes—may be general characteristics of all schizophrenic patients. In two studies (Kling et al., 1982; Berman, Torrey, and Daniel, 1989) these frontal lobe dysfunctions discriminated most normal from schizophrenic twins, even when both fell within the range of normal controls. Some authors (Daniel and Weinberger, 1991) argue this evidence indicates that when nonspecific variation in brain morphology and physiology is properly controlled for, subtle neuropathological features characteristic of the disorder can be identified in all or most diagnosed patients. In this sense, they maintain that many symptoms result from a single underlying cause, similar to disorders such as mental retardation and epilepsy. At present, most evidence indicates that no morphological abnormality has been observed which can serve as the basis for the diagnosis of schizophrenia, and no morphological deviation has been demonstrated to consistently differentiate schizophrenic patients from controls. Among the findings that seem to be consistently reported in the neuropsychological literature is the role of frontal lobe disturbance in the origins of many schizophrenic symptoms (Maher and Deldin, 2001). However, the source of the disturbance remains obscure, and frontal lobe dysfunctions are implicated in many other processes, including affective disorders and aging. In addition, evidence indicates that the activity of specific brain areas to patterns of behavior is subject to wide individual variation. For these reasons, it is probably best for researchers to focus on conducting longitudinal studies of the underlying brain-based dysfunctions that are associated with specific symptom groupings and physiological markers (e.g., impaired eye tracking, P50 inhibition deficits) rather than studying a broad diagnostic group such as schizophrenia.

Neurobiological studies focus on nodal areas of dysfunction and their connections. This approach is perfectly reasonable, but like all other approaches that study only single levels, etiological models based on this approach are under the assumption that a single underlying causal agent (nodes of brain dysfunction) is responsible for the disorder. There are empirical and philosophical reasons to question this assumption. It is important to recall that each level of analysis is simply another level of description which does not necessarily indicate cause.

Chapter 9

Antipsychotic Medications and Neurochemical Theories

The introduction of antipsychotics into clinical practice was the result of serendipity. The chemical class of traditional antipsychotic medications, the phenothiazines, was first synthesized over a century ago. Phenothiazine was used as an antiseptic in veterinary practice for years, but it was the discovery of its antihistaminic effects that gave primary impetus for its further development after 1937. About that time a phenothiazine derivative, promethazine, was observed to potentiate barbiturates and was soon adopted as a preoperative medication by surgeons (Owens, 1998). The French surgeon Henri Laborit later noted that a new phenothiazine derivative, chlorophenothiazine, had fewer antihistaminic effects than promethazine but produced a greater reduction in autonomic activity. Laborit also noticed that the medication seemed to produce a calm, unemotional indifference to the environment in many patients and suggested it might be of interest to psychiatrists. The earliest published case of the use of this group of drugs to treat psychotic symptoms was in 1951 (Owens, 1998). Since that time antipsychotic medications have played a significant role in the revolutionary changes which have occurred in the care and treatment of the seriously mentally ill.

Several names are used to refer to the chemical classes of drugs first used in the treatment of schizophrenia and other psychoses. The drugs are often referred to as *antipsychotics,* although the term *neuroleptics* is also widely used. Neuroleptic literally means "seizing or acting upon the nervous system." The term *neuroleptic syndrome* was introduced to refer to some of the changes caused by these drugs. Neuroleptic syndrome includes decreased psychomotor activity, decreased affect, affective indifference, decreased initiative and interest in one's surroundings, psychomotor slowing, and suppression of complex cognitive processes and behavior. These effects can be beneficial in some cases but unfortunately are also similar to the negative symptoms of schizophrenia.

Today the terms *antipsychotics* and *neuroleptics* are often used inter-changeably to refer to those drugs that reduce psychotic symptoms. The in-troduction of newer medications has led to the adoption of the term *typicals* to refer to the original neuroleptic agents. Use of the term *anti-schizophren-ics* would not be appropriate since the effects of these drugs are nonspecific and not confined to the disorders known as schizophrenia (Owens, 1998).

EFFICACY OF TYPICAL ANTIPSYCHOTICS

Antipsychotic drugs are currently the principal first-line treatment for schizophrenia and play an important role in the treatment of psychotic symptoms whatever the causes, including those associated with schizo-affective disorder, mood disorders with psychotic features, and psychotic symptoms associated with drug abuse and organic brain disorders. These drugs are also used to sedate agitated, explosive, nonpsychotic individuals, to manage a variety of severe disorders in children, and to manage the symp-toms of movement disorders such as Tourette's syndrome and Huntington's disease as well as neurodegenerative disorders such as Alzheimer's.

Antipsychotic drugs are effective in suppressing specific positive symp-toms of psychosis such as hallucinations, delusions, and thought distur-bance. These drugs also contribute to improved symptom remission rates and shorter hospital stays. About 60 to 70 percent of all acute psychotic pa-tients show some improvement on antipsychotic medications, 25 to 30 per-cent respond poorly, and about 8 percent are nonresponders. In comparison, about 23 percent of acute psychotic patients show improvement on placebos (Davis, 1976; Tuma and May, 1979).

The efficacy of antipsychotic medications has been demonstrated in nu-merous double-blind placebo-controlled studies. Nevertheless, most schiz-ophrenic patients on antipsychotic medications do not regain prebreakdown levels of functioning. Antipsychotics have proven effective for positive symptoms—delusions and hallucinations—but they are generally thought to be less effective for negative symptoms such as alogia, apathy, anhedonia, shyness, social withdrawal, and affective flattening. The side effects of the typical antipsychotics can also make it difficult to differentiate *primary* (caused by the disorder) from *secondary* negative symptoms that result from the effects of long-term hospitalization and the effects of antipsychotic medications. Heterogeneity of drug response among patients with the same diagnosis and symptoms also complicates research.

Antipsychotics reduce the likelihood of symptom exacerbation, although most studies of long-term maintenance have not extended beyond two years (Owens, 1998). Projections of efficacy rates beyond two years suggest that prophylactic antipsychotics delay relapses rather than prevent future acute flare-ups. Complete long-term symptom control with medication is estimated to occur in about 20 percent of all cases (Owens, 1998).

Currently six classes of antipsychotics are available in the United States that are now referred to as typical antipsychotics: phenothiazines, thioxanthenes, butyrophenones, dibenzoxapines, dihydroindolones, and dibenzodiazepines. These six classes of compounds differ chemically but have similar pharmacological effects. Their efficacy rates are also similar, although the severity of side effects varies among classes. Some classes of antipsychotics are more soporific (sleep inducing) whereas others are much less so; some have fewer extrapyramidal side effects (tremors, stiffness, shuffling gait) than others. Tables are available that rate each of the FDA-approved antipsychotic medications for their side effect profiles (Owens, 1998).

The most limiting aspect of the use of typical antipsychotic drugs is associated with effects known as extrapyramidal symptoms or pseudoparkinsonism (Owens and Firth, 1982). Patients often do not follow through on aftercare medication recommendations because of these side effects which mimic aspects of the symptoms of Parkinson's disease. All typical antipsychotic medications produce varying degrees of extrapyramidal effects, although such effects vary from individual to individual and are dose related.

The drugs usually require up to three weeks to induce full clinical benefits. Therefore, it is likely that complex changes in the brain are induced which are related to these changes. At present these changes are not well understood. At a behavioral level, the drugs reduce initiative and interest in the environment. Emotional reactivity is also diminished. Animal studies indicate that the drugs block the effects of reinforcing electrical self-stimulation of the medial forebrain bundle and reduce hyperactivity and aggressiveness. Spontaneous motor activity is reduced, and many of the drugs cause extreme muscular rigidity in high doses. Extrapyramidal side effects include parkinsonian-like tremors, dystonia, akinesia, and tardive dyskinesia.

Patients who receive the drugs for prolonged intervals may manifest symptoms of excess dopamine-like activity. Prolonged blockade of dopamine receptors results in an increase in the number of dopamine receptors in the corpus striatum. This increase is associated with the occurrence of a chronic iatrogenic (treatment-related) neurological disorder called *tardive dyskinesia*. Tardive motor disorders develop at about the rate of 4 percent per year for the first five to six years of typical antipsychotic drug treatment (Kane et al., 1986). The symptoms of tardive dyskinesia include aimless movements of the tongue, face, mouth, or jaw, including movements such as smacking of the lips, chewing, and protrusion of the tongue. In the extremities symptoms may include rapid, jerky chorioform movements and writhing athetoid movements. Estimates of the incidence of tardive dyskinesia range from 10 to 50 percent in patients who are on antipsychotic medications long term. Additional parkinsonian symptoms may include akinesia, rigidity, masked facies, stooped posture, and a shuffling gait. A deficiency in the striatonigral gamma-aminobutyric acid (GABA) pathway, possibly induced by chronic understimulation of this pathway as a result of dopamine receptor blockade by typical antipsychotics, has been proposed as the underlying cause of tardive dyskinesia (Gunne and Haggstrom, 1985).

Akathesia is characterized by an unpleasant sense of restlessness that leads the patient to pace constantly, a symptom that mimics agitation. Photosensitivity in the form of sunburn sensitivity, rash, or purplish pigmentation may occur in some patients. The phenothiazines can also increase prolactin secretion with subsequent development of amenorrhea in women and gynecomastia (breast enlargement) in men. Reduced sex drive may also be associated with endocrine changes. A rare but potentially fatal blood disorder—agranulocytosis—may occur in one in 10,000 patients on phenothiazines. This risk is as high as 2 percent of patients on the atypical antipsychotic clozapine.

Despite the many side effects and potential drawbacks that can occur, the risk-benefit ratio of antipsychotic medications is generally considered to weigh heavily in favor of the use of these medications to control psychotic symptoms. In addition, the likelihood of symptom relapse is significantly delayed through prophylactic use of these medications. Thus, despite limitations and risks, the balance in favor of the benefits of antipsychotic medications is believed to be substantial.

THE DOPAMINE HYPOTHESIS

Dopamine is one of the principal catecholamines in the brain. In most areas of the brain it is a precursor of norepinephrine. However, in areas lacking the enzyme necessary to transform dopamine, it is the presumed primary neurotransmitter. The dopaminergic system plays a modulatory role in a wide variety of mental, motor, endocrine, and autonomic nervous system functions (Carlsson, 1987). It also appears to be involved in the integration of neocortical structures with older subcortical structures. The fact that antipsychotic medications exert their therapeutic actions by blocking dopamine receptors suggests dopaminergic neurons in the brain must be either directly or indirectly involved in the regulation of processes involved in psychotic symptoms.

The involvement of dopamine in the symptoms of psychosis and of schizophrenia is supported by indirect evidence from pharmacological studies. Drugs that induce excessive levels of dopamine, such as amphetamines or L-dopa, can lead to or worsen psychotic symptoms such as paranoid ideation, manic excitement, or delirium. Conversely, drugs that block or interfere with dopaminergic transmission of nerve impulses reduce acute psychotic symptoms (Carlsson, 1983). In addition, the dose-equivalent efficacy of antipsychotic drugs in reducing psychotic symptoms is a direct function of their efficacy in blocking dopamine receptors (Snyder, 1978).

Supersensitivity of dopamine receptors has been proposed to be the cause of schizophrenia; however, there are a number of reasons why qualifications of the dopamine hypothesis of schizophrenia are necessary. First, antipsychotic drugs act not only on schizophrenia but on other psychotic conditions as well (Carlsson, 1987). Second, not all patients or symptoms of schizophrenia respond to antipsychotic medications. Last, these drugs also act on a variety of other neurotransmitters, although their antipsychotic action is highly correlated with the action on dopamine (Carlsson, 1983). Carlsson (1987) proposed a revision to the original hypothesis of dopaminergic hyperfunction in schizophrenia. He suggested that the disorder may be caused by a more subtle dopaminergic dysfunction or by an imbalance between dopaminergic and other systems.

Dopamine Pathways

The major dopamine pathway of the brain has its cell bodies in a nucleus of the brainstem called the substantia nigra. Its dopaminergic nerve cells extend through long axons that ascend to the corpus striatum, a part of the brain involved in the smooth coordination of the arms and legs. The degeneration of this pathway in Parkinson's disease causes the characteristic symptoms of rigidity, decreased movement, and tremor. Antipsychotic drugs cause parkinsonian-like symptoms by blocking the dopamine receptors in this region. A second pathway has cell bodies in an area of the brainstem referred to as the tegmentum. Axons from cells in this area spread to parts of the limbic system having to do with emotional regulation, including the olfactory tubercle, the nucleus accumbens, and the central nucleus of the amygdala. The oldest part of the cortex, the cingulate cortex, also receives dopamine input. The effects of dopamine blockers on these limbic and paleocortical areas that are involved in the regulation of emotions are thought to be most significant in reducing symptoms of schizophrenia. Other dopamine pathways have cell bodies in the hypothalamus with axons extending to the pituitary gland. One pituitary hormone, prolactin, stimulates lactation and inhibits ovarian and testicular hormone secretions.

Dopamine Receptors

There is evidence relating the antipsychotic efficacy of typical neuroleptics to the blockade of dopamine (DA) receptors, particularly those receptors (D_2) that inhibit the enzyme adenylate cyclase (Stoof and Kebabian, 1981).

D_1 receptors stimulate adenylate cyclase and until recently were not thought to be involved in the antipsychotic action of typical antipsychotics because of a lack of correlation between antipsychotic potency and D_1 receptor affinity (Meltzer, 1989). That view is probably mistaken. It now appears that the two receptor subtypes must cooperate in order to elicit antipsychotic behavioral responses (Carlsson, 1987). The consensus is that blockade of mesolimbic and mesocortical D_2 receptors is the primary basis for the antipsychotic efficacy of typical antipsychotic medications. The motoric effects of these drugs are due to their effects on D_2 receptors in the basal ganglia (Meltzer, 1989).

Carlsson (1987) cites evidence that dopaminergic neurons appear to play an important modulatory role in a variety of mental, motor, endocrine, and autonomic functions. These neurons also appear to possess a complex intrinsic control mechanism. As relatively recent mechanisms, from an evolutionary perspective, dopaminergic systems appear to be involved in the integration of the activities of neocortical and older subcortical systems. The neostriatum, including the nucleus accumbens in particular, appears to be intricately involved in this integration.

The complicated and vulnerable process of integrating the newer structures of the neocortex with older subcortical structures is thought to play an important role in the origins of psychosis. Carlsson (1987) speculates that psychosis may not be due to dopaminergic hyperfunction, as many theorists postulate, but may be the result of a more subtle dysfunction or an imbalance between dopaminergic and other systems.

ATYPICAL ANTIPSYCHOTICS

The problem of tardive dyskinesia and other side effects associated with neuroleptic medications led to the search for agents that block dopamine receptors in the limbic and mesocortical areas without affecting the corpus striatum or pituitary gland. Researchers have searched for drugs with increased likelihood of benefit and reduced risk of extrapyramidal side effects on the assumption that drugs which do not induce these effects will be less likely to cause tardive dyskinesia (Creese, 1983). The consensus is that blockade of D_2 dopamine receptors in the limbic and mesocortical areas of the brain is the basis for the efficacy of typical antipsychotic medications, while the adverse effects of these drugs on motor behavior are due to a similar effect on D_2 dopamine receptors located in the basal ganglia (Meltzer, 1989). The most promising class of antipsychotic drugs to emerge is referred to as the *atypical antipsychotics*. Of these, clozapine was the first that was FDA approved.

No hard-and-fast criteria differentiate typical from atypical antipsychotic drugs. One characteristic that differentiates the typical from the atypical antipsychotic drugs is the difference between doses that produce catalepsy in animals and doses that block hyperactivity. Evidence suggests that the dose of an atypical antipsychotic required to combat psychosis (the assumed analogue to animal hyperactivity) is lower than the dose required to induce catalepsy (extrapyramidal symptoms). This "window" is larger for the atypical drugs than for the typicals. In general, the atypical drugs are thought to be more specific to a given type of dopamine receptor, less likely to produce neurologic side effects, and less likely to elevate prolactin levels (Deutch et al., 1991). These characteristics, however, are probably not related to one another or to a common underlying mechanism.

FDA approval of clozapine in 1989 made it possible to evaluate the effects of the first of the atypical antipsychotic medications. Results indicated that clozapine was more effective than typicals in treating both positive and negative symptoms of schizophrenia and did so with reduced risk of movement disorders (Jibson and Tandon, 1998). Clozapine was found to be effective in treating about 30 percent of previously treatment-resistant patients and appeared to have a limited capacity to produce tardive dyskinesia and elevation of prolactin release (Meltzer, 1989). Unfortunately, the utility of clozapine has been limited by its potential (risk factor is approximately 2.5 cases/1,000) to produce a potentially fatal disorder (agranulocytosis, a metabolic-type bone marrow suppression which can lead to reduced white blood cell counts). This potential complication requires frequent and expensive blood count monitoring.

At present, clozapine is used primarily as an alternative medication for treatment of refractory psychotic patients who have not responded to typical medications. A second problem with the drug is that seizure thresholds are lowered by clozapine, with a cumulative one-year incidence of about 4 percent of patients on this drug (Jibson and Tandon, 1998).

The introduction of a second atypical antipsychotic, risperidone (Risperdal) in 1994, allowed for additional applications of this class of drugs. Risperidone appears to have minimal risk for agranulocytosis and has significantly lower risk for inducting extrapyramidal symptoms at therapeutic dose levels. Recently other atypicals, olanzapine (Zyprexa), ziprasidone (Geodon), and quetiapine (Seroquel), have also been FDA approved.

Pharmacology of the Atypicals

The receptor profiles of the atypical antipsychotic agents vary in terms of binding affinities for various neurotransmitter receptors (Jibson and Tandon, 1998). However, there are similarities in their pharmacological profiles. First, these agents all retain the property of D_2 antagonism to varying degrees. Risperidone and olanzapine are potent D_2 antagonists, and clozapine is a weak antagonist. The atypical antipsychotics are also potent serotonin ($5HT_{2a}$) antagonists. Each of the atypicals also exhibit significant differences in activity at various muscarinic, cholinergic, histaminergic, noradrenergic, and other serotonin sites. Currently there are no antipsychotics that do not block D_2 receptors (Jibson and Tandon, 1998), and serotonin receptor ($5HT_{2a}$) antagonism appears to be associated with decreased propensity for extrapyramidal symptoms.

Each of the atypical antipsychotics has proven to be as effective as conventional antipsychotic agents in treating psychotic symptoms in short-term trials (four to six weeks) (Beasley et al., 1996), and clozapine has been demonstrated to be more effective than typicals in the treatment of neuroleptic refractory patients (Jibson and Tandon, 1998). Negative-symptom improvement with all atypical antipsychotics is also slightly superior to that obtained with conventional agents. Secondary negative symptoms are particularly likely to respond to these agents.

How do these medications selectively block D_2 receptors? The mesolimbic dopamine pathway has a limited number of presynaptic $5HT_{2a}$ receptors. The atypicals block serotonin 2 ($5HT_{2a}$) receptors in all pathways. Serotonin normally inhibits dopamine release in these pathways. When $5HT_{2a}$ is blocked it increases dopamine release in the mesocortical, tuberoinfundibular, and nigrostriatal pathways. Enhanced dopamine release offsets the side effects of dopamine blockade. The result is antipsychotic effects without severe cognitive slowing and extrapyramidal or prolactin-related side effects. Both positive and negative symptoms of schizophrenia are reduced in severity in most patients in response to these medications. Thus, the paradox of typical antipsychotics sometimes making negative symptoms worse while reducing positive symptoms is largely resolved by the atypicals.

The side effect profiles of the atypical antipsychotics differ and are dose related, but overall the side effects can be significant. Clozapine commonly induces hypotension early in treatment and is associated with anticholinergic effects such as constipation, hypersalivation, sedation, weight gain, and tachycardia. The risk of agranulocytosis is 1 to 2 percent in the first six months of treatment. The side effects of risperidone include drowsiness, orthostatic hypotension, lightheadedness, anxiety, akathesia, constipation, nausea, nasal congestion, weight gain, and prolactin elevation. Side effects of olanzepine include somnolence, dry mouth, nausea, lightheadedness, ortho-static hypotension, dizziness, constipation, headache, akathesia, weight gain, and transient elevation of hepatic transaminases. Prolactin elevation occurs transiently. The side effects of sertindole include nasal congestion, weight gain, and tremor (Jibson and Tandon, 1998).

An important advantage of the atypical antipsychotics is associated with their limited extrapyramidal side effect profile compared with typical anti-psychotics. This means that fewer patients are likely to discontinue treatment due to unpleasant side effects. The antipsychotic effects of all anti-psychotic medications begin when D_2 receptors are about 60 percent occupied by the medication. Side effects such as tremor and rigidity of muscles begin at about 80 percent occupancy. The lower rates of side effects of the newer drugs indicate that it is easier to remain within the 60 to 80 percent receptor site occupancy range with these medications, possibly because they block the receptor sites for shorter periods of time and because they also act as se-rotonin antagonists (Kapur et al., 2000). The atypicals are also more effec-tive for reducing the severity of negative symptoms and for symptoms of anxiety and depression that are often present in psychotic patients (Carlsson and Carlsson, 1990).

THE HYPERDOPAMINERGIC HYPOTHESIS AND GLUTAMATE

Grace (1991) proposed that dopamine neurons may exhibit two modes of firing—either a burst of impulses or a steady pacemaker-like mode. He sug-gests that these two firing patterns may result in different types of dopamine release. The rapid mode causes rapid, phasic increases of dopamine in the synaptic cleft. The steady tonic firing pattern could result in dopamine re-lease that does not result in a large increase in dopamine levels. Additional evidence indicates that basal levels of dopamine in the nucleus accumbens may be regulated by the excitatory neurotransmitter glutamate. Grace sug-gests that schizophrenic patients may have a reduced level of tonic dopa-mine release in the nucleus accumbens, secondary to decreased glutamate activity which results from hippocampal deficiencies. As a result, dopamine turnover could be reduced, but responses to phasic releases of dopamine would be increased. The result would be that active symptoms result from increased phasic dopamine release and negative symptoms from decreased tonic dopamine levels. Thus, Grace believes that antipsychotic drug treat-ment blocks phasic dopamine releases.

Recent studies have focused on the role of glutaminergic physiology due to the relationship between dopaminergic and glutaminergic systems. Recall that glutamate is an excitatory neurotransmitter which acts on several types of receptors. The drug phencyclidine (PCP), initially used as an anesthetic, has been known for many years to have psychotomimetic properties. It has been widely abused in the United States since the 1960s. What makes PCP particularly interesting is that in addition to the paranoia induced by dopamine agonists, the psychotomimetic effects include cognitive impairment and negative symptoms such as apathy, negativism, and thought disorganization. The PCP binding site is thought to be within the ion channel of a glutamate receptor subtype (NMDA, or N-methyl-D-aspartate). The drug appears to block the ion channel in the NMDA receptor complex, resulting in diminished glutaminergic neurotransmission. A related finding suggests that both dopaminergic and glutaminergic terminals converge on sections of pyramidal neurons in the cortex, indicating a possible common site of action for both dopamine agonists and PCP (Bergson et al., 1995). Some researchers now believe that modulation of glutamate release by dopamine receptors may mediate some of the effects of dopamine in psychosis (Gao, Krimer, and Goldman-Rakic, 2001). For this reason the potential therapeutic role of agents that act on glutamate receptors is being actively explored as a direction in which to develop a new and potentially more effective class of antipsychotic agents (Fahy, Woodruff, and Szmukler, 1998).

Drugs that enhance glutaminergic neurotransmission may be discovered which are more effective than the atypicals in reducing negative symptoms and thought disorganization. Researchers are currently attempting to identify and test substances that enhance glutaminergic transmission using agonists of the glutaminergic NMDA receptor, since pilot research indicates drugs that activate this receptor complex are effective in reducing negative symptoms (Goff et al., 1995).

SCHIZOPHRENIA: A NEUROTRANSMITTER IMBALANCE SYNDROME?

It is fairly clear that the antipsychotic action of neuroleptics is achieved as a result of their action as D_2 antagonists. PET studies indicate that between 65 to 80 percent of D_2 receptor occupancy by neuroleptics is obtained in the striaum and that the density of dopamine receptors in the human cerebral cortex is very low (Farde et al., 1988). Thus it is unlikely that the antipsychotic action of these drugs is located primarily in the cortex. Carlsson and Carlsson (1990) propose that the cerebral cortex is capable of controlling its sensory input and arousal by means of a negative feedback loop involving the striatal complexes, the thalamus, and the mesencephalic reticular formation. This feedback loop is composed of several parallel components representing motor, cognitive, and emotional functions. The afferent and efferent connections of the dorsal and ventral striatum are organized so that the dorsal striatum receives afferent input largely from the neocortex, whereas the ventral striatum is mainly innervated by the limbic cortex. In either case the afferent fibers are glutaminergic. There is also a glutaminergic supply to the striatum from the thalamus. Efferent fibers from the dorsal and ventral striatum project to the pallidum and in turn innervate different thalamic nuclei. The dorsal projections go to the ventrolateral nucleus, which projects to the neocortex. The ventral striatum projects to nuclei in the thalamus which in turn project to the frontal and limbic cortex and the amygdala. Some fibers leaving the pallidum innervate the mesencephalic reticular formation rather than the thalamus.

It appears that part of this feedback system deals with precisely targeted functions, whereas others, involving parts of the thalamus and reticular formation, may be engaged in the control of cortical arousal. Carlsson and Carlsson propose that these systems provide a means for the cerebral cortex to control its sensory input by adjusting a thalamic filter, as well as by controlling the activity of subcortical arousal systems. They propose that the mesostriatal dopamine pathways play a modulatory role by exerting an inhibitory influence on the striatum, which in turn acts to inhibit thalamic/mesencephalic reticular formation activity. Stimulation of dopaminergic mechanisms functions to counteract this inhibition. The corticostriatal glutamate system acts in the opposite direction by stimulating the inhibitory function of the striatum.

Carlsson and Carlsson propose that a deficient corticostriatal glutamatergic function can lead to functional disturbances similar to those caused by dopamine agonists, such as amphetamines. In addition, phencyclidine (PCP, "angel dust") is a psychotogenic substance that appears to target one of the major glutamate receptors. In other words, PCP is a glutamate antagonist. Thus the catalepsy and psychomotor inhibition induced by PCP is the result of eliminating the dopaminergic function that in turn releases the active inhibitory impact of the dopaminergic striatal system. The authors suggest that schizophrenia could be caused by a dopamine-glutamate imbalance. They argue that our understanding of the role of dopamine as an essential stimulant for a variety of brain functions (mental and motor) must be revised. It is true that when dopamine is reduced mental and motor activity go down. However, it now appears that the lack of activity which occurs when dopamine activity is reduced is due to an active inhibition exerted by the corticostriatal glutaminergic pathway via the striatum on the thalamus and mesencephalic reticular formation. If this inhibition is removed by blocking glutamate receptors, psychomotor activity occurs in the absence of dopaminergic stimulation. Thus the corticostriatal glutaminergic pathway is a strong suppressant of a number of arousal mechanisms.

The inhibitory action of the corticostriatal glutaminergic pathway on brain activity appears to be selective, in that it allows for targeted and purposeful responses to external stimuli. This in turn suggests that the selection of purposeful programs, as well as the switch from one program to another, is an important function of corticostriatal glutamate. The corticostriatal pathway appears to act as an antagonist to the mesostriatal dopaminergic system. Thus, just as a psychotic condition can be induced, aggravated, or alleviated by manipulation of the dopaminergic system, manipulation of the corticostriatal pathway may have similar consequences. Evidence of the psychotogenic actions of PCP, ketamine, and other substances support this view. Carlsson and Carlsson hypothesize that schizophrenia may be induced by a deficiency of the corticostriatal glutamate pathway. If this is the case, glutaminergic agonists may possess antipsychotic properties. However, if schizophrenia is a heterogenous disorder, as Carlsson and Carlsson suspect, neurotransmitter imbalances of various kinds may also be important.

SUMMARY

Typical antipsychotic medications are generally effective in reducing the intensity and severity of positive psychotic symptoms. These drugs reduce agitation, distress, confusion, hallucinations, and the intensity of delusional preoccupation in the majority of patients. Typical antipsychotic medications may also compound some negative symptoms, and their side effect profiles include extrapyramidal symptoms and elevated prolactin, problems which decrease the likelihood of outpatient medication compliance. These drugs also increase risk for tardive dyskinesia, a serious and permanent neurological condition. Typicals act by blocking D_2 receptors in all major dopamine pathways, including the mesocorticolimbic, nigrostriatal, and tuberoinfundibular pathways. Dopamine blockade in the mesolimbic pathway appears to be associated with their antipsychotic effects. Blockade of mesocortical, nigrostriatal, and tuberoinfundibular pathways is associated with unwanted side effects.

Although the therapeutic effects of typical antipsychotic drugs are closely associated with D_2 receptor blocking, this does not necessarily indicate that deficits or excesses of dopamine or abnormalities in sites affected by these drugs are the cause of schizophrenia. It is possible that dopamine-blocking drugs may ameliorate positive symptoms indirectly by reducing all forms of affect and willed or spontaneous activity. In this way there is less likelihood of the patient having experiences that are related to psychotic symptoms. The downside is that there is a price to pay for these benefits. Symptoms such as auditory hallucinations, agitation, and the compelling quality of delusional beliefs may be reduced, but patients often find it more difficult to think, to feel, to concentrate, and to act spontaneously (Hirsch, 1982).

Typical antipsychotic medications are generally more effective and act more quickly than atypicals in reducing the active symptoms of acute psychosis. Despite their intimidating side effect profiles, it is important to recognize that these effects are dose related and in some cases infrequent. These medications have benefited and continue to benefit millions of patients. In the great majority of patients the benefits far outweigh the risks and untoward side effects of these drugs. There is no question that judiciously prescribed typical antipsychotic medications have an important role to play in the amelioration and prophylactic treatment of symptoms.

Atypical antipsychotic medications, to varying degrees, have lower potentials for impairing cognitive functions, inducing tardive dyskinesia, and inducing extrapyramidal side effects, although these benefits are dose related. These reduced side effect profiles are due to the fact that these drugs appear to functionally selectively block D_2 receptors in the mesolimbic pathways without blockade of D_2 receptors in mesocortical (cognitive slowing), nigrostriatal (extrapyramidal), or tuberoinfundibular (elevated prolactin) pathways. The blockade of mesolimbic D_2 receptors is thought to be the basis of the atypicals' antipsychotic effects. However, there is a substantial body of evidence indicating that $5HT_{2a}$ receptor blockade is also essential for the therapeutic effects of atypical antipsychotic drugs.

Although significant advances have occurred in the pharmacotherapy of schizophrenia with introduction of the atypical medications, the molecular biology of how the medications work is not well understood. Recent speculation and research on next-generation antipsychotic medications is focused on the neurotransmitter glutamate.

Carlsson and Carlsson hypothesize that the corticostriatal glutaminergic system exerts an inhibitory influence on dopaminergic excitatory pathways and allows for selective responding to external stimuli. They hypothesize that schizophrenic symptoms may be induced by a deficiency of the corticostriatal glutamate pathway. If this is the case, glutaminergic agonists may become the new mainline drugs for the treatment of schizophrenia.

It is possible that antipsychotic medications produce benefits that have nothing directly to do with the origins of the symptoms they effect. Whatever neurochemical changes are associated with improvement in schizophrenic symptoms, questions remain about whether the changes induced by antipsychotic drugs alter primary or secondary dysfunctions or compensatory mechanisms or decrease activity in critical brain pathways that have to do with the influences of limbic and midbrain structures on higher cortical processes (Bray and Owen, 2001). We do not know that antipsychotic medications work by correcting some etiologically significant biochemical defect, but these medications have unquestionably helped many people. The downside is that the limited solutions they provide are too often viewed as less expensive alternatives rather than supplements to supportive psychosocial rehabilitation programs. Antipsychotic drugs help people regain some control over their distress and agitation, but they do little to enhance energy, social awareness, or those skills needed to effectively engage with others or to cope with social expectations. In fact, the evidence suggests that long-term rates of social recovery have not improved in tandem with widespread use of antipsychotic drugs (Harding et al., 1987; Hegarty et al., 1994; Warner, 1994). Obviously, maximizing the recovery of schizophrenic patients requires far more than provision of medications.

SECTION IV:
COGNITIVE-BEHAVIORAL,
NEUROCOGNITIVE,
AND NEURODEVELOPMENTAL
RESEARCH

Neurocognitive theorists generally assume that vulnerability-linked impairments appear prior to the onset of acute schizophrenic symptoms and endure into the residual phase. These impairments are thought to result from prenatal or perinatal insults of genetic, viral, autotoxic, or mechanical origin and appear as abnormalities of cognitive functions and motor control (Spaulding and Poland, 2001). Impairments in higher levels of cognitive functioning may not become apparent until late adolescence or early adulthood, presumably after the dysfunctional neurological substrates of these systems are fully activated by hormonal and neurological changes. The enduring deficits in social cognition that persist through chronic and residual phases of schizophrenia are assumed by neurocognitive theorists to result from two factors: (1) the cumulative effects of basic neurocognitive impairments on the individual's ongoing ability to acquire normal modes of social cognition during development (compromised acquisition) and (2) the continuing effects of specific vulnerability-linked residual neurocognitive impairments in basic processes (active impairments) (Spaulding and Poland, 2001).

These factors are associated with the development of two relatively distinct approaches to cognitive therapy. One approach associated with the active impairment model seeks to identify and remediate the specific neurocognitive impairments that are characteristic of many schizophrenic patients. The specific processes targeted in therapy are chosen on the basis of evidence from laboratory studies and are referred to as neurocognitive deficits, such as impaired attentional and memory processes. The research and theory that is the foundation for the neurocognitive (active impairments) approach is summarized in Chapter 10. The second approach attempts to modify cognitive activities that may be thought of as signs of the compromised acquisition factor, including impaired social skills, faulty attributions, and negative self-schema. This approach focuses on higher-level cognitive processes, such as beliefs, attributions, and social problem-solving skills. It evolved largely from previously developed cognitive-behavioral therapies. Research and therapeutic strategies associated with this approach are summarized in Chapter 11.

Chapter 10

Neurocognitive
and Neurodevelopmental Research

NEUROCOGNITIVE INDICATORS OF VULNERABILITY

Since the 1980s, the Kraepelian view of schizophrenia as a disorder of early adult onset with progressive deterioration has been supplanted by a neurodevelopmental perspective. According to this model, schizophrenia is a consequence of early abnormalities (most likely genetically based and/or from prenatal sources) in neural development (Green, 1998). These abnormalities are thought to occur early in development but may remain unnoticed or dormant until the affected areas of the brain mature (Weinberger, 1987). Several predictions can be derived from this point of view (Green, 1998): (1) basic information processing problems are core features of the disorder; (2) these difficulties will be relatively pervasive; (3) the processing difficulties will be relatively mild, compared with disorders of disconnection; and (4) the signs will occur relatively early in life and prior to the onset of symptoms.

Most neurocognitive theories assume that the deficits which are the basis for most schizophrenic symptoms have to do with deficits in the ability to adequately process stimuli from the environment (Broen and Storms, 1966; Dawson and Nuechterlein, 1984). Many schizophrenic patients have difficulties selecting relevant stimuli, sustaining attention, and shifting focus appropriately. They have problems recognizing and identifying relevant stimuli, and in storing, recalling, and using them appropriately (Nuechterlein and Dawson, 1984). Patients are often slow to process stimuli and do poorly on short-term and recognition memory tasks. As the processing task becomes more complex, performance is more impaired (Calev, Venables, and Monk, 1983). When competing information is introduced (as in dichotic listening tasks) schizophrenic patients show greater intrusion of irrelevant stimuli (Dawson and Nuechterlein, 1984) and require more time between target and masking stimuli to identify a target stimulus accurately (Green,

Nuechterlein, and Mintz, 1994). In some cases these attentional impairments do not change significantly when patients are in an active or residual symptom phase of the disorder or when medications decrease active symptoms (Nuechterlein, 1991).

Dawson and Nuechterlein (1984) speculate that the reduced capacity of patients to process information impedes molar cognitive functions involved in what are referred to as "executive" functions. As a result, conscious effort may be required to complete cognitive tasks that are normally done automatically. Difficulties with executive functions such as planning, problem solving, and the ability to alternate attention among several tasks are evidenced in schizophrenic patients' impaired performance on measures such as the Wisconsin Card Sort Test (Heaton, 1981). When patients are asked to match cards that go together and are given feedback indicating whether a match is right or wrong but are not told specifically which characteristics on which to match (e.g., color, shape, size, or number), schizophrenic patients tend to make many errors and to give a relatively high number of perseverative responses. Response perseveration on the Wisconsin test continues in spite of trial-by-trial performance feedback and seems to indicate a deficit in executive functions. Impairment of performance on the Wisconsin Card Sort Test is widely thought to be associated with decreased activation of the prefrontal cortex, an area of the brain thought to be involved in schizophrenia (Weinberger, Berman, and Zec, 1986).

Research on electrodermal responses indicates that about half of all schizophrenic patients evidence high levels of orienting skin conductance (sweat gland activity) responses when faced with novel stimuli, while the other half are classified as "nonresponders" (Dawson and Nuechterlein, 1984). The authors speculate that electrodermal responders may allocate processing capacity indiscriminately to stimuli, while nonresponders may fail to allocate sufficient processing capacity.

Other researchers have focused on hemispheric laterality or the differential activation of the right and left cerebral hemispheres for motor, perceptual, cognitive, and emotive functions (Nasrallah, 1982). Studies using a wide range of measures indicate that there is a lateralized dysfunction in the left cerebral hemisphere of schizophrenic patients which may be central to patients' inability to respond cognitively. Additional research indicates that information processing dysfunctions occur at a high rate among first-degree family members of patients, particularly their children (Nuechterlein and Dawson, 1984).

Eye tracking deficits, in the form of saccadic intrusions into smooth-pursuit eye tracking movements, have been reported on average in around 65 percent of schizophrenic patients, 40 percent of first-degree relatives, 30 to 50 percent of bipolar patients, and 8 percent of controls (Holzman and

Matthysse, 1990; Siever, 1991). Impairment in eye tracking is reportedly related to poor premorbid personality, worsening symptom course, and severity of thought disorder but is not related to other positive symptoms (Siever, 1991). Thus eye tracking dysfunction holds promise as a potential psychophysiological measure of an underlying disturbance in cognitive processing that reflects a genetically determined abnormality. This is consistent with the idea that eye tracking deficits are signs of a predisposition which is inherited as a latent trait which may be variably expressed as chronic schizophrenia. This interpretation is supported by additional evidence that eye tracking deficits are observed twice as frequently in monozygotic as in dizygotic twins (Holzman et al., 1980). Other deficits reported to occur with greater frequency in remitted as well as symptomatic patients, in at-risk populations, and in first-degree relatives of patients are the continuous performance and span of apprehension tests (Asarnow, Granholm, and Sherman, 1991; Mirsky, Ingraham, and Kugelmass, 1995). These neurocognitive deficits may be better predictors of posthospital social and occupational functioning than are clinical symptoms (Green, 1998). Servan-Schreiber, Cohen, and Steingard (1996) developed an analogue model that explains neurocognitive deficits of schizophrenic patients in terms of an inability to represent and maintain context. That is, schizophrenic performance deficits in measures of working memory and behavioral inhibition are thought to be indicators of a failure to adequately represent and maintain context in situations so that stimuli are not processed in the appropriate associational and contextual frameworks. As a result, working memory is impaired and the ability to inhibit inappropriate responses is diminished.

Research on social cognitive ability assesses several areas of functioning, including the ability to accurately recognize emotions in others, the ability to correctly infer what others are thinking, and the ability to understand social roles and the implicit rules that govern most social interactions (Penn et al., 1997). Schizophrenic patients tend to have difficulties in all of these areas, including the ability to correctly recognize emotions portrayed in faces and voices (Mueser et al., 1996). These deficits are related to patients' abilities to successfully assume work responsibilities in the community.

Neurocognitive research has contributed to a shift from a focus on symptoms to basic processing deficits as "primary" features of schizophrenia. The usefulness of neurocognitive deficits as predictors of outcome and as targets for direct therapeutic interventions, as well as the impact of atypical neuroleptics on these deficits, are being studied. One large study found that 90 percent of diagnosed schizophrenic outpatients evidenced impairments on a measure of at least one neurocognitive domain (e.g., attention, memory, motor functioning), and nearly 75 percent showed deficits on two domains (Palmer et al., 1997). It is possible that neurocognitive deficits rather than symptoms will eventually become the targets of treatment interventions since these features may be the most important aspects of the disorder (Green, 1998).

NEURODEVELOPMENTAL PRECURSORS TO CLINICAL SYMPTOMS

A premise of the neurodevelopmental model is that risk for schizophrenia is related to problems which may begin as early as the second trimester and involve misinformed communication within regions of the brain due to problems in neural migration. A number of reasons have been set forth to support the view that schizophrenia is a neurodevelopmental disorder. First, the typical onset of the disorder is during adolescence, a time when many important changes are occurring in the brain and hormonally. Second, the structural abnormalities associated with onset of schizophrenia do not appear to progress with time (Weinberger, 1995). Further support comes from evidence that some schizophrenic patients evidence signs of neuromotor and cognitive dysfunctions during childhood (Walker et al., 1996). Additional developmental antecedents reported include behavior problems at school, lower IQ and achievement test scores, and motor skills deficits (Walker, Savoie, and Davis, 1994). Follow-back studies indicate that preschizophrenic children evidence significantly more behavior problems than their healthy siblings during childhood, and the severity of these problems increases with age (Baum and Walker, 1995; Neumann and Walker, 1996).

These models postulate that the neurodevelopmental brain abnormalities that predispose to schizophrenia occur early in development, intranatally or perinatally, most likely during the second half of gestation (Weinberger, 1987). This assumption is supported by several postmortem studies indicating abnormal cortical cytoarchitecture indicative of possible early errors in developmental neurogenesis or migration (Weinberger, 1995). Other theorists postulate that schizophrenia may result from later neurodevelopmental errors such as an abnormality in periadolescent synaptic pruning in the central nervous system or a defect in the myelination of key corticolimbic pathways (Feinberg, 1983).

Attempts to understand the neural circuitry of schizophrenia have moved away from a focus on generalized abnormalities such as enlarged ventricles, cortical atrophy, and abnormal functioning in other discrete brain structures to a focus on multiple functional circuits involving cortico-subcortical loops or modular disruptions. Several loops—the dorsolateral circuit (thought to mediate "executive" functions such as planning and working memory), the anterior cingulate (thought to mediate motivation), and the lateral orbitofrontal circuit (context-appropriate behavioral responses)—are widely thought to be involved in schizophrenia. Walker and colleagues (1996) maintain that neurodevelopmental deficits in these circuits are the reasons why many schizophrenic patients in the premorbid phase manifest dysfunctions that include motoric, cognitive, and socioemotional deficits which escalate with age and appear to be congenital. Walker and colleagues suggest there may be two premorbid behavioral subtypes of schizophrenia, one characterized by early onset of behavioral dysfunctions that increase in severity through adolescence and another that shows an unremarkable behavioral course until adolescence. Walker and colleagues (1996) hypothesize that schizophrenia is caused by an abnormality of dopamine transmission in the striatum which disrupts the functioning of neural circuits which connect this subcortical region with multiple areas of the cortex, including frontal, limbic, and motor circuits.

Development of the human cerebral cortex extends into late adolescence/early adulthood, with different circuits activated at different developmental periods. The motor circuit is dominant during the first two years of life, while frontal and limbic circuits do not reach maturity until late adolescence/early adulthood. Hyperkinetic movement abnormalities observed by Walker and colleagues in preschizophrenic children are thought to represent an abnormality in the motor circuit that is associated with overactivity of striatal dopamine pathways involved in the striatal-thalamic-cortical motor circuit. Walker and colleagues (1996) hypothesize that hyper-dopamine activity in the limbic circuit which results from striatal dopamine receptor abnormalities may lead to the co-occurrence of movement and thought abnormalities. However, because these circuits develop at different rates, the expression of the underlying striatal pathology changes with age. The authors conclude that the clinical syndrome schizophrenia is only one of several developmentally linked manifestations of the diathesis, the initial expressions of which coincide with maturation of the limbic and frontal circuits. The authors believe that cases of schizophrenia and schizophrenia spectrum disorders involve an underlying neuropathology which results in a heightened sensitivity to dopamine because of unspecified abnormalities in dopamine receptors. As a result, these individuals are more sensitive to increased dopamine activity and to stress. This sensitivity is assumed to be the expression of a genetic diathesis. During the developmental years it is assumed that the diathesis interacts with exposure to life stressors to render the individual increasingly vulnerable. The cumulative effects of stress are hypothesized to be the source of individual differences in the extent of childhood behavioral dysfunction among schizophrenic patients, as well as differences in the course and onset of the symptoms.

The neurodevelopmental approach is supported by evidence from epidemiological and neurohistological studies that indicate neural migration during the second trimester of pregnancy may be adversely affected by genetic or environmental factors, such as exposure to influenza virus (Mednick et al., 1988). These abnormalities in neural migration appear to be reflected in subtle but measurable physical characteristics and abnormalities in motor development. For example, schizophrenic patients have been reported to evidence an unusual frequency of minor physical abnormalities, mixed laterality, and neuromotor functioning compared to controls (Green et al., 1989; Walker, Savoie, and Davis, 1994). These neurodevelopmental characteristics are thought to be latent traits of underlying genetic vulnerability (Matthysse, Holzman, and Lange, 1986).

A second point of view considers neurodevelopmental deficits as stressors that are understood in the framework of a vulnerability-stress model of schizophrenia (Zubin and Spring, 1977). According to this model, neurodevelopmental stressors have to be combined with genetic predisposition in order for schizophrenia to occur. It should be noted that "stressors" in this case refer to the neurodevelopmental consequences of physical environmental influences (e.g., prenatal exposure to influenza) rather than psychosocial factors such as poverty, job loss, or abuse.

THERAPIES FOR NEUROCOGNITIVE DEFICITS

At least two comprehensive approaches to the treatment of neurocognitive impairments in schizophrenia have been developed, in addition to a number of specific therapeutic strategies (Corrigan, Hirschbeck, and Wolfe, 1995; Spaulding and Poland, 2001). These approaches share the goal of attempting to develop specific strategies for improving cognitive abilities that are impaired in chronic schizophrenic patients.

Integrated psychological therapy (IPT) was developed to provide strategies to improve a number of basic neurocognitive functions identified as deficiencies in experimental research (Brenner et al., 1994). IPT is designed to proceed in a stepwise fashion, beginning with structured group activities requiring various combinations of molecular cognitive abilities and operations. Subprograms gradually progress to address molar processes associated with aspects of social cognition. IPT sessions begin with efforts to improve basic vigilance and learning-based processes of information acquisition and short-term memory storage and retrieval processes. They then progress to units covering molar processes such as social skills and social competence. The molecular cognitive differentiation subprogram includes activities designed to develop concept manipulation abilities. In this program a sorting task is introduced, and the group is encouraged to develop strategies for sorting objects of different color, size, and shape. The more general social perception subprogram includes activities designed to develop skills for processing social information (e.g., detailed examination and description of pictures of people involved in different social contexts). The activities included in all subprograms are graduated in complexity and amount of required social interaction.

Initial studies of the effects of IPT indicate that the approach has significant effects on measures of symptom functioning, neurocognitive measures, and interpersonal problem-solving skills (Spaulding et al., 1999), although at least one study indicates that the gains resulting from neurocognitive remediation efforts did not generalize to broader executive and social cognitive measures of functioning (Wykes et al., 1999). Although IPT appears to be promising, more research is needed to enhance our understanding of the variables that facilitate and impede generalization of improvements in molecular neurocognitive processes to ecologically valid indices of social cognitive processes.

Cognitive enhancement therapy (CET) (Hogarty and Flesher, 1999a) is a second comprehensive model that draws from research studies in experimental psychopathology. CET is also influenced by developmental theories of social cognition and is based on the assumption that a fundamental problem of schizophrenic patients is impaired apprehension of the gist of social problems and situations. This approach does not assume that the more molar components of social cognition are necessarily a compilation of molecular processes. The ability to perceive and respond to the gist of social situations is viewed instead as a rapid form of conceptual apprehension.

CET assumes that the gist or big picture of various social situations is normally inferred from a relatively small amount of information when that information correlates with implicit social schemata stored in memory about declarative relationships, social roles, cues, and procedural scripts. Normally this information is learned in the course of development. In the case of schizophrenia normal elements of social cognition are not developed. It is assumed that impairments in the social cognitive processes required for identifying and acting on the gist of social situations and interactions is a fundamental deficit that limits the social performance of schizophrenic patients.

Controlled-outcome studies of CET indicate that this approach is effective in enhancing social competence and performance (Hogarty and Flesher, 1999a,b; Spaulding et al., 1999). The biggest problem in evaluating the short-term and long-term effects of both CET and IPT on molar cognitive processes is in developing ecologically valid measures of social functioning and social cognition. At present we do not have well-validated measures nor do we have a good understanding of the specific attentional, perceptual, memory, or executive processes required to function socially. However, initial research findings indicate that both IPT and CET are likely to grow in influence.

SUMMARY

Vulnerability-stress models of schizophrenia (Nuechterlein and Dawson, 1984) have stimulated the search for neurocognitive indicators of vulnerability that are independent of current symptom picture. Several neurocognitive measures hold promise for eventually serving as objective indices of vulnerability for at least some percentage of cases of schizophrenia. The indices supported by research include impaired performance on measures of attention (Cornblatt and Erlenmeyer-Kimling, 1985), impaired processing of complex information, deficits in maintaining a steady attentional focus, problems distinguishing relevant from irrelevant stimuli and in forming consistent abstractions, deficits in sensory inhibition and autonomic responsivity, eye tracking deficits, impairments in processing interpersonal information, and coping skills deficits (David and Cutting, 1994; Nuechterlein and Dawson, 1984). It is clear that neurocognitive abnormalities are present in a large percentage of schizophrenic patients, and these markers are likely to provide useful indicators of the boundaries between subpopulations of schizophrenic patients as well as important clues to the relationship between these groupings and the pathophysiological changes associated with these dysfunctions.

Some researchers believe that we should begin using these neurocognitive deficits as the basis for grouping patients in studies and as targets for therapeutic interventions, rather than continuing to use a heterogenous grouping such as schizophrenia. Others maintain that measures of neurocognitive deficits should be used as indicators of risk or vulnerability and as clues for guiding brain imaging studies but should be treated as correlates of broad clinical symptom syndromes. One problem in using any measure as an alternative to diagnosis is that each deficit occurs in a certain portion of nonschizophrenic controls and does not occur in a certain percentage of schizophrenic patients. Therefore, the measures cannot be used as an alternative means of diagnosing schizophrenia, although they may provide information about vulnerability markers.

Substantial evidence shows that behavioral problems are often manifest in childhood for at least a subgroup of schizophrenic patients (Neumann and Walker, 1996). Preliminary evidence also indicates that a large portion of patients and a significant number of their healthy biological relatives evidence a variety of information processing and perceptual deficits (Green, 1998; Toomey et al., 1999). This suggests that impairments in neurocognition and social cognition may predate the onset of symptoms and that a genetic diathesis for these deficits may be present. Neurodevelopmental theorists suggest that the emergence of schizophrenia in adolescence can be explained by an interaction of early brain lesions and a disruption of later postnatal brain maturational processes in which genetic factors and environmental variables play a role (Keshavan, 1997).

Keshavan suggests that the net result of the complex interplay of these causative factors may be a multimodal network dysplasia in certain critical cortical-subcortical systems or modules, with clinical expression of symptoms varying with the particular networks predominantly involved. Neurodevelopmental theorists postulate that some process disrupts the neuronal winnowing process which naturally occurs during adolescence. This process leads to a deficit in the organization of cortical, lower limbic, and midbrain centers that have to do with the coordination of higher-order cognitive processing with emotions, memory storage, and other functions. The result is a brain-based developmental deficit that significantly increases risk for schizophrenia. At this time, however, these findings need to be replicated in diverse populations, and the etiological and therapeutic models they have spawned remain speculative. Several questions remain to be answered before the neurodevelopmental origins of schizophrenia can be considered to be valid: (1) What brain abnormalities unique to schizophrenic patients unambiguously point to derailment in one or more neurodevelopmental processes? (2) Can these pathologies be reliably demonstrated in individuals at the time when the brain is undergoing the proposed abnormal developmental changes? (3) Can it be demonstrated that putative etiological factors predictably cause the observed developmental neuropathology?

If reliable neurocognitive and social cognitive deficits can be identified in some or most schizophrenic patients and their normal relatives and not in carefully matched controls, the next step will be to identify the neural mechanisms that are the basis for each of the deficits. Neurodevelopmental and neurocognitive researchers are optimistic that advances in developmental neurobiology, neurocognition, and neuroscience make it reasonable to expect that answers to these questions are attainable in the near future.

Chapter 11

Cognitive-Behavioral Approaches and Therapies

Behavioral psychologists and neurobiological theorists share several assumptions about what science is and how it should be conducted, although behaviorists are not biological reductionists. First, both approaches favor a view of science referred to as *physicalism.* Physicalism in science dictates that valid scientific statements must be about physical events which are capable of verification. A second assumption, *operationalism,* dictates that scientific statements must be tied as closely as possible to descriptions of those concrete operations involving the manipulation of physical events which are the basis for the statement. Behavioral psychology represents the implementation of these principles to the study of human beings and advocates limiting the subject matter of psychology to the study of observable activities. Thus, thoughts, memories, and meanings are considered to be of little or no explanatory value unless these constructs can be reduced to operational statements about objectively observable physical events. Mental constructs are viewed as misleading and mistaken ways of representing what occurs, constructs that function only to obscure and obstruct scientific progress.

B. F. Skinner (1971), perhaps the best-known behaviorist, maintained that, apart from genetic factors, human behavior is controlled solely by environmental contingencies. Speculations about mental activities and their relationship to the past simply function to obscure the relationships between behavior and environmental events.

Behaviorists do not consider schizophrenia to be an entity or disease; in their view the term refers to a variety of learned maladaptive behaviors. Consequently, there is no specific behavioral theory of schizophrenia because behaviorists argue there is no such illness; there are only certain maladaptive behaviors controlled by environmental contingencies that tend to be evidenced by people called schizophrenic.

APPLIED BEHAVIORAL ANALYSIS

The task of the behavior therapist is to observe and record the frequencies of problem behaviors and their relationship to environmental contingencies. Once these relationships are documented, changes in contingencies can be engineered to decrease maladaptive behaviors and increase adaptive behaviors. The behavioral approach leads practitioners to focus on the consequences of behaviors and the context in which the behaviors occur. Applied behavioral analysis has gained increased acceptance as a strategy for dealing with particularly problematic behaviors among long-term patients in mental institutions, along with a variety of other severely disabled populations.

Ayllon (1966) was among the first to publish detailed case studies of the systematic application of the behavioral perspective to the treatment of schizophrenic patients. One of his early, groundbreaking case presentations described a chronic patient who occupied a disproportionate amount of staff time and energy in attempts to prevent her from wearing excessive layers of clothing. The patient's most problematic psychotic "symptom" consisted of wearing six or more dresses, multiple pairs of stockings, various sheets and towels wrapped around her body, and a turbanlike headdress made of several towels. The patient also typically carried several cups in one hand while holding a large bundle of clothing and a large purse in the other.

Ayllon first worked with the nursing staff to establish a baseline of the frequency of the psychotic behavior by weighing the articles worn or carried that exceeded the patient's normal body weight. It was established that on an average day she wore or carried at least twenty-four pounds of clothing and articles above her body weight. A reinforcement program was implemented that involved weighing the patient daily. Graduated reductions in excess weight of worn or carried articles were the behaviors to be reinforced. Body weight plus twenty-four pounds was designated as the initial baseline weight, with gradual reductions set as goals as each limit was successfully met. Failure to meet the required weight resulted in the patient missing the meal at which she was weighed and offered a bland but nutritious alternative. When she missed the weight goal the nursing staff stated, "Sorry, you weigh too much; you'll have to weigh less." Whenever the patient discarded more clothing than required, the weight requirement was adjusted to correspond to this new maximum limit.

Gradually, the patient shed her excess clothing to meet the graduated weight requirements until, at the end of eleven weeks of treatment, her clothing averaged about three pounds. Initially the patient reacted angrily when denied access to her meals because of too much clothing. She on various occasions shouted, cried, and threw chairs around. The staff ignored this behavior, and she gradually began to shed assorted items that she carried in her arms. Next, she stopped wearing the shawls, capes, and elaborate head-gear of towels. Then off came the eighteen pairs of stockings that had been part of her daily attire for a very long time. After fourteen weeks of treatment the patient began to routinely dress normally and started to participate voluntarily in social events in the hospital. Later her parents came to visit and insisted on taking her home for the first time during her nine years of hospitalization. They remarked that they had not wanted to take her home previously because her excessive clothing made her look like a "circus freak." This case is an excellent example of the application of a reinforcement approach to the treatment of a psychotic symptom. Notice that the therapist did not ask about mental constructs implied in questions about *why* the patient might be wearing the clothes. He simply established clear reinforcement contingencies to reinforce gradual steps in the direction of more appropriate dress.

Reinforcement techniques have also been applied on a group scale in the form of "token economy programs." Token economies are attempts to restructure mental hospital wards so that patients are rewarded for engaging in desirable behaviors such as participation in groups, social interactions, cleaning their living areas, participating in job training, and so on. Tokens are used as a form of script that can be exchanged for privileges, privacy, or other desirable outcomes. In this way, adaptive behaviors are reinforced, and the deterioration and social decline that is associated with prolonged hospitalization can be limited or even reversed (Kazdin and Bootsin, 1972).

Behavior therapy with psychotic patients was considered a truly radical approach to the treatment of the chronically mentally ill during the 1960s. The behaviorists' pragmatic focus on changing specific behaviors, rather than vaguely defined symptoms of mental disorders, brought about many positive changes and helped introduce a more optimistic, solution-oriented view of working with chronic schizophrenic patients. In addition, this approach increased awareness of the effects of context and the consequences of psychotic behaviors. With the introduction of token economies, task groups, skills training, and other behaviorally oriented treatments, patients in large institutions were no longer medicated and warehoused. Studies on the effects of the hospital milieu based on social theories also contributed greatly to a growing awareness of the importance of the current interpersonal and social context on patient behaviors and outcome (Wing and Brown, 1970).

Behavior therapists demonstrated that psychotic behaviors can be changed by the same reinforcement contingencies that influence us all. The practical "can-do" approach stimulated renewed energy directed toward the rehabilitation of chronic institutionalized patients. Today the impact of the behavioral approach is evident on mental hospital wards across the United States.

Patients must earn points and pass through levels in order to be eligible for privileges. They are no longer viewed as helpless, untreatable victims of a brain disorder, to be medicated and left to wander either in the community or on the hospital grounds, but as individuals who are capable of improvement and rehabilitation. The behavioral approach was an important contributor to this change in perspective.

It became apparent to many practitioners during the 1970s that the assumptions of behaviorism are both enabling and limiting. Many psychologists concluded that human beings cannot be adequately understood or influenced when one is restricted to strategies and concepts based solely on observable behaviors and their environmental consequences. Cognitive processes, such as the ability to learn by observation, to anticipate future events, and to form a mental schema that determines how we interpret and respond to events, also had to be taken into account.

THE COGNITIVE-BEHAVIORAL APPROACH

An early form of the blended cognitive-behavioral approach to psychosis was suggested by Beck (1952) in an article titled "Successful Outpatient Psychotherapy of a Chronic Schizophrenic with a Delusion Based on Borrowed Guilt." However, Beck's cognitive approach was not widely influential in the literature on schizophrenia until the 1990s. A key assumption of the cognitive-behavioral approach is that people develop and maintain cognitive sets or schemata by which they attempt to make sense of the world and organize experiences. Dysfunctional schemata are the source of many maladaptive emotions and patterns of behavior. Psychopathological symptoms are assumed to result from cognitive distortions in schemata that result in inaccurate or inflexible beliefs which in turn lead to distortions and contextually inappropriate behaviors.

The basis for the cognitive distortions in schizophrenia is attributed primarily to underlying neurocognitive deficits or diatheses by some cognitive-behavioral theorists and to life experience by others. Maher (1974), for example, assumes that delusions result from neurologically based abnormal perceptual experiences. Other theorists do not assume a necessary biological dysfunction as the cause of delusions and argue that the cognitive processes associated with the development of many schizophrenic symptoms may differ from normal only in degree (Strauss, 1991).

Cognitive therapists do not generally concern themselves with the importance of detailed exploration of the past or with hidden meanings in the symptoms or thinking of patients. They stress the importance of cognition but maintain a focus on the importance of behavioral focus. Delusions are understood as the consequences of inappropriate cognitive schemata that are resistant to counterevidence and lead to the misinterpretation of experiences (Roberts, 1992). The goal of therapy is to gradually challenge the underlying assumptions and dysfunctional cognitive schemata that are assumed to be the basis for the false beliefs and thereby change the behavioral disturbances that result from these mistaken beliefs.

BROAD-SPECTRUM COGNITIVE THERAPY

Most cognitive therapists, unlike their behavioral colleagues, emphasize that therapy must be founded on a secure empathic base and a sense of understanding. The praxis of cognitive therapy is based on the notion of collaborative empiricism which involves specific requirements for planning, motivation, and methods that should be discussed and clarified with the patient on an ongoing basis. The goals of cognitive therapy are to bring about a restructuring of patients' core understandings of themselves and their relationship to the environment. This process involves strategies to bring about alterations of prevailing dysfunctional meaning structures and their replacement with more adaptive alternatives. Specific behavioral strategies, such as relaxation and other stress reduction methods, may be introduced to supplement cognitive change strategies.

Perris (1989) lists several types of cognitive distortions common to schizophrenic patients. The identification and alteration of these patterns of cognitive distortion is the goal of many of the therapeutic strategies devised by cognitive therapists.

1. *Predicative thinking.* Logic errors of identity are based on identical predicates rather than identical subjects, e.g., George W. Bush is from Texas. I am from Texas. Therefore I am a world leader.
2. *Premature assignment of meaning.* Ambiguous stimuli are assigned meaning before they are adequately processed. Therefore, information is distorted before it is understood. This process often contributes to the formation of persecutory delusions.
3. *Egocentric overinclusion.* Overinclusion refers to the tendency to include material in a thought sequence that is irrelevant to the major theme of the thought. This often results from the confusion of fantasy and external reality that is characteristic of many schizophrenic patients.
4. *Failure to distinguish between meanings and causes in arriving at certainty.* This distortion consists of replacing the idea of a cause with a personal meaning when attempting to rationally answer the question why? certain external events occur. For example, a patient might interpret a failure to exchange greetings as evidence of his or her inferiority or as a sign of a plot to poison his or her food.

5. *Loss of symbolic thinking.* This grouping refers to the tendency of patients to lose their ability to think symbolically or metaphorically, causing language to be taken literally. As a consequence, many schizophrenic patients are unable to interpret proverbs even though their initial cognitive ability was adequate to do so.
6. *Concrete concepts and their transformation to perception.* This concept refers to the tendency of schizophrenic patients to avoid abstract thought and to transform concepts to perceptual phenomena. For example, patients may hear their own thoughts and feelings expressed as if they were external voices.

Jacobs (1980) postulates that during the initial experience of a delusion, knowing precedes thinking rather than the normal sequence of thinking preceding knowing. Metathinking allows for thinking about thinking and allows one to select and direct the contents of thoughts. He maintains that the capacity for metathinking is severely impaired in schizophrenic patients. Jacobs believes that dysfunctional (delusionogenic) preconceptions are developed early in life, become automatic, and predispose the individual to later development of delusions. These dysfunctional assumptions are peremptory, i.e., they are experienced as imperatives that do not allow for refutation. In this sense, Jacobs postulates that knowing must precede thinking, at least in areas of peremptory thoughts. The combination of delusionogenic preconceptions and defective development of the capacity for metathinking processes combine to increase risk for later development of delusions. Finally, these preconceptions or delusionogenic automatic thoughts are reinforced through a dysfunctional feedback system, so that they become self-confirming and therefore more frequent, eventually assuming a delusional level. Jacobs (1980) proposes that the initial stage of therapy should help patients become aware of and trained in the components of metathinking. The second phase should focus on the recognition and gradual correction of specific controlling delusional misconceptions.

Jacobs (1980) described several typical delusionogenic assumptions that are common among patients. Examples include "If you are not responsible for something negative then I must be to blame" and "If I were to lose you I would not exist any longer." Perris (1989) described several additional delusionogenic distortions: "I cannot be loved therefore it is meaningless to try to relate to people," "If I keep to myself I cannot be hurt," and "I must be careful since people are out to harm me."

Arieti (1962), a psychodynamic theorist, also described four goals and strategies for working with delusions that apply to Jacobs's description of the second stage of therapy.

1. To help patients become aware that they adopt a referential attitude, seeking external cues to justify a frame of mind
2. To make patients aware of the tendency to make concrete the indefinite mood of feeling threatened
3. To encourage them to recognize situations in which they use primitive logic to maintain their delusions
4. To help them become conscious of their circumscribed or limited insight, meaning that patients may perceive limited stimuli correctly but tend to expand this experience at a concrete level, distorting the rest of reality

Cognitive therapists assume that lasting changes in a patient's personality and behavior must be associated with changes in fundamental dysfunctional beliefs. At this time little is known about the degree to which such changes can be brought about long term. Perris (1989) recommends that the strategies used to deal with delusions should be tailored to the pervasiveness and extent of the beliefs. When delusions dominate to such an extent that meaningful communication about other topics is difficult, he recommends that initial therapeutic contacts should be directed toward attempts to influence the pervasiveness of the beliefs, and efforts to alter degree of conviction should be deferred to a later stage. Even in cases of less pervasive delusions he recommends not focusing on these symptoms during the initial stages of therapy. Therapeutic work should instead focus on issues such as automatic thoughts and cognitive distortions related to self-image and only gradually move to discussion of delusional beliefs as progress is evidenced in correcting distortions of self-image. He suggests that the therapist must function as a "beacon of orientation" rather than push the patient beyond his or her actual preparedness.

In addition to attempts to change delusional and other dysfunctional beliefs, cognitive therapists use specific techniques to treat other aspects of schizophrenic disorders. Techniques such as self-instruction, problem solving, and social skills training are focused on particular social, behavioral, and cognitive deficits. These interventions are often done in groups. In self-instructional training, patients are coached to recognize situations in which they are likely to exhibit schizophrenic behavior and encouraged to incorporate and apply a set of corrective self-instructions designed to help them initiate alternate behaviors (Meichenbaum and Cameron, 1973). Social skills training programs have been developed to attempt to compensate for the deficits evidenced by schizophrenic patients (Bellak and Hersen, 1979; Liberman, Mueser, and Wallace, 1986), and recent innovations have integrated strategies for altering dysfunctional cognitions within the group format.

In contrast to earlier descriptions of therapy with less severely disturbed nonpsychotic patients, cognitive therapy with schizophrenic patients often involves a radical reconstruction of the patient's basic schema and requires a lengthy process involving several stages (Perris, 1989). This process may often include discussion of memories. In the cognitive reappraisal process the focus of memory discussions is one way in which dysfunctional convictions have been incorporated in memories of different past situations and one way in which they have been consistently reconfirmed. The reappraisal process is used to help the patient become aware of his or her capabilities that have been used to deal with situations in the past. Past psychotic episodes are thought to offer particularly rich opportunities for integration.

In summary, broad-based cognitive therapy of schizophrenic patients attempts to bring about restructuring of patients' understanding of themselves and their relationships (past, present, and future) to the environment. The process of therapy involves the use of strategies designed to bring about alterations of prevailing dysfunctional meaning structures and to encourage their replacement with more adaptive alternatives. The therapeutic process, as conceptualized by Perris (1989), Liotti (1988), and others who have worked extensively with seriously disturbed patients, can be thought of as occurring in two parts. The first involves correction of cognitive distortions, i.e., the ways the patient understands and processes external and internal stimuli. Therapeutic changes may occur directly or indirectly as a result of strategies such as having the patient decenter or consider alternative interpretations or by using various problem-solving strategies. Whatever the strategy, the goal is always to attempt to alter the core cognitive distortions that continuously activate and maintain the central dysfunctional schema. It is not enough that dysfunctional schemata are questioned and undermined; new more functional constructs must also be developed. As therapy proceeds, the patient is encouraged not only to consider the dysfunctional consequences of core assumptions and to learn strategies to counteract their continued influence but also to consider more functional alternatives. An important part of this process is to help the patient become aware of the capabilities he or she already has and has used in the past.

The goal of broad-based cognitive therapy is more than changing specific symptomatic behaviors, it is to bring about what can be likened to a paradigm shift, a change in the basic schemata by which the patient defines himself or herself, the world, and the particular ways he or she is prone to act in certain situations. The specifics of cognitive therapy approaches to working with schizophrenic patients are described in more detail in the following sections.

SYMPTOM-FOCUSED COGNITIVE INTERVENTIONS

Davidson, Lambert, and McGlashan (1998) have applied the cognitive approach to the treatment of delusions. In the initial phase of treatment the therapist attempts to identify each delusion and to assess the degree of conviction with which the belief is held. The therapist targets the least firmly held beliefs for intervention. Two strategies are used to gently challenge the patient's delusional beliefs and to introduce alternative interpretations (Chadwick and Lowe, 1994). The initial strategy involves verbal challenge in which the therapist questions the evidence for the delusional belief and points out discrepancies in the patient's account. Once seeds of doubt about the accuracy of these beliefs are introduced, the therapist begins to offer alternative explanations to account for the evidence and experiences that are the basis for the beliefs and to encourage the patient to consider alternative ways of looking at the evidence. The second strategy involves encouraging the patient to engage in small behavioral experiments to test the evidence for the beliefs. These tests are carefully planned and negotiated with the patient to assure their relevance and acceptance and to increase the likelihood that they have the potential to invalidate the delusion. Next, the patient is asked to carry out the tests, and the results are discussed in subsequent sessions. Dialogues and small homework assignments are structured to gradually introduce alternative interpretations to the experiences that form the apparent foundation for the delusional beliefs. The desired outcome is to guide the patient so that delusional beliefs are eventually let go and replaced by more adaptive explanations.

Other cognitive-behavioral approaches include a "normalizing" approach, based on the assumption that delusional beliefs represent extremes on a continuum of degrees of conviction of belief which ranges from normal to psychotic. The goal is to gradually move delusional beliefs and extreme behaviors toward the normal range. This process is accomplished through a process of first identifying, then attempting to understand, explain, and normalize previous and current confusing and frightening experiences (Kingdon and Turkington, 1994). Techniques such as verbal challenge, behavioral assignments, and teaching coping strategies are incorporated as the therapy progresses and additional aspects of delusional ideation are identified. The etiological importance of the concept of a "delusional mood" that is associated with increased suggestibility experienced during stressful times is emphasized by the authors of this approach. They maintain that increased anxiety, confusion, and other disturbing feelings associated with a delusional mood increase suggestibility and contribute to the misperceptions and misattributions which culminate in delusional beliefs. Delusions are understood as serving to alleviate confusion and unpleasant feelings by providing explanations and reasons for these experiences, no matter how unusual the beliefs may seem to others. By identifying and better understanding the origins of the confusing and frightening experiences associated with onset of the delusional mood, Kingdon and Turkington believe the patient will become more open to alternative interpretations of memories of experiences associated with the acute disturbed affective state or "delusional mood." Kingdon and Turkington (1994) reported the results of the application of this approach for a cohort of sixty-four patients over a five-year period. Participants in the cognitive-behavioral therapy program, designed in accordance with their model, evidenced lower readmission rates and more symptomatic improvement than did controls.

Fowler, Garety, and Kuipers (1995) developed a different approach to cognitive therapy with schizophrenic patients based on six steps:

1. engagement and assessment;
2. teaching self-management coping strategies;
3. collaborative development of new ways of understanding symptoms based on a vulnerability-stress model;
4. using cognitive strategies to challenge delusional beliefs;
5. using cognitive therapy techniques to challenge dysfunctional assumptions; and
6. teaching relapse prevention and disability management strategies.

Support for the effectiveness of this approach is based on case studies (Garety, 1992) and a study of nineteen patients (Fowler, 1992). The authors noted that the ability to benefit from the therapy was symptom related. Patients with predominantly negative symptoms generally had difficulty participating in the therapy and did not show improvement; patients with predominantly positive symptoms participated in an average of twenty-two sessions and evidenced significant benefit. Garety and colleagues (1994) also reported that patients participating in this approach to cognitive therapy showed significantly greater reductions in overall symptom severity and delusional conviction than did controls.

Another clinical research group developed an individual approach to changing delusions and hallucinations in treatment-refractory patients and a combined individual and group approach to working with acute patients (Chadwick and Birchwood, 1994; Drury et al., 1996a,b). In this approach verbal challenge techniques are used to gradually structure discussions of the feasibility of delusional beliefs. Gradually, alternative possibilities and interpretations for the patient's experiences are introduced in sessions to provide alternative interpretations to the events associated with the delusions. Behavioral assignments are planned to help provide evidence of the accuracy or error of the delusional beliefs. Hallucinations are approached in a similar fashion. First, the important dimensions of hallucinated voices are identified, including the identities, power, source, and meaning of the voices. Then, verbal challenge and planned reality-testing strategies are introduced to offer alternative explanations of the hallucinations and to develop plans for how the patient might deal with the voices differently. Work with acute patients includes both individual and group sessions in which participants are encouraged to discuss the adaptive and dysfunctional aspects of one another's beliefs, to consider alternative interpretations of these beliefs, and to learn new coping strategies. Negative attitudes toward psychosis, such as expectations of permanent disabilities and dependency, are also challenged. The discussion of the functional and dysfunctional beliefs in group context is considered to be especially important since many schizophrenic patients tend to live in their own worlds of fantasy and rarely voluntarily subject their beliefs to interpersonal consideration and discussion.

Additional components of the comprehensive program designed by Chadwick and Birchwood (1994) include family sessions that focus on stress and symptom management and a structured ward program that emphasizes interpersonal skill development. Studies of the effects of this program on small samples using behavioral baseline measures indicate that delusions and auditory hallucinations can be significantly changed toward the normal range through verbal challenge and planned reality-testing strategies (Chadwick and Birchwood, 1994; Chadwick and Lowe, 1994). A controlled trial of acute inpatients also indicated that cognitive therapy was significantly more effective than supportive (control) therapy in reducing positive symptoms and delusional convictions by week seven (Drury et al.,1996b). At a nine-month follow-up, 95 percent of the cognitive therapy participants showed significant reductions in symptoms versus 44 percent of controls. These differences were observed for positive but not for negative or disorganization symptom patients.

In summary, programmatic attempts to extend cognitive therapy techniques, developed originally for treatment of symptoms of anxiety and depression, to the treatment of schizophrenic patients appear to be effective in bringing about reductions in symptoms such as delusions and auditory hallucinations.

SOCIAL COGNITION AND SCHIZOPHRENIA

That aspect of social cognition referred to as "theory of mind" focuses on the fact that we tend to assume other people have minds like our own and consequently base our behavior on what we assume about the beliefs and intentions of others. We demonstrate this process whenever we infer hidden intentions behind what someone says or does or whenever we recognize states of false belief and predict the consequences of those false beliefs. This capability to infer the intentions of others suggests that most people must be capable of developing, to varying degrees, two separate mechanisms for mental representation. The first mechanism manages primary representations which have to do with physical aspects of the world. For example, humans learn that wood burns when it is ignited and produces fire, which is hot and can burn but can also be used for cooking. Propositions at this level are either true or false. The second, more developmentally advanced, mental mechanism handles metarepresentations which concern mental states such as beliefs, desires, and imagination. Metarepresentations are not judgments about physical reality. They are judgments about the beliefs, desires, and intentions of others; therefore, judgments about literal truth or falsity do not directly apply. In order to use metarepresentations humans must have developed and continue to utilize a social cognitive ability referred to as "theory of mind." Many human activities such as deceiving, imagining, pretending, understanding humor, irony, and satire, and recognizing the meaning of discrepancies between verbal communications and nonverbal gestures require the capacity for metarepresentations or a theory of mind.

It is widely believed that people with autism and Asperger's syndrome lack those theory of mind functions which would enable them to interact appropriately. Some theorists postulate that people with schizophrenia resemble people with autism and Asperger's syndrome because they evidence significant impairments in the mechanisms which enable them to form metarepresentations of aspects of their own experiences and those of others. Frith (1992) postulates that schizophrenic patients to varying degrees lose the ability to reflect during their first episode and never fully recover it. Thus patients may know that other people have minds but have lost the ability to infer the contents of these minds or to recognize their own intentions. Patients may lose the ability to reflect on the contents of their own minds even though they continue to evidence limited behavioral routines in their interactions with people that do not require inferences about mental states.

The ability to reflect is relative rather than all or nothing. There is a wide range of such abilities in the normal population, including naive, concrete, literal-minded, humorless, and object-focused individuals. Likewise, among schizophrenic patients loss of theory of mind functions, although significant in all cases, varies considerably among patients. Frith believes schizophrenia may be thought of as a disorder that results from either the failure to develop or the loss of the capacity for normal social cognitive functions. Autistic individuals normally develop reflective abilities. As a consequence, they are unaware that other people have different beliefs and intentions and, therefore, do not develop delusions about the intentions of others. Schizophrenics, in contrast, appear to develop normal reflective abilities and then during adolescence or young adulthood lose this ability. When the ability to form social cognitions is lost later in development patients may continue to "feel" and "know" the truth of their experiences but are unable to correct their mistaken beliefs. Frith argues that this inability to correct mistaken beliefs results from loss of the ability to form or maintain those metarepresentations which are essential for ongoing awareness of one's own goals and intentions and those of others.

Three types of cognitive impairments underlie the primary signs and syndromes of schizophrenia, according to Frith (1992):

1. Lack of awareness of one's own goals and intentions leads to negative symptoms such as *abulia* or poverty of will. Abulia is postulated to arise as a result of an early developmental disruption that gradually results in a complete or nearly complete inability to represent intentional behavior. Lack of awareness of one's own intentions leads to a cycle which results in additional deficits in self-monitoring. The result is that ultimately the patient may become unable to evaluate the experience of his or her own actions.
2. Formal thought disorder is thought to result from a failure to take into account other people's state of knowledge.
3. Faulty awareness of the intentions of others contributes to mistaken beliefs as evidenced in delusions of persecution and ideas of reference.

Research supports several of Frith's predictions regarding the relationship between theory of mind deficits and symptom patterns (Corcoran, 2001). The implications of Frith's model for cognitive therapy are that the capacity for metarepresentations must be restored for symptom improvement to occur.

COGNITIVE-BEHAVIORAL INTERVENTION PROGRAMS TAILORED TO SYMPTOM PHASE

A treatment model developed in Australia (McGorry et al., 1998) focuses on the development and evaluation of targeted cognitive interventions that can be used in three distinct phases of psychosis: prepsychotic, early first-episode recovery, and incomplete recovery. The authors adopted a stress-vulnerability framework that includes both pharmacologic and cognitive interventions to bring about change. Focus is placed on early-onset or relapse symptom detection, utilizing an extensive community-based referral network, and intensive early treatment of prepsychotic, emergent psychotic, and prolonged recovery symptoms.

The program is based on a model that regards psychotic disorders as a collection of illnesses in which disturbances of central nervous system (CNS) functions result in a mix of symptoms and cognitive-emotional disturbances. The biological disturbance is assumed to derive from the interaction of genetic or environmentally based biological vulnerabilities that contribute to but are typically not sufficient for the expression of psychosis. The therapeutic model assumes that a series of contributory causes including both distal and proximal psychological and social influences such as trauma, current life events, social conditions, and difficult life transitions are required for onset of psychosis and influence the course of the disorder.

Intervention is based on several principles. The first tenet is that intervention should be delivered at the earliest opportunity. The second tenet is that the psychotic or prepsychotic person should be instrumental in his or her own recovery and come to be personally responsible for follow-up treatment and his or her own quality of life. The third tenet of the model is that at-risk and first-presentation clients have different needs from those with chronic problems. The phase-oriented treatment program consists of a series of cognitively oriented interventions tailored to the phase of psychosis evidenced by the patient (Jackson et al., 1996).

Early Psychosis

The Early Psychosis Prevention and Treatment Team (EPACT) program was developed to prevent the onset of psychosis in at-risk adolescents and young adults and to avoid the disastrous disruptions of personal development, as well as secondary problems and social and family disturbances, that often follow onset of a major mental disorder. Since many people do not seek help prior to a first psychotic episode until positive symptoms have developed and been present for some time, a service system was developed to identify and offer treatment to at-risk young adults.

The program is implemented with referrals received from an extensive referral network that has been developed through community education activities which are designed to raise community awareness of psychosis in young people and to promote early recognition of warning signs and early referral. EPACT provides a twenty-four-hour, seven-days-a-week service which provides immediate assessment and, when justified, home-based treatment. The team attempts to minimize stress for all concerned by providing information and support at each stage of the assessment and treatment process. Home-based treatment is provided whenever possible, a case manager is introduced early in the process, and transport to the clinic is provided when required. Approximately 69 percent of all referrals to the EPACT program come from psychiatric sources and 25 percent come from families.

Eligible referrals are offered psychological treatment with the aim of reducing symptoms, enhancing coping, and delaying or preventing onset of psychosis. The specific interventions developed for individuals at high risk of transition to psychosis include five modules that focus on the topics of stress management, depression/negative symptom management, positive symptom management, comorbidity of symptoms, and group work. Interventions generally consist of three phases: (1) engagement and assessment, (2) cognitive therapy drawing upon the five treatment modules, and (3) relapse prevention. Follow-up studies indicate that approximately 40 percent of patients treated in this program progress to psychosis within one year of referral (Yung et al., 1996).

A second component of the early intervention program, the Personal Assessment and Crisis Evaluation Clinic (PACE), was developed for individuals who are at high risk for developing psychotic disorders in the near future. Young people thought to be at risk include those with a strong positive family history for psychotic disorders, schizotypal personality, a recent change in mental state, or subthreshold psychotic symptoms occurring several times a week or over a lengthy period. Patients accepted into PACE tend to have more general psychopathology, negative symptoms, and disability than patients recovering from a first episode of psychosis. These individuals receive interventions similar to those developed for persons attempting to recover from an initial episode of psychosis.

Cognitively Oriented Psychotherapy in Early Psychosis

Persons recovering from an initial episode of psychosis have gone through powerful, disturbing, and traumatic disturbances and have likely undergone at least transient cognitive impairments. These individuals often find it difficult to trust people or to relate to others. Self- and external stigma also threaten identity and self-esteem in ways that compound premorbid issues. Occurrence of acute psychosis can be likened to a personal "disaster" that threatens the coping resources and adaptational resource of the patient and family. Trauma models have therefore provided a heuristic in which McGorry and colleagues (1998) have attempted to understand some aspects of the phenomena associated with early psychosis. Raphael (1986) and Taylor (1983) suggest, for example, that trauma victims be provided with interventions as soon as possible after the disaster, which

1. promote a sense of mastery of the experience and over one's life in general;
2. promote support from significant members of the social group;
3. foster a search for meaning in the experience and encourage efforts to enhance self-esteem; and
4. facilitate working through the experience and of the emotions of fear, helplessness, anxiety, and depression that developed as a consequence.

The Cognitively Orientated Psychotherapy Program for Early Psychosis (COPE) is based on the disaster response model and is designed to assist people to adjust after the acute symptoms of their first psychotic episode have been reduced (McCann and Pearlman, 1990). Psychoeducation and cognitive techniques are used to challenge tendencies toward self-stigmatization and to help people understand and come to terms with their illness and recommence life goals. Prevention of secondary complications such as depression, anxiety, and substance abuse are additional goals of the COPE program. The main goal of the program is to assist clients in recovering from an initial episode of psychosis. The program is designed to help clients preserve a sense of self-identity and self-efficacy and to help them cope with the experience of psychosis and its secondary effects and with the disempowering effects of the hospitalization and treatment experience itself.

The cognitive component focuses on the importance of understanding how the person deals with being diagnosed as seriously mentally ill for the first time. Horowitz's (1986) information processing model of PTSD that focuses on "person schemata" as enduring or slowly changing views of self and others was adapted to provide a practical framework for the COPE program. Additional foundational material was derived from models of the readjustment process developed to assist people in recovery from disasters (Taylor, 1983). The model is described in detail by Jackson and colleagues (1996) and consists of an average of eighteen sessions designed for older adolescents and young adults experiencing their first episode of psychosis. The program has four primary goals:

1. To assess and understand the person's explanation of his or her disorder and gain an appreciation of his or her attitude toward psychosis in general
2. To engage and develop a therapeutic relationship with the person
3. To promote an adaptive recovery by focusing on how the person is adjusting to the reality of having experienced a psychotic episode and the possibility of continuing symptoms or vulnerability and their effects on how the person perceives himself or herself

4. To manage secondary comorbid problems such as depression, anxiety, and stigma that might influence self-esteem (Edwards and McGorry, 1998)

Preventive Intervention in Prolonged Recovery

The approach adopted for patients placed in the prolonged recovery group or those patients with persisting symptoms is referred to as "systematic treatment of persistent psychosis" or STOPP. Components of the STOPP program include assessment of the person's symptom-related explanatory model, exploration of aspects of one's personal history and self-concept that contribute to the formulations of possible explanations for the persistence of symptoms, and fostering a rationale for working together. Normalized models for understanding aspects of psychotic experiences are introduced to participants, and strategies for coping with specific symptoms, heightened emotional states, and ongoing stressors are taught. Belief systems that may be the basis for positive symptoms are explored and indirectly challenged, while alternative explanations for experiences continue to be offered and reinforced. Therapists focus on attempting to make sense of the person's story in order to help the patient consolidate a sense of self. Opportunities for new experiences are introduced and discussed, and renewed contact with old interests is encouraged. The therapy is usually offered on a weekly or twice-weekly basis, although flexibility is emphasized in order to allow for cognitive deficits and distress associated with symptoms. The STOPP program recognizes and reinforces the view that different people recover at different rates and along different paths.

The strategies introduced in the STOPP program also have application to a relapse prevention model. The goal of the program is to foster the practical integration of cognitive-behavioral psychological treatments that are appropriately linked by phase of illness to biological and social interventions (McGorry et al., 1998).

Postdischarge Psychoeducational Family Illness Management Programs

Several family therapy approaches to understanding and treating schizophrenia were developed during the 1950s and 1960s. These models assumed that interactions within the family played a role in the onset and maintenance of schizophrenia (Lidz et al., 1957; Bateson et al., 1956). Evidence for the role of family factors in the etiology of schizophrenia has been seriously challenged, as evidence for the role of the family in preventing or triggering symptom relapse has accumulated at a rapid rate.

During the 1960s researchers in the United Kingdom (Brown, Birley, and Wing, 1972; Leff and Vaughan, 1981) began studying the degree to which the emotional characteristics of the family environment influenced the course rather than the onset of schizophrenic symptoms. By the late 1970s it was clear that high relapse rates among discharged schizophrenic patients could not be fully accounted for by medication noncompliance (Schooler et al., 1980). At about the same time, research indicated that highly stimulating forms of psychosocial interventions, and the stress associated with expressed emotion (EE) in some families, represented stressful forms of environmental stimulation that could evoke psychotic symptoms in vulnerable patients (Vaughan and Leff, 1976a,b). Researchers developed reliable measures of EE that were based on family interviews and rating scales (Brown and Rutter, 1966; Vaughan and Leff, 1976b).

The key components of EE were identified as high levels of critical comments, hostility, overinvolvement, and low levels of warmth directed by family members toward the patient. Each of the negative components of EE was found to be correlated with higher rates of relapse (Vaughan and Leff, 1976a,b). High ratings on warmth, in contrast, were associated with lower rehospitalization rates. Overall research indicates that patients discharged to high-EE families have a nine-month relapse rate of about 50 percent compared to 15 percent for low-EE families (Leff and Vaughan, 1981). These findings led several teams of clinicians to develop interventions to modify high-EE behaviors and family attitudes and thus decrease relapse rates (Leff and Vaughan, 1981).

The program designed by Leff and colleagues employs three main techniques: an educational component, a relatives group, and family therapy sessions conducted in the patient's home. Evaluation indicates that about half of high-EE families are able to change to the low-EE category after nine months of therapy and that these changes are associated with a significant reduction in relapse rate at follow-up. Studies conducted at different centers have consistently indicated that patients maintained on antipsychotic medication and provided with psychoeducational family interventions do better than controls or those provided with individual therapy over a one-year follow-up (Anderson, Reiss, and Hogarty,1986; Falloon et al., 1985; Hogarty et al., 1995; Leff et al., 1990). Differences between EE therapy and control groups are evidenced most notably in length of time between hospitalizations. Two-year relapse rates indicate that the average time to relapse is 9.2 months for controls and 14.2 months for family intervention groups (Leff and Vaughan, 1981).

Expressed emotion research has convincingly demonstrated that stressors in the natural environment which require schizophrenic patients to respond to complicated, vague, excessive, or emotionally charged expectations function as triggers for recurrence of symptoms in vulnerable individuals. These triggers elicit symptoms of both cognitive dysfunction and emotional upset. If external demands are excessive and the underlying deficit-based vulnerabilities are sufficient, patients may relapse, even while on adequate doses of antipsychotic medications (Anderson, Reiss, and Hogarty, 1986; Falloon et al., 1985; Hogarty et al., 1995; Leff et al., 1990). This evidence supports a model that involves the reciprocal influences between the patient's symptoms and the reactions of other important people. In particular, there appears to be an interaction effect in which problem behaviors and symptoms of the patient elicit frustration, distress, and concern from family members and others and prompt coping attempts on the part of family members (Kavanaugh, 1992). These coping attempts unfortunately often involve critical interactions that trigger negative emotions and lead to conflicts that exacerbate the patient's symptoms. Therapy adopts a cognitive approach which focuses on the interpretations each actor makes of the other's behavior and attempts to teach coping skills that will increase the chances of a positive outcome.

The interactive model of EE therapy (Kavanaugh, 1992) is based on a variant of the stress-vulnerability model of schizophrenia (Zubin and Spring, 1977). It assumes that the effects of events are moderated by the interpretations placed on them and by the skills available to deal with the life stresses that are experienced. This is consistent with an eclectic therapeutic approach which includes both use of antipsychotic medications to decrease arousal-based vulnerabilities and psychoeducational training for both patients and others.

The goal of psychoeducational training is to decrease behaviors and interaction patterns that are likely to contribute to an environment that will overtax the patients' adaptive capacities. Family interventions are important since about 40 percent of schizophrenic patients on discharge live with parents, 37 percent with a spouse, and 8 percent with some other relative or friend (Wing, 1987). Psychoeducational theorists maintain that communication abnormalities do not occur with any greater frequency or intensity in the families of schizophrenic patients than in the rest of the population in which a family member has suffered a mental disorder (Liberman et al., 1986). Schizophrenia is assumed to be caused by a brain disease, not psychosocial factors, but it is recognized that psychosocial factors can create stress which contributes to increased risk for relapse.

Several groups have developed family psychoeducational therapy programs based on the vulnerability-stress model (Falloon et al., 1985; Anderson, Reiss, and Hogarty, 1986; Leff et al., 1990). Although there are distinctive features to each program, they share many similarities. Most family psychoeducational programs include educational components and management strategies designed to lower the emotional climate of the home to which the patient is likely to be discharged while maintaining graduated expectations for the patient's performance. A common goal is to avoid overstimulation that tends to elicit positive symptoms and at the same time to avoid understimulation that might result in increased negative symptoms. Detailed treatment manuals for family interventions are available (Anderson, Reiss, and Hogarty, 1986; Falloon et al., 1985; Mueser and Glynn, 1995).

The goals of psychoeducational therapy, as described by Anderson, Reiss, and Hogarty (1986), are as follows:

> *Phase 1*—The goal is to connect with the family and to enlist their cooperation, to decrease guilt, emotionality, and negative reactions to the illness, and to reduce family stress.
> *Phase 2*—The goal is to increase the family's understanding of illness and patient's needs and to enhance social networks.
> *Phase 3*—Efforts focus on maintaining the patient in the community and supporting calibrated resumption of responsibility by the patient. Additional goals are to strengthen the marital/parental coalition and increase family tolerance for low-level dysfunctional behaviors on the part of the patient.
> *Phase 4*—Efforts focus on providing support for gradual reintegration of the patient into normal social roles in community systems (work, school) and continuing to maintain and improve effectiveness of family problem solving.

An important component of the Hogarty and Anderson program is a lengthy *social skills* training program that progresses over a two-year period. This component is based on behavioral social skills training techniques (Liberman et al., 1986) and focuses on social perception and performance. The skills training component emphasizes problem behaviors that are likely to be manifested in the family and, later, in the context of resocialization in social and vocational settings beyond the family. The goal of the training is to improve the social competence of patients by focusing on behaviors that are likely to elicit high levels of expressed emotion, particularly criticism. Despite the obvious utility of this approach, follow-up research indicates that social skills interventions have little lasting effect once sessions are stopped; as a consequence, therapy programs often include continuing sessions over extended periods of time to remind and prompt the use of strategies as new situations arise (Falloon et al., 1985).

Description of One Prototypic Family Psychoeducational Program

The family intervention program developed by Leff and Berkowitz (1996) includes an initial educational component implemented in the home during two sessions scheduled while the patient is still in hospital. The primary goal of educating the relatives about schizophrenia is to moderate unrealistic expectations and critical attitudes. The program is presented in simple, nontechnical language and focuses on the role of hereditary factors in causing the disorder.

Research indicates that 70 percent of all critical comments are focused on negative symptoms (apathy, lack of motivation, lack of emotional responsiveness, failure to participate in household activities) and only 30 percent are directed at positive symptoms. Relatives tend to attribute negative symptoms to personality attributes rather than to biological factors (Leff and Berkowitz, 1996). As a consequence, emphasis is placed on topics such as the patient's lack of control and the role of negative symptoms and prognosis after positive symptoms are controlled. The probability that the family member's schizophrenia, even when episodic, will most likely be a lifelong problem is emphasized.

The timescale of sessions can be long. Family sessions are usually held for one hour, once every two weeks, for at least nine months and often continue for several years at reduced frequency. Leff and Berkowitz (1996) emphasize the importance of therapists' perseverance and ability to be satisfied with small gradual changes and little in the way of positive feedback. Families with a schizophrenic member are faced with many pressing problems and concerns, and emotions often run high. As a consequence, in this program two therapists work together to balance possible inadvertent alliances with family members and to assist each other in avoiding being caught up in family conflicts. The authors emphasize that it is critical for therapists to avoid any form of explicit or implied criticism of family members no matter how poor or inappropriate their coping behaviors appear, since criticism triggers increased guilt and anger, and may lead to rejection of therapeutic help.

An important goal of the family sessions is to improve communication among members, since they often feel anxious, emotional, overwhelmed, and pressured by problems. This pressure can lead to streams of speech and emotions that can overwhelm the therapists. To compound matters, the patient is usually withdrawn and silent. Therefore, simple ground rules such as one person speaking at a time may take months to be observed and require frequent reminders to family members. These reminders must be given in a way that does not imply criticism or negative reactions to family members. A second rule that guides the long-term goals of family sessions is that everyone should be given an equal chance to speak. The authors note that typically the patient and other noncommunicative family members are not accustomed to this exercise and may remain silent. The therapists strive to prevent other family members from encroaching on the time allotted to the silent members and try to reassure the patient that he or she can have the full attention of the group even if he or she prefers to remain silent. This exercise emphasizes the importance of attending and listening attentively to others. A third rule of the sessions is that all statements about a person in the room must be addressed directly to that person. This rule is implemented to avoid discussions that talk about the patient as if he or she were not there or were a nonperson. The establishment of these rules is often a long-term and difficult process but one that can help effect important structural changes in the family by firming up boundaries between members, redressing power imbalances, and reinstating the patient to the status of a respected person.

A second goal of the sessions is to teach problem-solving techniques to the family members. The model of problem solving that is implemented is conceptualized as a straightforward behavioral approach, but it can be difficult to implement effectively. The first step is to explore the main concerns of the family. Relatives often expect that the patient will be completely cured on discharge from the hospital, particularly after the first episode, and are angry, confused, and disappointed when it becomes apparent that a cure has not been effected. Typically a flood of problems and concerns is expressed that focuses on negative symptoms such as the patient staying in bed all day, unwillingness to clean up after himself or herself, and poor personal hygiene. Lowering expectations during educational presentations and repeated emphasis on the importance of small advances by the patient are important goals throughout the program. During these discussions the patient often will refuse to participate and express his or her views or will deny that there is a problem. A long arduous process, with many sidetracks, is often required before a family consensus is reached on a problem list and a particular problem is in focus. During these discussions, high-EE family members often revert to personal attributions for both negative and positive symptoms, so the information provided in the educational program must be reintroduced. At times the patient's point of view on the nature of a problem can contribute to lowering high-EE reactions and to identification of an acceptable solution.

Once a particular problem is in focus, the next step is to establish in considerable detail what each family member does when faced with the patient's problematic behavior and to describe what he or she feels about the patient's attempts to cope. Once each family member's perspective on the problem has been explored, the problem is divided into small, manageable steps. The therapists must be skilled in discriminating between high- and low-EE solutions and guide the family toward the latter. Next, a detailed plan is developed that specifies exactly what each family member will do, including the precise timing and frequency of his or her efforts. Vague plans are typically not carried out. Each family member may not be assigned a specific role in the implementation of the plan, but it is emphasized that each member has a responsibility to see to it the plan is carried out. Feedback about the plan is requested at each subsequent session, and the importance of persistence rather than immediate success is emphasized. The goal is for each session to end with an agreed task.

As family members' negative attitudes are ameliorated, they are encouraged to seek sources of emotional satisfaction outside of their relationships with the patient. Lowering expectations of the patient facilitates this process. Conflicts between family members, for example, over one being too soft and the other being too demanding or punitive can trigger criticism and escalating emotions. The therapists must take control and shift the focus to a calm problem-solving discussion of the alternatives. Eventually the therapists must somehow manage, through this process, to transfer authority and control back to the family for them to get along without the therapists.

Leff and Berkowitz note that overinvolvement is often more difficult to alter than criticism and requires a longer timescale of intervention, since overinvolvement often dates to the patient's childhood and has to do with the actions of both parents. Parents readily appreciate the importance of increasing the patient's independence, but changing patterns so that parents and patients begin to let go of one another can be a difficult process. Therapy sessions at this juncture focus initially on the fears that the overinvolved relative has about what might happen if he or she is absent for even brief intervals.

The patient is also encouraged to take small steps toward independence in order to build confidence. During these sessions healthy siblings can at times be enlisted to assist with and participate in planned excursions out of the home. Anxieties about separation are often expressed by one or both parents and must be thoroughly discussed as steps toward independence are initiated. Extensive preparatory work is necessary for these anxieties to be effectively addressed and ameliorated, but this work is required before any meaningful reductions in overinvolvement can occur.

Families with a schizophrenic member may start with average-sized social networks, but their networks tend to shrink over time. It is common to find an elderly mother caring for a middle-aged son at home. Typically the caretakers have little or no social life outside of the home. Relatives are often reluctant to become more active outside the home because of fears of separating from the patient. Likewise, patients often feel deficient and find it difficult to mix with healthy individuals. They often find it less threatening to participate in clubs attended by other psychiatric patients. Arrangements must be made to accompany the patient to the initial club meetings and to increase leisure activities for patients and relatives. In some cases, transitional employment support services may be enlisted to help find full-time or part-time employment for the patient.

Evaluations of the effectiveness of family psychoeducational programs have consistently indicated positive effects of treatment in reducing recidivism (Falloon et al., 1985; Leff et al., 1990). Projections into the second year of follow-up of the Hogarty and Anderson cohort, for example, indicate that about 25 percent of family therapy patients, 35 percent of social skills patients, 22 percent of combined patients, and 57 percent of controls experienced a symptom relapse during follow-up. Generalization of the results must be tempered by evidence that expressed emotion, patient gender, and household expressed emotion are confounded. Studies indicate that "high-risk" patients for psychosocial interventions, based on the identification of high expressed emotion households, tend to include about 75 percent unmarried male patients living in parental households (Falloon et al., 1985). Low expressed emotion females are reported to be at about the same risk level for relapse as high expressed emotion males. The reasons for these gender-related effects are not clear.

Coping and Symptom Management

Liberman and colleagues (1986) developed programs designed to help patients identify and manage warning signs of relapse and to develop emergency plans and manage medication. Hogarty and colleagues (1995) developed a similar symptom-management program that attempts to foster increased awareness of signs of personal vulnerability, such as inner signs of affective disturbance, and to teach graduated coping strategies for dealing with warning signs and managing stress. The authors reported that relapses were decreased and indicators of personal and social adjustment increased over the three-year interval of their treatment program and follow-up (Hogarty et al., 1995).

Symptom-management programs generally consist of three subcomponents. The first focuses on education about schizophrenia and its treatment based on a vulnerability-stress-coping model. In this context participants are taught to assess early warning signs of relapse. The second subprogram deals with coping with stress. Stress-management techniques are taught in conjunction with lessons on identifying and recognizing signs of stress. In addition, crisis management and the prevention of relapse are incorporated into the stress-management component. Finally, focus shifts to identifying and fostering personal assets in order to improve quality of life. In these sessions the goal is to help patients develop a concept of self that is not exclusively defined in terms of their illness. One-year follow-up indicates that the success rate is about the same as psychoeducational interventions, with a 21 percent one-year relapse rate compared to a standard 38 percent one-year relapse rate.

A program developed by Schaub and colleagues in Germany (Schaub, 1998) intended for stabilized patients incorporates both psychoeducational components for families and patients and cognitive-behavioral techniques designed to improve patient coping strategies (e.g., role-playing, cognitive restructuring, problem solving). There are two versions of the program, a long version of twenty-four sessions distributed over two and one-half months and a shorter version of sixteen sessions that includes four outpatient sessions. The program is implemented in either an individual or group format and is always provided in combination with case management and short-term psychoeducational family groups for relatives. Families are provided information about schizophrenia from a stress-vulnerability perspective, along with related contemporary treatment approaches and guidelines for stress management. Communication training is included to help improve communication skills, and with the cooperation of the patient, an emergency plan is developed to handle crises. Family groups include a minimum of eight sessions (biweekly or monthly) and at least four single family sessions.

The patients' program consists of three subprograms. The first subprogram focuses on education about schizophrenia and its treatment from a vulnerability-stress-coping viewpoint. In these sessions patients are encouraged to share ideas, information, and experiences with their disorder in groups, along with the information provided by the therapist. Symptoms are explained as the result of a breakdown in coping that occurs when a vulnerable person is confronted with excessive demands. Participants are taught about their underlying biological vulnerability based on evidence from research on alterations in brain metabolism and information processing. It is made clear how stress increases vulnerability and how coping strategies and social support networks along with treatment can decrease the negative effects of stress. Discussions focus on inviting participants to share experiences that illustrate how stressors provoked exacerbations of symptoms and what was most helpful to them in coping with the stress. Participants are asked which changes in thinking, feeling, body sensations, and behaviors they are most likely to experience prior to relapse and to identify their own early warning signs. They are encouraged to monitor these signs during and after treatment. In collaboration with family members and case management staff, contracts are developed based on these warning signs that describe what steps are to be taken if the warning signs occur, and an emergency plan is developed. Topics such as diagnosis, positive and negative symptoms, course of illness, neuroleptics, and cognitive-behavioral therapies (psychoeducational family therapy, social skills training) are incorporated into the discussions, and their relevance for the vulnerability-stress model is explained.

The second component of the program focuses on coping with stress. Participants are asked to identify stressful situations in different areas of their lives and to classify them in terms of two groupings: illness related, such as negative symptoms (e.g., loss of energy, lack of motivation), positive symptoms (e.g., delusions, auditory hallucinations), and medication (side effects), or psychosocial stressors (e.g., relationships with people, work, living situation). A hierarchy of stressful situations is developed by each patient. Next, participants are encouraged to identify the signs of stress that are associated with each activating event, in terms of the cognitive beliefs, emotional reactions, coping responses, and the consequences that are most likely to occur. Stress-management techniques such as relaxation training, breathing techniques, and positive imagery are taught at the beginning of each session. Stressful situations described by participants are discussed in the group, and ideas about how to deal with the situation are considered. Role-playing is incorporated in the sessions to have participants practice solutions that they consider to be the best. Emphasis is placed on strategies to improve problem solving, social skills, and cognitive change. Problem-solving sessions include teaching steps such as brain-storming, discussing pros and cons, deciding on the best solution strategy, and planning implementation.

Social skills training components are adapted from other established programs, such as that of Bellack and colleagues (1997). The skills training components include sessions on listing personal competencies and deficits in skills and relevant strategies to be learned or unlearned. The goals of exercises are explained clearly, and information about the key elements of each skill are incorporated into individualized scenarios that are used in role-plays. Dysfunctional cognitions triggered by stressful situations are discussed, and cognitive restructuring techniques are taught to help participants confront dysfunctional thinking. Participants are also taught specific coping skills. Maladaptive coping strategies such as aggression, drug use, and behavioral excesses are identified. Adaptive strategies that have been used in the past are also identified, and plans are developed to deal with future stress. Recreational and social activities that are typically neglected when under stress are also identified, and incorporated into the plans, along with behavioral, cognitive, and social coping strategies.

The latter sessions of the second phase of training focus on issues of crisis management and relapse prevention. Warning signs are reviewed, and a detailed biographical analysis of the most recent relapse is developed. This analysis includes information about how the crisis developed, what happened prior to the crisis, how the patient tried to cope with the crisis, what worked and what did not, what he or she could have done that might have been more effective, and what he or she might do differently in the future.

The third component of the program developed by Schaub and colleagues (1997) focuses on improving quality of life. Lifestyle changes that promote health and well-being are discussed, and participants are helped to develop a self-concept that is not exclusively based on their illness. The focus is on emphasizing each participant's individuality and remaining possibilities in life. This includes identifying stressors, as well as pleasant situations in which patients tend to feel and act well. Participants are encouraged to identify and develop interests and to organize and plan leisure activities. Preliminary follow-up studies (Schaub et al., 1997) indicate that the coping-oriented treatment program has resulted in a lower one-year relapse rate. A randomized outcome study of thirty-seven patients is currently under way to assess course of illness, social integration, and quality of life over three years.

PERSONAL THERAPY (PT): A DISORDER-RELEVANT THERAPY

Hogarty and colleagues (1995) developed personal therapy (PT) as a supplement to their social skills and family psychoeducation/management approach designed to address sources of postdischarge patient destabilization and distress. PT is conceptualized as an attempt to reduce internal sources of affect dysregulation and loss of control. This approach is designed to equip patients with adaptive strategies that facilitate self-control of affect by helping them develop control over experiences of escalating affect that might lead to increased dysfunctional behavior.

PT is designed to help patients develop greater awareness and understanding of their subjective affective experience and to develop skills for enhanced control over and appropriate expression of feelings. PT also attempts to enhance the patient's sensitivity to the stages of recovery from schizophrenic episodes and to provide coping strategies that lessen vulnerability to stress. PT is designed to help patients develop both increased awareness and understanding of their subjective state, including intense emotions, to develop alternatives for control or expression of these feelings, and to increase awareness of the influence of these feelings on the reciprocal behavior of others. The therapy is designed to individualize the learning of adaptive strategies that are tailored to the patient's level of clinical recovery.

Phase 1 (Basic PT)

The goals of Phase I include therapeutic joining with the patient to establish a therapeutic alliance and empathic understanding, as well as fostering a sense of hopefulness about recovery. Phase I goals also include efforts to achieve clinical stabilization. The therapist and patient develop a "treatment contract" conceptualized as steps needed to maintain adjustment without psychosis, to develop enhanced awareness and foresight, to develop adaptive coping strategies, and eventually to integrate into the community. Issues such as establishment of the minimum effective dose of maintenance antipsychotic medication, supplemental medications when necessary, medication noncompliance, use of alcohol and illicit drugs, and the importance of contacting the therapist during crises are included in the contract. Families are seen to explain the treatment program and to establish a positive working relationship.

Psychoeducation is an integral part of all individual sessions. In addition, patients, once stabilized, participate in three group workshops with twenty-minute presentations. The first workshop focuses on the psychobiological nature of schizophrenia and is designed to explain how treatments work. The need for medication and the vulnerabilities that patients might suffer are discussed, and the need for a strong therapeutic alliance is emphasized. Problems of substance abuse are also reviewed.

Phase 1 includes discussion of a strategy for gradual resumption of responsibilities such as self-care and household tasks. In addition, a technique for increasing "internal coping" is introduced. Stressful situations volunteered by patients are evaluated and identified for "internal cues" of emotional dysregulation. The relationships between "stressors as triggers" and the range of cognitive, affective, behavioral, or somatic disturbances that follow are made explicit. Finally, basic, rudimentary social skills training is introduced, including exercises in stress avoidance and using positive prosocial statements when appropriate. Phase 1 occurs over a three- to six-month period. In order to proceed to Phase 2, the following criteria must be met:

1. Positive symptoms and living conditions must be reasonably stable.
2. A maintenance dose of antipsychotic medication should be achieved for at least two months.

3. The patient's attention span should permit at least a thirty-minute tolerance of discussions.
4. The patient should have achieved a basic understanding that schizophrenia is an involuntary and environmentally sensitive psychobiological illness.
5. There should be regular therapeutic attendance.
6. The patient should evidence use of positive comments and avoidance techniques as appropriate.

Phase 2 (Intermediate)

The goals of Phase 2 are development of enhanced self-awareness, regarding affective, cognitive, and behavioral states, and signs of increasing competence at self-regulation. Therapists focus on internal states but attempt to avoid precipitation of intense affects. As individual psychoeducation sessions continue, the presentations include descriptions of prodromal signs of relapse. These sessions include discussions of cues of distress as well as coping or avoidance strategies. The second session summarizes the adaptive techniques that have been or will be learned, including relaxation, social perception techniques, and the fundamentals of conflict resolution. The third session focuses on prevocational or vocational issues that patients may eventually encounter, including elements of resumption of vocational interests, work-related vulnerabilities, and interactions with co-workers and supervisors. Prior experiences with work or rehabilitation are included in these discussions. Introduction of discussions of work and other important and expressive roles is done gradually to avoid precipitation of less apparent vulnerabilities, and discussions include identification of early internal cues associated with stress.

As patients progress, they are provided training in relaxation techniques including diaphragmatic breathing and guided imagery, supported by audiotapes and music. Social skills training focuses on enhancing social behaviors judged to be deficient. Skills such as social perception and basic strategies for managing conflict are introduced.

Phase 2 highlights self-awareness of internal cues. Goals are typically achieved over a six- to eighteen-month interval. Patients progress to Phase 3 if the following criteria are met:

1. Stabilization has continued.
2. Basic understanding of the effects of stress on a vulnerable person with schizophrenia and his or her role in relapse is achieved.

3. Regular participation in role-play scenes has occurred and homework assignments have been completed.
4. There has been evidence of correct social perception in role-play sessions in the office and of application outside the office.
5. There is correct identification of at least one vulnerable affect, as well as one physical, affective, or cognitive cue.
6. Diaphragmatic breathing has been applied in the context of stress and progress has been achieved in relaxation.

Phase 3 (Advanced)

Phase 3 focuses on the relationship between patients' life circumstances and their internal states. Timing and pacing of reintegration and vocational initiatives are related to the maintenance and successful application of basic and intermediate strategies. Discussions focus on practical examples of problems with impaired attention, memory, and social cognition. New ventures that prove to be too stressful are reconsidered, and time is given to retreat to less complex tasks. Patients are encouraged to develop a greater sense of mastery by identifying unique prodromal symptoms that are predictive of relapse. Because patients often discount the need for continued maintenance medication, the necessity of continuing medication compliance is reinforced.

Advanced internal coping strategies include progressive relaxation training and a shorter tension-release procedure. Additional self-protective techniques are discussed in the context of social encounters, such as using public transportation, being in a crowd, or entering new social contexts. Advanced social skills training includes protocols such as criticism management and conflict resolution. Protocols address stressors identified in the expressed emotion literature. Criticism management sessions include correct identification and labeling of criticism, assessment of its validity, and a repertoire of responses designed to lessen the other person's intensity and to enhance the patient's social perception and negotiation skills. Finally, a simulated vocational setting and supported work placements are used to provide real life sources of stress. Unsuccessful encounters are included as material for individual PT sessions.

The authors are conducting two three-year trials of PT. Of 186 patients judged to be protocol eligible, schizophrenic or schizoaffective patients, ages seventeen to fifty-five, IQ above seventy-five, and without serious substance abuse or medical contradictions, 150 were enrolled in the program. Ninety-one patients completed three years of protocol treatment by 1995. Despite many unanticipated problems, evidence indicates that relapse is delayed and incremental gains in personal and social skills have been achieved over the three years of treatment.

SUMMARY

As is evident in the range and amount of material covered in this chapter, cognitive-behavioral therapies for schizophrenic patients have become the focus of a great deal of interest and innovative energy during the past decade or more. Cognitive therapists assume that a number of basic dysfunctional meaning structures exert influence over the patients' experiences of themselves and the external world. These dysfunctional schemata or working models enable the patient to comprehend events, predict future situations, and make plans but in ways that contribute to the development of symptoms. Most contemporary cognitive therapists accept Bowlby's (1973) assumption that it is possible for two or more schemata or models to be operating at one time, only one of which is conscious. Therefore, unconscious dysfunctional core schemata can systematically distort new experiences and constructions so that experience tends to reinforce dysfunctionality. Therapies are designed to alter cognitive distortions and to decrease symptoms and social deficits. Evidence indicates that targeted cognitive-behavioral interventions can be effective in reducing symptoms. Expressed emotion research indicates that psychoeducational interventions decrease the frequency of rehospitalization. Critics have pointed out, however, that cognitive-behavioral approaches do not adequately address the "nonspecific" aspects or deficits observed in schizophrenic patients (e.g., alogia, anhedonia, lack of motivation) and that their long-term effectiveness in reducing symptoms has not been established (Davidson, Lambert, and McGlashan, 1998). Thus, although cognitive-behavioral intervention programs appear to hold considerable promise as practical therapeutic programs, more research is needed to evaluate the degree to which coping skills generalize and are maintained in postdischarge living environments, as well as the impact of the interventions on a range of outcomes, including vocational and social-role functioning, quality-of-life indices, well-being, and service utilization.

SECTION V:
PSYCHODYNAMIC,
PHENOMENOLOGICAL,
AND FAMILY-BASED THEORIES

Psychodynamic theories of schizophrenia were dominant during the 1950s and 1960s. Much of this literature has fallen out of favor and is largely ignored for a variety of reasons, but perhaps because there is little beyond retrospective case studies to support any of the concepts and because outcome studies of this approach to therapy for schizophrenia have not been impressive. In addition, the advent of psychoactive drugs and brain-imaging technology quickly came to dominate the thinking of most psychiatrists who have worked to gain credibility within physical medicine.

Several prominent theories are presented in this book because, in the author's opinion, there is currently no basis to exclude the processes described by these theorists from playing a contributing role in at least some cases of schizophrenia. It seems implausible that models that so dominated professional thought just forty years ago could be of no value today.

Phenomenological theorists attempt to describe rather than explain in terms of causes. These descriptions enhance our understanding at a descriptive level of the experiences of many patients. As therapists, phenomenologists seem to adopt an existential approach to change. Phenomenology is a small voice in the wilderness of schizophrenia literature but one worth listening to.

Finally, family theory provides an interactive framework in which to think about schizophrenia. Early family research was influenced by psychodynamic thinking and adopted a dyadic model for conceptualizing pathogenic interactions. Later theorists moved in the direction of broader systems thinking and have tended not to work or write extensively about either the origins or treatment of schizophrenia. Evidence suggests, however, that the family environment must be considered as a potential contributing factor in at least some cases of schizophrenia.

Chapter 12

Psychodynamic Theories:
The Role of Early Experience

Psychodynamic theories of schizophrenia are based on a model that places emphasis on the formative role of early experience in the development of personality (Bruch, 1978). These theorists are most concerned with what is unique and idiosyncratic about the individual, that is, the information that can account for the development and organization of specific psychological characteristics. Psychodynamic theorists do not discount the role of genotypes in contributing to development but maintain that in many cases personality characteristics, including vulnerability to schizophrenia, also have roots in developmental disturbances. These disturbances are observed in the unique and specific experiences of each individual during the process of development.

The psychodynamic approach developed as an interpretive discipline rather than an observational science. Its strengths are based on the unique access therapists have to the patient's inner experiences. Psychodynamic therapists concern themselves with the patient's beliefs and subjective experiences and their significance and meaning in the context of an individual life. They draw on theory and evidence provided by patients in the context of therapy to formulate interpretations and explanations for the reality-distorting experiences of patients. Individual cases and their histories rather than laboratory research provide data for constructs and formulations.

From the psychodynamic perspective, experiences of childhood must interact with phenotypic expressions of genetic predispositions to determine how later events are cognized, why specific emotions are triggered or arise spontaneously, and how relations with others are experienced (Arieti, 1955). This approach emphasizes the importance of the reality that individuals with a schizophrenic genotype or diathesis must negotiate the same developmental tasks and milestones, and respond to the same cultural and interpersonal stresses as others, but their meaning and mode of resolution may differ as their constitutional differences interact with their experiences with primary caretakers (Robbins, 1993). A central assumption of the psycho-dynamic approach is that vulnerability for psychopathology is most likely to emerge, whatever the genotype or other biological risk factors, in the con-text of primary parenting that does not compensate for or that contributes to the emerging mental manifestations of constitutional predispositions.

Psychodynamic theorists view the diverse symptoms of schizophrenia, including withdrawal, dereistic thinking, confusion, awkward body move-ments, dependency, lack of social competence, flat affect, and rage reac-tions, as indicators of a deficiency in psychological functions. In contrast to the neuroses, the symptoms of schizophrenia are seen not as compromise resolutions of unconscious conflicts but as manifestations of underlying psychological deficits (Holzman, 1975). Psychodynamic theorists empha-size the role of early parent-child interactions in shaping the development of personality traits as well as differences in brain structure and function. Psychodynamic theorists maintain that constitutionally vulnerable children may grow up to be either dysfunctional or normal depending on the parent-ing they experience.

BACKGROUND

Eugen Bleuler was among the first to emphasize the value of paying at-tention to the content of patients' delusions and hallucinations. He consid-ered these symptoms to be understandable in the context of the patient's life history. The growing influence of Freud's psychoanalytic theory in the United States was a major factor that contributed to the increased impor-tance American diagnosticians placed on Bleuler's diagnostic system. Psy-chodynamic theorists place great emphasis on the significance of Bleuler's concept of the primary symptom of autism, since they believe that the unique cognitive/affective characteristics of schizophrenia are linked to this state and to its developmental successor—narcissism (Freedman, 1991).

Bleuler's concept of autism resembles Freud's concept of autoeroticism, in which an infant is assumed to have no concept of self. Analysts assume that this objectless developmental stage normally progresses to the narcis-sistic stage of ego development, during which the child develops a growing awareness of others and the world but continues to view and interpret others with minimal regard to the existence of factors and interests outside of the self. Gradually, under normal conditions, the child becomes capable of nor-mal object relations and reality-based thought if experiences are conducive to healthy ego development.

From a psychodynamic perspective, the primary symptom autism indi-cates that aspects of the patient's ego functions either failed to develop beyond the narcissistic phase of development or regressed back to this stage during a developmental crisis of adolescence or young adulthood. Psychodynamic theorists ask, "What are the experiences in the patient's personal history that created the framework through which the individual experiences the world with such powerful distorting elements?" Psychodynamic therapy is focused on development of ego functions that enhance the capacity for emotional control and intimacy rather than short-term goals related to symptom management.

Sigmund Freud

Freud had limited firsthand experience with psychotic patients. His efforts were directed primarily toward formulating a theoretical model and treatment for the psychoneuroses. Freud did publish one highly speculative paper on paranoid schizophrenia based entirely on his reading of the autobiographical memoirs of a Dr. Schreber. In this essay, Freud concluded that schizophrenia involved a conversion of the drive toward pleasure away from other people or objects and toward oneself. He observed that the psychodynamics of psychosis appear to involve two stages in which (1) the ego abandons object relations and (2) symptoms are formed as attempts to restore lost object relations but in a manner that is egocentric and cut off from meaningful object relations (the term *object relations* generally refers to intrapsychic representation of interpersonal relations).

Freud (1924) observed that the ego functions of schizophrenic patients during the active symptom phase regressed back to a level of narcissistic functioning that was characteristic of early infancy. In his view, the nucleus of psychosis is the break with reality that signals ego regression back to *primary narcissism,* a level of early functioning that existed during the first year of life, prior to the development of rudimentary ego functions. During this stage, both infants and psychotic patients are characterized by the inability to distinguish external reality from fantasy.

In schizophrenic regression, Freud believed, the individual withdraws from external reality and creates a narcissistic reality based on fantasy and primary process thinking. He viewed the two basic processes as typically co-occurring rather than sequential. The psychotic process, according to Freud, includes two components. *Symptoms of regression* signal a gradual or sudden collapse of ego functions that results from an overall inability to cope with the demands of life. These symptoms include primitive regressive behaviors, fragmented terrifying visions and fantasies, alterations of body sensations and sensory experiences, agitation, intense anxiety, a sense of

something uncanny taking place, feelings of depersonalization and derealization, and delusions of grandeur.

At the same time that symptoms of regression are occurring, *restitutional
symptoms* are initiated. These symptoms, Freud believed, represent attempts to shore up and restore some semblance of ego control and integration to experience. Delusions are attempts to restructure reality and to construct beliefs and explanations that make partial sense of chaotic psychotic
experiences and restore some semblance of ego control and object relating.
Auditory hallucinations in the form of accusatory and derogatory voices or
commands are understood as projections of superego processes.

Freud believed that the distortions of reality and cognition which are apparent in delusions help create a new reality, one that insulates and protects
the individual so life stresses and object relations do not continue to overwhelm the vulnerable ego. This adaptation is achieved at great cost in terms
of overall level of functioning and future adaptive potential.

In Freud's view, the level of narcissistic regression observed in schizophrenic patients rendered most of them incapable of forming a therapeutic
transference relationship. Therefore, schizophrenics were not considered
candidates for psychoanalytic therapy.

SULLIVAN'S INTERPERSONAL THEORY

During the first part of the twentieth century, American practitioners,
trained in the tradition of Adolph Meyer, were more open to Freud's
psychodynamic views than their European counterparts were. Two American psychiatrists, Harry Stack Sullivan and Frieda Fromm-Reichmann,
working independently, began to successfully apply psychodynamic concepts
to the understanding and treatment of schizophrenia. Sullivan (1931) described his therapy as a "modified psychoanalytic treatment." Fromm-Reichmann referred to her therapy as "psychoanalytically oriented psychotherapy."
Their approaches differed from Freud's in several important aspects, but both
shared at least two assumptions with traditional psychoanalytic theory:
(1) important mental processes take place outside of awareness, and these unconscious processes often contain the clues for understanding disturbed behavior, and (2) childhood experiences are of great significance for personality development and the development of mental disorders.

Sullivan (1953) developed a more comprehensive model of psychopathology than did Fromm-Reichmann. He later referred to this approach as
interpersonal theory. Sullivan conceived of development in terms of interpersonal experiences with significant people in the child's environment,
rather than Freud's notion of libidinal stages. He also assumed that the criti-

cal force in psychological development is not libido but the interpersonally based experience of anxiety. Sullivan described anxiety as the unpleasant sensation that is felt in the presence of lack of empathy or disapproval from significant adults. He believed that anxiety is the primary force which drives the development of personality and that excessive or overwhelming anxiety, produced by lack of validation, harshness, and confusing, contradictory stimulation, is the primary source of environmentally induced impairments which result in various mental disorders.

The motivating force that leads the child to develop the self-system is based primarily on the need to avoid or minimize experiences of anxiety. Protective strategies such as selective inattention, avoidance, and dissociation are used to manage anxiety and can later become dominant modes of functioning. These strategies may reduce anxiety in ways which result in rigid and inflexible inner representations (personifications) which distort interactions and relationships and restrict the range of experiences, relationships, and possibilities that are available to the individual. According to Sullivan, mental disorders are "interpersonal processes that are either inadequate to the situation in which the persons are integrated, or excessively complex reactions because of illusionary persons that are unconsciously integrated into the situation" (Sullivan, 1938, p. 130).

Sullivan viewed schizophrenia as representing the extreme outcome of lifelong patterns of dealing with anxiety, an extreme that may be exacerbated by current life circumstances and biological factors. He emphasized the importance of infancy, childhood, and preadolescent developmental experiences for the formation of the self-system and assumed the continued unconscious influence of stressful, perplexing, and painful childhood experiences into adulthood. Sullivan attempted to understand mental disorders not in terms of intrapsychic processes but as complications of an individual's styles of interacting that help manage anxiety.

Sullivan described four *security operations* by which the self-system manages anxiety. The first, *sublimation,* refers to the substitution, for a behavior pattern which arouses anxiety, of a more socially acceptable activity, such as art or scholarship, which also satisfies the motives that contributed to problems. *Selective inattention* occurs when the person ignores important information, such as anxiety-arousing feelings, in order to maintain the security of the self-system. *Obsessionalism* refers to the use of language and speech to create a false sense of control, as if words had magical potency to reduce anxiety. *Dissociation* is a process by which developmentally overwhelming experiences are split off from access to consciousness and form a part of the unconscious or "not-me" component of the self-system. These dissociated not-me processes continue to operate at an unconscious level in ways that allow the individual to ignore or block out important aspects of experiences and possibilities with others. Sullivan believed the dramatic and bizarre experiences and behaviors that occur during acute psychosis represent eruptions of dissociated aspects of the not-me aspects of the self-system. These eruptions occur when the accumulated effects of a lifelong pattern of dissociation-related ineffective interpersonal relating, anxiety avoidance, and life stresses combine to overwhelm the adaptive capacities of the individual.

Schizophrenia occurs when the self-system and self-esteem are not adequate to manage the demands of interpersonal living. Painful experiences with significant people in the past result in extreme uneasiness about intimacy and closeness with others. Individuals susceptible to schizophrenia are those with many dissociations of past experiences and related aspects of the self. Sullivan viewed the acute schizophrenic experience as indicating that the self-system had lost control of the contents of awareness so that it could no longer maintain dissociations and restrict from awareness the chaotic processes and experiences characteristic of infancy and early childhood. This loss of control is associated with the experience of an overpowering anxiety and sense of the uncanny that is characteristic of the early acute schizophrenic experience. The emergence of previously dissociated elements of the not-me personification in the context of the collapse of the self-system triggers the confusion, terror, and extreme sense of urgency characteristic of acute psychoses.

Sullivan viewed the intense feelings of vastness and grandeur mixed with smallness and vulnerability experienced during the acute psychotic phase as evidence of a return to the qualitative aspects of experiences that are characteristic during early infancy. The extreme sense of urgency and the preoccupations observed during the onset stages of schizophrenia are attempts to avoid a complete collapse of the self-system, which is sensed at a preverbal level of awareness. After the stage of acute excitement and urgency, some degree of control is gradually established by the individual over his or her experience through delusions and gradual withdrawal into negative symptoms.

Sullivan believed the person's life history determines the symptom pattern that is established as the patient struggles to establish some degree of control over his or her experience. Delusions are understood as attempts to establish a measure of control over chaotic mental processes through obsessional reconstructions of recent experiences. These reconstructions work to reintroduce meaning and organization to experience and to reduce confusion but are primitive in their logic and appear fantastic to others. Delusions are maintained with remarkable tenacity because they are the basis for reestablishing the self-system and its control over the contents of conscious experience. Disorganized/hebephrenic symptoms are adopted by individuals who, based on their genotypes and personal histories, have come to despair that interpersonal relationships can never be manageable and gratifying. The paranoid dynamism involves the transfer of blame onto others for feelings of insecurity that are rooted in early experiences. This transfer of blame is never stable or secure because the sources of insecurity date back to infancy and the empathic linkages experienced with significant people during this period when the child was unable to symbolize or discriminate the source of these feelings.

Sullivan viewed most schizophrenic patients as individuals who are temperamentally shy, sensitive individuals, and as a consequence have erected enormous defensive operations to protect themselves from the risks of lasting intimate contact with others. The interaction of genetic traits and childhood experiences contributes to a failure to develop the sense of self-esteem, trust, and ability to get along with and be close to others that makes human interaction and intimacy safe. Anticipating the good-poor premorbid adjustment distinction, Sullivan argued that anyone who once achieved a satisfactory, intimate sexual relationship with another person of comparable status would be unlikely to become a chronic schizophrenic patient. If the personality is reasonably well developed in other areas, the break with the path toward schizophrenia will be abrupt. If, on the other hand, the adolescent avoids or retires from interpersonal peer and heterosexual relations and turns to the juvenile world of submission to authoritarian adults, the schizophrenic process is likely to occur earlier in life and to be insidious.

Sullivan maintained that many schizophrenic patients would respond to psychosocial therapies and emphasized the importance of creating a therapeutic environment in the entire hospital unit as an essential part of treatment.

In summary, Sullivan (1953) viewed schizophrenic symptoms as the result of a confusion of interpersonal relations triggered by the appearance of referential processes that are ordinarily excluded from awareness. He believed that an important factor in the origin of the weakness of the schizophrenic self-system was primarily the result of an extreme lack of "favorable opportunity" experienced early in life. The goal of psychotherapy was to provide opportunities for interpersonal experiences to be incorporated into the self that help the person feel that he or she is now one of a meaningful group.

THE KLEINIAN SCHOOL

The British Object Relations School initiated significant post-Freudian steps toward understanding psychotic disorders. Melanie Klein (1946) was instrumental in formulating an early object relations model of psychosis. Klein speculated that the infant's experience consists largely of fantasies mixed with indistinguishable experiences of reality. An important aspect of these fantasies has to do with satisfying, or "good," and frustrating, painful, or "bad," experiences. Since fantasy and reality are not clearly distinguished by the infant, if the great majority of experiences are nourishing or good, the infant is predisposed to experience its own goodness and the goodness of objects in external reality. If frustrated often and not adequately emotionally nourished, the infant is predisposed to internalize a sense of its own badness and develops a persecutory set toward the object world.

The infantile defenses used to manage overwhelming bad or frustrating experiences identified by Klein are denial, splitting, projection, and introjection. She used the term *projective identification* to refer to a fantasy process in which parts of the self and internalized objects (representations of others) are split away from the self and placed in an external object (e.g., person or persons). This process allows threatening object representations to be symbolically controlled and managed while remaining objects of identification. In this manner, split-off memories, emotions associated with bad parts of the self that are felt to be dangerous or cannot be accepted based on early object relations, are symbolically placed outside of the self. Klein's concepts were later modified and expanded on by her students; among the most prominent were Wilfred Bion and Donald Winnicott.

Wilfred Bion

Wilfred Bion (1897-1979) practiced psychoanalytic therapy with psychotic outpatients in London for many years. His theorizing was shaped by his work with these patients. Bion, like Klein, postulated that early internal splitting and projective identification processes create a separate "schizophrenic" core of personality, which is unconscious and not integrated into the growth and development of the rest of the personality. This core emerges during subsequent psychotic episodes of acute ego failure and regression triggered by overwhelming anxiety and life events.

Bion (1984) believed that the intense fear experienced during an acute psychosis goes back to an early developmental position associated with experiences of "bad" self-object representations and results in a form of projective identification characterized by attempts to obliterate all anxiety-invoking intrapsychic representations of one's self and objects. He viewed the ability of the parent to act as a container for the negative or unmanageable aspects of the self during infancy as the key to understanding early development.

The concepts of *container* (holding other or parent and holding the environment) and *contained* (experiences of the infant that are too strong or primitive to be managed and must be properly processed and responded to) refer to processes that are essential to development of the self. Early experiences of being adequately contained play a determining role, according to Bion, in how the self manages certain fundamental polarities in human psychological functioning, such as the balance between power and vulnerability. In Bion's view, how the self experiences these polarities later in life, as integrated, unified, and whole and therefore having been held and contained, or as split, unintegrated, psychotic, and therefore not held, is a function of the quality of early experience. If the parent figures are able to function adequately as a container and hold the affect of the infant, for example to help the infant transform frustration and rage into manageable emotions, the infant will remain connected and learn to integrate these feelings. If the infant's intense feelings are not adequately held by the other, the self will develop in fragmented fashion and aspects of development will be arrested. In this case, the precognitive experiences of self and other associated with aspects of these experiences will continue to be separate or split off from the rest of development. Affects that are split off and not integrated into the self tend to be experienced as polarities (e.g., good versus evil, omnipotent power versus terrifying vulnerability, infinite love versus destructive rage). These polarities are often externalized and later expressed in the themes that are evident in psychotic delusions.

Bion's concept of holding refers to an action by parents that supplements the existing psychic infrastructure so that what might otherwise be experienced as overwhelming becomes manageable (Lewin and Schulz, 1992). In this way, effective holding provides security that allows for continued development and increased possibilities for self-realization. The role of the container is that of provider of a safe place for affects, impulses, and experiences that do not yet have a place in the self. The job of the container is to hold on to (respond to and help organize) the infant's yet to be placed, overwhelming affects, impulses, and experiences in a way that contributes to ownership and integration of these affects rather than to disavowal. The extent to which the container can perform this function depends on how capable he or she is to empathize and to feel, tolerate, and respond appropriately to the pressures that are evoked by the primitive reactions of the infant. The more vulnerable and "difficult" the infant, of course, the more challenging the parenting tasks.

Bion introduced the term *linking* to refer to the way people are able to connect themselves to the emotions of others in ways that help avoid splitting, fusion, annihilation, or fragmentation. He believed that people are able to establish foundational links with others that form the basis for an integrated self through early experiences of being appropriately held and contained. Failures of containing and linking undermine development of an integrated self and contribute to tendencies to fragment and push the self back toward isolation, narcissism, and identification with imaginary omnipotent powers.

Bion was struck by the level of fragmentation in schizophrenic thought and assumed a connection must exist between schizophrenic fragmentation and attacks on linking. He borrowed Klein's concept of projective identification to explain this fragmentation. Recall that projective identification refers to a mental activity characteristic of the infant in which some segment of the self is experienced as located in another person, with whom some segment of the self is identified and struggles to control. Bion assumed that the fragmentation of schizophrenic thought and language must originate with the infant's experience of disturbing sensations that he or she cannot organize or control. Through the mechanism of projective identification, the infant projects this disturbing and disorganized content onto the other. If the parenting figure is appropriately responsive to this content (acts as a container) and is able to help make sense out of and organize the experience for the infant, then the infant is able to introject it in a form that is bearable. If, however, the parent is not well attuned to the infant, for whatever reasons, and is unable to act as a container for the infant's projective identifications, the infant will become victim to these disorganized and terrifying experiences.

Holding means empathically containing the rages, the fears, and the narcissistic longings of the infant. The processes of containing and holding provided the foundations for the human psyche. Bion believed that our "selves" develop through a process of projection of *unbearable emotions* into holding/containing others (Glass, 1995). The more intimate we are in our relationships with others, the more likely we are to project and to be contained, and the more open we are to receive the split-off projections of our partners. The more emotionally distant we are, the more objectified our experience of others is likely to be, and the less vulnerable we are to their projections.

The "container" (the parenting person) ideally provides an empathic psychological environment with clear and consistent boundaries and limits; without these boundaries and limits, the self is not able to construct, develop, and sustain itself. Breaks in the linking process contribute to emotional and psychological problems. Denial of opportunities to experience linking either because of untoward events, refusal, unavailability, or inability of the parent to serve as a repository for the infant's feelings, or due to characteristics of the infant that interfere with the parent's ability to exercise this function, leads to an erosion of the link between infant and parent and fragmentation of the foundations of the self. In this way, the basis is established for arrests of aspects of development that can contribute to vulnerability to psychosis (Bion, 1984).

Bion believed that the damage done by disruptions of linking have lasting effects because these experiences result in the creation of "destructive introjects" which operate to destroy the possibility of links later in life. In extreme psychotic states all emotion is avoided, because released emotions are felt to be too threatening and powerful, since emotions are also links to objects. The chronic regressed psychotic is anhedonic (i.e., does not feel) since whatever feelings he or she retains are so full of anger that to "feel" would threaten psychological annihilation. Without access to effective linking mechanisms, however, we remain isolated and exist in an empty universe, devoid of meaningful connections and intimacy.

In normal development, the parent who is an effective container is able to hold those emotions and aspects of the self which otherwise threaten to overwhelm the infant. If powerful affects and impulses are not adequately contained, they will gradually be turned against the self and experienced as split-off feelings of anxiety, rage, envy, and despair. What is vital to the development of a functional self is the consistent presence of an *other* who can be an effective container. If the parenting figures avoid or cannot contain, accept, and soothe the infant, or simply return the projected unmanageable aspects of the self (e.g., respond with anger to the infant's rage, or anxiety to the infant's fear), these "parts" will remain unintegrated as split-off aspects inside the self structure, parts that drive unconscious emotional dynamics. If, on the other hand, the infant's urges and affects are contained, they can gradually be integrated, and the tendencies of the self toward intimacy and reciprocity will progress. The drive toward intimacy and connection will be stronger than narcissistic urges to isolate, to use, and to destroy.

An adequate holding environment, characterized by empathy, understanding, compassion, and tolerance, allows for the integration of experiences into a coherent self. When the link between self and other is disrupted or undermined, as with parenting figures who cannot or will not make themselves consistently available to hold the infant's projections, the self splits off the affect associated with these experiences. These split-off fragments of earlier experiences come back to distort consciousness and are experienced as overwhelming feelings of anger, resentment, despair, fear, and destructive tendencies that seem irrational and grossly inappropriate to the context.

In psychosis the intensity of these painful experiences and fears is such that they are externalized. Thus, it becomes impossible for the patient to recognize and integrate these emotion-charged memories and tendencies into his or her own being. Instead, they are experienced in the form of hallucinated voices and delusional ideas. Vulnerability to psychosis increases when the boundaries of the self are broken so that feelings can no longer be integrated and experienced as belonging to the self. The psychotic self experiences affects as external to the self, as omnipotent, secret, and sinister forces. In schizophrenia it is no longer that "I am filled with angry feelings," but that "The world is a dangerous and evil place."

Split-off psychotic parts of the self are externalized as the other and expressed in the form of symptoms such as delusions and hallucinations. The self that cannot maintain links to others in the form of intimate and empathic relationships has no true object. It becomes its own omnipotent/grandiose object. In schizophrenia, Bion believed the self regresses back to a form of narcissistic isolation from the other and to a narcissistic identification with omnipotent power. The ego ideal is projected as an identification with absolute power in a form of narcissistic fusion, expressed as grandeur, self as God-man or the universe.

Bion viewed psychosis as a universal human potential. This potential is expressed in both individual and group expressions of alienation, narcissism, grandiosity, and destructiveness, all ways of severing connections with the linking objects in the self. For Bion, the potential for psychosis is partly rooted in our early linking experiences of holding and being held, of containing and being contained. Most of us manage to keep our psychotic potential in check because of the qualitative balance of our early experiences and through our ongoing linking experiences throughout life, experiences that are based on our capacities for intimacy and empathic identification with others.

D. W. Winnicott

Donald Winnicott was both a pediatrician and a psychoanalyst who wrote and practiced from the 1950s through the early 1970s. Winnicott was also influenced by Melanie Klein but eventually moved away from Kleinian mentalistic concepts to an emphasis on the interaction of the child with the family environment. He did not develop a comprehensive theory of psychopathology but provided insightful descriptions of the interpersonal context of early development. Winnicott broke with traditional psychoanalytic theory and thought of emotional development not primarily in terms of the vicissitudes of the gratification of instinctual drives but in terms of the child's relationship with the parent. Winnicott (1975) saw the quality of the infant's experience as critical to the emergence of healthy psychological development. He also viewed the maternal environment that responds and adapts appropriately to the changing needs and capacities of the infant as critical to healthy development.

Winnicott believed that the infant gradually develops from an early experiencing state of subjective fusion or lack of self-object differentiation to a capacity to relate to objects (self-other and self-object differentiation). He believed that the integrity of this developmental process is a function of the quality of early experience. It is the quality of the environment provided by the parent early in life that Winnicott regarded as crucial to development of a person with an integrated sense of self and of life as meaningful, real, and connected. In early infancy the child has no concept of or relation to external reality. The availability of the mother to connect and superimpose comforting experiences, symbolized by the breast, provides the foundation for the infant's connection to reality. Winnicott coined the term the *good-enough mother* to describe the parental function of providing sufficiently for the child's needs to give a good start in life. The good-enough mother holds the baby together by being attuned to and responding appropriately both temporally and qualitatively to his or her needs and inner states. The quality of these experiences, in the context of the biological vulnerabilities of the individual, determines the degree to which the self develops good internal object representations that foster the integration of experiences into a coherent self-representation and allows the individual to build up a belief in a benign environment (Winnicott, 1965).

Winnicott believed that the parenting figure must be available to the infant when needed but not impinge, interfere, or smother when not needed. He or she must create a *holding environment,* a psychic and physical space in which the infant feels protected and appropriately responded to without being aware that he or she is protected. Nurturance and protection are not particularly important to development, according to Winnicott. Experiences of gradual, well-timed, and developmentally appropriate limits can also have a constructive impact on the psychological development. Gradually, the infant must realize that his or her wishes and desires are not omnipotent, that grunts and gestures do not magically create satisfactions; instead, they are provided by others. This growing realization is critical to the development of an awareness that the object world consists of many subjectivities and that satisfaction of desires requires not only their expression but also interactions and connections with others, who have their own desires and goals. Integration is linked to the quality of parenting that is experienced. Through appropriate experiences of nurturance and limits the infant slowly becomes an individual self in his or her own right, with clear boundaries that define an inside and an outside, a me and a not-me, and with the capacity for objectively perceived relationships. These capacities are developed or formed in dysfunctional ways as a result of the interaction of inborn vulnerabilities and the quality of parental provision.

Winnicott introduced the term *the environment mother* to refer to the parent's surrounding presence. He identified the ways in which the parent protects the baby from feelings of being overwhelmed, isolated, and losing relation to the body or orientation to the world. Winnicott believed the parent protects the baby from these experiences by three types of interactions: *holding, handling,* and *object presenting.*

Holding refers to both physical and emotional processes by which the parent contains the infant's feelings by empathizing and protecting him or her from too many distressing experiences. Protection is carried out in the way the parent holds, carries, feeds, speaks to, and responds to the baby, in ways that are sensitive to and understanding of the baby's needs and experience. Experiences of prolonged distress and startling or uncomfortable experiences such as loud noises and pain are to be avoided as much as possible. The function of the holding environment is to reduce to a minimum experiences that the infant cannot manage or which cause undue frustration, emotional distress, shut down, or feelings of being overwhelmed. A good holding environment that allows the infant to remain in a relaxed open state enables the baby to gradually develop a coherent, continuous stream of experience that is the foundation for the development of an authentic, positive, and integrated sense of self that exists across time and space.

Winnicott believed that the parent figures play a critical role in fostering the baby's psychological development by mirroring the baby's experiences. Through this mirroring process the parents provide images that are internalized as both self and other representations by the baby. During the earliest developmental stages parents are not yet clearly distinguished from self by the infant. When circumstances are such that the child is not provided with an adequately empathic, mirroring, and appropriate holding and protective environment, he or she will not be able to integrate experiences into an integrated and continuous whole. If experiences that trigger distress, discomfort, and negative emotions are too frequent or prolonged, the infant will increasingly split off and fragment experiences. As a consequence, the sense of self that develops will be highly vulnerable to anxieties and "fears of going to pieces." Winnicott believed to the extent that experience is fragmented, the infant develops a "false self" which hides the inner splitting of experience with the outward experience of compliance and conformity (Winnicott, 1975).

The second aspect of the predifferentiated stage of experience has to do with the parent's handling of the infant. Ideally, touch and handling will be gentle and sensitive to the baby's body and experience, and will foster the experience of integrated emotional and physical satisfaction, so that bodily sensation, emotion, and connection to objects can be gradually integrated into a stable and coherent mind-body self. The baby's sense of self is grounded in the safe and comfortable experiencing of his own body. Sensitive handling of the baby's body functions and sensations helps provide the foundation for development of a "true self" that is open to emotional, physical, and mental capacities and experiences. If the baby experiences insensitive or incongruent handling or is left alone for long periods in discomfort, he or she may develop splits between sensory and body experiences and mental life. As a result, he or she may distance from physical and sensory experiences and later in life adopt a depersonalized or ethereal mode of experiencing. Depersonalization and anhedonia as seen in schizophrenia represent an extreme loss of union of ego and body.

The third aspect of mothering identified by Winnicott is object presenting. This term refers to the manner in which the parent brings the outside world to the baby. Initially, object presenting is experienced through feeding experiences. The sensitive parent presents the nipple and later other objects in a way that is sensitive to the baby's state and enables the child to build a growing belief in the ability to connect, to act effectively, and to trust in the world. Object presenting must be appropriate to the development of the infant, however. Some level of dissatisfaction and frustration is necessary for the child to develop a clear sense of the object as separate from the self, an awareness of the not-me world. The immaturity of the infant must be balanced by the parent who is available and present to the infant without interfering or making inappropriate demands. Ideally the baby develops a sense of self-competence and trust in the world, which develops into a mature self that feels real and is capable of integrating the polarities of connectedness with others and a comfortable sense of autonomy and separateness.

Problems in object presenting can also arise when the infant is deprived of developmental opportunities by circumstances or parents who are excessively anxious and overprotective. An anxious parent may smother the infant with attempts to feed when the baby is not hungry, play before the child is ready, overprotect, or isolate the infant inappropriately. In such cases the infant may develop the implicit assumption that the world will be there to meet needs without any special effort on his or her part. The developing child may develop anxieties about intimacy for fear of merging, losing boundaries, or being taken over or *engulfed* by others. Boundaries between self and others in such cases may easily become confused. Later symptoms such as ideas of reference and influence (thinking others are talking about you, or alien thoughts are placed in one's head) and auditory hallucinations are viewed as expressions of extremes of these boundary deficits.

The child of parents who cannot respond may develop a "false self" position as martyr or caretaker, responding to the needs of others rather than being conscious of and expressing his or her "true" needs and possibilities. Others may develop a sense of distrust of others, a sense of separateness, social isolation, suspiciousness, and belief that one must go it alone. In such cases, self-sufficiency and autonomy become ideals that drive the false self-system.

Transitional Experiences

Gradually the child's experience of subjective omnipotence must be balanced by the experience of external reality so that the two exist in dialectical relation. Winnicott (1975) did not view development as a linear process characterized by distinct stages. People continue throughout life to have access to both modes of experience. The infant's experiences of omnipotence that are allowed by holding and facilitating interactions are critical early experiences which allow the infant to experience his or her own desires as valid and meaningful, without splitting or denial. Winnicott believed that between subject omnipotence and objective reality there is a third form of experience, *transitional experience.* In subjective omnipotence the infant cannot distinguish need from reality or self from other, so desired objects seem to appear as if created by fantasy. In experience organized by objective reality, the child is aware of his or her separateness and lack of control over the object. Winnicott described the "transitional object" as experienced as somewhere between subjectively created and separate and distinct. Transitional phenomena belong to the border world between the child's early omnipotent fusion with the mother and a dawning realization of separateness.

The transitional object is a symbol of the child's internal sense of unity with a giving, nurturing, good-enough parent. It facilitates the movement of the self away from its internal focus (subjective omnipotence) into a form of object relationship. It also facilitates the infant's use of symbol formation and leads the self away from omnipotence in a social direction. If this transition is blocked due to deficiencies in the parent's ability to adapt and provide for the infant's spontaneous impulses and needs, this failure may result in a split-off part of the self that is angry, despairing, and fearful of reality, intimacy, and connection with others. Cognition and language as well as spatial and motor skills may develop normally, but emotionally the self retains an infantile orientation. The transitional period requires the child to leave the world of omnipotent delusion and accept the reality of social and cultural illusions. The transitional object enables the infant to move beyond isolation into the world of trust and shared realities. "Environmental failure" increases the risk that critical aspects of the transitional phase will not be completed.

Winnicott viewed transition as an ongoing process that never ends for anyone, since people may both advance and regress during life struggles. If early development was successful, the risk of slipping back to a permanently impaired state is less. The psychotic regresses to a primitive level and may remain locked inside the omnipotent subjectivity of infancy. Winnicott believed that the transitional realm is also a source of deep-rooted experience and spontaneous creative energy within the self, which at the same time allows for self-expression of those parts of the self that remained connected to the object world. He viewed play, art, music, and religion as modes of experience in which the inner and outer worlds meet and are expressed, areas which are personal and which offer meaning and enrichment. A person who lives entirely in the realm of objective reality lacks passion, spontaneity, and creativity. A person who lives largely in the realm of subjective omnipotence, on the other hand, is self-absorbed, narcissistic, or autistic.

Winnicott referred to experiences that disrupt and interfere with the development of a coherent and integrated self as "impingements." Impingements refer to failures in holding, handling, and object presenting that disrupt the wholeness of experience. Impingements are not experienced as external failures by the infant, who has not yet developed a sense of separateness or self-object differentiation; they are simply overwhelming experiences that cannot be managed. If impingements become a significant part of the world of experience of the infant, the child will accommodate to this object world and construct defensive modes of splitting affects, sensations, thoughts, and self-other inner representations, at an unconscious level, that allow him or her to survive overwhelming experiences of anxiety, frustration, loneliness, and despair. The false-self modes of emotional shutdown, disconnectedness, self-denial, and extreme self-sufficiency are all modes of protection for the true self.

Winnicott (1975) believed that however hidden and undeveloped the true self may be, it is never completely extinguished. He was not interested in classification but did distinguish mental disorders into three broad groups: psychoneuroses, antisocial or delinquent disorders, and psychosis. He did not discount the possible role of genetic influences but placed emphasis on studying and describing the role of deficiencies in care during the early stages of formation of the self, particularly during the period of absolute dependency of the infant, in understanding the origins of psychosis. He believed that evidence of the role of genetics and neurochemistry in schizophrenia does not contradict his view that the disorder can be understood as a basic disorder of "being." He believed that vulnerability to schizophrenic psychosis is in part the result of an early failure of relationship, granted that the failure may in some cases be difficult to avoid due to the special characteristics and vulnerabilities of the child.

Winnicott viewed the infant as continually on the brink of "unthinkable anxiety" (1975, p. 127). It is the experience of the good-enough mother as a surrounding and comforting presence that holds the baby together. The baby is only capable of being aware of a sense of well-being or the opposite, an unbearable state which Winnicott called "annihilation." He described this state as like the experience of falling forever, of complete isolation having no relation to the body or to others, of having no orientation in time or space. He believed these horrific experiences surface later in life as acute psychotic states or intense borderline anxieties in which it seems as though one's very being is in danger.

Psychosis

When too many disintegrating experiences are suffered early in development, Winnicott believed that aspects of the child's psychological development cease, although other externally oriented aspects of the personality may continue to develop around these missing areas. Stressful experiences can cause a radical split with the self between the sources of energy, desire, creativity, and meaning within the self (the true self) and a compliant, prematurely fashioned, coping, externally oriented self (the false self). This split is the beginning of a psychological life that becomes increasingly dissociated from community, trust, and reality. As a consequence, a false self develops on the basis of compliance and denial; it cannot attain the independence or interconnectedness required of maturity. As the demands of life increase and pressures for independence, intimacy, and eroticism grow, and the home environment is experienced as increasingly confining, a struggle occurs within the individual. Regressive forces interfere with attempts at transition and reciprocity, anxieties, and old overpowering affects recur as the young adult struggles to establish and maintain contact and to avoid collapse and regression. At some point the false self may fail so that the fragmentation of acute psychosis becomes evident with the psychotic individual no longer able to experience himself or herself as whole, coherent, and continuous. Efforts to live in meaningful relationships, to empathize and to engage in human exchange may be given up. Omnipotent fantasies in the form of grandiose delusions become interwoven with self fragments experienced as voices, external forces, and magical but frightening influences. Boundaries between inner and outer and self and other dissolve; the sense of self as bounded in time and space is lost. The self may now seem capable of existing for eternity. It may be experienced as one with the universe. Omnipotent fantasies coexist with intense fears and feelings of vulnerability; the self is both omnipotent and victim.

Psychosis leads to recurring or permanent regressions in adult life and to pretransitional object modes of experiencing so that external reality becomes a threat, chronological time is transformed into psychotic time, and fragments of self are cut off from any form of intimate connection with others.

MARGARET MAHLER

Margaret Mahler (1978) did clinical work with psychotic children and conducted detailed observational studies of the development of normal children. Her theorizing focused on the nature of development of internalized object relations during childhood. Mahler conceptualized the psychological birth of the infant as a slowly unfolding interactive process she referred to as *separation-individuation.* Separation refers to the gradual development of a sense of separateness from and relation to the world of reality. Particular emphasis is placed on reality as experienced with regard to the experience of one's own body and to the principal representative of the world as experienced by the infant, the *primary love object.* Development of these processes continues throughout life, but particular emphasis was placed by Mahler on the developments that take place in the interval from the fourth to the thirty-sixth month. She referred to this interval as the separation-individuation phase. Mahler's descriptions of the separation-individuation process greatly influenced subsequent theorists who were looking for an alternative framework to Freud's libido theory in which to understand childhood development.

According to Mahler, the normal separation-individuation process follows an early symbiotic phase and involves the child's gradual achievement of separate functioning in the presence of and with the emotional availability of the mother. In optimal development the child is continually confronted with minimal threats of object loss that occur in the context of appropriate developmental readiness for and pleasure in independent functioning. In contrast, threats of object loss, object ambivalence, or unpredictable object absence that overwhelm the child's capacities interfere with the separation-individuation process.

Separation and individuation are conceived of as two complementary processes: separation refers to the child's gradual emergence from a symbiotic, fused relationship with a parent, and individuation refers to those achievements that mark the child's assumption of individuality. These processes are intertwined, but they may diverge so that a developmental lag in one may coincide with precocity in the other. For example, a child may develop locomotor abilities early and before internal regulatory mechanisms to manage separateness are developed. Or an enmeshed, anxious parent may interfere with the child's autonomous functions and delay development of awareness of self-other differentiation, even in the context of otherwise precocious cognitive, motor, and perceptual functions. Developmentally between the fourth and thirty-sixth month Mahler believed the initial state of lack of self-other differentiation of the young infant gradually becomes organized into internalized mental structures having to do with issues of separation and individuation.

At crucial times during infancy genetically prepared tendencies are activated to facilitate internalization of whatever interactions take place with the parenting figure as mechanisms to modulate, soothe, and cope with distress arising from internal sources. If the mother figure is unable to provide adequate buffering for the child, either because of the child's vulnerability or lack of capacity at that time, or if the parent figure provides confused, inconsistent, punitive, or enmeshed parenting, the consequence will be that the child will internalize deficient regulatory functions (Robbins, 1993). Later on, during times of stressful transitions or disappointments, the preschizophrenic may compensate for deficient regulatory functions with defensive autonomy, placatory behavior, substitution of idealized images or memories, and percepts. These attempts at restoration ultimately create more difficulties and anxieties, leading to further withdrawal from reality and a focus on dysfunctional substitutes and fantasies in place of more adaptive regulatory functions.

OBJECT RELATIONS AND DELUSIONS

James Glass (1985) identified four concepts of psychodynamic theory that are central to the understanding of delusions: (1) the splitting of the object world into good and bad and the origins of these experiences in infancy; (2) fusion and lack of ego boundaries, including problems in identity, body ego, and differentiating self and other; (3) the experience of the self and other as a unit exercising omnipotent control over the internal environment; and (4) the function of delusions in protecting the self from the explosive power of aggressive drives.

"Value" for the very young infant depends on the gratification or frustration of drive states. If a drive is gratified, the universe is experienced as good; if it is not gratified, the world is experienced as bad. The balance of good and bad experiences during early infancy is critical to later experience because the concepts of good and bad are projected outward onto others and internalized in the formation of the self. The initial objects (sources of drive gratification) on which experiences are projected are the parents. If experience is often bad, not only are the object and the world bad, but in taking in the badness (frustrating aspects) of others, part of the self, too, becomes bad. These identifications lead to views about the self (as bad or good or part bad or good) and others (as bad or good or part bad or good). Each part (bad or good) of internalized experience is separable and retains its own identifications, memory fragments, meanings, and values. The infant experiences self, others, and the world in a totalistic fashion: when the self is experienced as bad it is completely, absolutely, and irrevocably bad. When it is good, it is completely and irrevocably good. The same principle holds for the other. When the other (the mother) is bad, she is completely bad and threatening. When she is good, she is all gratifying and perfect. This splitting is inherent in the object relations of the infant. The infant "knows only absolute perfection and complete destruction; it belongs to the early time in life when only black and white existed, good and bad, pleasure and pain, but nothing in between" (Reich, 1973, p. 301).

Delusions recreate the infant's dichotomous mode of valuing and experiencing. Many delusions encapsulate either images of power and omnipotence or terrifying situations of victimization and destruction. These dichotomous images relate to the psychoanalytic view of schizophrenic delusions as signs of massive regression back to the infantile universe that was split into images of good and bad, omnipotent and weak (Reich, 1973). Tolerance and tentativeness of understanding are present neither in the mental content of the infant nor in the delusional schizophrenic patient. What stands out are the tendencies toward fragmented, dichotomous experiences, toward omnipotent cosmic identifications, and to unquestioning belief in the experienced/constructed reality.

Psychodynamic theorists do not assume that mothers or families "cause" schizophrenia, but they do argue that these factors can in some cases be important contributing factors to vulnerability to the disorder. Schizophrenia is viewed not as the direct result of bad parenting but as a grouping of symptoms which can result from the interactions and compounding effects of any number of social, genetic, physiological, and intrapsychic processes. The early parent-child relationship is viewed as potentially critical to all personality development, including the development of schizophrenia.

Mahler (1978) described the process of introjection, or taking into the self images of goodness and badness. This splitting process is intensified through the continuing psychological, cultural, and social maturation of the self. As a result, some children develop a "brittleness" that may be manifested in a fragmented self-image, emotional and social awkwardness, and a stiffness or lack of coherence of body experience. The rigid separation of good and bad self and other representations contributes to the infant's lack of certainty and confusion over self boundaries. If the infant never learns to adequately distinguish where the self begins and ends, the result is a failure to develop a separate identity that is independent and not heavily contaminated by introjected memories and images. This can lead to an underlying fear of "engulfment" by the other, which can be triggered by the stresses and demands of emotional closeness. Fear of closeness can become a continual threat against which the growing child must continually defend himself or herself.

Engulfment and reengulfment can function as both powerful fears and powerful needs. They are experienced as ambivalence, a powerful need to avoid closeness, and a powerful need to fuse, to find a defining attachment to a nurturing, omnipotent object relationship. Lacking a sense of boundaries, the infant searches for a defining attachment, or what is described as a "need to fuse" with the nurturing object. The need to fuse is expressed in schizophrenic delusions of grandeur, as imagery of enormous power and significance, as representations of unconscious attempts to fuse with an all-powerful object. Closeness to any human being, however, threatens engulfment or loss of a sense of ego boundaries to an object/person that has the power to absorb those boundaries. The schizophrenic defense against risk of such loss involves withdrawing emotional closeness and trust from other human beings. Delusions compensate for this withdrawal by providing substitute gratifications and by re-creating the early feelings of union with omnipotent figures.

The splitting of the object world is an important source of rigidity in the infant's experience that continues and emerges in the experience of the adult schizophrenic. Splitting the object world, and simultaneously one's own ego, into good and bad parts impairs the capacity for ambivalence in relationships that is crucial to movement toward autonomy and growth. Angry, negative feelings that are split off from the ego during infancy may reappear during adolescence in association with the struggle to separate from dependency on the family and to develop autonomy. The stresses of separation, of integrating feelings of sexual desire, of coping with peer pressures and the growing need for and cultural expectations of increased autonomy may activate feelings of inadequacy, anger, and fear that have been kept under control during childhood. The result is vulnerability and increased risk for an acute psychotic episode.

The splitting of the object world was the child's solution to inborn vulnerability and the pain of "longings and losses," but this split defines all later development and makes for greater difficulty in resolving later object-related conflicts. In schizophrenic patients, the fixation of ego development due to split self-object representations is so strong and the tendencies to regression so great that whatever ego functions have developed in the form of rational, relational, and social structures dissolve. Ego functions become absorbed in the split-off parts of infantile unconscious processes. The self, as a coherent personality structure, ceases to exist in an interpersonal context. The schizophrenic functions in an autistic universe of emotions that derives from inner conflicts of an ego that was split during childhood. The split in the ego between good and bad results in delusional imagery in which good is equated with power and omnipotence and bad with victimization and images of destruction and annihilation. Anger or indifference becomes the safest form of human contact, and intimacy becomes an impossibility.

In schizophrenia, vulnerabilities are expressed in the form of dependency conflicts; severe anxiety in relation to both aggression and attachment; fluctuations between omnipotence and helplessness; problems around experiencing grief, loss, or separation; a punitive punishing conscience in place of normal guilt; idealistic goals of attainment contributing to a sense that any achievement is worthless; and a defect in integrating past experience in order to develop foresight or a future orientation (Schulz and Kilgalen, 1967).

People who are not schizophrenic also develop fantastic worldviews, whether in the form of political beliefs, religious cults, or alienated communities. Glass (1985) views delusional systems as posing both a threat to sociality and examples of the hidden aspects of human nature that are a part of the continuum of human experience. Schizophrenic delusions represent a form of survival against the fear of annihilation. The tendency to polarize political, ideological, and ethical experience into good and bad has similar beginnings. These phenomena-like delusions are products of psychodevelopmental processes that begin in infancy and are elaborated later in life.

ROBBINS' HIERARCHICAL SYSTEMS/ PSYCHOANALYTICAL MODEL

It is likely that no single theory will be adequate to exhaustively explain schizophrenia. Diathesis-stress models ignore or minimize the significance of mental events and include little more than cursory acknowledgment of the potential role of environmental contributors (Kringlen, 1987). As an alternative to reductionistic models, general systems theory postulates that natural phenomena are related by a process of hierarchical transformation along dimensions of evolution, development, and magnification, so that higher levels of system organization cannot be constructed or predicted from their discretely analyzable constituents. General systems theory includes the assumption that when human psychological, social, and cultural phenomena are analyzed into their constituent biological and physical parts, something essential is lost.

Robbins (1993) developed a biopsychosocial systems model of schizophrenia. He assumes that schizophrenia does not exist concretely at any single level, that it can be viewed with equal validity from a hierarchy of systems and viewpoints. Each level of organization from cell to society depends on its predecessor but is theoretically autonomous, based on new principles of structure, function, and meaning which cannot be predicted from or reduced to that predecessor. Levels of analysis, such as the neurobiological, psychodynamic, and sociological, signify the level of attention of the observer, not levels of truth or value. Schizophrenia, Robbins argues, must eventually be understood as a process that can be viewed from many perspectives.

Robbins emphasizes the point that the at-risk or constitutionally predisposed individual must attempt the same developmental stages and respond to the same social stressors as others, but meaning and mode of resolution may differ because of unique neurobiological and developmental events, which emerge as psychological characteristics. These characteristics interact with the unique aspects of the primary caretakers during development, who are also responding in terms of their own idiosyncratic ways to the stress of dealing with a difficult or "unusual" infant. He maintains there are four stages in the development of schizophrenia:

1. Phenotypic (characterological) vulnerability emerges as some combination of deficit and abnormality in the context of primary parenting that inadvertently expands rather than repairs the emerging mental manifestations of specific genetic weaknesses.
2. The family compounds the constitutional vulnerabilities by responding to the child's configuration of psychological vulnerabilities to express, or represent, and to compensate for traits, often because the problems and limitations of adult members have not been adequately processed in themselves. Family members of vulnerable children may, for example, simultaneously compensate for their child's limitations by a process that infantalizes and then denies the existence of those limitations. As a result, expectable intrapsychic structural developments do not occur, and the child fails to adequately learn socially consensual modes of thought and to develop essential age-appropriate interpersonal and self-care skills. These disabilities may, however, remain hidden so that the child is shielded from ordinary social consequences.
3. At the time the young adult is expected to separate from the family, to establish intimacy with others, and to assume adult responsibilities, the individual undergoes an adaptive disequilibration involving loss of the symbiotic cushion of the family, which has served to conceal the individual's unusual qualities from the scrutiny and expectations of outsiders. At the same time, the individual receives more realistic social feedback from outside the family, and social pressures increase. Increasingly, the vulnerable child's expectations and capabilities are mismatched with interpersonal realities.
4. The social and psychological skills prove inadequate in this period of developmental crisis; unfortunately, the only possible response available to the child is often regression and further maladaptation.

Core Vulnerabilities

The psychological nature of the constitutional vulnerability in schizophrenia is a matter of wide speculation. Robbins suggests that at least two basic constitutionally based areas of vulnerability are fundamental to vulnerability to schizophrenia. The first has to do with *organization-affinity* (a term with referents similar to Meehl's concepts of aversive drift), hypohedonia, and cognitive slippage. Lack of organization-affinity has to do with an aversion to close contact with other human beings, as well as a deficiency in the potential for adequate psychological differentiation and integration. Aversion to people contributes to problems in relatedness. Robbins maintains that integration and differentiation are facets of a single process by which differentiated elements are integrated into more complex units. In this sense, integration connotes affinity whereas its lack connotes aversion, or lack of affinity. Vulnerability in the area of organization and affinity is evidenced in the schizophrenic patient's aversion to other human beings and his or her related deficiency in skills of differentiation and integration.

Robbins (1993) assumes that an underlying central nervous system problem is an important contributing factor to the tendency to withdraw from relationships. Other sources of aversive drift are related to ongoing difficulties in maintaining age-appropriate self-object boundaries and differentiation. These problems contribute to an increased likelihood of problematic and painful interactions that only mount as problems continue and lead one to keep even greater distance from others. Robbins (1993) believes that a genetically disordered sensory-perceptual system may be an important contributor to the lack of integration and difficulties with attention and perception that have been documented in schizophrenics (Iacono, 1993; Mirsky et al., 1992; Nuechterlein et al., 1992). Symptoms such as hallucinations and delusions may in turn result from a partly biologically based failure to integrate cognitive, affective, sensory, and perceptual experiences as internally experienced elements of the mind, organized around differentiated self and object representations. In this way the hallucinations and delusions of schizophrenics represent failures of integration and differentiation that are reflected in the inability to recognize components of the self and to discriminate and make sensorimotor contact with others, experiences that are necessary precursors to mature thought. Delusions and hallucinations represent the long-term developmental consequences of a lack of affinity with others and with one's own thoughts.

The second vulnerability postulated by Robbins involves problems with intensity and regulation of stimulation, both external (sensation and perception) and internal (drive and affect). This vulnerability emphasizes the importance of problems with unsymbolized, poorly controlled emotions, particularly rage, and of failure to develop mental functions related to emotionality and self-control. Many schizophrenic patients have been noted to show a hypersensitivity to stimulation. Robbins believes that this hypersensitivity may be related to a diathetic predisposition that makes some individuals vulnerable to aversion in the presence of their own and others' emotions. Robbins views the tendency for unmanaged rage as a special instance of the schizophrenic's unique vulnerability to stimulus intensity, impaired affective regulation, and vulnerability to experiencing and handling emotions. Many psychodynamic writers have noted the potential for remarkable and indiscriminately destructive rage in schizophrenics (Fromm-Reichmann, 1954). These feelings are often easy to infer from the content of delusions and from the destructive acts that often precipitate hospitalization. In other cases rage is more difficult to recognize because it is unsymbolized; instead, it is enacted against the patient's own self-organization and those aspects of the self that constitute his or her uniqueness, aliveness, and self-expression. As a result, many schizophrenic patients, however intelligent, are socially inept, disorganized, and markedly lacking in energy, motivation, range of interests, and assertiveness in their daily lives. This colorless docility is particularly characteristic of chronic schizophrenics.

Robbins maintains that the schizophrenic does not relinquish the attachment to reality so much as he or she mounts a chronic and global attack on his or her own sensory-perceptual and cognitive capacities to perceive reality. He hypothesizes that the two core constitutional vulnerabilities combine to produce a third vulnerability: *nihilism,* or a deep aversion to the basic mental work involved in thinking, feeling, and being responsible for the content of one's mind. These core vulnerabilities account for the schizophrenic patient's aversion to object relations and for bearing feelings and thoughts about the self and others.

Robbins contrasts schizophrenics with "primitive" personalities, such as borderline patients, by noting that although primitive personalities are unable to bear and sustain affect and are easily overstimulated and emotionally volatile (like schizophrenics), relationships remain a priority in their lives and are used as symbiotic projection screens for noninternalized forms of cognition and affect. Primitive personalities have turned away from owning and bearing emotions but not from compensatory symbiotic human relationships. Schizophrenics have turned away both from owning emotions and from attempts to form compensatory human relationships. This turning away from human relatedness characteristic of most long-term schizophrenic patients is one reason Robbins believes constitutional factors as well as life history must play a role in vulnerability to schizophrenia.

The problems of developing a model that integrates the findings of diverse disciplines such as neuroscience, psychoanalysis, and family systems psychology have obviously not been resolved. Robbins' model is an attempt to begin that process. He posits that the development of schizophrenia must involve interactions of constitutional vulnerabilities, pathological early experiences, and developmental pathways that are not the same as normal developmental pathways. Robbins assumes that the intrapsychic problems in schizophrenia are intertwined with problems in early dyadic relationships. The content and structure of mental life emerges in the context of socialization. At the dyadic level, the primary parental caretaker can either confront and ameliorate the infant's constitutionally determined vulnerabilities to preschizophrenic vulnerabilities and character traits and teach him or her more mature ways of coping, or the parent might unconsciously stimulate these traits and contribute to a state which is symbiotic and negative for the child. This state is one in which both participants are simultaneously victimized and compensated for.

Object relations theory postulates that through countless interactions between the infant and the special combination of reflective mirroring and symbiotic participation provided by the parents the child progressively develops an awareness and representation of his or her own thoughts and feelings. Through these interactions the infant internalizes the basic foundations of the content and structure of his or her later mental functions. Progressive refinements, integrations, and differentiations lead to the gradual development of a cohesive self-system. Dysfunctional interactions occur when parent figures initiate projective-introjective interactions in which one or both attribute to their infant their own unconscious affects, meanings, needs, and agendas.

Differentiation and integration are aspects of a single process. As aspects of mental functions are differentiated from one another and from the caring person who has mirrored them, they are gradually integrated into organized configurations or structural entities that are increasingly differentiated from one another. This process of building complex representations and mental structures is the basis for their growing separateness and distinctive qualities. Schizophrenic patients have severe problems of psychic differentiation and integration. In schizophrenia the subjective aspects of mind are not differentiated from characteristics of other persons. As a result, integration of mental functions into a cohesive and stable sense of self is seriously impaired. Symptoms such as the incapacity to reflect on the self, aversion to emotional closeness, delusional thinking, hallucinations, and difficulties with affective state regulation are signs and consequences of this *failure of integration-differentiation.*

Robbins believes that some preschizophrenic individuals have not developed an internalized, mentally represented, coherent template of an early good-enough symbiotic relationship. As a result, the developing child, and later the schizophrenic patient, is unable to make a mental displacement of a primary relationship pattern to other persons. The schizophrenic's failure to differentiate, to own, and to integrate a cohesive self-structure is reflected in his or her later repudiation of the possibility of a facilitating symbiotic relationship with another person. Delusions are evidence of the undifferentiation of self from object and the lack of integration of mental content. Their content reflects a failure of differentiation of self from not-self and the loss of an integrative connection between mind and self-sense that is more severe than what is observed in any other disorder.

Another characteristic of schizophrenic mentation is a form of *global passivity*. This passivity is obscured during acute episodes but otherwise is a pervasive aspect of schizophrenic thought. Global passivity is expressed in a lack of assertiveness or the ability to adaptively process aggressive feelings. Rage and angry feelings are diffusely represented and directed inward or toward other persons, especially those whose attentions might stimulate self-awareness. Schizophrenic rage destroys all self-cohesion and triggers assaults on and rejection of others. The intensity of these feelings may not be directly expressed in actions but can be inferred from the content of delusions and hallucinations, the shutdown of thinking and feeling about the self and object world, and the urge toward emotional anesthesia. Hallucinations function as alternatives to the presence of real objects related to the self, as well as substitutes for capacities for affect representation and regulation.

A fourth facet of the schizophrenic mind identified by Robbins is a severely impaired capacity for social and interpersonal adaptation. Robbins relates this characteristic to a lack of development during infancy of rudimentary forms of sensorimotor-affective thinking that is characteristic of infants. This form of thinking is the basis for the infant's gradual development of stable recognition representations of which objects will foster development of continued mental development and which will not.

Robbins proposes that schizophrenia develops from genetic contributions that result in a variety of possible constitutional vulnerabilities. The combination of these vulnerabilities, in the context of difficulties in parenting the child during infancy and a disturbed family structure, results in schizophrenia. He argues that schizophrenia only appears to develop unexpectedly in early adulthood in a hitherto relatively normal person who is a member of a relatively normal family; however, signs of disturbance are present from the earliest stages of life. The role of dysfunctional family experiences in schizophrenia cannot be measured in terms of some psychological scale, but Robbins believes that the disturbed family system can be described at a dynamic level. Characteristics of the family function to amplify, compensate for, and deny the existence of the cognitive and affective characteristics of its most vulnerable member. The result is a developing child, adolescent, and young adult who is in a fragile state of equilibrium. This fragile state persists until the preschizophrenic member attempts to separate and make his or her way in the outside world.

There are numerous studies of family disturbances associated with schizophrenia (Bateson et al., 1956; Wynne and Singer, 1963; Lidz and Fleck, 1965; Lidz, 1973). This body of literature has been criticized for problems of methodology and limited sampling procedures, but Robbins argues the preponderance of the evidence is consistent and is sufficient to justify the assumption of an etiological role for parental failure to perceive and accurately evaluate the infant's gestures, needs, potentials, and vulnerabilities. To the extent that parental resentment is present, these feelings are likely to be disguised and enacted as overprotectiveness and a subtle authoritarian posture disguised as caring, which is expressed in the form of a rigid set of rules about reality and what things mean. These rules are often at odds with the perceptions of an outside observer. In the context of the interaction of the infant's constitutional propensities and deficiencies of control mechanisms, this propensity is increased in the context of family pathology. The result is that unrepresented anger is expressed in the form of diffuse, internalized ideation or fantasies that pose no obvious threat to the integrity of the family.

Robbins maintains that family members of schizophrenic patients do not lack in caring or love for the patient-to-be, they lack in the ability to provide appropriate and timely kinds of growth promoting forms of love. Everyone in the family suffers in this process, and no one intends for or takes pleasure in dysfunction. The interaction between the difficult characteristics of the child and the parent's own dynamics dictate the nature of the pathological developmental process. The challenges and stresses of having responsibility for rearing a child who is irritable, impulsive, inconsolable, explosive, clumsy, or disorganized, who cannot tolerate or respond appropriately to even normal levels of stimulation, is likely to trigger the parent's own vulnerabilities. A reparative family context may provide ministrations that prevent further activation of these phenotypic vulnerabilities. In situations where the primary family is unable to consistently provide adequate ministrations, circumstances and the ability of other relatives to compensate and provide effective alternatives also play an important etiological role.

Robbins believes that the child may become a receptacle for the projections of family members. He emphasizes, however, that the child is not simply a victim; family members also play caretaking and stabilizing functions for the patient who is unable to manage for himself or herself. At the same time, the preschizophrenic, as both child and adolescent, is exempted from having to grow up and be an independent adult. This disability is often masked in shared denial and by exaggerated beliefs that are parental projections.

At the level of the family, the vulnerabilities of the schizophrenic are symbiotically complemented by family dysfunctions. Immaturities and missing elements of age-appropriate self-care are compensated for by responses that impair rather than assist the child to develop capacities in himself or herself. As a result, the identity of the child is supplied through a combination of grandiose and devalued projections. The family supplies missing aspects of reality in the form of denial and inversions of reality. The infant with constitutional difficulties related to aversion to people, difficulties managing stimulation, problems with psychological integration and differentiation, difficulty controlling rage and converting it to adaptive interpersonal assertiveness, and aversion to the work of bearing and regulating emotion-laden thoughts presents a demanding and stressful parental burden in the best of circumstances. Such an infant is likely to overtax the parent's coping capacities to consistently lovingly mirror and contain the infant's mental capacities and manage his or her own frustrations, anger, disappointments, and feelings of being overwhelmed at the same time. Even the most mature parents might be provoked to respond inconstantly, to have difficulty responding to the infant's real needs.

Parents limited in their capacity to respond to the infant's true potentials are likely to substitute meanings, needs, and feelings of their own. The activation of vulnerability in a predisposed infant results in failure to learn age-appropriate self-care and interpersonal skills. Developmental deviations are formed in response to specific projections of the parents or family dynamics. These psychological dysfunctions are rarely identified until efforts to leave home, to become self-supporting, and to enter into and maintain intimate relationships and adult responsibilities are undertaken. Once the young adult loses the protective family cushion of symbiotic patterns, he or she is likely to experience what Robbins refers to as *adaptive equilibration,* compounded by regression. Families of schizophrenic patients are probably no more dysfunctional than families of many other patients, Robbins speculates; the essential difference seems to one of constitutional vulnerability.

Robbins maintains that contemporary scientific theories about the etiology and treatment of schizophrenia represent forms of objectification of the disturbed thinking of the schizophrenic and dysfunctional dynamics of the families. The schizophrenic is not viewed as a whole person; he or she is viewed as a collection of symptoms that are assumed to be somehow unconnected to his or her otherwise normal personality and normal family. Symptoms are thought to originate in a malfunction of the brain. This fragmented view mirrors the fragmentation of the schizophrenic mind, as well as this quality within his or her family.

Reductionistic explanations in terms of brain functions imply that the complexity of patients' mental processes are meaningless epiphenomena, reducible to and understandable in terms of neural parts. Robbins argues that this aspect of the larger culture contributes to and perpetuates the individual and family pathology that contributes to schizophrenia by enacting its elements in the guise of scientific objectivity and by supporting the family's response to the disturbed member. The expressions of patients are viewed as symptoms of an organic disease, expressions that have no meaning, even to the patient. Treatment is directed toward expunging these symptoms with drugs and persuading the patient to conceal his or her thinking. Patients are managed, directed, reinforced, educated, tranquilized, and rehabilitated as a member of a group for whom ordinary human expectations and responsibilities are forever closed. These views and treatments, Robbins argues, mirror and enhance the schizophrenic's alienation from others and function to further invalidate his or her experience and mirror similar processes of denial and distorted communication within the family.

Mental health treatments that deny any inherent validity to the patient's experience or mental processes and encourage him or her to do likewise, Robbins believes, only mirror the internal processes of schizophrenia. Society devotes great effort and resources to providing and discovering improved forms of diagnosis and pharmacological "care" for the schizophrenic patient but looks at him or her in pieces, not as a full human being but as a victim of unknown biological disease processes.

CONTEMPORARY PSYCHODYNAMIC THERAPIES

Psychodynamic approaches to therapy with schizophrenic patients have been modified over the past few decades to more directly deal with symptoms. Interpretation is de-emphasized, and a pragmatic approach to symptom management is more prominent. Several general principles characteristic of this modified approach can be identified (Holzman, 1975; McGlashan, 1984). Initial efforts are focused on limiting regression, reducing symptoms, strengthening defenses, sealing over psychotic experiences, and encouraging the development of stable, trusting object relationships between patient and staff. The importance of these relationships is emphasized and continued after the patient is discharged, since stable contacts with understanding persons are viewed as critical to counteract the tendencies toward fragmentation and fears of object disappearance characteristic of many schizophrenic patients. Therapists also provide reassurance and advice, maintain ongoing contact with the family members, and continue to work with the patient's family as a form of crisis intervention and education. Postacute treatments focus on exploration of previous conflicts and the complications of the patient's life brought about by the psychosis. Feelings of guilt and inner badness, experiences of inner emptiness and despair, and problems with good and bad object representations often become the focus of therapeutic discussions. Finally, as symptoms are stabilized, psychodynamic therapists emphasize competency skills building and the importance of reestablishing ego functions such as delaying gratification and limiting fantasies. Contemporary psychodynamic therapy of schizophrenic patients is reality oriented and supportive more than it is interpretive. It focuses on pragmatic and adaptive goals, including teaching of coping strategies, resolution of concrete problems, and assistance in identifying stressors and prodromal symptoms. In this area there are a number of similarities between psychodynamic and social-cognition approaches to therapy.

The increased emphasis on the importance of more supportive elements in therapy was stimulated in part by many psychodynamic and interpersonal theorists' recognition that schizophrenia is probably primarily a brain disorder and is a learned disorder only occasionally or secondarily (McGlashan, 1984). Coursey (1989) has outlined a number of issues that psychotherapy can nevertheless profitably address given this increased awareness of the etiological role of biological factors. First, patients need help to gain perspective on the disorder and understanding of the symptoms and what tends to make them come and go, to develop an enhanced ability to form a separate sense of self from the illness, to have opportunities to grieve over lost opportunities and their disability, and to relinquish former dreams and develop alternative, more realistic sources of self-esteem and meaning. Psychotherapists can also help patients manage medication more effectively, reality test their fantasies and suspicions, become more alert to the importance of prodromal signs, better utilize health and social service systems, counteract tendencies toward social and emotional withdrawal, and cope with the stigma and social consequences of the diagnosis. Finally, therapy can help patients deal with the universal human issues of loneliness, intimacy, sexuality, and family.

Coursey maintains that therapy must focus on helping people cope with the disabilities that are associated with this disorder, just as people need help coping with any disease. However, in the case of schizophrenia the task is doubly difficult since the brain-based "software" that guides psychological coping abilities is also compromised.

Some therapists advocate limiting any form of interpretive therapy to a very select group of patients with the following characteristics (Gunderson, 1975): young, intelligent, good premorbid functioning, with a history of achievement at work, as well as some degree of success in interpersonal relationships. They should be motivated, see themselves in need of help, and experience a sense of pain or struggle. They should exhibit some degree of capacity for self-observation, problem solving, self-control, and the ability to integrate experiences.

These characteristics are likely to be present in only a small minority of patients. Despite the marked changes in expectations and approach that have occurred among psychodynamic therapists regarding therapy with schizophrenic patients, there is evidence available which indicates that psychotherapy can have important positive effects on schizophrenic patients (Grinspoon, 1969; Karon and VandenBos, 1970; Rogers et al., 1967). Other research indicates that evidence for long-term effects of interpretive therapy with this population is not encouraging (McGlashan, 1984; Stone, 1986).

SUMMARY

Psychodynamic theories dominated the clinical literature on schizophrenia from the period prior to the onset of World War II until the early 1970s. The resurgence of biological thinking beginning in the 1960s was associated with growing rejection and marginalization of this approach so that today few mainstream researchers believe that psychodynamic theory is of value in furthering our understanding of schizophrenia. Psychodynamic theories are criticized because of the burden of parental blame they imply, as well as the ambiguity of their constructs and the retrospective narrative form of the data on which they are founded. These concerns touch on a core issue in the field of psychopathology: What value should be given to constructs based on clinical understanding and observation? Positivists argue that a theory is not scientific unless it generates testable predictions. Psychodynamic theories are not based on quantitative data or laboratory studies, but they do generate predictions that are testable in principle if difficult to test in practice. Accurate information on unconscious processes or child-rearing practices, for example, is difficult to obtain retrospectively. Additional problems are associated with the study of small and select patient groups. Nevertheless, evidence of the etiological role of psychosocial variables, such as dysfunctional patterns of family communication and expression, is available (Goldstein, 1985; Tienari et al., 1994). Experimental research with non-human primates also indicates that early stressful experiences can have lasting effects on both behavior and brain processes. Biological systems, even highly heritable ones including the brain itself, have been demonstrated to be vulnerable to changes induced by relatively brief exposures to adverse early experiences (Suomi, 1997). Research indicates that even relatively brief early separation experiences can play a crucial role in the development of later behavioral, neurochemical, and brain dysfunctions. Given this evidence, "it is hard to believe that humans would not be at least as potentially sensitive to the long-term behavioral and physiological effects of adverse early experiences as their evolutionary cousins appear to be" (Suomi, 1997, p. 113). Psychodynamic theory attempts to understand human development and reduce suffering based on retrospective reconstructions of symptoms and associations. From this perspective, early family-based experiences, as well as genes and neurons, are assumed to be potential contributors to vulnerability to schizophrenia. As is true for all monistic theories, psychodynamic theory is both limited and limiting because its constructs deal with only one level of analysis, the intrapsychic-dyadic level, and are based on retrospective reconstructions in which it seems impossible to separate the evidence from the influences of the biases of the analyst. Yet this limitation does not mean that empathic, subjective understanding of the context and origins of another person's suffering does not have an important role to play in long-term recovery or in helping us to understand the origins of this disorder.

Chapter 13

Phenomenology and Schizophrenia

The diagnostic revolution which culminated in the revisions introduced in DSM-III was predicated on the belief that diagnosis of mental disorders should be based on "objective" signs. This approach treats subjective, contextual information about problems as secondary (Alpert, 1985). The operationalistic approach continued in DSM-IV-TR fosters a disjunction between objective signs and subjective symptoms and has limitations in terms of its ability to deal with the question of "otherminds" (Parnas, 1995). The origins and limitations of an objective approach to diagnosis arise from the effects of two influences on contemporary thought: (1) Cartesian dualism (that mind and body are logically distinct) and (2) the empiricist claim that knowledge must be justified by an appeal to observation of "sensory data."

Parnas (1995) argues that diagnosis limited to sensory data and based on Cartesian assumptions must inevitably confront the age-old dilemma of empiricist psychology, i.e., the problem of "other minds, or knowing and understanding the experience of others." Since it is not possible to have sensory contact with other minds, empiricists insist that we can only observe behaviors and obtain self-reports. Subjective understanding and narrative data are not scientifically admissible. Phenomenologists, on the other hand, propose that mind and body are abstractions from the more basic concept of "person." Second, they assert that personal experience is an abstraction from the more primary concept of "intersubjective experience." The phenomenological approach views mental concepts as anchored in social interactions. Thus, comprehension of another person is based on two aspects: (1) the primacy of intersubjectivity and (2) the unique status of the body in framing all human experience. The prominent French phenomenologist Merleau-Ponty ([1945] 1962), for example, viewed the human body as the medium which subtends our cognition of the world. The body is privileged by being both intrinsically perceiving and perceived. Parnas (1995) uses the example of someone touching his or her toe to illustrate these points. At the moment of touch one cannot distinguish the aspect of touching from the aspect of being touched. In this sense, each person lives and experiences himself or herself simultaneously as an object and as a subject. Our recognition of other persons as being inhabited by a similar consciousness is linked to and grounded in experiences of bodily involvement in the world. Phenomenologists maintain that the tacit identification of body image as the basis for self-identity implies that the body is both subject and object simultaneously. Perceiving another as like oneself involves perceiving another person as displaying a state of consciousness, a consciousness that is visible in the expressions and movements of the body. The perception of a schizophrenic patient dully inspecting his or her empty hands, for example, is a perception of his or her behavior as well as his or her experiencing. It is a perception of the patient's phenomenological experience, of which behavior is just the place (Tatossian, 1979).

The phenomenological concept of each person "having a world" implies that each of us has a specific situatedness in the world and its enaction. Phenomenologists view descriptions of a "schizophrenic world" as important and legitimate, not as simply distorted copies of the real world but as examples of particular patterns or ways of being in the world. As cognitive science moves toward the idea of mind as an emergent and autonomous network with self-organizing properties, in which changes are triggered but not specified by internal or external inputs (Maturana and Varela, 1988), adoption of mental phenomena as emergents implies an important shift in focus from speculation about the causal role of localized brain dysfunctions in schizophrenia. These changes imply the potential usefulness of a shift of focus from the search for underlying brain dysfunctions to an approach that recognizes the role of self-organizing mental functions and problems with the integration of brain processes in the unpredictable evolution of psychopathology.

Phenomenological theorists emphasize the role of self-organizing functions in all human functioning including schizophrenia. As such, they are concerned with a person's inner world of experience (Jaspers, 1923) or the meaning of phenomena (Bovet and Parnas, 1993).

Phenomenological studies are based on phenomenological philosophy (Heidegger, 1975; Merleau-Ponty, [1945] 1962) and aim to identify and describe the essential features of the human being in the world. Human beings are understood as processes rather than objects, as evolving systems of projects and understandings, continually struggling to understand themselves and their experiences of the world, not simply as automatisms driven by bundles of neurons and neurochemicals. The task of phenomenological inquiry is to develop an unprejudiced understanding of others' worlds, of self, and modes of being in the world as they are encountered in experience. Attempts at causal explanations in terms of deterministic forces are not part of this approach. Phenomenological inquiries into schizophrenia attempt to describe what it means for schizophrenic patients to be, their experiences of the self and of being in the world. This does not mean that phenomenologists do not allow for the possibility that schizophrenia may also be the outcome of epigenetic processes and predisposing traits such as early aggressiveness, introversion, social anxiety and general fearfulness, cognitive slippage, or difficulties with establishing emotional rapport (Parnas and Jorgenson, 1989). It does mean that phenomenologists focus instead on several aspects of schizophrenic patients based on their understandings. For example, first they suggest that the *schizophrenic defect in common sense* may be manifested in a lack of intuitive feeling for what is adequate and a lack of a sense for the "rules of the game" of human behavior (Blankenburg, 1969; Bovet and Parnas, 1993). Second, these individuals appear to be diminished in the ability to project themselves into possible futures and to anticipate events. That is, individuals vulnerable to schizophrenia have difficulties in self-temporalization; from a phenomenological perspective, they appear to live mainly in the "waiting mode." Temporalization is expressed in two different approaches to the future (Heidegger, 1975): an activity or anticipation mode, in which we feel ourselves going toward the future coming toward us, and a waiting mode, in which we feel the future coming toward us. In the latter case, the ability to project oneself into possible futures and anticipate is diminished. In the waiting mode the future is seen as a repetition of the past, as a prearranged destiny, and consequently, there is reduced ability to transcend the immediate. A third aspect of schizophrenic vulnerability is manifested in weak intersubjective ties. Relationships are lacking in emotional force and influence and tend to become stereotyped and routine.

Phenomenologists do not attempt to explain what causes, in terms of neurobiology, developmental experiences, or social forces, an individual to develop vulnerability. They focus instead on describing the vulnerabilities that comprise this picture in terms of lived expressions. The normal individual, for example, is immersed in intersubjectivity, searching in himself or herself for the main clues to the future. The vulnerable individual, in contrast, is poorly framed by intersubjective ties and is forced to look for guiding clues in the "outer world," rendering the outer world self-referential. If the vulnerable individual finds himself or herself committed to a situation that unduly threatens autonomy, the route to escape the threat is not to attempt to alter the reality of the external situation but to reshape the context of being in the world either by a delusional reshaping of experience or by senseless behavior.

DELUSIONS AND THE RELATIONSHIP
TO THE OUTER WORLD

Bovet and Parnas (1993) propose that the "metaphysical taint" in the delusions of schizophrenics conveys something essential about the nature of the relationship between the schizophrenic individual's self and the outer world. The schizophrenic patient's autistic vulnerability functions to impede ties to the world and to others. As a result, schizophrenic delusions are characterized by two features: (1) the other in the delusional dialogue is not considered as another ontic (individual subjectivity) being, and (2) the ontological elements of the communication dominate because they lack ontic embodiment. The result is that the listener to schizophrenic communication is confronted with an "empty ontological matrix" lacking in meaningful engagement with other people. The onset of schizophrenic delusions represents the emergence of a new life paradigm and the radical transformation of the patient's mode of being in the world.

Bovet and Parnas (1993) maintain that the phenomenon of emergence of mental functions makes sense only when the result is understood from a general systems perspective. Self-consciousness and sense of self emerge in the context of intersubjectivity and historicity. Since the emergence of self is constituted in the interpersonal world, the authors believe that the autistic defect in schizophrenia must be rooted in an impairment in the biological constitution that is the basis for the capacity for inter-subjectivity. This impairment, under certain circumstances or in combination with other vulnerabilities, may result in a series of life experiences that over time culminate in delusion formation.

Delusions are expressions of the emergence of a new meaning structure comprising the deluded person and his or her transformed world. This new structure is an expression of the intentional attributions of the schizophrenic and his or her ontological counterparts in the world. Delusions, in other words, represent the emergence of a new "order of being," one that is originally rooted in a possible biological predisposition, referred to as "autistic vulnerability."

THE PROCESS OF DELUSION FORMATION

The development of delusions can be understood as consisting of four stages from a phenomenological perspective: (1) the initial phase, as *das Trema*, an experience similar in meaning to a term used by actors to describe a state of extreme tension before going on stage when there is a sense of no escape as possible, only the likelihood of success or failure; (2) the *apophantic* phase, in which delusional beliefs are constructed (from the Greek word *apophainein* meaning "becoming apparent"), which in this context refers to the revelatory quality of the delusional experience; (3) the *apocalyptic* phase, in which the patient's organized, executive-level psychological functioning crumbles; and (4) the *consolidation* or outcome phase, in which the delusional reality transforms the person's mode of living in the world and relationships with people (Conrad, 1958).

During the initial phases (1 and 2) of the schizophrenic transformation there is a gradual elevation of tension. This tension is experienced as pressure that narrows the field of experience into a profound sense of uncanniness, or the single expectation of something highly significant to one's life that is impending. The narrowing of the experiential field that results leads to a further increase in tension. Thus the individual in *das Trema* is in a rapidly intensifying state of "abnormal awareness of significance" (Jaspers, 1923). During the trema many situations are experienced as somehow unreal or fabricated. This experience in turn leads to a "delusional mood," an awareness and form of experience that represents a profound transformation of the structure of experiencing, and in turn leads to a revelatory phase in which the delusional perception is crystallized.

The *apophantic* phase is associated with the connection between the elements of earlier fragments of experience into the formation of the perceptual whole or Gestalt of delusional meaning. Single elements of the Gestalt may have contextual relevance, but in the apophantic phase the connections between the elements of the experience become integrated into a single underlying meaning or significance. Everything that one has experienced, perhaps for a lifetime, suddenly seems connected. A profound form of revelation is experienced in which the schizophrenic individual now "understands" what was previously only alluded to. From a phenomenological perspective, the resolution of *das Trema* that is specific to schizophrenia is associated with a global transformation of the structure of experiencing. There are obvious parallels between the revelatory experience of delusional perception and the experiences of nonschizophrenic individuals (Blankenburg, 1995). The difference is that normal people are able to assimilate such experiences in ways that amplify or at least do not seriously impair their social functioning and future possibilities. For schizophrenics, however, the experience of *das Trema* and the delusional transformation leads them to exist thereafter in the mode of a limiting prearranged destiny, so that the possibility of a future in the context of caring involvement with other human beings and ambitions is lost.

At a descriptive level, the "how" of delusional experiencing has to do with what is lost, as typified in delusions of control and of grandeur, i.e., the qualitative aspects of the mineness of experience. In schizophrenia either the experience of mineness is absent (delusions of control, thought insertion, influence) or it is inflated to an omnipotent level (grandeur), or both. In delusions the normal distinction between being and acting is lost, so that the meanings of the concepts of "to be" and "to act" are fused. Delusions are viewed as the only way the schizophrenic patient can express the "unthinkable" experiences that are associated with the acute schizophrenic experience of breakdown or dissolution of the self. They also allow for a semblance of self-reintegration, albeit in a severely impaired form that allows for little in the way of ambition, life possibility, or potential to live in the context of caring involvement with others.

SCHIZOPHRENIC AND NONSCHIZOPHRENIC DELUSIONS

Kepinski (1974) has attempted to describe the qualities of schizophrenic delusions that appear to distinguish them from nonschizophrenic delusions. First, many delusions of cognitively intact patients involve *ontological issues* and concerns that focus on the essence of being and existence in the cosmos. These expressions within a schizophrenic cosmology are often fantastic and magical in character. The schizophrenic's inner world becomes filled with secret energies and good and evil forces. Events seem to be connected and take on meanings that normally would be viewed as coincidental.

The second quality that characterizes schizophrenic delusions has to do with concerns about *cosmological issues* such as the end of the world. Feelings of impending disaster reach apocalyptic intensity in schizophrenia. As anxiety increases to crescendo during the acute stage, there is often the experience, fantasy, and preoccupation with explosion, apocalypse, war, cataclysm, and chaos. These themes are one of the features that make schizophrenic delusions different from nonschizophrenic delusions.

Finally, the *charismatic trend* contains issues having to do with meaning and sense of life and its true purpose. In schizophrenic delusions the patient is in the central position of the world. He or she may feel immortal, immaterial, almighty, as god or devil, and believe that the fate or well-being of the world depends upon his or her actions.

DASEINSANALYSIS

Ludwig Binswanger studied with and remained on friendly terms with Freud throughout his career but turned to the concepts of Heidegger's phenomenological philosophy to develop his unique approach to therapy.

Binswanger (1960) applied daseinsanalytic concepts to understanding the alterations in the structure of existence or world design that occur in schizophrenia. Binswanger's goal was twofold: (1) to reclaim the schizophrenic person from the structure of causal theories and (2) to discover the critical moments associated with the schizophrenic development of his or her unique world design or existential structure. Binswanger believed that such moments are associated with profound experiences of failure in the process of existence, during which the sequential character of experience becomes problematic. These interruptions, whatever their origins, create a vacuum that must be filled, a void in which it no longer seems possible to conduct one's life as one has.

Binswanger understood schizophrenic delusions as attempts, however inadequate, at coping with the anxiety of not being able to deal with life as it is. He described two phases to the schizophrenic experience. First, the individual tries to protect himself or herself against the emergence of the sensed dangers of the uncanny (a highly anxious experience triggered by anything which ought to remain obscure but somehow has become manifest). The emergence of the uncanny occurs after defensive measures fail. Subsequent experience is filled with an overpowering sense of the dreadful. As the individual's existential structure is overpowered by a sense of the uncanny and the dreadful—subjective experiences that are forms of the existential anxiety of not being able to cope with life—the schizophrenic abdicates intersubjectivity in favor of the feared alternative. As a result, the physiognomy of the world is transformed into a world of malice and persecution. Existence is reconstituted and restored through the formation of delusions, but existential possibilities are severely narrowed in the process.

Binswanger believed that the specific schizophrenic solution to the experience of existential void or the uncanny is the substitution of a set of rigid alternatives. In schizophrenia existence continues, but it is both protected and confined within delusional rigid alternatives that allow the individual to shut himself or herself off from others and from the world of possibility. Schizophrenic symptoms are both the consequences and manifestations of the breakdown in the natural sequential order of experience and of the resulting creation of a world of rigid alternatives that results in an existence with no exits. Through the process of delusion formation the experiences of the dreadful and uncanny, based on vague but powerful internal threats, are transformed and experienced as concrete threats from the external world. Delusions transform inner anxieties into external threats. This process, referred to as *mundanization* by Binswanger, serves to free the self from continuing to struggle to exist as an autonomous, responsible person.

Binswanger described four processes that form the basis of schizophrenic experience.

1. *The consistency of natural experience breaks down.* The torment characteristic of the lives of schizophrenics results from the fact that they are unable to come to terms with the anxiety and disorder of their experience. Their way out of this chaotic world is through the formation of delusions. Delusions allow the individual to reestablish a semblance of order and control over thoughts, impulses, and emotions.

2. *Existential consistency is split off into rigid alternatives.* The delusional schizophrenic patient adopts rigid alternatives and extravagant beliefs about issues such as good versus evil or power and vulnerability. These rigid alternatives lead to the fear of giving in to the dark side of the alternatives. The result is that the schizophrenic patient is convinced that to temporize, i.e., to become emotionally engaged in life, is impossible. As a result, the patient withdraws from involvements and lives in a world of delusion and fantasy.

3. *Covering is attempted.* The delusional schizophrenic patient engages in attempts to conceal or disguise the evil or dark side of the rigid alternative(s) that characterize his or her experience and cognition, which is unbearable. As a consequence, the focus of delusional beliefs is often about self-perfection and grandiose identifications.

4. *Existence is worn away.* The schizophrenic patient is eventually worn away by the struggle with inner forces that seem unbearable. The hopelessness of this experience leads to an extreme form of existential retreat and the renunciation of life as an independent dasein (being in the world).

Binswanger viewed the problem of schizophrenia as most clearly expressed in delusions of persecution. In these delusions, *dasein* comes to see the enemy everywhere and hostile intentions in everyone, and the self is experienced as a victim. By surrendering the will to others, the schizophrenic replaces the tension of disordered experience and being caught between rigid alternatives with a one-sided but consistent experience. Delusions enable the person to escape disordered experiences; they also (dis)enable the patient (dasein) to abandon the potential for being and to displace personal responsibility and guilt onto an outside force, a fate, or a world design.

Through the process of mundanization the individual escapes the human tasks of finding meaning and responsibility but does not completely escape the experience of anxiety. As a consequence, in schizophrenia those qualities of human beings which are existentially a priori (makes existence possible) become severely constricted so that existence is ruled by only a few categories. Delusions provide a meaning matrix for the patient, but it is one with only a few themes, within which all experiences appear and are interpreted, and within which the world and the self are reconstituted. Schizophrenia is in this sense a paradox, an attempt at denying being as a means of preserving being.

The task of the daseinsanalyst in therapy is to apprehend the transcendental structure that makes it possible for phenomena to be phenomena for the patient, i.e., the world design. In many cases of acute schizophrenia the world design is most evident in delusions. Delusions reduce everything in the world that is significant to the rule of a single or few categories and alternatives. Delusions severely narrow existence but make it manageable. The more simplified and constricted the world design to which the individual existence has committed itself, the greater the underlying anxiety and sense of vulnerability must be. The severity of the disorder is judged in terms of the degree to which the freedom of dasein has been surrendered, not specific symptoms.

The daseinsanalyst strives to understand and remain acutely aware of the immediately given phenomena of the patient's world, without distortion or the objectification of causal theories. Therapists stress the importance and value of understanding the uniqueness of each individual and his or her life situation. Dreams, symptoms, and transference issues are understood as reflections of each person's mode of being in the world, rather than the results of deterministic developmental forces. The goal of therapy is to assist each person to attain a meaningful and purposeful life within the context and range of possibilities of his or her unique potential. This is achieved through a careful process of understanding and confrontation with the implications of one's self-imposed restrictions and limitations on living, carried out in the context of an empathic therapeutic relationship. Inherited dispositions and painful experiences in one's past life are not thought of literally as "causes" of problems but as conditions associated with the initiation of inhibitions against fully living and experiencing one's full potential for interpersonal and interworldly relationships.

The concepts of daseinsanalysis and Sartre's existential philosophy influenced several clinicians to develop experimental communities in which individuals are allowed to live through their psychotic experience in the context of a protected community that provides acceptance and support. R. D. Laing was among the most prominent of these antiestablishment clinicians. He cofounded one of the earliest such experimental programs called Kingsley Hall in London in 1965. Laing (1967) argued that individuals provided with a safe and accepting context might not regress to a permanent psychotic state as so many do but could potentially use the experiences of the acute psychotic episode as an opportunity to move beyond previous self-limiting modes of being. The Kingsley Hall project was a mixed success. Not surprisingly, the operation of a loosely organized residence with few rules, no paid supervisory staff, and composed largely of psychotic individuals proved more difficult to fund and operate than was anticipated. However, some individual case histories written about the experiment and its effects suggest that many of the participants benefited significantly from the experience (Edgar, 1984). Kingsley Hall closed after several years, but the model in modified form was adopted by several subsequent community-based programs, the most prominent of which is Soteria House (Mosher, 1995), described in more detail in Chapter 14.

SUMMARY

Phenomenologists attempt to understand and describe phenomena based on their intersubjective understanding of "what is" as expressed by the "other." They do not attempt to explain "what is" in terms of causal concepts based on other levels of analysis. The search for evidence about possible causal pathways and contributing factors is not part of this approach to knowledge. Broad principles, when developed, are used to describe common aspects of the mode of being in the world that may be associated with certain symptoms, such as delusions of persecution or influence. Phenomenologists focus on what is unique about human beings as meaning-creating individuals, rather than as objectified outcomes of deterministic forces. They assume that human beings above all strive to create a "meaning world" that is liveable, in the context of all the factors that may have contributed to each person's vulnerabilities.

Phenomenological therapists (Binswanger, 1960; Boss, 1963) strive to develop an understanding of each person's unique mode of being in the world. This form of empathic understanding is thought to be the basic path to opening possibilities for change and for the patient's initiating steps toward reengagement in life. The phenomenological approach attempts to apply a subjective rather than a causal perspective to understanding schizophrenia. It implies a perspective in which the importance of intentionality is emphasized. This suggests that it is essential to develop an understanding of symptoms not only in terms of causal processes but also in terms of each individual's efforts to create a liveable meaning world.

Chapter 14

Schizophrenia and the Family

Clinicians have long observed that psychosis in young adults is associated with disturbances in family relationships. Freida Fromm-Reichmann (1948) among others noted that family members of young-adult schizophrenic patients do not seem to recognize appropriate boundaries or to be adequately responsive to one another's existence as separate persons. Object-relations theorists described this pattern and referred to it as a form of psychological symbiosis in which a vulnerable child is responded to and comes to perceive himself or herself largely in terms of the projected wishes, anxieties, and needs of the parents (Mahler, 1952). In this manner, Mahler argues, the vulnerable child may become increasingly alienated from his or her true potential, as identity is formed on the basis of substitute sources of fulfillment of displaced parental issues and needs.

It is important to recognize that although family theories focus on only the possible etiological role of parenting and family dysfunction, these attempts to understand the role of the family in the development of schizophrenia are not necessarily in conflict with genetic-biological views. Genetic vulnerabilities must interact with environmental and family factors from the outset of development. Since the family is the primary mediator between the child's biological-genetic makeup and society, it is reasonable to assume that the family environment can play a role in the development of most mental disorders. After all, in most developed countries the primary family has the responsibility to socialize, nurture, and selectively foster valued aspects of personality development in the child. It makes sense that the family environment must play a role in all aspects of personality development (Lidz, 1978).

The assumptions that served as the basis for much early research on the contributing role of family processes in the development of schizophrenic disorders were these:

1. Schizophrenic reactions often develop in a family milieu which is subtly disturbed in a manner distinguishable from patterns associated with most other diagnostic syndromes.

2. These disturbances begin relatively early in the life of the patient.
3. Disordered family relationships may be a necessary but not sufficient condition for the development of schizophrenia (Goldstein and Rodnick, 1975).

Sanislow and Carson (2001) point out that research on the family and interpersonal processes within the family which might contribute to the development of schizophrenia reached its zenith in the 1950s and has declined ever since. The authors list five principal reasons for this decline:

1. Family research is very difficult to carry out in a precise and controlled way, far more so than the technology-driven research into biological processes so prevalent in the twenty-first century.
2. Some early but insufficiently controlled findings of apparent familial aberrancy (e.g., double binding) have proven to be nonspecific for schizophrenia and somewhat routine in families that have exclusively normal offspring.
3. Dysfunctional behavior in family members, it has been shown, is reactive to the presence of a disturbed family member rather than antecedent to such disturbance; indeed, these sequences may be the norm.
4. Research on the possible intrafamilial origins of schizophrenia has, understandably, not been popular among parent groups who have sometimes perceived that they are unfairly blamed for the disorder.
5. The so-called decade of the brain, the 1990s, for the most part, obviated thinking and research along these lines in mainstream psychiatry.

The authors point out the importance of recognizing the difficulties of parenting and note that most parents they have encountered who have had the "bad luck" of having raised a child who later became schizophrenic did the very best they could to ensure the happiness, health, and success of their child. Concepts of blame or schizophrenogenic parenting are counterproductive and simply add to the unjustified guilt that too many parents already harbor. Nevertheless, like Sanislow and Carson, this author believes that open inquiry into the developmental processes associated with the familial environment is a necessary component of any comprehensive attempt to discover the sources of schizophrenia. Many of the models and studies presented in this chapter suffer from significant flaws in interpretation, design, and execution. Nevertheless, they represent the beginnings of serious attempts to build a knowledge base that is relevant to any comprehensive attempt to understand schizophrenia.

MURRAY BOWEN AND THE WASHINGTON GROUP

Murray Bowen conducted studies of the families of schizophrenic patients at the National Institute of Mental Health during the 1950s. He was the first to admit entire families to the hospital for study. Fourteen families participated in Bowen's early research for intervals varying from six months to three years. All families included an adolescent or young-adult patient who was chronically and severely disturbed. The families lived full-time on the hospital ward, which allowed researchers to intensively observe the families in a variety of interactions over extended periods. In all families that included a mother-father-patient trio, Bowen and his colleagues (Bowen, Dysinger, and Basamania, 1959) noted a form of "emotional divorce" between the parents. Typically there was an "overadequate-inadequate" complementary interaction pattern between the parents that was associated with this emotional divorce. An additional characteristic of the families was that they all had a great deal of difficulty making decisions. Conflicts typically began early in the marriage. Often the wife became markedly more emotionally invested in the child than in the husband. According to Bowen, Dysinger, and Basamania most fathers reacted to this relationship between wife and child by establishing a pattern of aloof distance from both. Bowen (1960) referred to this pattern of emotional divorce and enmeshment as the "interdependent triad." He noted that mothers of patients in his study tended to make two demands on the child. One was a covert emotional demand that the patient remain dependent. The second was that the child is and must become a gifted and special person. Another pattern noted by Bowen and his associates was the mothers' tendencies toward overinvestment in the patient, as expressed in excessive worries, intrusiveness, and concerns. Mothers' worries about the schizophrenic child tended to focus on a range of concerns including health problems, attractiveness, posture, dress, gender characteristics, and body build. Bowen believed it was as though the mothers could function better and deal with their own anxieties and unhappiness by projecting certain aspects of their anxieties and frustrated needs and ambitions onto their children. Those children who later became schizophrenic somehow were more likely to fit into these family dynamic and parental projections and to accept the role as their identity.

Bowen and his group also stressed the importance of the father's emotional divorce from the mother as a significant contributing factor. The mothers of patients were described as particularly overinvolved and overadequate in relation to this child. The fathers were described as emotionally distant and only peripherally attached to both mother and child, although not necessarily distant from other children in the family. Bowen developed the idea that it takes about three generations of dysfunctions for schizophrenia to occur, suggesting that schizophrenia develops as a consequence of a progressive pattern of immaturity and dysfunctional interactions that are passed through several generations. He believed that the crucial development in the impact of family process on risk for schizophrenia has to do with those interactional processes in which a functional bind develops in which the child must deny important aspects of himself or herself to meet the needs and expectations of one or both parents, and the parents project their anxieties and needs onto the child.

Bowen described the relationship between selected members of the families as having formed an undifferentiated ego mass, from which attempts at differentiation triggered intense anxiety. In this context, both parent and child are caught in a spiraling process of "having to be for one another." The developmental process of being and becoming primarily to meet projected parental needs increasingly arrests the inherent emotional and social growth and potential of the child to develop in ways that are organismically congruent, while aspects of cognitive functioning and physical growth may remain unaffected. Therefore, the child may or may not evidence clear signs of vulnerability until adolescence or young adulthood and the seemingly abrupt onset of acute psychosis. The initial schizophrenic breakdown occurs during adolescence because the natural growth of the child threatens the parent-child relationship. The dilemma of the preschizophrenic child at this point is to find a balance between natural urges to develop and become independent and to establish social and intimate relationships outside of the primary family versus the need to "be" for the projected parental needs. Bowen believed that adolescent schizophrenic patients were most likely to show lasting improvement only after the parents became more emotionally invested in each other and the child was able to begin to develop an individual identity. Therapeutic efforts are directed toward facilitating changes in the way family members interact, rather than focusing on the cognitions or intrapsychic memories and meanings of the individual patient.

Bowen's observations should be viewed as tentative and limited in application since his research did not include an adequate sample on which to base a sound or convincing model of family process and its role in the development of schizophrenia. His observations are consistent with tendencies to develop a range of emotional problems, rather than providing evidence that is specific to schizophrenia (Howells, 1968). Additional limitations of family research in general include the following: (1) It is often impossible to determine the degree to which theory guides observations rather than observations guiding theory formation; (2) post hoc inferences about the role of processes prior to the onset of symptoms cannot differentiate cause from effect; and (3) intensive studies of interpersonal processes are extremely difficult and time consuming to document; as a result, sample sizes are typically very small and often highly select (Howells, 1968).

THEODORE LIDZ AND THE YALE GROUP

Theodore Lidz was also a pioneer family researcher. Lidz and his wife, Ruth Lidz, published an early study of the childhood family environments of fifty schizophrenic patients, noting that 90 percent of these homes were seriously disturbed. The authors concluded that the families in which schizophrenic patients grow up do not provide a proper milieu to foster healthy ego development. The effects of a deficient family environment and constitutional vulnerabilities, Lidz believed, contributed to risk for schizophrenia. Deficiencies in basic family processes, such as appropriate levels of nurturing, providing structure, socialization, and enculturation, were the most important family-based contributing factors noted by Lidz (1973; 1978).

Lidz viewed aberrant symbolic processes that distort perception, meaning, and logic as the critical characteristics of schizophrenia. He noted that many schizophrenic patients have withdrawn into an autistic world. Autistic withdrawal and delusions function to insulate patients from an overwhelming and anxiety-provoking world and help to maintain self-esteem in the context of a reshaped representation of reality. Lidz argued that the family plays a role in this process both by providing the constitutional base for temperament and genetically based vulnerabilities and by schooling the child in the day-to-day interactions of family and social life.

Much of the intensive observational research that formed the basis for many of the Yale Group's concepts was obtained from an intensive study of a highly select group of seventeen families of young, unmarried patients from intact families (Lidz et al., 1965). Lidz adopted the view of Parsons and Bales (1955) that the father tends to be the leader of the family in terms of adaptive-instrumental roles, and the mother is primary in socializing and modeling the integrative-expressive roles as a framework for their observations. Of the families studied, Lidz and colleagues noted that none of the fathers appeared to adequately fill his role as leader, instructor, and role model for adaptive-instrumental roles. Five patterns characterized the participant families:

1. Fathers of female patients in particular tended to be in ongoing serious conflict with their wives.
2. Some fathers turned or redirected their hostility toward their children.
3. Several fathers had markedly exalted concepts of themselves.

4. A number of the fathers were generally inadequate and were failures in their social and professional lives.
5. Several very passive men were totally dominated by their wives.

Lidz and colleagues (1965) characterized the mother's task in the family as (1) providing nurturance and fostering a sound foundation for ego autonomy; (2) contributing positively to a family system that provides integrating directives to the child; and (3) transmitting the basic adaptive roles of the culture to the child, including shared cultural meanings. The authors noted that none of the mothers in the sample fulfilled these functions adequately. Some were handicapped by their husband's psychopathology that dominated family life, other mothers treated the child as an extension of themselves and were often inappropriately intrusive and impervious to the needs and unique characteristics of the child. Mothers of schizophrenic sons tended to seek compensation for their dissatisfaction with their marriage by finding completion through their "special" sons. These mothers were often engulfing, chronically dissatisfied, and critical of their husbands; as a result, their sons became both dependent on their mothers and fearful of age-appropriate close relationships with women. Mothers of schizophrenic daughters were also caught up in unhappy marriages and preoccupied with their dilemmas.

The main findings reported by Lidz and colleagues (1965) were these:

1. In 60 percent of the families of schizophrenic patients, one or both parents evidenced serious personality problems, and 3 percent evidenced psychotic features. Irrationality is thus transmitted within the family.
2 Parents mutually dissatisfied in their relationship made structurally inappropriate emotional demands on their child to serve as a substitute for what was missing in their lives.

Lidz and colleagues did not suggest that bad parenting or unhappy marriages directly produced schizophrenia. They argued that family disturbances impair the ego development of the child and are an additional factor, along with a possible biological diathesis, that contributes to vulnerability.

Each of the marriages of the parents of schizophrenic patients studied by Lidz and colleagues were lacking in three basic requisites for adequate family functioning: (1) role reciprocity, in which spouses are able to establish reciprocal interrelated patterns of interaction with each other and with their children; (2) mutual trust and communication between all members of the family; and (3) consistent maintenance of clear boundaries between generations so that distinctions between parents and children and generationally appropriate levels of confidences, decision making, and emotional support are not confused.

Two predominant patterns characterized schizophrenic family communications. The first, *defective rationality,* referred to a range of patterns having to do with the mother's confused ideation under pressure or when anxious, as well as paranoid, suspicious ways of thinking on the part of fathers. The second pattern was termed *defective communication* and referred to a family context in which children were socialized to sacrifice their own needs and potentials in order to meet the needs and support the defenses of one or both parents. One or both of the parents in these families were often described as markedly impervious to feeling or perceiving the needs of the child. Disturbing situations within the families were denied or masked, so that family members learned to act as if the situation did not exist.

Lidz and colleagues (1965) proposed that the structure and functional stability of the normal family rests on the parents' ability to form a mutually satisfying coalition, to maintain appropriate boundaries between the generations, and to adhere to and function adequately in culturally appropriate sex-linked roles. They hypothesized that increased vulnerability to schizophrenia results from ego deficiencies that grow out of a complex interaction of constitutional factors and the vulnerable child's special tendency to incorporate into his or her own ego development the distortions of day-to-day family interactions.

Two general dysfunctional patterns were observed in the families of the schizophrenic patients: (1) *schizmatic families* in which the parents are in ongoing conflict, often undercutting the relationship of the other with the child in ways that the marriage is stabilized but the internal psychic structure of the child is ruptured by two irreconcilable but seemingly omnipotent parents; and (2) *skewed families* in which one parent does not establish appropriate boundaries between himself or herself and the child and continues to be inappropriately intrusive yet insensitive to the developmental needs of the child. In both patterns the child is used to stabilize a marriage in which a meaningful coalition is absent and conflict is either overt or latent, and the child is used to complete missing aspects of a parent's life. The result of growing up in these family contexts is that the child does not develop appropriately and does not develop age-appropriate self-boundaries and ego functions or alternative objects for identification outside of the family.

Lidz noted that many parents of the schizophrenic patients in his study had difficulty differentiating their own needs and vulnerabilities from those of their children or adequately recognizing that the child has different perceptions and innate characteristics. As a result, appropriate generational boundaries were not formed and maintained in the family. Gradually, the child and parent became involved in a reciprocal pattern of dysfunctional communication and interaction, but the child, being more dependent, must accommodate the needs of the parents.

Schizophrenic patients are characterized by poor self-boundaries, expressed in failures to differentiate between self and others and between feelings, impulses, and thoughts that arise from within versus what takes place outside the self. These developmental failures represent a form of egocentricity that Lidz believes resembles Piaget's description of the sensorimotor stage. Normally infants transition out of this stage as they establish object constancy and differentiate self from other. Lidz concluded that the development of schizophrenic patients, because of inborn vulnerabilities that interact with the family environment, becomes arrested at this early egocentric stage. Egocentricity refers to the tendency to distort reality to meet internal needs and to overvalue cognitive processes as a means of altering reality. Egocentricity reappears each time the child moves into a new developmental stage that has not been mastered. During these transitional periods fantasy and reality are confused, and words and thoughts become confused with the objects they symbolize. Schizophrenic patients, according to Lidz, demonstrate aspects of egocentricity that are evident in their symptoms. Eventually, vulnerable individuals reach a developmental stage during adolescence or young adulthood when they are confronted with psychosocial demands and tasks such as achieving independence and intimacy. These tasks are particularly difficult for vulnerable individuals because of the consequences of their earlier developmental failures and ongoing enmeshment. Given a poor foundation for grounding experience in reality, with a life history of permeable and confused boundaries between self and other, the vulnerable individual regresses to egocentric modes of function under the pressures of developmental transitions that overwhelm his or her capacity to cope. During this process of ego failure and regression, trivial events may take on heightened meaning, supernatural powers seem to be at work, experience often seems to be controlled, influenced, or directed, and need-based fantasies replace reality.

During the phase of acute schizophrenic ego fragmentation, the patient may come to believe that everything arises from within and that he or she is central to all that is happening; logical categories break down, attentional focusing and filtering mechanisms are disrupted; and inappropriate associative processes develop so that everything that occurs seems connected to everything else. Powerful insights are often experienced, the results of a fusion of fantasy with internal emotions and needs that increasingly takes precedence over accurate perceptions of external reality. As a result, thought becomes increasingly egocentric.

Lidz (1973) believed that the breakdown in category formation which frequently occurs in schizophrenia can be attributed to fundamental failures in developmental processes which foster the development of clear differentiation between fundamental categories such as self and not-self, self and parent, and maleness and femaleness. The failure of these categorizations, which are necessary for reality-based thought, allow for bizarre fantasies and the fusion of impulses with events, so that experiences increasingly represent expressions of intercategorical processes. He observed that many of the disturbances observed in schizophrenic patients parallel the types of egocentric cognitions observed in children. Therefore, Lidz argued, it is not necessary to assume that these patterns must always be caused by brain dysfunctions. These problems could also have to do with developmental failures that result from a combination of constitutional and developmental factors.

In summary, the family research conducted by Lidz and colleagues was among the earliest to focus on the role of triadic interactions within the family in the development of psychopathology. The findings reported were interesting but based on anecdotal and descriptive data and derived from observations of small and selected samples of patients and their families. An additional criticism of this work is that the parental and family characteristics described are not unique to schizophrenic patients and, in fact, are similar to those described in studies of families of other groups of patients (Slater and Roth, 1969).

Y. O. ALANEN AND FINNISH FAMILY RESEARCH

Y. O. Alanen and a group of Finnish researchers have reported findings on family dysfunction associated with schizophrenia that complement the American studies published by Bowen and Lidz. Alanen studied families of a group of schizophrenic patients living in the Helsinki area and a comparison group of controls. The research team reported that the families of schizophrenic patients could be divided into two groups: "chaotic" and "rigid." Chaotic families included parents suffering from psychosis or severe personality disorders and were characterized by unpredictable communication. Rigid families showed unusually formal, restrictive, and confining attitudes, so that the children were tightly bound by their parents. Symbiotic relationships in rigid families were observed between schizophrenic sons and their mothers in particular. Almost two-thirds of the parents evidenced personality disorders—about equally divided between mothers and fathers—which had an obvious adverse effect on the ego functioning of the child. In contrast, only 20 percent of control families of mentally ill but nonschizophrenic patients showed disturbances, and these were less severe (Alanen, 1997).

Alanen (1997) conceptualizes the role of the family in risk for schizophrenia in terms of a reciprocal interactive process between parents and child. Children identify with and unconsciously learn from their parents, and these early interactions provide the foundation for sociocultural development. Emotional relationships are of primary significance because their emergence is so closely tied to gratification of biological needs. Early experiences of emotional gratification are inseparably attached to the mother's responses to and ability to gratify the infant's biological needs. These early emotional bonds form the foundation for all later object relations; however, Alanen believes that early frustrations and unsatisfactory mother-child relationships alone cannot account for the origins of schizophrenia. The process of individuation is understood as a long-term developmental process that continues throughout childhood and adolescence.

Successful development of ego functions into adulthood requires that self-object relationships continue to move in the direction in which one experiences other individuals as separate from oneself with their own needs, potentials, and goals. Internal self and object representations must be clearly differentiated and relationships based on a sense of mutual respect and concern for others' needs and potentials. Projective identifications in which the needs of the parents distort the relationship with the child, such that the child becomes a support for the parents' own needs and emotional balance, are important factors in vulnerability to schizophrenia. If these developmental processes are impaired, problems will become most apparent when the individual must deal with the challenges of adolescence and early adulthood. The issues associated with these developmental tasks include managing strong sexual urges, establishing a relationship and finding a sexual partner, establishing independence from one's family, becoming self-supporting, and developing occupational competence. Young persons who experience difficulties with self-object differentiation experience increasing difficulties establishing satisfactory relationships with peers and will likely experience a greater number of disappointments that add to their vulnerability. Psychosis in adolescence and young adulthood is understood by Alanen as a developmental effort that has failed because of the interaction of various biological and family-based vulnerabilities.

Alanen concluded the following on the basis of his study of families of patients and controls:

1. Factors related to vulnerability to schizophrenia are not limited to the early mother-child relationship; family disturbances include patterns of symbiosis and disengagement that involve both parents and processes that continue through adolescence.

2. Parent personalities and their effects on parent-child relationships are critically important, but the temperament and characteristics of the child also influence the parents.
3. Primitive defense mechanisms—particularly projective identification—hinder individual development and are common occurrences in the families of schizophrenic patients.
4. The persistence of symbiotic needs is typical in schizophrenic vulnerability. In schizophrenic patients these needs may be understood as delayed needs to retain primitive self-object relationships, as well as ambivalent needs to develop new self-objects that would make further personality development possible.
5. The overall pattern of intrafamilial relations—including the influences of the children on their parents—is crucially important in understanding the development of schizophrenia.

THE PALO ALTO GROUP—JACKSON, BATESON, HALEY, WEAKLAND, SATIR, AND WATZLAWICK

Don Jackson was a pioneer family researcher and therapist during the 1950s who observed that improvements in young schizophrenic patients were often associated with notable changes in the behavior of other family members. Jackson noted that in some cases the responses of family members to signs of improvement worsened the patient's symptoms. In other cases members began to show signs of distress as the patient improved. He conceptualized his observations in terms of patterns of family interactions that function to maintain a status quo, or "family homeostasis." Jackson defined family homeostasis as a process in which change in one family member results in compensatory changes in other family members that functions to maintain a dynamic equilibrium within the family system.

Jackson later collaborated with anthropologist Gregory Bateson, who was attempting to apply the concepts of cybernetic models to understand the role of group patterns of communications, interactions, and messages and their impact on patterns of behavior. A third researcher, Jay Haley, joined the group during the mid-1950s. Haley's initial contribution was to note the similarity between some schizophrenic symptoms and the lack of ability to discriminate between logical types as described by Whitehead and Russell (1910). An important component of the theory of logical types is that there is and must be a discontinuity between different types or classes, in this case the generational levels of family unit. John Weakland, a psychologist, later joined the group.

In 1956 Bateson, Jackson, Haley, and Weakland published a report on their studies of the patterns of communication that they observed in many families of schizophrenic patients (Bateson et al., 1956). The group observed that the families they studied were unusually prone to breach the necessary discontinuity between generational levels or types. They further hypothesized that psychopathology can result from the breaching of logical types that occurs in the communications between parents and children. In the extreme this situation can lead to behaviors that resemble the symptoms of schizophrenia. The authors noted that in any situation in which multiple levels of meaning are communicated, such as play, drama, humor, sports, family interactions, and business transactions, different levels of communication occur simultaneously. If the individual is to understand the situation appropriately and respond in the expected manner, it is critical that he or she is able to discriminate between levels of messages. For example, in the metamessages communicated in the context of play or humor, discrimination between levels of messages is vital to the appropriate reactions of others, otherwise conflict or confusion will likely occur. Haley noted that schizophrenic symptoms reflect an inability to differentiate between levels of messages or logical types of communications. The authors next addressed the question of how such a deficit develops and why it is maintained.

Bateson and colleagues (1956) observed that schizophrenic patients tend to exhibit deficiencies in three areas of functioning:

1. They have difficulty assigning the correct level or communicational mode to the messages they receive from others.
2. They have difficulty assigning the correct level or communicational mode to their own messages.
3. They have difficulty assigning the correct communicational level to their own thoughts and perceptions.

The Palo Alto Group next focused on the role of sequential patterns of interaction in the current interpersonal context. They used the term *double bind* to describe the sequences associated with the communications and behaviors observed in families of schizophrenic patients. Bateson and colleagues specified five ingredients of a clinically significant double-bind pattern:

1. Two or more persons, i.e., some combination of mother, father, and/or siblings
2. A repeated experience, so that the double-bind structure comes to be an habitual experience

3. A primary negative injunction, such as, "Do not do X or I will punish you in some way" or "If you do not do such and such, I will punish you"
4. A secondary injunction conflicting with the first at a more abstract level and, like the first, enforced by punishment or signals that threaten
5. A tertiary negative injunction prohibiting the victim from escaping from the situation

Three additional conditions were also required for the double-bind situation to result in schizophrenic symptoms.

1. The relationship of the persons involved must be an intense one; that is, one in which the individual feels it is vital that he or she discriminate accurately what sort of message is being communicated so that he or she can respond appropriately.
2. The other person in the relationship is expressing two orders of message, and one of these denies the other.
3. The individual is unable to comment on the messages being expressed to correct his or her discrimination of what order of message to respond to; that is, the individual cannot comment on the inconsistencies or contradictions he or she is faced with.

The researchers emphasized that the concept of the double bind refers only to communication sequences that include contradictions between messages occurring at different levels. They viewed the double bind as a necessary but not sufficient condition for schizophrenia to occur and at the same time a by-product of schizophrenic communication (Bateson et al., 1963). The double bind is conceptualized in terms of people caught in an ongoing interactional system that produces conflicting definitions of a relationship and associated distress. In this sense, Bateson and colleagues argued, there is no "victim" and no "perpetrator" but simply people communicating and being caught up in interactional patterns that have the characteristics of a double bind.

Haley (1959) extended the communication model and defined most psychological problems as behaviors that are part of a sequence of acts between several people. As a consequence, he stressed the importance of involving the entire social unit of the patient in therapy. He defined the social unit as including the patient's family, professionals providing services and making administrative decisions, school personnel, and agents of the court system. With this expanded definition, the goal of therapy becomes preventing the repetition of sequences associated with attempts to cope with symptoms and the introduction of greater complexity and alternatives in systems interactions (Madanes, 1981). Any intervention that alters repetitive sequences and increases the likelihood of occurrence of alternative patterns can potentially alter the interactional system in lasting ways and, as a consequence, reduce symptoms. Therapy for any disorder then involves the presentation of "strategic" interventions designed to bring about changes in recurring interaction patterns associated with the occurrence of a particular problem. Disturbances in structure such as appropriate interactions within family hierarchies, triangles in which one parent is enmeshed with a particular child and the other is distant or disengaged, are additional examples of interactional patterns that are thought to be associated with symptoms.

In summary, the Palo Alto Group introduced systems thinking and communication theory into the literature on schizophrenia. Their work represented an important transition from a dyadic to a broader family and social systems perspective. The communications model had a significant impact on the work of many other researchers and theorists, including Singer and Wynne, and Laing. There is also correlational evidence available that double-bind communications are observed more often in schizophrenic families than in comparison groups (Ringuette and Kennedy, 1966; Bateson, 1978). However, reliable ratings of double-bind communications are difficult to obtain. The double-bind concept has generated a great deal of interest since it was introduced. However, it is important to note that it has not been adequately validated as a causal factor in the development of schizophrenia. The double-bind hypothesis did, however, contribute to a paradigm shift toward systems thinking about the role of families and other social institutions in psychopathology.

EXPERIMENTAL FAMILY STUDIES— MISHLER AND WAXLER

Mishler and Waxler (1968) conducted quasi-experimental studies of communication in the families of schizophrenic patients. The authors studied the content of recordings of discussions among family triads, including parents and an adult schizophrenic child. Family discussions during eighty-eight sessions were completed by forty-nine families. Participants in the study included families of both good and poor premorbid adjustment patients as well as a control group of families that did not include a diagnosed schizophrenic member. Several interesting findings were reported based on this study. First, blind analyses of transcripts suggested that families of schizophrenic patients were more rigid than controls. This rigidity was evident in higher levels of instrumental focus and lower levels of expressive behavior in families of patients. The authors interpreted this rigidity as reflecting a form of collective defense against the expression of feelings and stabilization through a rigid pattern of interpersonal and role relationships. Second, the authors reported more frequent signs of reversal of generational roles between father and son in families of schizophrenic male patients. Mothers and sons, in contrast, tended to jointly assume strong power positions, while the fathers exerted relatively little real influence within the family. Third, normal families were more likely to assume a direct mode of interpersonal influence (e.g., statements such as "Please stop talking about that"), while members of schizophrenic families, particularly mothers, relied on indirect controls such as guilt inducement or distraction. The authors concluded that the high frequency of indirect control strategies observed in schizophrenic families suggests the power hierarchy is more ambiguous in these families. Finally, the authors reported that in normal families children of both sexes tended to be more responsive and likely to focus on the comments and opinions of others than in patient families. Consequently, family discussions tend to lack meaningful continuity and supportive references to the ideas and comments of one another.

The research conducted by Mishler and Waxler represents one of the few experimental studies of family communication in schizophrenia. Unfortunately, limitations resulting from small sample size and observations based on postdiagnosis family discussions limit the ability to generalize based on this series of studies.

THE ROCHESTER RESEARCH GROUP— WYNNE AND SINGER

The family communication research of Lyman Wynne, Margaret Singer, and colleagues was published in a series of papers that extends over nearly two decades (Singer and Wynne, 1963, 1965; Wynne, 1977). Wynne was an established schizophrenia researcher who published a number of clinical papers on family dynamics and schizophrenia. He first collaborated with the psychodiagnostician Margaret Singer in a study of a sample of twenty schizophrenic children, twenty neurotic children (ten aggressive and ten withdrawn), and twenty schizophrenics who became acutely mentally ill during late adolescence or young adulthood. The families were recruited from newspaper ads and matched on

1. age of the child,
2. age of parents,
3. number of children in family,

4. educational and occupational level of parents, and
5. participation of at least the mother in psychotherapy.

The authors developed a method to study communication deviance in these families by using standardized interviews and psychological tests.

Results of the study indicated that the researchers were able to blindly differentiate parents of the schizophrenic children from the parents of neurotic children at a highly significant level. Parents of neurotic children were also differentiated from the parents of the two schizophrenic groups at a significant level. The authors reported that the following characteristics could be used to differentiate the groups:

1. Parents of schizophrenic children feel more dissatisfied and critical. They tend to avoid closeness, but they tend to tell coherent stories in response to stimulus cards and depict people, events, feelings, and consequences more clearly than parents of young-adult schizophrenics.
2. Parents of young-adult schizophrenics tend to feel unhappy and hopeless, have frustrating relationships, and convey an overall lack of direction. They tell stories that lack unity or closure, perceive events, feelings, and consequences in global terms, and have fragmented attention spans.
3. Parents of withdrawn neurotic children tell unified stories and have well-defined percepts but tend to dwell obsessively on details and appear introspective.
4. Parents of acting-out neurotic children are moody, active, have clear percepts, and are not very introspective.

Using the criteria developed by Singer and Wynne (1963), two psychologists blindly and separately examined parental joint Rorschach responses and rated them for disordered thought processes. Parents of young-adult schizophrenics were rated as evidencing the greatest number of responses in which both parents displayed abnormalities. The proportion of parents showing communication deviances in each group was 95 percent for schizophrenic patients, 60 percent for withdrawn neurotics, and 20 percent for schizophrenic children. No such abnormalities were noted for those with conduct disorders. The authors concluded that the form and style of parents' thinking, attentional focus, and communication was associated with the patterns of abnormal thought development in their children.

During their years of collaboration, Singer and Wynne studied over 600 families in their research projects. They concluded that disordered styles of communication are a distinguishing feature of families with young-adult schizophrenics. The authors found that a modification of the Rorschach procedure in which two or more individuals attempt to establish a consensually shared view of the ambiguous blots provided a useful format for evaluating family communication patterns. Each participant is asked to label what he or she "sees" and to offer an interpretation of its meaning to the others. The authors observed that parents of young-adult schizophrenics shared meanings that were reliably rated as difficult to follow, comprehend, and visualize. Patterns of deviance on the Rorschach protocols of the parents formed six factors derived from thirty-two categories of deviances. The six factors were

1. odd, hard to follow, ambiguous remarks;
2. failures to sustain task focus;
3. unstable perceptions and thinking;
4. nihilistic and idiosyncratic task orientation;
5. extraneous, illogical, contradictory comments; and
6. abstract, indefinite, discursive vagueness.

The types and severity of communication disorders in the parents predicted severity of psychiatric disorder in adolescent and young-adult schizophrenic patients. Singer and Wynne introduced the terms *amorphous* and *fragmented* to refer to the patterns of communication disorders observed in young-adult patients. A third style represented a "mixed" form of amorphous and fragmented, and a fourth was referred to as "stably constricted." The last style was characteristic of families of paranoid patients who speak coherently but split off aspects of reality. Amorphous schizophrenics show laconic, impoverished, and poorly differentiated focusing, similar to "process" patients. Patients with fragmented communications have relatively more clear, differentiated styles of attending and communicating but suffer from a failure in articulation and integration of their ideas; as a result, they are highly vulnerable to emotional stress and show abrupt, paranoid attention to task-irrelevant stimuli.

The authors reported that by studying parental communication they could predictively describe the forms of disorder that their offspring present. Singer was able to successfully identify the parents of schizophrenic patients and to predict their level of severity of ego disorganization based on a five-point rating scale of their Rorschach protocols with a high level of accuracy, using blind ratings of the protocols. Using the four characteristic family features mentioned previously, Singer was able to match a sample of thirty-six patients with their own families with only six errors, a highly significant result (Singer and Wynne, 1965).

In summary, the research conducted by Singer and Wynne indicates that the communication patterns of parents can be consistently linked to the diagnosis of their adolescent and young-adult offspring. Many years of research by these investigators, including detailed testing over 280 families, failed to show a family with a schizophrenic member that did not evidence significant levels of communication deviance. Singer and Wynne (1965) were able to discriminate reliably between the parents of schizophrenics and those of neurotics and normals at about 78 percent accuracy. They developed a detailed and reliable rating method for use in scoring transcripts of protocols. The transition in research focus from specific to more general concepts of dysfunctional patterns of family communication that occurred during the 1980s was in large part the result of the studies published by Singer and Wynne.

NONREACTIVE FAMILY RESEARCH

Several studies have been published which indicate that deviant parental communication need not always be a reaction to the presence of a schizophrenic family member in the household and that in some cases evidence of communication deviance is present years before the onset of schizophrenia. Rolf and Knight (1981), for example, related outcomes in diagnosed schizophrenic males to family variables obtained during the patients' childhood years. The data were collected from records that were obtained at the time the children and parents were seen for a variety of nonpsychotic adjustment problems. Results indicated that poor outcome of schizophrenic symptoms in adult patients was associated with parental marital dysfunction and signs of serious disturbance in one of the parents.

The UCLA Family Project

A substantial body of clinical and research evidence indicates that dysfunctional relationships and disordered styles of communication are observed more often in families with young-adult schizophrenics than in comparison groups (Bowen, 1960; Hirsch and Leff, 1975; Laing and Esterson, 1964; Lidz and Lidz, 1949; Mishler and Waxler, 1968; Singer, Wynne, and Toohey, 1978). This evidence is often dismissed by critics because it was gathered after the patients had been diagnosed. For this reason, one cannot say for certain whether the disordered communication was present prior to onset of the symptoms (a contributing factor) or developed in response to living with a psychotic family member (a consequence). However, the prospective study conducted by Tienari and colleagues (1994) described in Chapter 7 is an exception to this criticism. The Finnish research is ongoing but, thus far, provides evidence for the role of family dysfunction in the etiology of schizophrenia. The UCLA Family Project (Asarnow et al., 1982; Goldstein et al., 1978; Goldstein, 1985) is a second source of evidence of the possible etiological role of family communication disturbance. This research was a prospective study designed to follow a sample of sixty-four adolescents and their families who sought help from a psychological clinic for their moderately disturbed teenager over fifteen years of age. Each family participated in an extensive evaluation and was rated on three pathological styles of communication. Family communication styles were evaluated at the outset of treatment and long before the onset of any psychotic symptoms in the adolescents. The parental communication styles evaluated were communication deviance (Singer, Wynne, and Toohey, 1978), affective style (Doane, West, and Goldstein, 1981), and expressed emotion (Hirsch and Leff, 1975). Communication deviance refers to an inability of the parent or parents to establish and maintain a shared focus of attention during transactions with another person. Negative affective style refers to low-frequency behaviors by the parents such as personal criticism, guilt induction, critical intrusiveness, and excessive noncritical intrusiveness. Expressed emotion reflects attitudes of criticism and/or emotional overinvolvement.

The troubled adolescents and a number of their siblings were followed at two subsequent time periods, five and fifteen years after the initial family assessments, at which times blind diagnostic evaluations were completed. Of the original sample of sixty-four teenagers, follow-up was possible on fifty cases, of which forty-five had all three parental measures available.

Development, at fifteen years follow-up, of schizophrenia spectrum disorders within the subsample was significantly associated with the combined parental communication pattern of high communication deviance, negative affective style, and high expressed emotion. When data for siblings was included, the predictive value of high communication deviance was even greater. Using the criteria for schizophrenia spectrum disorders employed in the Danish-American adoption studies for all offspring, the percent of spectrum cases for high communication deviance families was 70 percent, compared to 9 percent for low communication deviance families. These results indicate that disturbed patterns of intrafamilial communication and affect expression antedated the onset of schizophrenia spectrum disorders.

Asarnow and colleagues (1982) concluded that evaluations of symptom outcome among the schizophrenia and schizophrenia spectrum cases indicated that when the adolescent's problems in controlling negative affect were combined with a tendency for the parents to interact with the adolescent in a predominantly negative manner during the initial evaluation, outcome at the fifteen-year follow-up was poor. When parental communication deviance and affective style were employed as joint predictors, precise identification of the adolescents destined to develop schizophrenia spectrum disorders was possible (Doane, West, and Goldstein, 1981).

Without a reliable genetic marker for the predisposition to schizophrenia spectrum disorders is it impossible to separate the relative contributions of disordered family interactions from genetic factors. It is clear, however, that disturbed family communications can be an important contribution to risk for schizophrenia and schizophrenia spectrum disorders.

Finnish-American Adoption Studies

The research conducted by Tienari and colleagues (1994) described in detail in Chapter 7 represents a third prospective study in which measures of parental family functioning were obtained prior to the onset of any signs of schizophrenia or schizophrenia spectrum disorders. Index adoptees in this ongoing study developed more and more serious psychopathology at follow-up, but most of these disorders were concentrated in those children reared by adoptive parents who evidenced high levels of communication deviance. Index adoptees raised by adoptive parents who did not show signs of communication deviance evidenced substantially less psychopathology. These results indicate that both genetics and parental disturbance have an impact on outcome of both index and control cases.

It should also be noted that the Finnish adoption study included the same communication deviance scoring criteria developed by Singer and Wynne as the UCLA study. The Finnish research also indicates that a disturbed and disturbing rearing environment contributes to risk for later schizophrenia spectrum disorders (Tienari et al., 1994).

Of course, the assumption of family deviance as a contributor to risk for schizophrenia and schizophrenia spectrum disorders must also explain the fact that most siblings of the patient do not develop the disorder. Family researchers argue that the interactions and subculture of the family are not constant, either over time or among offspring. Countless factors, including familial resemblances, birth order, situational parental discord, gender, subtle developmental strengths or liabilities, and so on, can dramatically influence the developmental context and experiences of different children reared in the same family. These differences are summarized perhaps too glibly in Meehl's (1962) diathesis-stress model under the heading of a "bad luck" factor.

SUMMARY

Family research has sensitized clinicians to the potential role of ongoing interaction patterns and communications in the onset and maintenance of symptoms of many disorders. However, the majority of family research, other than expressed emotions studies, is subject to several methodological limitations, perhaps the most important being that the data on which much of the family research is based are derived from retrospective studies of small, select groups of first-admission patients. Second, matched controls are not included in the designs. The studies published by Goldstein and colleagues and Tienari and colleagues are important exceptions to most of these criticisms.

Esterson (1970) argues that the methods of phenomenological and dialectical analysis are more appropriate for studies that focus on interactions within families and that criticisms given from an experimental perspective are largely irrelevant to this body of literature. Many family researchers, like psychodynamic theorists, develop constructs derived from clinical understandings based on intensive interactions and interpretations that provide a different order of information than experimental studies. These observations and predictions are often difficult or impractical to test in the real world. Early family researchers were initially guilty of ignoring or appearing to ignore the role of genetic and biological contributors and placing exclusive emphasis on family dysfunctions as the cause of schizophrenia. This error is inherent in all attempts to understand complex human phenomena from a single perspective. The evidence seems clear that in most cases schizophrenia is not caused by either bad or neglectful parenting or disturbed family communication. Single-cause explanations of this complex group of disorders are too simplistic. The evidence published by Goldstein, Tienari, and others does indicate that family dysfunction can play a contributing role in the development of schizophrenia. To what degree, in which circumstances, and in interaction with which genetic risk factors and brain-based disturbances remains to be determined.

SECTION VI:
LIFE IN THE COMMUNITY

This section describes several innovative programs that have been developed to meet the needs of schizophrenic patients living in the community. These needs are the most inadequately addressed aspect of the treatment and understanding of schizophrenia today. The reader will have some idea of these needs and what can be accomplished with proper dedication and funding after reading this material.

Chapter 15

Schizophrenia and Life in the Community

Deinstitutionalization, which began in the mid-1950s, had and continues to have dramatic effects on the treatment and well-being of schizophrenic patients. In 1955, 77 percent of all episodes of psychiatric care were in inpatient settings and 63 percent were in state hospitals. By 1990, 26 percent were inpatient episodes and 16 percent were in state hospitals (Redlick et al., 1994). The figures are even lower today. Several factors contributed to the dramatic decline in the U.S. inpatient mental hospital population since the 1950s. Today, patients are typically stabilized on high doses of medications in hospitals and returned to the community within a relatively short period of time, unless they are severely impaired or aggressive. However, the problems of a "revolving door" of chronicity have not disappeared. Rather than warehousing patients for indefinite periods as was done in the past, hospitalizations are now used mostly for crisis stabilization. Unfortunately, after the crisis is stabilized and the patient is released, far too little is offered in the way of effective follow-up and supportive services. No one is advocating a return to the warehousing of mental patients that occurred during the first half of the twentieth century, but more than thirty years after implementation of the deinsitutionalization movement in the United States, a great deal more remains to be accomplished, particularly in providing adequate community-based programs for the seriously mentally ill. Comprehensive, integrated, and adequately funded systems of care for discharged schizophrenic patients need to be established in every community but, in fact, rarely are.

The revolving-door phenomenon of admission and frequent readmission of schizophrenic patients and lack of adequate community-based services is obviously related to the increase in the homeless population in our cities. It is estimated that about one-third of all homeless adults in the United States have a major mental disorder (Baum and Burns, 1993). There are many paths to homelessness among the mentally ill, but lack of access to subsidized housing and the absence of a proactive, comprehensive, integrated system of care in most communities are important sources of this problem. Most mentally ill persons who are already vulnerable to stress and lacking in skills are unable to deal with the stresses of tenancy problems, managing finances, and living independently and the expectations of self-initiated access to mental health services. Once on their own, many are likely to fail to respond to day-to-day realities such as bills and disability administrative requirements, to stop taking medications, to abuse alcohol or drugs, to have problems with financial management, to be taken advantage of by others, and eventually to become overwhelmed, disorganized, and unable to cope with the demands of living outside the hospital.

The young-adult dual-diagnosis schizophrenic patient presents a particular challenge. Young-adult patients lacking social supports who are aggressive, bizarre in dress or behavior, rebellious, and abuse drugs constitute a large segment of both the revolving-door participants and the homeless mentally ill population. Emphasis on rapid tranquilization and quick release from hospital to poorly organized community care systems serves only to further alienate these individuals.

Deinstitutionalization ended the warehousing of severe mental patients but, in turn, resulted in a new and more complex set of problems. We have been fairly successful in managing some of the active symptoms of schizophrenia with medication but have not accomplished enough in the way of implementing the kinds of programs and services which are needed to increase the likelihood that mental patients of all types will not only remain out of the hospital for longer intervals but also will be able to engage in productive activities and develop an increased sense of self-esteem. Given the extreme vulnerability to stress, problems with daily living responsibilities, and frustrations in dealing with bureaucratic requirements encountered by most patients, it is not surprising that many become dependent on mental institutions and have difficulty maintaining even marginal functioning in the community (Glass, 1989).

COMMUNITY SUPPORT AND RECOVERY

Wing and Brown (1970) studied the effects of level of services and interpersonal climate of mental hospitals on the long-term adjustment of chronic patients. They found that a substantial part of the variance in outcome and long-term adjustment was a function of the amount of time patients spent in activities and were exposed to increased contact with the outside world and an optimistic staff. They concluded that many of the negative symptoms attributed to disease processes appear to result from neglect of the social milieu provided for patients. Research by the World Health Organization (Jablensky et al., 1992) also indicated that recovery rates are better in developing countries, with good outcome rates about double those observed in the developed world. The reasons for these differences are not entirely clear, but likely contributors are that people with symptoms of mental illness in developing countries receive more appropriate forms of social support and more acceptance in their communities, are less likely to be stigmatized, and are more likely to assume meaningful work in agricultural economies (Warner, 1994).

Traditional treatment approaches focus on containing disturbances and minimizing symptoms. These goals are important, but they are often implemented in ways that artificially disconnect the individual from aspects of his or her prior history and possibilities for social participation and role functioning. Most hospitalized schizophrenic patients have good reasons for feeling unprepared for and frightened of the challenges that face them when returning to the outside world. Discharge means losing the security of the role of patient in the context of the hospital routine and the structure of being cared for and supervised around the clock by the staff.

There are advantages and disadvantages to hospitalization. The role of mental patient defines the individual in the language of mental disorders and patienthood and infantilizes the individual. On the other hand, being a hospitalized mental patient provides containment, protection, limits, security, relief from terror, and a place to receive assistance. Symptoms may be controlled by medications so that they may not disrupt the patient's ability to perform the routine chores of daily living, but many behaviors including those that create anxiety, conflict, and misunderstandings in social relationships and work-related social environments are not altered by medications. Today, life outside of the hospital too often means little more than continuation of the nonperson status of the hospitalized patient. Patients are discharged to live alone, isolated and often too confused to cope with the demands of life in the community. Most caseworkers are so burdened with heavy caseloads that they can provide only perfunctory services to those who are most visible.

Patients' efforts to assume meaningful and productive social roles, if undertaken at all, are frequently associated with failure, rejection, and disappointment. Failure to establish any form of meaningful socially acceptable role participation pushes the patient further in the direction of his or her delusions, so that an inner fantasy life increasingly comes to function as a source of refuge. The low-status, marginal, and paternalistic treatment of schizophrenic patients both in and out of the hospital contributes to a process of continued demoralization that effectively reduces opportunities for a productive and meaningful social life. The stereotype of the schizophrenic as a person suffering from a chronic, incurable brain disease is a contributor to the negative transformation of a patient's sense of identity and reinforces a sense of inferiority, alienation, and separateness. There are no easy answers to these problems, and schizophrenic patients are not always cooperative and compliant, but we can do much better than what passes as typical community-based services for the long-term mentally ill.

Glass (1989) suggests that it may be more productive to also think of schizophrenia in terms of economic and political concepts. What is lacking in much of the clinical literature is a belief that some form of shared public life which involves both productive activity and participation is possible for most schizophrenic patients. Clinical theories focus on what is wrong with the patient, conceptualized in terms of brain or chemical dysfunctions, cognitive processing errors, skill deficits, or unconscious conflicts. They ignore the importance of work, meaningful interpersonal relations, and the politics of persons, institutions, and bureaucracies as factors that are related to long-term outcome. Feelings of placelessness and loss of personhood are reinforced by what patients encounter when attempting to return to society. The most important long-term issue in providing adequate and appropriate services to schizophrenic patients is how to best provide opportunities for experiences that are likely to foster a viable sense of individuality and integrity along with some degree of manageable productive contact with and involvement in society.

Admittedly, the symptoms of schizophrenia, the tendency for active symptoms to be episodic in nature, and the social stigma associated with this disorder make it extremely difficult to successfully integrate patients into meaningful social roles in the community and the workplace. Lack of access to affordable and appropriate housing further contributes to difficulties in successful integration into the community. More than 65 percent of hospital-discharged schizophrenic patients are sent to live with their families, most often because there is no other place for them to go. Others live in group homes, nursing homes, and marginal apartments (Levine, Lezak, and Goldman, 1986), and many rotate between the streets, hospitals, jails, and homeless shelters.

There is a need to rethink how we understand and treat chronic mental disorders such as schizophrenia. It is not that successful models have not been developed which can provide a framework for planners. Chronic patients may be impaired, but this impairment does not necessarily rule out the capacity to act on specific economic and social opportunities. Meaningful forms of public participation, especially in the form of employment, give patients opportunities to develop an identity that lies outside the focus of the medical model.

Glass (1989) suggests we must develop programs that represent a synthesis of caring treatments which treat the vulnerability of patients, creating an environment that gradually defuses the impact of psychosis and the tendency to further withdrawal into internal psychotic processes. Efforts at rehabilitation must facilitate the feelings of efficacy and community essential to development of the public self. Incentives must be provided to explore ways of developing coproduction models and innovative organizational approaches in both rural and urban environments, models designed to encourage and support enterprises that harness the productive potential of chronic patients. Provision of meaningful opportunities to develop a sense of place, understood as involving both productivity and community, would do much to reduce the problems of alienation, homelessness, and recidivism among the mentally ill (Warner and Polak, 1995). In addition, adoption of social policies that encourage active involvement rather than impairment would help. For example, today a patient who finds full-time or part-time employment risks permanently losing his or her disability payments.

The functions of an adequate community treatment program are succinctly expressed in the following guidelines (Warner and Polak, 1995):

1. Adopt total responsibility for the disabled client's welfare, including helping the patient acquire such material resources as food, shelter, clothing, and medical care
2. Aggressively pursue the client's interests, ensuring that other social agencies fulfill their obligations or actively searching for patients who drop out of treatment, for example
3. Provide a range of supportive services which can be tailored to fit each patient's needs and which will continue as long as they are needed
4. Educate the patient to live and work in the community
5. Offer support to family, friends, and community members

MODEL PROGRAMS

Fountain House

The original Fountain House program was established in New York City during the early 1960s. The program has grown into a highly successful organization that serves as a model for the rehabilitation of the chronically mentally ill living in the community (Beard, Propst, and Malamud, 1982). There are wide variations in the settings and operations of clubhouse programs that have been established around the country and abroad; however, most have modeled themselves to varying degrees after the Fountain House program. John Beard, a staff member who joined the organization shortly after it was established, is credited with instituting many key components of the Fountain House philosophy and organization including the transitional employment program.

Two key elements are essential to the success of the Fountain House model (Richardson, 1987). First, the philosophy is based on a belief in the potential usefulness and productivity of all participants. This belief means, for example, that members take responsibility for the bulk of the day-to-day running of the clubhouse. The Fountain House prevocational day program is organized into six work units: kitchen, reception, clerical, education, research, and snack bar. Each new member is asked to select a unit and a key staff liaison worker and to participate in the activities of these units as well as twice-daily unit meetings. The goal is to foster opportunities for interacting and relating to other members and staff in the context of a meaningful work environment. Prevocational day-program members are encouraged to participate in their assignments and to develop basic work habits such as punctuality, improved concentration, and acceptance of supervision. They are not criticized but instead are encouraged and given opportunities to develop and become involved. The assumption at Fountain House is that everyone has a need to become involved with others and to engage in meaningful, productive activities and will do so if they feel safe in that context and have a reasonable expectation of success.

The New York Fountain House program attracts a daily attendance of over 350 members. A clubhouse program of this size requires a complex organization in which many responsibilities must be assumed by members. The staff-to-member ratio is kept low to assure this. Members and staff work alongside one another in the day-to-day operation of the program, with an emphasis on egalitarian relationships. Member involvement in running the program and maintaining the facility fosters a sense of personal investment and having meaningful responsibilities and expectations. Staff members focus on providing opportunities for growth and encouraging and promoting members' strengths rather than diagnosing or developing treatment plans.

When a member feels ready and has participated successfully in the day program for a sufficient amount of time (usually around six months), he or she may be eligible to enter into the transitional employment program. This program offers opportunities for part-time work in entry-level jobs in various industries and business organizations where members receive regular wages. Currently over 100 members in the New York program go out to work on a part-time basis. The remainder of their day is spent at the clubhouse. In many cases two members fill one job placement. Some placements involve teams or groups of six to ten members working together. Over forty different employers in New York City employ Fountain House members. Staff members negotiate with employers for new positions, and work units of staff and members are responsible for managing and supervising the placements. This means that staff must spend time on the jobs to familiarize themselves with the work demands, since they may at times have to fill in for a member and work the job. Members work in their part-time jobs for six months or more before helping train another member who may be about to replace them. About 50 percent of members move on to full-time work.

The transitional employment program is organized so that if members are unable to attend work there is always another member or staff worker available to take their places. In this way, businesses are assured of continuity of workers. In turn, employers are more willing to hire those members who may have a long record of hospitalizations, little formal education, or a poor work record. Most members find the transition from working in the clubhouse environment to working in a transitional employment position an intimidating prospect. Many members have never held a job before and are afraid of failure and uncertainty. Members are not pressured to take jobs, however long they have been participating in the clubhouse program, and are assured that whenever a placement does not work out they can return to full-time participation in the day program without criticism or censure. It is not unusual for members to try several placements before completing one successfully. There is no time limit on how long it may take for members to move into the transitional employment program or on how long they may stay in the program and work on a part-time basis. These decisions are left to individual members.

Weekly dinners are held at Fountain House for all members on transitional employment placements. Members sit down to a meal prepared and served by fellow members and staff, and each member is asked to stand up to describe his or her achievements and problems for the week. These presentations in front of an audience of fifty or more people are often followed by informal problem solving and social conversations with fellow members and staff after dinner. Mutual support and help among members is a fundamental component of the program. Fountain House attempts to build on the universal human need to have a sense of belonging and purpose that comes from meaningful relationships and involvement in productive activities. Few if any schizophrenic patients become immune to these needs.

When the goals and philosophy of the program are effectively implemented the clubhouse model can do much to counteract the tendencies for withdrawal, dependency, and lack of initiative that characterize many schizophrenic patients. Establishing the complete package of an effective clubhouse program and adequate opportunities for transitional employment requires great effort, commitment, perseverance, and effective community outreach. Staff members must have a clear understanding of and commitment to their role as enablers, i.e., people who encourage, involve, support, and guide rather than instruct or do for. If the staff is not able to create a genuine climate of belief in each member's potential to become involved and gradually assume responsibilities in the clubhouse and a work placement in the community, then it will not happen. The difficulties of obtaining adequate funding, finding appropriate facilities and locations, and creating and maintaining job placement programs and an effective social milieu are daunting.

There are also several important issues and needs, such as housing and aftercare, that are not incorporated directly into the clubhouse model. Nevertheless, the New York Fountain House program serves as a prototype for many community-based programs for the long-term mentally ill. Fountain House has demonstrated that many long-term patients can reenter the social world and become involved in meaningful and useful activities. The focus on the public self through provision of opportunities for meaningful and productive social roles and an accepting social environment has demonstrated the unrecognized potentials of schizophrenic patients. Unfortunately, the few community-based clubhouse programs that have attempted to adopt the Fountain House model are only partial mirrors of the original.

A Program of Assertive Community Treatment (PACT)

Test and colleagues (1991) listed several areas that must be addressed by treatment programs if course and outcome of schizophrenia are to be improved. These are (1) to decrease biological vulnerability through provision of medications; (2) to foster coping and protective factors through social skills training, work rehabilitation and training, and social support, and (3) to decrease sources of environmental stress (e.g., by providing assistance in securing adequate and supportive living and work environments and in meeting basic needs). Unfortunately, components two and three of this model are inadequately addressed in most community programs (Test, 1992). There are many reasons for this failure. First, community services are fragmented so that sheltered workshops, day centers, halfway houses, rehabilitation services, and access to psychoactive medications are often housed in different locations and administered by different personnel. This fragmentation makes it difficult if not impossible for patients to negotiate the system. Second, services are typically provided based on the ability and willingness of the patient to come to that agency and seek services. Many schizophrenic patients are unable or unwilling to consistently initiate requests for services, hence they drop out of treatment or do not follow up and often relapse. Third, patients rarely receive individualized services.

Since the 1970s, a group in Madison, Wisconsin, has implemented a comprehensive community care and research program designed to meet these gaps in services (Stein and Test, 1980). Their efforts have evolved into a comprehensive, integrated care model called PACT (Program of Assertive Community Treatment). An important part of the PACT model is the concept of a "core services" team. The core services team is a community-based, multidisciplinary mental health team tasked to serve as a fixed reference point of responsibility for a defined group of clients. The team is responsible for assisting clients to meet their needs in all aspects of their lives, seven days a week, twenty-four hours a day. The original Madison PACT interdisciplinary team consisted of fourteen staff who were responsible for 120 young adults diagnosed with schizophrenia.

The PACT core team provides clients with medication, supportive and problem-solving therapy, assistance in finding appropriate housing, occupational rehabilitation and placement, crisis intervention around the clock, and whatever else is needed in terms of biopsychosocial services. The team serves as a fixed point of responsibility, in order to avoid the fragmentation that so often exists in community services. This core services team allows for continuity in functional areas in time as well as continuity of caregivers.

A second important innovation is that the PACT team is mobile. Team members use assertive outreach to provide most services where the client is rather than only in offices. Staff members meet with clients in residences, neighborhoods, or work sites. This form of assertive outreach is effective in significantly reducing the number of drop-outs and allows for effective provision of services when and where the client needs them.

A third aspect of the PACT program is that services are individualized to address the diversity of persons diagnosed with severe mental illness as well as the fact that a person with such a disorder is constantly changing. PACT services and interventions are provided to meet the current needs and preferences of each client, based on a thorough clinical and functional assessment and an individualized treatment plan. The core team also provides medication which is often delivered to the clients in their homes. One-on-one contacts frequently focus on problem solving and providing emotional support. Staff members attempt to educate clients about their illness, to help the client develop ways to manage symptoms, and to provide individualized psycho-educational sessions to family and relevant community members such as landlords and supervisors. A team member is on call twenty-four hours a day to provide crisis intervention or brief hospital admission when needed. Staff members also help clients locate living arrangements in the community and spend a great deal of time doing outreach where clients live. Activities of daily living, including money management, grocery planning and shopping, laundry, housekeeping, and learning about transportation, are all concerns of the core services staff. Staff members act as coaches, both teaching clients how to manage these tasks and providing them with support when new or difficult moments occur.

The PACT program is based on the assumption that work plays an important role in providing meaning and structure in an individual's life. The program uses a "supported employment" model in which each client is assisted in securing a paying job in the community that matches the client's current interests, skills, and abilities. In addition to assistance in locating jobs, core team members may work with the client and the employer at the site. Work with clients and employers may involve helping to structure the job environment so that clients work in spite of continuing psychotic symptoms. The goal of the PACT program is to provide interventions that decrease vulnerability and help build protective factors such as social skills and supports, meaningful and appropriate work opportunities, and resources to weaken the effects of environmental stressors. Emphasis is on helping clients find environments in which they can function, as well as on decreasing the severity of their symptoms.

Staffing of the PACT core team includes various mental health professions, with at least 75 percent holding bachelor's or master's degrees in mental-health-related fields and no more than 25 percent trained at only the paraprofessional level. All team members work with all clients. Team members also share responsibilities for treatment plans so that no single person is responsible for a specific caseload of clients.

Evaluation of the PACT program indicated that clients experienced markedly less time in psychiatric hospitals, exhibited fewer symptoms, and lived more independently than controls (Stein and Test, 1980). PACT clients also spent more time in sheltered employment and belonged to more social groups. Similar findings have been reported in other settings where the PACT model has been adopted (Bond et al., 1990; Morse et al., 1992). Overall costs and benefits of the PACT program indicate that the costs were similar to traditional care although its benefits were greater. Once clients were discharged from the program, many of them lost the advantages relative to controls. This demonstrates that programs for patients should not only provide comprehensive services but must also provide these services long term. An ongoing study of young-adult schizophrenic patients (Test et al., 1991) indicates that PACT clients spend significantly less time in psychiatric hospitals or nursing homes than do controls, and this advantage continues as long as services are provided.

Kingsley Hall and Soteria House

In 1965 R. D. Laing and his colleagues opened a facility called Kingsley Hall in London. Laing maintained that a community-based, protective, supportive, normalizing environment could facilitate recovery of psychotic persons and avoid the disintegrative effects of institutionalization. Kingsley Hall closed after several years, but the concepts implemented there influenced Loren Mosher, an American psychiatrist at the National Institute of Mental Health. Mosher decided to support the implementation of a program in the United States modeled after Laing's Kingsley Hall project. The name of the project was "Soteria," meaning "salvation or deliverance" in Greek.

The goal of Soteria House was to provide a protective, supportive, normalizing environment as an alternative to medication and hospitalization for acute schizophrenic persons. The project was also designed as a research study and involved random assignment of persons newly diagnosed as having schizophrenia and deemed in need of hospitalization. The sample was limited to newly diagnosed (less than thirty days previous hospitalization), young-adult, unmarried patients that were reliably diagnosed by three independent raters. Newly diagnosed schizophrenic individuals were alternately given a choice of standard psychiatric treatment and hospitalization or Soteria House.

Most psychiatric hospitals are organized around a medical model in which medical doctors have final authority and decision-making powers, medications are the primary therapeutic intervention, and patients are seen as having a disease involving permanent disability and dysfunction that is to be "treated" by the professional staff. The model proposed as the theoretical base for the day-to-day operation of Soteria House was based on an interpersonal phenomenological approach to schizophrenia. The Soteria focus was on attempts to understand and share the psychotic person's experience and one's reactions to it without judging, labeling, derogating, or attempting to invalidate it. The rationale for Soteria was rooted in the moral treatment approach of the nineteenth century (Bockoven, 1963), the tradition of intensive interpersonal therapy in schizophrenia (Fromm-Reichmann, 1948; Sullivan, 1952), the view that growth can occur from psychosis (Menninger, 1959), the ideas of the "antipsychiatrists" (Laing, 1967; Szasz, 1970), and evidence that psychiatric disorders are often responses to life crises (Brown and Birley, 1968).

The Sorteria approach involved around-the-clock application of interpersonal phenomenologic interventions by nonprofessional staff, usually without neuroleptic drug treatment, in the context of a small, homelike, supportive environment. This approach focuses on the development of a nonintrusive, noncontrolling, empathetic relationship with the psychotic person. There are no formal therapeutic sessions at Soteria, but a great deal of helpful relating takes place as staff gently attempt to build bridges that help the individual connect his or her emotional turmoil to the life events which seem to have precipitated psychological disintegration.

The original Soteria House opened in 1971 in the San Francisco Bay Area. A second facility (Emanon) was opened in 1974. Soteria housed twelve residents, with one or two new residents admitted each month. Two specially trained nonprofessional staff, a man and a woman, were always on duty at any one time. In addition, one volunteer was also present in the evening. Overall there were six paid nonprofessional staff, a house director, and a quarter-time psychiatrist at each facility. Staff generally worked thirty-six- to forty-eight-hour workweeks to enable them to interact with residents continually over a relatively long period. Staff and residents shared responsibility for household maintenance, meal preparation, and cleanup. Residents who were not functioning well were not expected to do an equal share of work or complete all tasks to which they had agreed. Soteria House staff considered all facets of the psychotic experience to be "real." Staff tried to provide an atmosphere that would facilitate integration of the psychotic experience into the continuity of the individual's life, rather than to invalidate or treat these experiences as symptoms of a diseased brain. Limits were set if residents were clearly a danger to themselves, others, or the program as a whole. Antipsychotic drugs were ordinarily not used for at least the first six weeks of residence. If the resident showed no change by that time, drugs were prescribed. The community mental health clinic (CMHC) comparison ward consisted of two locked units of thirty beds each. The staff to patient ratio was excellent (1:1.5). Antipsychotic medications in high doses were typically administered on admission. Staff members were well trained and enthusiastic and believed they were doing a good job. Patients were quickly evaluated and placed in other sections of the treatment network when stabilized.

Six-week and two-year outcome data from the participants admitted between 1971 and 1976 were collected. Results indicated that Soteria and control participants were comparable at intake and that both groups improved significantly and comparably in terms of reduced symptoms of psychopathology at six-week follow-up. All control participants were given neuroleptic medications compared to 3 percent of Soteria patients. At the two-year evaluation, the 1971 to 1976 Soteria cohort was significantly more likely to be living independently, to work at high levels of occupational functioning, and to have fewer readmissions than controls. The cost for care for the first six months was about the same for both groups, since Soteria participants stayed about five months versus an average of one month of hospitalization for controls. These results were essentially replicated in a second cohort study (1976-1982) conducted at Emanon House (Mosher, 1995). The author concluded the following:

1. Interpersonally based therapeutic milieus are as effective as neuroleptic drugs in reducing the acute symptoms of psychosis in the short term, in newly diagnosed schizophrenic patients.
2. Therapeutic community personnel did not require advanced degrees or extensive training and experience in order to be effective. They did need to be sure this is something they wanted to do and to be tolerant, flexible, positive, enthusiastic, and psychologically strong.
3. Two-year outcomes were as good as or better than those of hospital-treated controls.
4. Positive long-term outcomes achieved were at least partially a result of the spontaneous growth of social networks around the facilities.

A second generation Soteria-like facility (called Crossing Place) opened in the Washington, DC, area in 1977. Crossing Place differed in that it served a more diverse client base, admitting any individual deemed in need of psychiatric hospitalization, regardless of diagnosis, length of illness, severity of symptoms, or functional impairment. In 1990, Mosher was instrumental in supporting the opening of a Crossing Place replication in Montgomery County, Maryland. These facilities differ somewhat from Soteria in that they are more organized and oriented toward practical goals. Psychosis is often not addressed directly by staff members, and neuroleptics are used to control psychotic episodes when necessary. An evaluation of the Montgomery County program (Mosher, 1995) indicated that the community-based alternative programs were equal in clinical effectiveness, but the alternative programs cost about 40 percent, or $19,000 a year, less per person to operate.

Mosher (1995) identified several important therapeutic ingredients of these alternative programs:

1. The residential setting allows for interactions with the community.
2. The facility is small and homelike, with space for about ten persons to sleep (six to eight clients and two staff).
3. The primary task of the staff is to understand the immediate circumstances and relevant background that precipitated the crisis necessitating admission.
4. Within the relationship between staff and client, staff will carry out the roles of companion, advocate, caseworker, and helper.

5. Staff is trained to prevent unnecessary dependency and as much as possible support autonomous decision making on the part of clients.
6. Access and departure are made as easy as possible, and clients are free to maintain their connection to the program any way they choose: phone calls, drop-in, advice, time with staff or clients.

Despite evidence of the effectiveness of these programs (Mosher, 1995), Soteria and the demedicalized approach it represents are rarely mentioned in mainstream literature. The original Soteria project ended in 1983, due to loss of federal funding. However Dr. Luc Ciompi initiated the opening of a Soteria House in Bern, Switzerland, in 1984. The success of this program, in which about two-thirds of newly diagnosed persons with schizophrenia recover from symptoms in two to twelve weeks with little or no drug treatment (Ciompi, 1997), prompted the beginning of additional projects in other European countries. These programs are continuing.

THE IMPORTANCE OF WORK

Evidence from the World Health Organization International Pilot Study strongly suggests that availability of meaningful work is important for recovery from schizophrenia (Jacobs, Wissusik, and Collier, 1992; Warner, 1994). Despite evidence that work has beneficial effects on the long-term outcome of patients, many obstacles face former patients who attempt to find employment. Consequently, only 15 percent of former psychiatric patients are employed in the United States (Consumer Health Sciences, 1997). In contrast, in industrialized countries that have provided employment assistance programs and adopted policies eliminating obstacles to finding work, a large segment of released patients are able to find and sustain employment. In Bologna, Italy, for example, nearly half of all former patients were employed continuously during the previous three months, and more than one-fifth were working full time. In Verona, Italy, nearly 60 percent of schizophrenic patients living in the community were employed, one-quarter of them full-time.

There are many reasons for these differences in rates of employment. First, in the United States and Britain the disability pension regulations are so restrictive in terms of allowable earned-income levels that there is no economic incentive to work. The problem is even greater for veterans who receive more generous disability payments. Current disability pension regulations provide disincentives to work and to symptom improvement. Rather than disincentives, seriously mentally ill people need wage subsidies to encourage them to work and to enable them to afford decent living conditions.

Beyond traditional sheltered workshops, long-term patients need access to transitional and continuous training, placement, and on-the-job support and intervention. The New York Fountain House model provides one example of the kinds of services that can be developed. Unfortunately, the spectrum of job-related services for the mentally ill in most communities in the United States falls far short of what is needed. Worker cooperatives have been developed in the United States (Fairweather et al., 1969) and in several European countries (Warner and Polak, 1995; Warner, 2000) that provide important alternatives to existing services. In Italy, business consortiums employ a mixed workforce, including mentally ill workers, to run businesses as varied as a hotel, café, restaurant, renovation company, transport business, and furniture workshop. Other companies in the northeast of Italy run cleaning businesses, pay telephone collection enterprises, plant nurseries, and/or provide contractual services for nursing home aides.

Gheel, Belgium, has long served as a model of the effectiveness of a program designed to integrate patients into the social fabric of the community and to provide meaningful opportunities for productive work. In the United States, Fairweather and colleagues (1969) demonstrated the effectiveness of patient-run cooperative janitorial and landscaping enterprises during the 1960s. Lack of political will and a focus on symptom management are primary reasons why most communities in the United States continue to overlook the importance of developing comprehensive and effective community support programs for the long-term mentally ill.

THE COMMUNITY NEEDS
OF THE SEVERELY MENTALLY ILL

In order to reduce the likelihood of rehospitalization, the severely mentally ill must have an integrated and comprehensive system of care in the community that has reliable adequate funding and clear lines of responsibility and accountability. Such systems exist in a few progressive communities, but few states or community boards have shown the level of commitment required to implement truly comprehensive programs.

H. Richard Lamb (1998), a community psychiatrist, outlined the basic components of a system designed to provide a modicum of adequate community care for the severely mentally ill population. Lamb proposes that changes will have to occur at many levels. Some of the proposals are controversial, but his list provides a starting point for serious discussions of the many changes necessary to improve the situation of the long-term mentally ill.

Lamb's initial proposals focus on macrolevel organizational issues. First, government agencies must designate and adequately fund programs in specific regions or core entities that are manageable in size, and these core agencies must be held responsible and accountable for the care of the severely mentally ill living in that area. Staff should be assigned to individual patients for whom they hold overall responsibility.

Lamb believes that some of the laws adopted in the 1970s that made commitment more difficult remedied abuses in public hospital care but also made it more difficult to provide involuntary treatment for mentally ill persons when acute exacerbations of their illnesses occur. He suggests that legal changes are needed to facilitate a prompt return to active inpatient treatment when necessary and to facilitate the option of outpatient civil commitment, which includes mandating treatment at a mental health outpatient facility. These changes, Lamb argues, would facilitate access to care in the community, rather than "freedom" for mentally ill persons to make decisions about their lives without consideration for the well-being of themselves and others. Lamb contends that outpatients who have impaired judgment and cannot make appropriate decisions or adequately care for themselves in the community should have access to conservatorship status, which is easier to obtain. The conservation should, at a minimum, have powers related to residential placement, involvement in treatment, and management of money. In Lamb's view, when adequately trained mental health workers are able to assume conservatorship and adequate supervisory oversight is in place, both the patients' rights can be protected and staff members can use their authority to require that patients participate in treatment and take medications in order to prevent relapse. These proposed changes raise civil rights concerns, but Lamb argues that with adequate checks and balances such a system would go a long way toward providing greater opportunities for many patients to lead stable lives in the community. Many mental health workers and family members of patients who must deal with managing acute psychotic crises and patients' refusal to take medications would undoubtedly support Lamb's proposals.

Lamb argues that when people are acutely psychotic they cannot make reasonable or rational decisions about their lives or their futures. As they recover patients should of course be granted a greater role in making decisions about their lives, but recurrences and relapses of psychosis are often unpredictable and interventions must be provided in a timely manner. Having to coordinate treatment decisions with legal proceedings can result in delays that can be devastating for patients and their family members.

Lamb believes a second major organizational change must be implemented so that funding sources and service agency functions can be coordinated in such a way that one overarching agency in each community receives funding and is responsible for the overall provision of services for the chronically and severely mentally ill population. This change would go a long way to avoid the turf issues and the fragmentation of funding and responsibility that so often result in lack of cooperation and inefficiency in providing services.

At a microlevel, service providers must be trained to act not only as counselors but also as advocates for patients to gain access to supports, such as Federal Housing Administration subsidized housing and disability payments. Disability payment policies should also be altered to allow for a graduated return to full-time or part-time work without penalty or reduction of payments. Advocacy and assistance in obtaining access to Medicaid services are also essential to any comprehensive community living support program package.

Adequate mental health and rehabilitation services should be available when necessary and provided seamlessly through both inpatient and outreach programs. Outreach services should include assertive community contact with patients in the community. Assertive aftercare means that staff must go to patients' living settings to provide services if patients do not or cannot come to the treatment facility. The services provided should include assessment, crisis intervention, formulation of individualized treatment plans, and access to medication and psychosocial treatments. Rehabilitation services must also be made available that include meaningful opportunities for socialization, living and social skills training, and vocational assistance.

An appropriate community-based services system for the seriously mentally ill must assure that each patient has an ongoing therapeutic relationship with a mental health professional or case manager, who is ultimately responsible for coordination of that individual's care. Each case manager should work with the patient to formulate an individualized treatment and rehabilitation plan that includes pharmacotherapy, monitoring of the patient, and assistance in accessing and providing services. This case management approach requires adoption of a truly multidisciplinary and democratic treatment model in which teams provide services in a coordinated and assertive manner, with single-point accountability for the care of individual patients and seamless continuity and coordination of care.

In model programs, such as the Madison, Wisconsin, assertive community program (Stein, 1992), the staff works in small teams and responds to crises around the clock in order to reduce the use of hospitalization. In the long run providing crisis services, including rapid access to medication, emergency housing, and counseling, will be more effective and less costly than hospitalization. Staff members should routinely go to the patients wherever they are located in the community to provide medication monitoring and vocational, social, supportive, and recreational services. Patients cannot be expected or required to seek and maintain contacts with staff.

Housing opportunities should include a range and adequate number of graded, stepped, supervised community living opportunities that are designed to facilitate independent community living for the mentally ill population. Settings that offer multiple levels of supervision, ranging from more to less intensive, should be made available by each program. The alternatives should range from fully independent living to halfway houses, supervised satellite apartments, foster care, family care, and temporary crisis hostels.

Since at least half of all severely mentally ill patients return to their families after leaving the hospital, services such as ongoing, long-term psychoeducational services should also be made available to these homes, as well as other supports. Programs such as the family psychoeducational and individual patient treatment programs described by Hogarty and colleagues (1995) should also be made available so that families are not left on their own.

No matter how many services and treatments are provided, there will be patients who are so disabled, disorganized, or dangerous that access to long-term settings must be available. Unfortunately, jails have become inappropriate holding places for many mental patients living in the community who commit petty crimes (Torrey, 1997). Lack of access to hospital beds and current criteria for civil commitment and conservatorship have added to the large and growing mentally ill population that is incarcerated. Hospital services or locked, highly structured community alternatives (Lamb, 1997) should also be made available to provide services to those who cannot return to or stay in the community.

SUMMARY

The deinstitutionalization movement of the 1970s ended the day of the total asylum for the long-term mentally ill. As a result, we have markedly reduced the average daily census of mental hospitals, but many of the problems of long-term institutionalization have been transformed into other problems. Now we have the phenomena of the homeless mentally ill, mental patients filling and being victimized in jails and prisons, and the "revolving door" through which patients are repeatedly readmitted, medicated for a few weeks, and discharged, only to be readmitted again within a short period.

Deinstitutionalization, as it has been implemented, has not solved the problems or necessarily improved the lot of many patients; it has simply moved the problems to different settings. Until policies are adopted to implement comprehensive changes in the manner in which mental health services are provided, the problems and personal and social costs of severe mental illness will continue to mount, and we will never know what many individuals diagnosed as schizophrenic are truly capable of. There is now wide agreement that successful life in the community and elimination of the revolving door of admission, discharge, and readmission in rapid succession for people with serious mental disorders requires provision of certain key elements. These services include timely access to psychoactive medications, health care, and meaningful assistance in meeting basic needs such as housing, food, and social support (Kane and Marder, 1993). Basic services are presently integrated into most existing community care programs. Typically lacking, however, are several key elements:

1. fixed responsibility and empowerment;
2. sufficient staff, administrative flexibility, and resources to see that these services are provided around the clock;
3. continuity of responsibility for care across time, so that responsibility is not transferred to other providers and organizations as a client goes through periods of recovery and relapse;
4. appropriate levels of effort to assure that all patients have support and meaningful opportunities and incentives to find and maintain employment (Franklin et al., 1987); and
5. an adequate spectrum of supportive employment and appropriate housing opportunities.

Cost-benefit analyses indicate that comprehensive programs based on the PACT model are not more costly than traditional care and the benefits are clearly greater (Weisbrod, Test, and Stein, 1980). Patients, mental health workers, families, administrators, and the public need to recognize the limits that are likely to exist to the patient's capacities and that many patients may be dependent on others for support and assistance for the rest of their lives. Deficit and disorganization syndromes may require continuous shelter, time, and energy from providers. This should be expected for some patients, and sufficient resources and support should be provided to both patients and family members. Lack of sufficient support leads to disillusionment, burnout, and ultimately to neglect, as evidenced in our city streets.

Provision of long-term comprehensive and assertive community care can significantly increase the likelihood that many severely mentally ill individuals can live in the community with fewer rehospitalizations and improved quality of life. Medications are helpful in managing symptoms, but these treatments must be integrated with comprehensive systems of psychosocial and rehabilitative services in order to provide meaningful alternatives to institutionalization.

We have learned that the ideal of deinstitutionalization must be supplemented by development of comprehensive and adequately funded systems of care. Much of the knowledge about what works and what does not has been developed. What has been lacking is the social and political will to authorize, plan, adequately fund, and organize the changes required to implement these models. Properly funded community care is unlikely to occur as long as we focus nearly all of our hopes and money on finding "breakthrough" discoveries of brain defects and drugs to improve the lot of schizophrenic patients. The current priority given to biological solutions only justifies the status quo and helps divert funds and attention away from the critical social policy requirements and programs that are necessary to improve the quality of life and prognosis of patients today. Needs—such as increases in access to decent, affordable housing; access to job training, placement, coaching, and employment opportunities and incentives; access to settings that foster and support meaningful social contacts, outreach workers, and centers to help with acute crises—are unlikely to be adequately provided as long as the mainstream focus and priorities are based on the expectation that biological research will soon provide the "cure" for schizophrenia. Until we develop models which help us to understand that the problems we refer to as schizophrenia are the outcome of a complex and probably highly varied set of biopsychosocial problems, it is unlikely that current priorities will change.

Chapter 16

Conclusion

Schizophrenia is the diagnostic category most associated with images of frightening, bizarre, and unpredictable behaviors. We learn about cultural stereotypes of madness early in life and are socialized to avoid evidencing thoughts, feelings, and behaviors that are viewed as unrealistic or "mad." Cultural views of reality are "givens," and transgressions of these views are ridiculed and censured. Folklore, humor, and the media help to maintain stereotypes of madmen who are depicted as dangerous violators of the rules of proper thought and behavior. The image of the deluded schizophrenic serves as a centerpoint that helps reinforce social values and assumptions about proper thought and behavior. In this sense, schizophrenia serves as a symbol, one that plays a role in defining and maintaining contemporary views of social reality and social order (Claridge, 1990).

Of course, schizophrenia is more than a symbol; the term also refers to a group of severely debilitating problems that are associated with great suffering. The mainstream view is that schizophrenia is a neurodevelopmental disorder which results from the interaction of genetic predisposition, biologically acquired diathesis (e.g., prenatal infection or perinatal complications), and environmental or interpersonal stressors (e.g., poverty, social disorganization, or disturbed family functions). Despite a great deal of research on the role of genetic and neurocognitive factors in the etiology of schizophrenia, it is important to bear in mind that schizophrenia was initially and continues to be used as a somewhat arbitrary terminological convention, one that has not as yet been reliably validated against any marker. No one has reliably identified anything that is unique to schizophrenic patients after more than a century of effort. We still do not know for certain that the term refers to a homogenous group of problems or to what extent the problems are the result of biological disease (Kerr and Snaith, 1986). Schizophrenia was introduced as and remains a provisional term which refers to heterogenous disorders that share a few phenotypic features.

Many experts since Eugen Bleuler have suspected that schizophrenia is not a single disorder. We continue to use the term in the singular for want of acceptable alternatives, but serious questions remain about whether schizophrenia is merely a loose descriptive term and whether clear qualitative differences can be reliably established between schizophrenia and other serious disorders (Bentall, 1990). If schizophrenia is a heterogenous group of disorders, then contributing factors (including polygenes, neurotransmitter imbalances, prenatal viral infections, modular brain dysfunctions, early difficulties in parent-child attachment formations, family communication disturbances of various kinds, or all of these) may be relevant to some cases and not others. A systems model much more complex than Meehl's will be necessary to account for the multiple interacting developmental pathways that can result in this grouping.

Schizophrenia currently serves as a convenient abstraction that facilitates useful communication among clinicians and has limited treatment implications. Neurocognitive and neurobiological research has provided promising leads, but questions remain about whether the differences reported can be replicated in large and diverse populations of patients and whether they are etiological, correlational, or iatrogenic effects of chronic disturbances and treatments. Research indicates that subtle idiopathic neuropsychological impairments (e.g., impaired sensory gating, attentional set, modulation of arousal, unusual interhemispheric organization, impaired eye tracking, and other cognitive, affective, and linguistic difficulties) are observed more often in patients and their relatives than in controls (Nuechterlein and Dawson, 1984). The range of deficits reported is impressive, and in some cases the deficits may not be the result of the consequences of medications, institutionalization, or clinical course (Green, 1998), but these findings remain preliminary. The validity of the concept of a unitary brain-based disorder called schizophrenia will be established only when broad evidence is available that the diagnosis is associated with reliable clusters of symptoms. In addition, consistent evidence of precursors and/or deficits must be associated with the symptoms and not in carefully matched controls. When these correlates are identified in large samples prior to treatment, and when specific treatment interventions are shown to consistently alleviate the symptoms of all or most patients, then the construct will be validated.

Research has not yet indicated that there is some monolithic disorder or set of traits that characterizes patients and follows predictable rules of genetic transmission (Watt, 1984). Rather, the evidence suggests that individual variations in multiple characteristics which may not be dysfunctional in themselves contribute to later vulnerability to schizophrenia. The biological impairments thought to result from genetic vulnerability have not been reliably identified, and the evidence for a physical environmental (e.g., birth complications, viral infections, structural brain damage) etiology of schizophrenia in some unspecified portion of cases is provocative but equivocal

(Mesulam,1990). Psychosocial factors are often dismissed by contemporary researchers, but serious scholars who have carefully reviewed the literature have concluded that even though much of the evidence for psychosocial contributors is circumstantial, it is stronger than the evidence that gene-controlled biochemical changes contribute to the onset of symptoms (Mesulam, 1990). Although most contemporary researchers espouse some form of a diathesis-stress model which allows for the interaction between biological and psychosocial variables, few studies are actually designed to examine this interaction. In fact, much of the contemporary literature either explicitly or implicitly denies that psychosocial factors play any role in the etiology of schizophrenia, despite substantial evidence to the contrary. This distortion has resulted in imbalanced allocations of resources both for research and for the treatment of discharged schizophrenic patients.

Vulnerability-stress models incorporate the assumption of a graded continuum of risk for schizophrenic symptoms which can be manifested along a range from severe to mild disorder or as traits which are not associated with signs of overt illness (Chapman et al., 1994; Gottesman and Shields, 1982; Meehl, 1962). Research on family communication (Tienari et al., 1994; Goldstein, 1985) and expressed emotion (Leff and Vaughan, 1981) indicates that the quality of developmental experiences and interactions in the family can also contribute to the likelihood of developing schizophrenic symptoms. This suggests that the factors which contribute to risk for the symptoms of schizophrenia are likely to be multifactorial and multi-layered (Scheflen, 1981).

Schizophrenia may refer to a continuum of developmental disorders, the contributing causes of which may range from genetic, prenatal, and perinatal brain function deficiencies to adverse developmental, social, and culture-based experiences. If schizophrenic symptoms result from the interaction of biological factors and environmental events, these problems are unlikely to be associated with a single biological etiology and pathology (Widiger, 1997). No one can assert with credibility at this time whether schizophrenia is one disorder or several, to what extent genetics may play a role in any individual case, or what brain-based dysfunction is correlated with any particular set of symptoms. Genetic research indicates that individuals inherit unspecified vulnerabilities which increase risk for schizophrenia as well as several other mental disorders. On the other hand, a large percentage of people become schizophrenic who have no identifiable first- or second-degree relatives who have been diagnosed as schizophrenic, and many individuals with two schizophrenic parents do not become schizophrenic themselves. Obviously, other factors beyond genetics must play a role in risk for schizophrenia. Are we to believe that these other contributing factors are limited in every case to prenatal and perinatal biological factors?

The evidence supports the concept of a continuum of genetic effects with varying phenotypic expressions that may increase risk for a range of serious mental disorders (Claridge, 1990), suggesting a dimensional risk model in which genetic influences have the same status as other quantitative characteristics, such as intelligence, extraversion, anxiety proneness, quality of mood tone, activity level, or susceptibility to hypertension. It is also worthwhile to recognize that other psychological patterns strongly resemble aspects of schizophrenia. Claridge (1990), Glass (1985), and others have pointed to the similarities between the religiously or politically fanatical, the mystic, and other more socially contained forms of deviance and schizophrenic patients. These individuals are not considered to be brain diseased. It is true that many people diagnosed as schizophrenic display behaviors which are more threatening to others, and they are temporarily or permanently unable to act appropriately and to support themselves, whereas clairvoyants and fanatics are considered to be merely eccentric. But the question of why biological explanations exist for one group and psychosocial explanations for the other is more than rhetorical.

It is probably most fruitful to think in terms of individual case-specific weightings of etiological factors in schizophrenia, since it is likely to be the case that different symptom patterns are not related to different etiological factors but are related to different combinations and weightings of factors (Alanen, 1997). If, for example, a biological predisposition to schizophrenia is associated with impairments of integrative processes that occur between different functional brain centers, as Andreasen and colleagues (1996) suggest, these processes are just as likely to involve the coevolution of predisposing factors and family-based interactions as birth injuries. Impairments of neuromodular organization are inevitably accommodated, compromised, or complicated by numerous developmental and adult psychosocial experiences. Multifaceted developmental aberrations may develop as a result of the effects of the combined and interactive effects of genetic, physical-environmental, and psychosocial factors—aberrations that may include one or more indicators such as deficiencies in hierarchical neural organization, neurotransmitter instabilities, unstable affect, inhibition difficulties, impaired sensory and perceptual processing, impaired ego functions, social awkwardness, eccentric beliefs, and difficulties in developing and maintaining relationships. Early signs of aberrations undoubtedly make parenting more difficult, especially if the impairments trigger underlying parental anxieties and conflicts in the context of other family-based and socioenvironmental stresses and deficiencies. In order for the assumption that schizophrenia is caused by a discrete biological etiology and pathology to apply to the majority of cases, one would have to assume that at-risk individuals have been unaffected by the many other factors which affect psychological development, and that evidence of the effects of early stress on the physiological and behavioral development of nonhuman primates is entirely irrelevant (Suomi, 1997).

Beyond diagnostic and theoretical issues there is an urgent need to broaden our perspective regarding serious mental disorders. Most long-term schizophrenic patients live markedly impoverished and marginalized lives. Patients' needs extend beyond the provision of medications (Pilgrim, 1990; Warner, 1994). The extent of these needs and the harsh realities of the day-to-day existence of schizophrenic patients in the community are rarely mentioned in research discussions of schizophrenia. The provision of adequate funding for services to significantly increase the possibilities for an adequate quality of life has too often been overlooked in the quest for a biological etiology and "cure" for schizophrenia. A second glaring problem in the ongoing economic climate is limited access to psychotherapy for schizophrenic patients. Spending time talking with patients, getting to know them as people, and understanding their hopes, fears, and memories has become an endangered practice, threatened by misguided fiscal policies and theoretical biases.

A great deal of commitment, energy, creative thought, and financial resources has been devoted to the study of schizophrenia, and there have been some good results. Today the new atypical antipsychotic medications help many patients gain control over symptoms without unpleasant and debilitating side effects. New brain scan technologies and knowledge of neurotransmitters have contributed to important advances in the formulation of models of schizophrenia. Genetic research has advanced with development of gene-mapping technologies and offers potential in unraveling the role of genetic factors. Cognitive-behavioral and family-oriented therapists have developed practical programs to help patients maintain and develop skills to foster improved community adjustment. Psychodynamic and family researchers have sensitized us to the importance of quality parenting and family functioning in psychological development. Community-based services and support programs are much more available and comprehensive today than during the 1970s. We have made progress, but a great deal more must be done. Universal access to quality, comprehensive community-based services and interventions, provided in combination with new and more effective drugs and psychological treatments, is critical if we are to improve the lives and outcomes of people diagnosed with schizophrenia. Despite many unknowns and questions, the field has not been static. Perhaps answers will come within the next few decades, or we will decide that the wrong questions are being asked. Beneath the surface of the bizarre utterances and ideas presented by schizophrenic patients there are individuals who suffer, struggle, and attempt to cope with a world that is far more stressful and confusing than most of us can fathom. Hopefully, we will continue to make both the scientific progress and the social commitments necessary to improve the quality of their lives so that each patient has enhanced opportunities to reach his or her full potential.

It is time to acknowledge what we do not know and to advocate for increased support to help make the lives of discharged patients more livable.

References

Chapter 1

Andreasen, N.C. (1997). The evolving concept of schizophrenia: From Kraepelin to the present and future. *Schizophrenia Research, 28,* 105-109.

Bleuler, E. (1903). Dementia praecox. *Journal of Mental Pathology, 3,* 113-120.

Bleuler, E. (1920). Storung der assoziationsspannug/Ein elemantarsymptom der schizophrenie (Association disturbance/an elementary symptom of schizophrenia). *Allgemane Zeischrift der Psychiatie, 74,* 1-21.

Bleuler, E. (1923). *Lehrbuch der Psychiatrie* (Textbook of Psychiatry). Berlin, Germany: Springer.

Bleuler, E. (1924). *Textbook of psychiatry.* Translated by A.A. Brill from *Lehrbuch der Psychiatrie,* Fourth edition. New York: Macmillan.

Bleuler, E. ([1911] 1950). *Dementia praecox or the group of schizophrenias.* Translated by J. Zinkin. New York: International Universities Press.

Defendorf, A.R. (1902). *Clinical psychiatry.* Adapted from the sixth German edition of Kraepelin's *Lehrbuch der Psychiatrie.* New York: Macmillan.

Gottesman, I.I. (1991). *Schizophrenia genesis: The origins of madness.* New York: W.H. Freeman.

Kraepelin, E. (1883). *Kompendium der Psychiatrie* (Compendium of psychiatry). Leipzig: Abel.

Kraepelin, E. (1907). *Textbook of psychiatry,* Seventh edition. Translated by A.R. Diefendorf. London, UK: Macmillan.

Kraepelin, E. (1919). *Dementia praecox and paraphrenia.* Translated by M. Barclay and edited by G.M. Robertson. Edinburgh, Scotland: E. and S. Livingstone.

Kringlen, E. (1994). Is the concept of schizophrenia useful from an aetiological point of view? A selective review of findings and paradoxes. *Acta Psychiatrica Scandinavia, 90* (Supplement 384), 17-25.

Meyer, A. (1912). The value of psychology in psychiatry. *British Psychological Society, 5,* 911-914.

Palha, A.P. and Esteves, M.F. (1997). The origin of dementia praecox. *Schizophrenia Research, 28,* 99-103.

Reider, R.O. (1974). The origins of our confusion about schizophrenia. *Psychiatry, 37,* 197-208.

Spitzer, R.L., Williams, J.B., and Skodel, A., Eds. (1983). *International perspectives on DSM-III.* Washington, DC: American Psychiatric Press.

Stierlin, H. (1967). Bleuler's concept of schizophrenia: A confusing heritage. *American Journal of Psychiatry, 123,* 996-1000.

Wrobel, J. (1990). *Language and schizophrenia.* Philadelphia, PA: John Benjamins Publishing.

Chapter 2

American Psychiatric Association (1952). *Diagnostic and statistical manual*, First edition. Washington, DC: Author.

American Psychiatric Association (1968). *Diagnostic and statistical manual*, Second edition. Washington, DC: Author.

American Psychiatric Association (1980). *Diagnostic and statistical manual of mental disorders*, Third edition. Washington, DC: Author.

American Psychiatric Association (1987). *Diagnostic and statistical manual of mental disorders*, Third edition, Revised. Washington, DC: Author.

American Psychiatric Association (1994). *Diagnostic and statistical manual of mental disorders*, Fourth edition. Washington, DC: Author.

Andreasen, N.C., Arndt, S., Alliger, R., Miller, D., and Flaum, M. (1995). Symptoms of schizophrenia: Methods, meanings, and mechanisms. *Archives of General Psychiatry, 52,* 341-351.

Baron, M., Gruen, R., Rainer, J., Kane, J., Asnis, L., and Lord, S. (1985). A family study of schizophrenic and normal control probands: Implications for the spectrum concept of schizophrenia. *American Journal of Psychiatry, 142,* 447-455.

Berner, P., Katschnig, H., and Lenz, G. (1986). The polydiagnostic approach in research on schizophrenia. In A. Freedman, R. Brotman, I. Silverman, and D. Hutson, Eds., *Issues in psychiatric classification.* New York: Human Sciences Press.

Brockington, I.F. (1992). Schizophrenia: Yesterday's concept. *European Psychiatry, 7,* 203-207.

Brockington, I.F., Roper, A., Buckley, M., Copas, J., Dubas, J., and Thorpe, A. (1991). Bipolar disorder, cycloid psychosis and schizophrenia: A study using "lifetime" psychopathology ratings, factor analysis and canonical variate analysis. *European Psychiatry, 6,* 223-236.

Carpenter, W.T., Strauss, J.S., and Bartko, J.J. (1973). Flexible system for diagnosis of schizophrenia. Report from the WHO International pilot study of schizophrenia. *Science, 182,* 1275-1278.

Carpenter, W.T., Strauss, J.S., and Bartko, J.J. (1974). The diagnosis and understanding of schizophrenia. Part I: Use of signs and symptoms for the identification of schizophrenic patients. *Schizophrenia Bulletin, 11,* 37-49.

Cooper, J.E., Kendell, R.E., Gurland, B., Sharpe, L., Copeland, J., and Simon, R. (1972). *Psychiatric diagnosis in New York and London.* London, UK: Oxford University Press.

Endicott, J., Nee, J., Cohen, J., Fleiss, J., and Simon, R. (1986). Diagnosis of schizophrenia: Prediction of short term outcome. *Archives of General Psychiatry, 43,* 13-19.

Endicott, J., Nee, J., Cohen, J., Fleiss, J., Williams, J., and Simon, R. (1982). Diagnostic criteria in schizophrenia: Reliabilities and agreement between systems. *Archives of General Psychiatry, 39,* 884-889.

Feighner, J.P., Robins, E., Guze, S., Woodruff, R., Winokur, G., and Munoz, R. (1972). Diagnostic criteria for use in psychiatric research. *Archives of General Psychiatry, 26,* 57-63.

Gottesman, I.I. and Shields, J. (1972). *Schizophrenia and genetics: A twin study vantage point.* New York: Academic Press.

Guze, S.B., Cloninger, R., Martin, R., and Clayton, P.J. (1983). A follow-up in a family study of schizophrenia. *Archives of General Psychiatry, 40,* 1273-1276.

Harrow, M., Carone, B., and Westermeyer, J. (1985). The course of psychosis in early phases of schizophrenia. *American Journal of Psychiatry, 142,* 702-707.

Kendell, R.E., Cooper, J., Gourlay, A.J., Copeland, J., Sharpe, L., and Gurland, B. (1971). The diagnostic criteria of American and British psychiatrists. *Archives of General Psychiatry, 25,* 123-130.

Kendler, K.S. and Gruenberg, A. (1984). An independent analysis of the Danish adoption study of schizophrennia: IV. The relationship between psychiatric disorders as defined by DSM-III and the relatives and adoptees. *Archives of General Psychiatry, 41,* 555-564.

Kety, S.S., Rosenthal, P., Wender, P., and Schulsinger, F. (1968). The types and prevalence of mental illness in the biological and adoptive families of adopted schizophrenics. In D. Rosenthal and S.S. Kety, Eds., *The transmission of schizophrenia* (pp. 231-253). New York: Pergammon.

Kraepelin, E. (1919). *Dementia praecox and paraphrenia.* Translated by R.M. Barclay and edited by G.M. Robertson. Edinburgh, Scotland: Livingston.

Laing, R.D. (1967). *The politics of experience.* London, UK: Penguin.

Langfeldt, G. (1939). *The schizophreniform states.* New York: Oxford University Press.

Langfeldt, G. (1956). The prognosis in schizophrenia. *Acta Psychiatirca et Neurologia Scandinavia, 23,* Supplement 110, 7-66.

Langfeldt, G. (1960). Diagnosis and prognosis of schizophrenia. *Proceedings of the Royal Society of Medicine, 53,* 1047-1051.

Magaro, P. (1980). *Cognition in schizophrenia.* Hillsdale, NJ: Erlbaum.

McGlashan, T.H. (1991). The schizophrenia spectrum concept: The Chestnut Lodge followup study. In C.A. Tamminga and S. Schulz, Eds., *Advances in neuropsychiatry and psychopharmacology,* Volume I: Schizophrenia research (pp. 193-201). New York: Raven Press.

Schneider, K. (1959). *Clinical psychopathology,* Fifth edition. Translated by M.W. Hamilton. New York: Grune and Stratton.

Siever, L.J. (1991). The biology of the boundaries of schizophrenia. In C.A. Tamminga and S. Schulz, Eds., *Advances in neuropsychiatry and psychopharmacology,* Volume I: Schizophrenia research (pp. 181-191). New York: Raven Press.

Spitzer, R.L., Endicott, J., and Robins, E. (1978). Research diagnostic criteria: Rationale and reliability. *Archives of General Psychiatry, 35,* 773-782.

Stephens, J.H., Astrup, C., Carpenter, W.T., Shaffer, J., and Goldberg, J. (1982). A comparison of nine systems to diagnose schizophrenia. *Psychiatry Research, 6,* 127-143.

Szasz, T. (1957). The problem of psychiatric nosology: A contribution to a situational analysis of psychiatric operations. *American Journal of Psychiatry, 114,* 405-413.

Wing, J.K., Cooper, J.E., and Satorius, N. (1974). *The description and classification of psychiatric symptoms: An instruction manual for the PSE and Catego System.* London, UK: Cambridge University Press.

Wing, J. and Nixon, J. (1975). Discriminating symptoms in schizophrenia. *Archives of General Psychiatry, 30,* 853-859.

Winters, K., Weintraub, S., and Neale, J. (1981). Validity of MMPI code types in identifying DSM-III schizophrenics. *Journal of Consulting and Clinical Psychology, 49,* 486-487.

Chapter 3

Andreasen, N. and Flaum, M. (1991). Schizophrenia: The characteristic symptoms. *Schizophrenia Bulletin, 17,* 27-49.

Andreasen, N.C. and Grove, W. (1986). Evaluation of positive and negative symptoms in schizophrenia. *Psychiatry and Psychobiology, 1,* 108-121.

Angermeyer, M., Kuhn, L., and Goldstein, J. (1990). Gender and the course of schizophrenia: Differences in treatment outcomes. *Schizophrenia Bulletin, 16,* 293-307.

Arndt, S., Andreasen, N.C., Flaum, M., Miller, D., and Nopoulos, P. (1995). A longitudinal study of symptom dimensions in schizophrenia. *Archives of General Psychiatry, 52,* 352-360.

Astrup, C. and Odegaard, O. (1961). Internal migration and mental illness in Norway. *Psychiatric Quarterly, 34,* 116-130.

Bates, C. E. and van Dam, C. (1984). Low incidence of schizophrenia in British Columbia coastal Indians. *Journal of Epidemiology and Community Health, 38,* 127-130.

Beck, J.C. (1978). Social influences on the prognosis of schizophrenia. *Schizophrenia Bulletin, 4,* 86-101.

Belcher, J.R. (1989). On becoming homeless: A study of chronically mentally ill persons. *Journal of Community Psychology, 17,* 173-185.

Beratis, S., Gabriel, J., and Hoidas, S. (1994). Age at onset in subtypes of schizophrenic disorders. *Schizophrenia Bulletin, 20,* 287-296.

Bland, R C. and Orn, H. (1979). Schizophrenia: Diagnostic criteria and outcome. *British Journal of Psychiatry, 134,* 34-38.

Bleuler, M. (1978). *The schizophrenic disorders: Long-term patient and family studies.* New Haven, CT: Yale University Press.

Book, J.A. (1953). A genetic and neuropsychiatric investigation of a North Swedish population (with special regard to schizophrenia and mental deficiency). *Acta Genetica, 4,* 1-100.

Bradbury, T.N. and Miller, G. (1985). Season of birth in schizophrenia, A review of evidence, methodology, and aetiology. *Psychology Bulletin, 98,* 569-594.

Breier, A., Schreiber, J., Dyer, J., and Pickar, D. (1991). National Institute of Mental Health Longitudinal Study of Chronic Schizophrenia. *Archives of General Psychiatry, 48,* 239-246.

Buchanan, R.W., Kirkpatrick, B., Heinrichs, D., and Carpenter, W.T. (1990). Clinical correlates of the deficit syndrome of schizophrenia. *American Journal of Psychiatry, 147,* 290-294.

Carone, B., Harrow, M., and Westermeyer, J. (1991). Posthospital course and outcome in schizophrenia. *Archives of General Psychiatry, 48,* 247-253.

Carpenter, W.T., Kirkpatrick, B., and Buchanan, R. (1990). Conceptual approaches to the study of schizophrenia. In A. Kales, C. Stafanis, and J. Talbot, Eds., *Recent advances in schizophrenia* (pp. 93-113). New York: Springer-Verlag.

Castle, D.J. and Murray, R. (1991). The neurodevelopmental basis of sex differences in schizophrenia. *Psychological Medicine, 21,* 565-575.

Castle, D.J., Scott, K., and Wessely, S. (1993). Does social deprivation in utero or in early life predispose to schizophrenia? *Social Psychiatry and Psychiatric Epidemiology, 28,* 1-4.

Ciompi, L. (1980). Catamnestic long-term study of the course of life and aging of schizophrenic patients. *British Journal of Psychiatry, 136,* 413-420.

Ciompi, L. (1981). The social outcome of schizophrenia. In J.K. Wing, P. Kielhotz, and W. Zinn, Eds., *Rehabilitation of patients with schizophrenia and depression.* Bern, Switzerland: Hans Huber.

Ciompi, L. and Muller, C. (1976). *Lebensweg und Alter der Schizophrenen* (Wellbeing and age of schizophrenics). Berlin, Germany: Springer.

Crocetti, G.J., Lemkau, P., Kulcar, Z., and Kesic, B. (1971). Selected aspects of the epidemiology of psychoses in Croatia, Yugoslavia. III. The cluster sample and the results of the pilot survey. *American Journal of Epidemiology, 94,* 126-134.

Crow, T.J. (1985). The two-syndrome concept: Origins and current status. *Schizophrenia Bulletin, 11,* 471-485.

Dixon, L. and Rebori, T. (1995). Psychosocial treatment of substance abuse in schizophrenic patients. In C.L. Shriqui and H.A. Nasrallah, Eds., *Contemporary issues in the treatment of schizophrenia* (pp. 749-764). Washington, DC: American Psychiatric Press.

Dohan, F.C., Harper, E., Clark, M., Rodriguez, R., and Zigas, V. (1983). Where is schizophrenia rare? *Lancet, 2,* 101.

Eaton, W.W. (1991). Update on the epidemiology of schizophrenia. *Epidemiological Review, 13,* 320-328.

Fenton, W.S. and McGlashan, T. (1991). Natural history of paranoid, hebephrenic, and undifferentiated schizophrenia. *Archives of General Psychiatry, 48,* 969-977.

Flor-Henry, P. (1990). Influence of gender in schizophrenia as related to other psychopathological syndromes. *Schizophrenia Bulletin, 16,* 211-227.

Gainullin, R.G., Shmaonova, L., and Trubnikov, V. (1986). Clinico-demographic characteristics and features of the social and occupational adjustment of schizophrenic patients in three population groups inhabiting the North-Eastern region of the USSR (a clinical epidemiological investigation). *Zhurnal nevropatolgii i psihiatrii* (Korsakov), *86,* 713-719.

Goldstein, J. and Tsuang, M. (1990). Gender and schizophrenia: An introduction and synthesis of findings. *Schizophrenia Bulletin, 16,* 179-183.

Gur, R.E., Gur, R., Skolnick, B., and Resnick, S. (1988). Effects of task difficulty on regional cerebral blood flow: Relationships with anxiety and performance. *Psychophysiology, 25,* 392-399.

Haas, G., Glick, I., Clarkin, J., and Spencer, J. (1990). Gender and schizophrenia outcome: A clinical trial of an inpatient family intervention. *Schizophrenia Bulletin, 16,* 277-292.

Hafner, H., Maurer, K., Löffler, W., Bustamante, S., an der Heiden, W., Riecher-Rössler, A. et al. (1995). Onset and early course of schizophrenia. In H. Hafner and W. Gattaz, Eds., *Search for the causes of schizophrenia,* Volume III (pp. 43-66). Heidelberg, Germany: Springer-Verlag.

Harding, C., Brooks, G., Ashikaga, M., Strauss, J., and Breier, A. (1987). The Vermont longitudinal study of persons with severe mental illness: II. Long-term outcome of subjects who retrospectively met DSM-III criteria for schizophrenia. *American Journal of Psychiatry, 144,* 727-735.

Harding, C., Zubin, J., and Strauss, J. (1992). Chronicity in schizophrenia revisited. *British Journal of Psychiatry, 161,* 231-246.

Hegarty, J.D., Baldessarini, R., Tohen, M., Waternaux, C., and Oepen, G. (1994). One hundred years of schizophrenia: A meta-analysis of the outcome literature. *American Journal of Psychiatry, 151,* 1409-1416.

Hoffman, B.F. (1985). Course and outcome in schizophrenia. In M.N. Menuck and M.V. Seeman, Eds., *New perspectives in schizophrenia* (pp. 86-103). New York: Macmillan.

Hollingshead, A.B. and Redlich, F. (1954). Schizophrenia and social structure. *American Journal of Psychiatry, 110,* 695-701.

Jablensky, A. (1986). Epidemiology of schizophrenia: A European perspective. *Schizophrenia Bulletin, 12,* 52-73.

Jablensky, A. (1988). Epidemiology of schizophrenia. In P. Bebbington and P. McGuffin, Eds., *Schizophrenia: The major issues* (pp. 65-70). London, UK: Heinemann Publishing.

Jackson, J.H. (1932). *Selected writings of John Hughlings Jackson.* J. Taylor, G. Holmes, and F. Walshe, Eds. New York: Basic Books.

Kashner, T.M., Rader, L., Rodell, D., Beck, C., Rodell, L., and Muller, K. (1991). Family characteristics, substance abuse, and hospitalization patterns of patients with schizophrenia. *Hospital and Community Psychiatry, 42,* 195-197.

Kay, S.R. and Singh, M. (1989). The positive-negative distinction in drug-free schizophrenic patients. *Archives of General Psychiatry, 46,* 711-718.

Kendell, R.E., Cooper, J., Gourlay, A.J., Copeland, J., Sharpe, L., and Gurland, B. (1971). The diagnostic criteria of American and British psychiatrists. *Archives of General Psychiatry, 25,* 123-130.

Kohn, M.L. (1975). Social class and schizophrenia: A critical review and reformulation. In R. Cancro, Ed., *Annual review of the schizophrenic syndrome* (pp. 177-180). New York: Brunner/Mazel.

Kraepelin, E. (1899). *Psychiatrie: Ein Lehrbuch fur Studierende und Aerzte* (Psychiatry: A textbook for students and physicians), Fifth edition. Leipzig, Germany: University of Leipzig.

Lewine, R.J. (1988). Gender and schizophrenia. In H.A. Nasrallah, Ed., *Handbook of schizophrenia,* Volume 3 (pp. 432-436). Amsterdam: Elsevier.

Lewis, S.W. and Murray, R. (1987). Obstetric complications, neurodevelopmental deviance, and risk of schizophrenia. *Journal of Psychiatric Research, 21,* 413-421.

McGlashan, T. (1984). The Chestnut Lodge follow-up study: II. Long-term outcome of schizophrenia and the affective disorders. *Archives of General Psychiatry, 41,* 586-601.

McGlashan, T.H. (1994). Psychosocial treatments of schizophrenia. In N.C. Andreasen, Ed., *Schizophrenia: From mind to molecule* (pp. 189-218). Washington, DC: American Psychiatric Press.

Pogue-Geile, M.F. and Harrow, M. (1984). Negative and positive symptoms in schizophrenia and depression: A follow-up. *Schizophrenia Bulletin, 10,* 371-387.

Ram, R., Bromet, E., Eaton, W., Pato, C., and Schwartz, J. (1992). The natural course of schizophrenia: A review of first admission studies. *Schizophrenia Bulletin, 18,* 185-207.

Regier, D.A., Farmer, M., Rae, D., Myers, J., Kramer, M., Robins, L., George, L., Karno, M., and Locke, B. (1993). One-month prevalence of mental disorders in the United States and sociodemographic characteristics: The Epidemiological Catchment Area study. *Acta Psychiatrica Scandinavica, 88,* 35-47.

Rennie, T.A. (1939). Follow-up study of five hundred patients with schizophrenia admitted to hospital from 1913 to 1923. *Archives of Neurology and Psychiatry, 42,* 877-891.

Satorius, N., Jablensky, A., Ernberg, G., Shapiro, R., and Korton, A. (1987). Course of schizophrenia in different countries: Some results of a WHO international comparative 5-year follow-up study. In H. Hafner, W. Gattaz, and W. Jazarik, Eds., *Search for the causes of schizophrenia* (pp. 107-113). New York: Springer.

Satorius, N., Jablensky, A., and Korten, A. (1986). Early manifestations and first contact incidence of schizophrenia in different cultures. *Psychological Medicine, 16,* 909-928.

Satorius, N., Jablensky, A., and Shapiro, R. (1978). Cross-cultural differences in the short-term prognosis of schizophrenic psychoses. *Schizophrenia Bulletin, 4,* 102-113.

Satorius, N., Shapiro, R., Kimura, M., and Barrett, K. (1972). WHO International Pilot Study of Schizophrenia. Preliminary communication. *Psychological Medicine, 2,* 422-425.

Silverton, L. and Mednick, S. (1984). Class drift and schizophrenia. *Acta Psychiatrica Scandinavica, 70,* 304-309.

Stein, L.I. (1992). A system approach to reducing relapse. Paper presented at the annual meeting of the American Psychiatric Association, Washington, DC, May.

Strauss, J.S. and Carpenter, W.T. (1978). The prognosis of schizophrenia: Rationale for a multidimensional concept. *Schizophrenia Bulletin, 4,* 56-67.

Torrey, E.F. (1980). *Schizophrenia and civilization.* New York: Jason Aronson.

Torrey, E.F., McGuire, M., O'Hare, A., Walsh, D., and Spellman, M. (1984). Endemic psychosis in western Ireland. *American Journal of Psychiatry, 141,* 966-970.

Torrey, E.F., Torrey, B.B., and Burton-Bradley, B. (1974). The epidemiology of schizophrenia in Papua New Guinea. *American Journal of Psychiatry, 131,* 567-573.

Turner, R.J. and Wagenfeld, M. (1967). Occupational mobility and schizophrenia: An assessment of the social causation and social selection hypotheses. *American Sociology Review, 32,* 104-113.

Vailant, G.F. (1978). The distinction between prognosis and diagnosis in schizophrenia: A discussion of Manfred Bleuler's Paper. In L.C. Wynne, R.L. Cromwell, and S. Matthysse, Eds., *The nature of schizophrenia: New approaches to research and treatment* (pp. 167-177). New York: Wiley.

Warner, R. (1994). *Recovery from schizophrenia: Psychiatry and political economy,* Second edition. London, UK: Routledge.

Wasylenki, D., Goering, P., Lancee, W., Farkas, M., and Harrison, M. (1985). Psychiatric aftercare in a metropolitan setting. *Canadian Journal of Psychiatry, 30,* 329-336.

Wiersma, D., Nienhuis, E., Sloof, C., and Giel, R. (1998). Natural course of schizophrenic disorders: Followup of a Dutch incidence cohort. *Schizophrenia Bulletin, 24,* 75-83.

Chapter 4

Andreasen, N.C., Arndt, S., Alliger, R., Miller, D., and Flaum, M. (1995). Symptoms of schizophrenia: Methods, meanings, and mechanisms. *Archives of General Psychiatry, 52,* 341-351.

Arndt, S., Alliger, R.J., and Andreasen, N.C. (1991). The distinction of positive and negative symptoms: The failure of a two-dimensional model. *British Journal of Psychiatry, 158,* 317-322.

Bentall, R.P. (1990). The syndromes and symptoms of psychosis: Or why you can't play 20 questions with the concept of schizophrenia and hope to win. In R.P. Bentall, Ed., *Reconstructing schizophrenia* (pp. 23-60). London, UK: Routledge.

Bentall, R.P., Jackson, H., and Pilgrim, D. (1988). Abandoning the concept of "schizophrenia": Some implications of validity arguments for psychological research into psychotic phenomena. *British Journal of Clinical Psychology, 27,* 303-324.

Bleuler, E. ([1911] 1950). *Dementia praecox or the group of schizophrenias.* Translated by J. Zinkin. New York: International Universities Press.

Bovet, P. and Parnas, J. (1993). Schizophrenic delusions: A phenomenological approach. *Schizophrenia Bulletin, 19,* 579-597.

Brockington, I.F. (1992). Schizophrenia: Yesterday's concept. *European Psychiatry, 7,* 203-207.

Brown, R. (1973). Schizophrenia, language, and reality. *American Psychologist, 28,* 395-403.

Cuesta, M.J. and Peralta, V. (1995). Psychopathological dimensions in schizophrenia. *Schizophrenia Bulletin, 21,* 473-481.

Gruszecka, A. (1923). Transtywuzm, utrata granic osobowosci i myslenie pierwotna w schizofrenii. (Transitivism, loss of personality and primitive thinking in schizophrenia.) *Towarzystwo Pryja ciot Nauk.* Poznan, Poznanskie: Komiski Lekarskey.

Jaspers, K. (1963). *General psychopathology,* Seventh edition. Translated by J. Hoenig and M. Hamilton. Chicago, IL: University of Chicago Press.

Lansky, M.R. (1977). Schizophrenic delusional phenomena. *Comprehensive Psychiatry, 18,* 157-168.

Lenzenweger, M.G. and Wetherington, E. (1991). Examining the underlying structure of schizophrenic phenomenology: Evidence for a three-process model. *Schizophrenia Bulletin, 17,* 368-376.

Levi-Strauss, C. (1969). *The savage mind.* Chicago, IL: University of Chicago Press.

Levi-Strauss, C. (1973). *From honey to ashes.* New York: Harper.

Liddle, P.F. (1987). The symptoms of chronic schizophrenia: A reexamination of the positive-negative dichotomy. *British Journal of Psychiatry, 151,* 145-151.

Liddle, P.F. (1995). Inner domains within the domain of dementia praecox: Role of supervisory mental processes in schizophrenia. *European Archives of Psychiatry and Clinical Neuroscience, 245,* 210-215.

Maher, B.A. (1966). *Principles of psychopathology: An experimental approach.* New York: McGraw Hill.

Maher, B.A. (1990). The irrelevance of rationality in adaptive behavior. In M. Spitzer and B.A. Maher, Eds., *Philosophy and psychopathology* (pp. 143-156). New York: Springer-Verlag.

Maher, B.A. and Spitzer, M. (1993). Delusions. In P.B. Sutker and H. Adams, Eds., *Comprehensive handbook of psychopathology,* Second edition (pp. 263-293). New York: Plenum.

Murray, R. (1986). Schizophrenia. In P. Hill, R. Murray, and A. Thorley, Eds., *Essentials of postgraduate psychiatry,* Second edition (pp. 174-191). London, UK: Grune and Stratton.

Searles, H. (1960). *The nonhuman environment.* New York: International Universities Press.

Searles, H.F. (1965). *Collected papers on schizophrenia and related subjects.* New York: International Universities Press.

Siirala, M. (1963). Schizophrenia: A human situation. *American Journal of Psychoanalysis, 23,* 29-31.

Storch, A. (1924). *The primitive archaic forms of inner experience and thought in schizophrenia.* New York: Nervous and Mental Disease Publication Co.

Strauss, R. (1969). Hallucinations and delusions as points on continua: Rating scale evidence. *Archives of General Psychiatry, 21,* 581-586.

Sullivan, H.S. (1952). *Schizophrenia as a human process.* New York: W. W. Norton.

Tamminga, C.A. (1999). *Schizophrenia in a molecular age.* Washington, DC: American Psychiatric Press.

Wrobel, J. (1990). *Language and schizophrenia.* Philadelphia, PA: John Benjamins Publishing Co.

Chapter 5

Campbell, R.J. (1989). *Psychiatric dictionary,* Sixth edition. New York: Oxford University Press.

Cannon, T.D. (1998). Neurodevelopmental influences in the genesis and epigenesis of schizophrenia: An overview. *Applied and Preventive Psychology, 7,* 47-62.

Chapman, L.J., Chapman, J.P., and D.C. Fowles, Eds. (1993). *Progress in experimental personality and psychopathology research,* Volume 16. New York: Springer.

Cornblatt, B.A. and Erlenmeyer-Kimling, L. (1985). Global attentional deviance as a marker of risk for schizophrenia: Specificity and predictive validity. *Journal of Abnormal Psychology, 94,* 470-486.

David, A.S. and Cutting, J. (1994). *The neuropsychology of schizophrenia.* Hillsdale, NJ: Erlbaum.

Day, R. (1986). Social stress and schizophrenia. From the concept of recent life events to the notion of toxic environments. In G. Burrows, T. Norman, and G. Rubenstein, Eds., *Handbook of studies on schizophrenia: Part I: Epidemiology, aetiology and clinical features* (pp. 71-82). New York: Elsevier.

Dohrenwend, B.P. and Egri, G. (1981). Recent stressful life events and episodes of schizophrenia. *Schizophrenia Bulletin, 7,* 12-23.

Erlenmeyer-Kimling, L. (1996). A look at the evolution of developmental models of schizophrenia. In S. Matthysse, D. Levy, J. Kagan, and F. Benes, Eds., *Psychopathology: The evolving science of mental disorder* (pp. 381-390). New York: Cambridge University Press.

Erlenmeyer-Kimling, L., Cornblatt, B., Rock, D., Roberts, S., Bell, M., and West, A. (1993). The New York High-Risk Project: Anhedonia, attentional deviance, and psychopathology. *Schizophrenia Bulletin, 19,* 141-153.

Eysenck, H.J. (1992). The definition and measurement of psychoticism. *Personality and Individual Differences, 13,* 757-785.

Fowles, D.C. (1992). Schizophrenia: Diathesis-stress revisited. *Annual Review of Psychology,* Volume 43 (pp. 303-336). Palo Alto, CA: Annual Reviews.

Goldstein, M.J. and Doane, J.A. (1982). Family factors in the onset, course and treatment of schizophrenia-spectrum disorders. *Journal of Nervous and Mental Disease, 170,* 692-700.

Gottesman, I.I. and Shields, J. (1982). *Schizophrenia: The epigenetic puzzle.* Cambridge, England: Cambridge University Press.

Guze, S.B. (1989). Biological psychiatry: Is there any other kind? *Psychological Medicine, 19,* 315-323.

Iacono, W.G. (1993). Smooth pursuit oculomotor dysfunction as an index of schizophrenia. In R.L. Cromwell and C.R. Snyder, Eds., *Schizophrenia: Origins, processes, treatment, and outcome* (pp. 76-97). New York: Oxford University Press.

Kuipers, L. (1979). Expressed emotion: A review. *British Journal of Clinical Psychology, 18,* 237-243.

Leff, J., Kuipers, L., Berkowitz, R., and Eberlein-Fries, R. (1982). A controlled trial of social intervention in the families of schizophrenic patients. *British Journal of Psychiatry, 141,* 121-134.

Lidz, R. and Lidz, T. (1949). The family environment of schizophrenic patients. *American Journal of Psychiatry, 106,* 332-345.

Lyon, M., Barr, C., Cannon, T., Mednick, S., and Shore, D. (1989). Fetal neural development and schizophrenia. *Schizophrenia Bulletin, 15,* 149-161.

McGlashan, T.H. (1991). The schizophrenia spectrum concept: The Chestnut Lodge followup study. In C.A. Tamminga and S. Schulz, Eds., *Advances in neuropsychiatry and psychopharmacology,* Volume I: *Schizophrenia research* (pp. 193-201). New York: Raven Press.

McGlashan, T.H. (1994). Psychosocial treatments of schizophrenia. In N.C. Andreasen, Ed., *Schizophrenia: From mind to molecule* (pp. 189-218). Washington, DC: American Psychiatric Press.

McGuffin, P., Asherson, P., Owen, M., and Farmer, A. (1994). The strength of the genetic effect. Is there room for an environmental influence in the aetiology of schizophrenia? *British Journal of Psychiatry, 164,* 593-599.

Mednick, S.A., Watson, J., Huttunen, M., Cannon, T., Katila, H., Machon, R., Mednick, B., Hollister, M., Parnas, J., Schulsinger, F., et al. (1998). A two-hit working model of the etiology of schizophrenia. In M.F. Lenzenweger and R. Dworkin, Eds., *Origins and development of schizophrenia* (pp. 27-66). Washington, DC: American Psychological Association Press.

Meehl, P.E. (1962). Schizotaxia, schizotypy, schizophrenia. *American Psychologist, 17,* 827-838.

Meehl, P.E. (1972). Specific genetic etiology, psychodynamics, and therapeutic nihilism. *International Journal of Mental Health, 1,* 10-27.

Meehl, P.E. (1989). Schizotaxia revisited. *Archives of General Psychiatry, 46,* 936-946.

Meehl, P.E. (1990). Toward an integrated theory of schizotaxia, schizotypy, and schizophrenia. *Journal of Personality Disorders, 4,* 1-99.

Meehl, P.E. (1993). The origins of some of my conjectures concerning schizophrenia. In L.J. Chapman, J.P. Chapman, and D.C. Fowles, Eds., *Progress in experimental personality and psychopathology research,* Volume 16 (pp. 1-10). New York: Springer.

Neill, J. (1990). Whatever became of the schizophrenogenic mother? *American Journal of Psychiatry, 64,* 499-505.

Norman, R.M. and Malla, A.K. (1993). Stressful life events and schizophrenia I: A review of the literature. *British Journal of Psychiatry, 162,* 161-166.

Nuechterlein, K. (1987). Vulnerability models for schizophrenia: State of the art. In H. Hafner, W. Gattz, and W. Janarzik, Eds., *Search for the causes of schizophrenia* (pp. 127-139). Berlin, Germany: Springer.

Nuechterlein, K.H. and Dawson, M.E. (1984). Information processing and attentional functioning in the developmental course of schizophrenic disorders. *Schizophrenia Bulletin, 10,* 160-203.

Nuechterlein, K.H., Dawson, M., Gitlin, M., Ventura, J., Goldstein, M.J., Snyder, K., Yee, C., D., and Mintz, J. (1992). Developmental processes in schizophrenic disorders: Longitudinal studies of vulnerability and stress. *Schizophrenia Bulletin, 18,* 387-425.

Rabkin, J. (1980). Stressful life events and schizophrenia: A review of the research literature. *Psychological Bulletin, 87,* 408-425.

Rado, S. (1956). *Psychoanalysis of behavior.* New York: Grune and Stratton.

Risch, N. (1990). Genetic linkage and complex diseases, with special reference to psychiatric disorders. *Genetic Epidemiology, 7,* 3-16.

Sanislow, C.A. and Carson, R. (2001). Schizophrenia: A critical examination. In P.B. Sutker and H. Adams, Eds., *Comprehensive handbook of psychopathology* (pp. 403-441). New York: Kluwer/Plenum.

Tienari, P., Sorri, A., Lahti, L., Naarala, M., Wahlberg, K., Moring, J., Pohola, J., and Wynne, L. (1987). Genetic and psychosocial factors in schizophrenia: The Finnish adoptive family study. *Schizophrenia Bulletin, 13,* 477-484.

Torrey, E.F. (1980). *Schizophrenia and civilization.* New York: Jason Aronson.

Valone, K., Norton, J., Goldstein, M.J., and Doane, J. (1983). Parental expressed emotion and affective style in an adolescent sample at risk for schizophrenia spectrum disorders. *Journal of Abnormal Psychology, 92,* 399-407.

Vaughan, C.E. and Leff, J.P. (1976). The influence of family and social factors on the course of psychiatric illness. *British Journal of Psychology, 129,* 125-137.

Zahn, T.P. (1986). Psychophysiological approaches to psychopathology. In M.G. Coles, E. Donchin, and S.W. Purges, Eds., *Psychophysiology: Systems, processes and applications* (pp. 508-610). New York: Guilford.

Zubin, J. and Spring, B. (1977). Vulnerability—A new view of schizophrenia. *Journal of Abnormal Psychology, 86,* 103-126.

Zuckerman, M. (1999). *Vulnerability to psychopathology.* Washington, DC: American Psychological Association Press.

Chapter 6

Engel, G.L. (1980). The clinical application of the biopsychosocial model. *American Journal of Psychiatry, 137,* 129-136.

Gottesman, I.I. and Shields, J. (1982). *Schizophrenia: The epigenetic puzzle.* London, UK: Cambridge University Press.

Kleinman, A. (1988). *Rethinking psychiatry.* London, UK: Free Press.

Meehl, P. (1962). Schizotaxia, schizotypy, schizophrenia. *American Psychologist, 17,* 827-837.

Robbins, M. (1993). *Experiences of schizophrenia: An integration of the personal, scientific, and therapeutic.* New York: Guilford.

von Bertanlanffy, Ludwig (1952). *Problems of life.* New York: Wiley.

von Bertanlanffy, Ludwig (1967). *Robots, men and minds.* New York: Braziller.

von Bertanlanffy, Ludwig (1968). *General systems theory.* New York: Braziller.

Chapter 7

Barondes, S.H., Alberts, B.M., Andreasen, N.C., Speller, J., Barnes, T., and Curson, D. (1997). Workshop on schizophrenia. *Proceedings of the National Academy of Sciences of the USA, 94,* 1612-1614.

Barr, C., Mednick, S., and Munk-Jorgensen, P. (1990). Exposure to influenza epidemics during gestation and adult schizophrenia. A 40-year study. *Archives of General Psychiatry, 47,* 869-874.

Benjamin, L.A. (1976). A reconsideration of the Kety and associates study of genetic factors in the transmission of schizophrenia. *American Journal of Psychiatry, 133,* 1129-1137.

Bleuler, M. (1978). *The schizophrenic disorders: Long-term patient and family studies.* New Haven, CT: Yale University Press.

Boyle, M. (1990). *Schizophrenia: A scientific delusion?* New York: Routledge.

Bray, N.J. and Owen, M.J. (2001). Searching for schizophrenia genes. *Trends in Molecular Medicine, 7,* 169-174.

Cadenhead, K.S., Light, G., Geyer, M., and Braff, D. (2000). Sensory gating deficits assessed by the P50 event-related potential in subjects with schizotypal disorder. *American Journal of Psychiatry, 157,* 55-59.

Cancro, R. (1985). The schizophrenic disorders: Nosology and etiology. In M. Menuck and M. Seeman, Eds., *New perspectives in schizophrenia* (pp. 31-41). New York: Macmillan.

Cassou, B., Schiff, M., and Stewart, J. (1980). Genetique et schizophrenia: Reevaluation d'un consensus (Genetics and schizophrenia: Reevaluation of a consensus). *Psychiatrie de l'enfant, 23,* 87-201.

Fisher, M. (1973). *Genetic and environmental factors in schizophrenia.* Copenhagen, Denmark: Munksgaard.

Freedman, R., Adler, L., Olincy, A., Waldo, M., Ross, R., Stevens, K., and Leonard, S. (2002). Input dysfunction, schizotypy, and genetic models of schizophrenia. *Schizophrenia Research 54,* 25-32.

Gottesman, I.I. (1991). *Schizophrenia genesis: The origins of madness.* New York: W.H. Freeman.

Gottesman, I.I. (1993). Origins of schizophrenia: Past as prologue. In R. Plomin and G. McClearn, Eds., *Nature, nurture and psychology* (pp. 231-244). Washington, DC: American Psychological Association.

Gottesman, I.I. and Shields, J. (1982). *Schizophrenia: The epigenetic puzzle.* New York: Cambridge University Press.

Green, A., Svejgaard, A., Platz, P., Hoffman, B., and Odum, N. (1985). The genetic susceptibility to insulin-dependent diabetes mellitus: Combined segregation and linkage analysis. *Genetic Epidemiology, 2,* 1-5.

Green, M.F. (1998). *Schizophrenia from a neurocognitive perspective.* Boston, MA: Allyn and Bacon.

Gurling, H.M.D., Read, T., and Potter, M. (1991). Genetic linkage studies of schizophrenia. In P. McGuffin and R. Murray, Eds., *The new genetics of mental illness* (pp. 98-111). Oxford, UK: Butterworth-Heinemann.

Heston, L.L. (1966). Psychiatric disorders in foster home reared children of schizophrenic mothers. *British Journal of Psychiatry, 112,* 819-825.

Jackson, D.D. (1960). A critique of the literature on the genetics of schizophrenia. In D. Jackson, Ed., *The etiology of schizophrenia* (pp. 37-87). New York: Basic Books.

Jones, P. and Murray, R. (1991). Aberrant neurodevelopment as the expression of the schizophrenia genotype. In P. McGuffin and R. Murray, Eds., *The new genetics of mental illness* (pp. 113-129). Oxford, UK: Butterworth-Heinemann.

Joseph, J. (1998). The equal environment assumption of the classical twin method: A critical analysis. *Journal of Mind and Behavior, 19,* 325-358.

Joseph, J. (1999a). A critique of the Finnish adoptive family study of schizophrenia. *Journal of Mind and Behavior, 20,* 181-194.

Joseph, J. (1999b). The genetic theory of schizophrenia: A critical overview. *Ethical Human Sciences and Services, 1,* 123-141.

Karlsson, J.L. (1988). Partly dominant transmission of schizophrenia in Iceland. *British Journal of Psychiatry, 152,* 599-603.

Kendler, K., McGuire, M., Gruenberg, A., and Walsh, D. (1995). Schizotypal symptoms and signs in the Roscommon family study. *Archives of General Psychiatry, 52,* 296-303.

Kendler, K., Neale, M., Kessler, R., Heath, A., and Eayes, L. (1994). Parental treatment and the equal environment assumption in twin studies of psychiatric illness. *Psychological Medicine, 24,* 579-590.

Kendler, K. and Robinette, D. (1983). Schizophrenia in the National Academy of Sciences-National Research Council Twin Registry: A 16 year update. *American Journal of Psychiatry, 140,* 1551-1563.

Kety, S.S. (1988). Schizophrenic illness in the families of schizophrenic adoptees: Findings from the Danish national sample. *Schizophrenia Bulletin, 14,* 217-222.

Kety, S.S., Rosenthal, P., Wender, P., and Schulsinger, F. (1968). The types and prevalence of mental illness in the biological and adoptive families of adopted schizophrenics. In D. Rosenthal and S.S. Kety, Eds., *The transmission of schizophrenia* (pp. 231-253). New York: Pergammon.

Kringlen, E. (1967). Schizophrenia in twins: An epidemiological-clinical study. *Psychiatry, 29,* 172-184.

Lewontin, R., Rose, S., and Kamin, L. (1984). *Not in our genes: Biology, ideology, and human nature.* New York: Pantheon.

Lidz, T., Blatt, S., and Cook, B. (1981). Critique of the Danish-American studies of the adopted-away offspring of schizophrenic parents. *American Journal of Psychiatry, 138,* 1063-1068.

McGuffin, P. (1991). Models of heritability and genetic transmission. In H. Hafner and W. Gattaz, Eds., *Search for the causes of schizophrenia,* Volume II (pp. 109-125). Berlin, Germany: Springer-Verlag.

McGuffin, P., Asherson, P., Owen, M., and Farmer, A. (1994). The strength of the genetic effect: Is there room for an environmental influence in the aetiology of schizophrenia? *British Journal of Psychiatry, 164,* 593-599.

Meehl, P.E. (1993). The origins of some of my conjectures concerning schizophrenia. In L.J. Chapman, J.P. Chapman, and D.C. Fowles, Eds., *Progress in experimental personality and psychopathology research,* Volume 16 (pp. 1-10). New York: Springer.

Mirsky, A.F., Lochhead, S., Jones, B., Kugelmass, S., Walsh, D., and Kendler, K. (1992). On familial factors in the attentional deficit in schizophrenia: A review and report of two new subjects samples. *Journal of Psychiatric Research, 26,* 383-403.

Moldin, S.O. and Gottesman, I.I. (1997). Genes, experience, and chance in schizophrenia: Positioning for the 21st century. *Schizophrenia Bulletin, 23,* 547-561.

Murray, R.M., Lewis, S., and Reveley, A. (1985). Towards an aetiological classification of schizophrenia. *Lancet, 1*, 1023-1026.

Neale, J. and Oltmanns, T. (1980). *Schizophrenia*. New York: Wiley.

O'Driscoll, G.A., Lenzenweger, M., and Holzman, P. (1998). Antisaccades and smooth pursuit eye tracking and schizotypy. *Archives of General Psychiatry, 55*, 837-843.

Ott, J. (1986). The number of families required to detect or exclude linkage subtypes and schizophrenia. *American Journal of Human Genetics, 39*, 159-165.

Pam, A., Keinker, S., Ross, C., and Golden, R. (1996). The equal environment assumption in MZ-DZ comparisons: An untenable premise of psychiatric genetics? *Acta Geneticae Medicae et Genelloggiae, 45*, 349-360.

Pulver, A.E. (2000). Search for schizophrenia suceptibility genes. *Biological Psychiatry, 47*, 221-230.

Risch, N. (1990). Linkage strategies for genetically complex traits 1. Multilocus models. *American Journal of Human Genetics, 46*, 222-228.

Rose, S., Kamin, L., and Lewontin, R. (1984). *Not in our genes*. London, UK: Penguin.

Rosenthal, D. (1970). *Genetic theory and abnormal behavior*. New York: McGraw-Hill.

Rosenthal, D. (1971). Genetic research in the schizophrenic syndrome. In R. Cancro, Ed., *The schizophrenic reactions: A critique of the concept, hospital treatment, and current research* (pp. 245-258). New York: Brunner Mazel.

Rosenthal, D., Wender, P.H., Kety, S.S., Schulsinger, F., Welner, J., and Ostergaard, L. (1968). Schizophrenic's offspring reared in adoptive homes. In D. Rosenthal and S.S. Kety, Eds., *The transmission of schizophrenia* (pp. 377-391). Oxford, UK: Pergammon.

Schneider, F. and Deldin, P.J. (2001). Genetics and schizophrenia. In. P. Sutker and H. Adams, Eds., *Comprehensive handbook of psychopathology,* Third edition (pp. 371-402). New York: Kluwer/Plenum.

Slater, E. and Cowie, V. (1972). *The genetics of mental disorders*. Oxford, UK: Oxford University Press.

Snyder, S. (1976). Drugs for schizophrenia. *Medical World News,* May 17, p. 24.

Straub, R.E., Jiang, Y., MacLean, C., Hawi, Z., Makishev, M., and Martin, R.B. (2002). Genetic variation in the 6p22.3 gene DTNBPa, the human ortholog of the mouse dysbindin gene, is associated with schizophrenia. *American Journal of Human Genetics, 71*, 337-348.

Straub, R.E., MacLean, C., Ma, Y., Kendler, K., and MacLean, C. (2002). Genome-wide scans of three independent sets of 90 Irish multiplex schizophrenia families and followup of selected regions in all families provides evidence for multiple susceptibility genes. *Molecular Psychiatry, 7*, 542-559.

Straub, R.E., MacLean, C., O'Neill, R., and Hawi, Z. (1995). A potential vulnerability locus for schizophrenia on chromosome 6p24-22: Evidence for genetic heterogeneity. *Nature Genetics, 11*, 287-293.

Tallent, R.A. and Gooding, D. (1999). Working memory and Wisconsin Card Sorting Test performance in schizotypic individuals: A replication and extension. *Psychiatry Research, 89*, 161-170.

Thaker, G.K. (2000). Defining the schizophrenia phenotype. *Current Psychiatry Reports, 2,* 398-403.

Tienari, P. (1968). Schizophrenia in monozygotic male twins. In D. Rosenthal and S.S. Kety, Eds., *The transmission of schizophrenia* (pp. 165-189). New York: Pergammon.

Tienari, P., Sorri, A., Lahti, I., Naarala, M., Wahlberg, K., Moring, J., and Pohjola, J. (1985). Interaction of genetic and psychosocial factors in schizophrenia. *Acta Psychiatrica Scandinavica, 71* (Supplementum No. 319), 19-30.

Tienari, P., Sorri, A., Lahti, L., Naarala, M., Wahlberg, K.E., Moring, J., Pohola, J. and Wynne, L. C. (1987). Genetic and psychosocial factors in schizophrenia: The Finnish adoptive family study. *Schizophrenia Bulletin, 13,* 477-484.

Tienari, P., Wynne, L., Moring, J., Lahti, I., Naarala, M., Sorri, A., Wahlberg, K., Saarento, O., Seitamaa, M., Kaleva, M., et al. (1994). The Finnish adoptive family study of schizophrenia. *British Journal of Psychiatry, 164* (Supplement 23), 20-26.

Torrey, E.F. (1988). *Nowhere to go: The tragic odyssey of the homeless mentally ill.* New York: Harper and Row.

Torrey, E.F. (1992). Are we overestimating the genetic contribution to schizophrenia? *Schizophrenia Bulletin, 18,* 159-170.

Wender, P.H., Rosenthal, D., Kety, S., Schulsinger, F., and Welner, J. (1974). Cross-fostering: A research strategy for clarifying the role of genetic and experiential factors in the etiology of schizophrenia. *Archives of General Psychiatry, 30,* 121-128.

Wynne, L.C., Singer, M.T., Bartko, J., and Toohey, M. (1975). Schizophrenics and their families: Recent research on parental communication. In J.M. Tanner, Ed., *Psychiatric research: The widening perspective.* New York: International Universities Press.

Chapter 8

Akil, M. and Lewis, D. (1996). Reduced dopamine innervation of the prefrontal cortex in schizophrenia [Abstract]. *Society for Neuroscience Abstracts, 22,* 1679.

Andreasen, N.C. (1997). Linking mind and brain in the study of mental illnesses: A project for a scientific psychopathology. *Science, 275,* 1586-1593.

Andreasen, N.C., Arndt, S., Alliger, R., Miller, D., and Flaum, M. (1995). Symptoms of schizophrenia: Methods, meanings, and mechanisms. *Archives of General Psychiatry, 52,* 341-351.

Andreasen, N.C., Arndt, S., Swayze, V., Cizadlo, T., Flaum, M., O'Leary, D.S., Ehrhardt, J.C., and Yuh, W.T.C. (1994). Thalamic abnormalities in schizophrenia visulaized through magnetic reasonance image averaging. *Science, 266,* 294-298.

Andreasen, N. and Carpenter, W. (1993). Diagnosis and classification of schizophrenia. *Schizophrenia Bulletin, 19,* 199-214.

Andreasen, N.C., Nasrallah, H.A., Dunn, V., Olson, S.C., Grove, W.M., Ehrhardt, J.C., Coffman, J.A., Crossett, J.H.W. (1986). Structural abnormalities in the frontal system in schizophrenia: A magnetic reasonance imaging study. *Archives of General Psychiatry, 43,* 136-144.

Andreasen, N.C., O'Leary, D., Cizaldo, T., Arndt, S., Rezai, K., Boles Ponto, L.L., Watkins, G.L., Hichwa, R.D. (1996). Schizophrenia and cognitive dysmetria: A positron emission tomography study of dysfunctional prefrontal-thalamic-cerebellar circuitry. *Proceedings of the National Academy of Sciences of the United States of America, 93,* 9985-9990.

Andreasen, N.C., Paradiso, S., and O'Leary, D. (1998). "Cognitive dysmetria" as an integrative theory of schizophrenia: A dysfunction in cortical-subcortical-cerebellar circuitry? *Schizophrenia Bulletin, 24,* 203-218.

Berman, K.F., Torrey, E.F., and Daniel, G. (1989). Prefrontal cortical blood flow in monozygotic twins concordant and discordant for schizophrenia. *Schizophrenia Research, 2,* 129-138.

Bloom, F.E. (1993). Advancing a neurodevelopmental origin for schizophrenia. *Archives of General Psychiatry, 50,* 225-227.

Bogerts, B. (1993). Recent advances in the neuropathology of schizophrenia. *Schizophrenia Bulletin, 19,* 224-227.

Bogerts, B., Lieberman, J., Ashtari, M., Bilder, R., Degreef, G., Lerner, G., Johns, C., and Masiar, S. (1993). Hippocampus-amygdala volumes and psychopathology in chronic schizophrenia. *Biological Psychiatry, 33,* 236-246.

Bray, N.J. and Owen, M. (2001). Searching for schizophrenia genes. *Trends in Molecular Medicine, 7,* 169-174.

Buchanan, R.W., Breier, A., and Kirkpatrick, B. (1993). Structural abnormalities in deficit and nondeficit schizophrenia. *American Journal of Psychiatry, 150,* 59-65.

Buchanan, R.W. and Carpenter, W.T. (1997). The neuroanatomies of schizophrenia. *Schizophrenia Bulletin, 23,* 367-372.

Buschbaum, M.S., Someya, T., Teng, C.Y., Abel, L., Chin, S., Najafi, A., Haier, R.J., Wu, J., and Bunney, W.E. Jr. (1996). PET and MRI of the thalamus in never-medicated patients with schizophrenia. *American Journal of Psychiatry, 153,* 191-199.

Carlsson, M. and Carlsson, A. (1990). Schizophrenia: A subcortical neurotransmitter imbalance syndrome? *Schizophrenia Bulletin, 16,* 425-432.

Carpenter, W.T. and Kirkpatrick, B. (1988). The heterogeneity of the long-term course of schizophrenia. *Schizophrenia Bulletin, 14,* 645-652.

Casanova, M., King, M., Atkinson, D., Friston, J., Fletcher, R., and Orzeck, P. (1990). Morphometry of brain structures in schizophrenia. *Proceedings of the American Psychiatric Association (Annual Meeting)* (p. 300). New York: APA.

Cleghorn, J.M. and Albert, M.L. (1990). Modular dysjunction in schizophrenia: A framework for a pathological psychophysiology. In A. Kales, C. Stafanis, and J. Talbot, Eds., *Recent advances in schizophrenia* (pp. 86-98). New York: Springer-Verlag.

Csernansky, J.G. and Bardgett, M. (1998). Limbic-cortical neuronal damage and the pathophysiology of schizophrenia. *Schizophrenia Bulletin, 24,* 231-248.

Daniel, D.G. and Weinberger, D.R. (1991). Ex multi uno: A case for neurobiological homogeneity in schizophrenia. In C.A. Tamminga and S. Schulz,

Eds., *Advances in neuropsychiatry and psychopharmacology,* Volume I: *Schizophrenia research* (pp. 227-235). New York: Raven Press.

Daviss, S.R. and Lewis, D. (1995). Local circuit neurons of the prefrontal cortex in schizophrenia: Selective increase in the density of calbindin-immunoreactive neurons. *Psychiatry Research, 59,* 81-96.

DeLisi, L.E., Hoff, A.L., and Schwartz, J. (1991). Brain morphology in first-episode schizophrenic-like psychotic patients: A quantitative magnetic resonance imaging study. *Bilogical Psychiatry, 29,* 159-175.

Fletcher, P.C. (1995). Patterns of cerebral blood flow associated with hallucination types. *Cognition, 57,* 109.

Frith, C.D. (1992). *The cognitive neuropsychology of schizophrenia.* Hove, Sussex, England: L. Erlbaum.

Goldberg, T.E. and Weinberger, D.R. (1988). Neuropsychological studies of schizophrenia. *Schizophrenia Bulletin, 14,* 179-184.

Kirkpatrick, B., Amador, X., Yale, S., Bustillo, J., Buchanan, R., and Tohen, M. (1996). The deficit syndrome in the DSM-IV field trial part II: Depressive episodes and persecutory beliefs. *Schizophrenia Research, 20,* 79-90.

Kling, A.S., Kurtz, N., Tachiki, K., and Orzeck, A. (1982). CT scans in sub-groups of chronic schizophrenics. *Journal of Psychiatric Research, 83,* 375-384.

Kraepelin, E. (1919). *Dementia praecox and paraphrenia.* Translated by M. Barclay and edited by G.M. Robertson. Edinburgh, Scotland: E. and S. Livingstone.

Levy, D. (1996). Location, location, location: The pathway from behavior to brain locus in schizophrenia. In S. Matthysse, D. Levy, J. Kagan, and F. Benes, Eds., *Psychopathology: The evolving science of mental disorder* (pp. 132-141). Cambridge, England: Cambridge University Press.

Lewis, S.W. and Murray, R. (1987). Obstetric complications, neurodevelopmental deviance and risk of schizophrenia. *Journal of Psychiatric Research, 21,* 413-421.

Liddle, P.F., Friston, K., Firth, C., and Hirsch, S. (1992). Patterns of cerebral blood flow in schizophrenia. *British Journal of Psychiatry, 160,* 179-186.

Maher, B.A. and Deldin, P. (2001). Schizophrenia: Biopsychological aspects. In P. Sutker and H. Adams, Eds., *Comprehensive handbook of psychopathology,* Third edition (pp. 341-370). New York: Kluwer/Plenum.

McCarley, R.W., Shenton, M., and O'Donnell, B. (1993). Auditory P300 abnormalities and left posterior superior temporal gyrus volume reduction in schizophrenia. *Archives of General Psychiatry, 50,* 197-203.

McGuire, P.K. and Frith, C.D. (1998). Hallucinations and cerebral blood flow. *Psychological Medicine, 26,* 663.

McGuire, P.K., Silbersweig, D.A., Wright, I., Murray, R.M., Frackowiak, R.S., and Frith, C.D. (1996). The neural correlates of inner speech and auditory verbal imagery in schizophrenia: Relationship to auditory verbal hallucinations. *British Journal of Psychiatry, 169,* 148-159.

O'Donnell, P. and Grace, A. (1994). Tonic D2-mediated attenuation of cortical excitation in nucleus pons recorded in vitro. *Brain Research, 634,* 105-112.

O'Donnell, P. and Grace, A. (1995). Synaptic interactions among excitatory afferents to nucleus accumbens neurons: Hippocampal gating of prefrontal cortical input. *Journal of Neuroscience, 15,* 3622-3639.

O'Donnell, P. and Grace, A.A. (1998). Dysfunctions in multiple interrelated systems as the neurobiological bases of schizophrenic symptom clusters. *Schizophrenia Bulletin, 24,* 267-283.

Pakkenberg, B. (1993). Leucotomized schizophrenics lose neurons in the mediodorsal thalamic nucleus. *Neuropathology and Applied Neurobiology, 19,* 373-380.

Pennartz, C.M., Dollerman-van der Weel, M., Kitai, S., and Lopes da Silva, F. (1992). Presynaptic dopamine D1 receptors attenuate excitatory and inhibitory limbic inputs to the shell region of the rat nucleus accumbens. *Journal of Neurophysiology, 67,* 1325-1334.

Rao, M.L. and Moller, H. (1994). Biochemical findings of negative symptoms in schizophrenia and their putative relevance to pharmacological treatment. *Pharmacopsychiatry, 30,* 160-172.

Roberts, G.W. and Bruton, C. (1990). Notes from the graveyard: Schizophrenia and neuropathology. *Neuropathology and Applied Neurobiology, 16,* 3-16.

Seeman, P. (1987). Dopamine receptors and the dopamine hypothesis of schizophrenia. *Synapse, 1,* 133-152.

Silbersweig, D.A., Stern, E., Firth, C.D., Cahill, C., Holmes, A., Grootoonk, S., Seaward, J., McKenna, P., Chua, S.E., Schnorr, L., et al. (1995). Brain activtion patterns associated with hallucinatory experiences. *Nature, 378,* 176-180.

Spitzer, M. (1993). The psychopathology, neuropathology, and neurobiology of associative and working memory in schizophrenia. *European Archives of Psychiatry and Clinical Neuroscience, 243,* 57-70.

Stevens, J.R. (1997). Anatomy of schizophrenia revisited. *Schizophrenia Bulletin, 23,* 373-383.

Suddath, R.L., Christison, G.W., Torrey, E., Casanova, M., and Weinberger, D. (1990). Anatomical abnormalities in the brains of monozygotic twins discordant for schizophrenia. *New England Journal of Medicine, 322,* 789-794.

Ulas, J. and Cotman, C. (1993). Excitatory amino acid receptors in schizophrenia. *Schizophrenia Bulletin, 19,* 105-117.

Weinberger, D.R. (1987). Implications of normal brain development for the pathogenesis of schizophrenia. *Archives of General Psychiatry, 44,* 660-669.

Wible, C.G., Shenton, M., Hokama, H., Kikinis, R., Gulevich, G., and Slominski, R. (1995). Prefrontal cortex and schizophrenia. *Archives of General Psychiatry, 52,* 279-288.

Wolkin, A., Sanfilipo, M., Wolf, A., Angrist, B., and Alligor, R. (1992). Negative symptoms and hypofrontality in chronic schizophrenia. *British Journal of Psychiatry, 49,* 959-963.

Chapter 9

Beasley, C.M., Tollefson, G., Tran, P., Satterlee, W., Sanger, T., and Hamilton, S. (1996). Olanzepine versus placebo and haloperidol: Acute phase results of the

North American double-blind olanzepine trial. *Neuropsychopharmacology, 14,* 111-123.

Bergson, C., Mrzljak, L., Smiley, J.F., Pappy, M., Levenson, R., and Goldman-Rakic, P.S. (1995). Regional, cellular, and subcellular variations in the distribution of D1 and D5 dopamine receptors in primate brain. *Journal of Neuroscience, 15,* 7821-7836.

Bray, N.J. and Owen, M. (2001). Searching for schizophrenia genes. *Trends in Molecular Medicine, 7,* 169-174.

Carlsson, A. (1983). Antipsychotic agents: Elucidation of their mode of action. In M.J. Parham and J. Bruinvels, Eds., *Psycho- and neuropharmacology* (pp. 197-206). Amsterdam, Netherlands: Elsevier.

Carlsson, A. (1987). The dopamine hypothesis of schizophrenia 20 years later. In H. Hafner, W. Gattaz, and W. Janzarik, Eds., *Search for and the causes of schizophrenia* (pp. 111-130). Berlin, Germany: Springer-Verlag.

Carlsson, M. and Carlsson, A. (1990). Schizophrenia: A subcortical neurotransmitter imbalance syndrome? *Schizophrenia Bulletin, 16,* 425-432.

Creese, I. (1983). Classical and atypical antipsychotic drugs: New insights. *Trends in Neurosciences, 6,* 479-481.

Davis, J.M. (1976). Recent developments in the drug treatment of schizophrenia. *American Journal of Psychiatry, 133,* 208-214.

Deutch, A.Y., Moghaddam, B., Innis, R., Krystal, J., Aghajanian, G., Bunney, B., and Charney, D. (1991). Mechanisms of action of atypical antipsychotic drugs: Implications for novel therapeutic strategies for schizophrenia. *Schizophrenia Research, 4,* 121-156.

Fahy, T., Woodruff, P., and Szmukler, G. (1998). The aetiology of schizophrenia. In G. Stein and G. Wilkinson, Eds., *Seminars in general adult psychiatry,* Volume 1. Washington, DC: American Psychiatric Association Press.

Farde, L., Wiesel, F., Halldin, C., and Sedvall, G. (1988). Central D_2-dopamine receptor occupancy in schizophrenic patients treated with antipsychotic drugs. *Archives of General Psychiatry, 45,* 71-78.

Gao, W.J., Krimer, L., and Goldman-Rakic, P. (2001). Presynaptic regulation of recurrent excitation by D1 receptors in prefrontal circuits. *Proceedings of the National Academy of Sciences of the USA, 98,* 295-300.

Goff, D.C., Tsai, G., Manoach, D., and Coyle, J. (1995). Dose-finding trial of D-cycloserine added to neuroleptics for negative symptoms in schizophrenia. *American Journal of Psychiatry, 152,* 1213-1215.

Grace, A.A. (1991). Phasic versus tonic dopamine release and the modulation of dopamine system responsivity: A hypothesis for the etiology of schizophrenia. *Neuroscience, 41,* 1-24.

Gunne, L.M. and Haggstrom, J. (1985). Pathophysiology of tardive dyskinesia. In D.E. Casey, T. Chase, A. Christensen, and J. Gerlach, Eds., *Dyskinesia: Research and treatment* (pp. 191-193). New York: Springer.

Harding, C.M., Brooks, G., Ashikaga, T., Strauss, J., and Breier, A. (1987). The Vermont longitudinal study of persons with severe mental illness: II. Long-term outcome of subjects who retrospectively met DSM-III criteria for schizophrenia. *American Journal of Psychiatry, 144,* 727-735.

Hegarty, J.D., Baldessarini, R., Tohen, M., Waternaux, C., and Oepen, G. (1994). One hundred years of schizophrenia: A meta-analysis of the outcome literature. *American Journal of Psychiatry, 151,* 1409-1416.

Hirsch, S. (1982). Medication and physical treatment of schizophrenia. In J.K. Wing and L. Wing, Eds., *Psychoses of uncertain aetiology: Handbook of psychiatry 3* (pp. 74-87). Cambridge, UK: Cambridge University Press.

Jibson, M.D. and Tandon, R. (1998). New atypical antipsychotic medications. *Journal of Psychiatric Research, 32,* 215-228.

Kane, J.M., Woerner, M., Borenstein, M., Wegner, J., and Lieberman, J. (1986). Integrating incidence and prevalence of tardive dyskinesia. *Psychopharmacology Bulletin, 22,* 254-258.

Kapur, S., Zipursky, R., Jones, C., Shammi, C., Remington, G., and Seeman, P. (2000). A positron emission tomography study of quetiapine in schizophrenia: A preliminary finding of an antipsychotic effect with only transiently high dopamine D_2 receptor occupancy. *Archives of General Psychiatry, 57,* 553-559.

Meltzer, H.Y. (1989). Clozapine: Clinical advantages and biological mechanisms. In S.C. Schultz and C. Tamminga, Eds., *Schizophrenia: Scientific progress.* New York: Oxford University Press.

Owens, D.G. (1998). The drug treatment of schizophrenia. In G. Stein and G. Wilkinson, Eds., *Seminars in general adult psychiatry,* Volume 1. Washington, DC: American Psychiatric Press.

Owens, D.G. and Firth, C. (1982). Spontaneous involuntary disorders of movement: Their prevalence, severity and distribution in chronic schizophrenics with and without treatment with neuroleptics. *Archives of General Psychiatry, 156,* 620-634.

Owens, D.G. and Johnstone, E. (1980). The disabilities of chronic schizophrenia: Their nature and the factors contributing to their development. *British Journal of Psychiatry, 136,* 384-395.

Snyder, S.H. (1978). Dopamine and schizophrenia. In L.C. Wynne, R. Cromwell, and S. Matthysse, Eds., *The nature of schizophrenia.* New York: Wiley.

Stoof, J.C. and Kebabian, J.W. (1981). Opposing roles for D-1 and D-2 dopamine receptors in the efflux of cyclic AMP from rat neostriatum. *Nature, 294,* 366-368.

Tuma, A.H. and May, R.R. (1979). And if it doesn't work, what next? A study of treatment failures in schizophrenia. *Journal of Nervous and Mental Disease, 167,* 566-571.

Warner, R. (1994). *Recovery from schizophrenia: Psychiatry and the political economy,* Second edition. New York: Routledge and Kegan Paul.

Chapter 10

Asarnow, R.F., Granholm, E., and Sherman, T. (1991). Span of apprehension in schizophrenia. In S.R. Steinhauer, J. Gruzelier, and J. Zubin, Eds., *Handbook of schizophrenia: Neuropsychology, psychophysiology, and information processing,* Volume 5 (pp. 335-370). Amsterdam, Netherlands: Elsevier.

Baum, K. M. and Walker, E. (1995). Childhood behavioral patterns of adult symptom dimensions in schizophrenia. *Schizophrenia Research, 16,* 111-120.

Brenner, H., Roder, V., Hodel, B., Kienzie, N., Reed, D., and Liberman, R. (1994). *Integrated psychological therapy for schizophrenic patients.* Toronto, Canada: Hgrefe and Huber.

Broen, W.E. and Storms, L. (1966). Lawful disorganization: The process underlying a schizophrenic syndrome. *Psychological Review, 73,* 256-279.

Calev, V., Venables, P., and Monk, A. (1983). Evidence for distinct verbal memory pathologies in severely and mildly disturbed schizophrenia. *Schizophrenia Bulletin, 9,* 533-542.

Cornblatt, B.A. and Erlenmeyer-Kimling, L. (1985). Global attentional deviance as a marker of risk for schizophrenia: Specificity and predictive validity. *Journal of Abnormal Psychology, 94,* 470-486.

Corrigan, P.W., Hirschbeck, J., and Wolfe, M. (1995). Memory and vigilance training to improve social perception in schizophrenia. *Schizophrenia Research, 17,* 257-265.

David, A.S. and Cutting, J. (1994). *The neuropsychology of schizophrenia.* Hillsdale, NJ: Erlbaum.

Dawson, M.E. and Nuechterlein, K.H. (1984). Psychophysiological dysfunctions in the developmental course of schizophrenic disorders. *Schizophrenia Bulletin, 10,* 204-232.

Feinberg, J. (1983). Schizophrenia caused by a fault in programmed synaptic elimination during adolescence? *Journal of Psychiatric Research, 17,* 319.

Green, M.F. (1998). *Schizophrenia from a neurocognitive perspective: Probing the impenetrable darkness.* Boston, MA: Allyn and Bacon.

Green, M.F., Nuechterlein, K., and Mintz, J. (1994). Backward masking in schizophrenia and mania: Specifying the mechanism. *Archives of General Psychiatry, 51,* 939-944.

Green, M.F., Satz, P., Gaier, D., Ganzell, S., and Kharabi, F. (1989). Minor physical anomalies in schizophrenia. *Schizophrenia Bulletin, 15,* 91-99.

Heaton, R.K. (1981). *Wisconsin card sorting test manual.* Odessa, FL: Psychological Assessment Resources.

Hogarty, G. and Flesher, S. (1999a). A developmental theory for cognitive enhancement therapy of schizophrenia. *Schizophrenia Bulletin, 25,* 677-692.

Hogarty, G. and Flesher, S. (1999b). Practice principles of cognitive enhancement therapy for schizophrenia. *Schizophrenia Bulletin, 25,* 693-708.

Holzman, P.S., Kringlen, E., Levy, D., and Haverman, S. (1980). Deviant eye tracking in twins discordant for psychosis: A replication. *Archives of General Psychiatry, 37,* 627-631.

Holzman, P.S. and Matthysse, S. (1990). The genetics of schizophrenia: A review. *Psychological Science, 1,* 279-286.

Keshavan, M.S. (1997). Neurodevelopment and schizophrenia: Quo vadis? In M.S. Keshavan and R. Murray, Eds., *Neurodevelopment and adult psychopathology.* New York: Cambridge University Press.

Matthysse, S., Holzman, P., and Lange, K. (1986). The genetic transmission of schizophrenia. Application of a Mendelian latent trait structure analysis to eye tracking dysfunctions in schizophrenia and affective disorder. *Journal of Psychiatric Reearch, 20,* 57-76.

Mednick, S.A., Machon, R., Huttunen, M., and Bontett, D. (1988). Adult schizophrenia following paternal exposure to an influenza epidemic. *Archives of General Psychiatry, 45,* 189-192.

Mirsky, A.F., Ingraham, L., and Kugelmass, S. (1995). Neuropsychological assessment of attention and its pathology in the Israeli cohort. *Schizophrenia Bulletin, 21,* 193-204.

Mueser, K., Doonan, B., Penn, D., Blanchard, J., Bellack, A., and DeLeon, J. (1996). Emotion recognition and social competence in chronic schizophrenia. *Journal of Abnormal Psychology, 105,* 271-275.

Nasrallah, H.A. (1982). Laterality and hemispheric dysfunction in schizophrenia. In F.A. Henn and H.A. Nasrallah, Eds., *Schizophrenia as a brain disease* (pp. 273-294). New York: Oxford University Press.

Neumann, C.S. and Walker, E.F. (1996). Childhood neuromotor soft signs, behavior problems and adult psychopathology. In T.H. Ollendick and R. Prinz, Eds., *Advances in Clinical Child Psychology, 18,* 173-203.

Nuechterlein, K. (1991).Vigilance in schizophrenia and related disorders. In S.R. Steinhauer, J. Gruzelier, and J. Zubin, Eds., *Handbook of schizophrenia,* Volume 5 (pp. 397-433). Amsterdam, Netherlands: Elsevier.

Nuechterlein, K.H. and Dawson, M.E. (1984). Information processing and attentional functioning in the developmental course of schizophrenic disorders. *Schizophrenia Bulletin, 10,* 160-203.

Palmer, B., Heaton, R., Paulsen, J., Kuck, J., Braff, D., Harris, M., Zisook, S., and Jeste, D. (1997). Is it possible to be schizophrenic yet neuropsychologically normal? *Neuropsychology, 11,* 437-446.

Penn, D.L., Corrigan, P., Bentall, R., Racenstein, J., and Newman, L. (1997). Social cognition in schizophrenia. *Psychological Bulletin, 121,* 114-132.

Servan-Schreiber, D., Cohen, J., and Steingard, S. (1996). Schizophrenic deficits in the processing of context: A test of neural network simulations of cognitive functioning in schizophrenia. *Archives of General Psychiatry, 53,* 1105-1112.

Siever, L.J. (1991). The biology of the boundaries of schizophrenia. In C.A. Tamminga and S. Schulz, Eds., *Advances in neuropsychiatry and psychopharmacology,* Volume I: *Schizophrenia research* (pp. 181-191). New York: Raven Press.

Spaulding, W.D. and Poland, J. (2001). Cognitive rehabilitation for schizophrenia: Enhancing social cognition by strengthening neurocognitive functioning. In P. Corrigan and D. Penn, Eds., *Social cognition and schizophrenia* (pp. 217-247). Washington, DC: American Psychological Association.

Spaulding, W.D., Reed, D., Sullivan, M., Richardson, C., and Weiler, M. (1999). Effects of cognitive treatment in psychiatric rehabilitation. *Schizophrenia Bulletin, 25,* 275-289.

Toomey, R., Seidman, I., Lyons, M., Farone, S., and Tsuang, M. (1999). Poor perception of nonverbal social-emotional cues in relatives of schizophrenic patients. *Schizophrenia Research, 40,* 121-130.

Walker, E.F., Neumann, C., Baum, K., and Davis, D. (1996). The developmental pathways to schizophrenia: Potential moderating effects of stress. *Development and Psychopathology, 8,* 647-665.

Walker, E.F., Savoie, T., and Davis, D. (1994). Neuromotor precursors of schizophrenia. *Schizophrenia Bulletin, 20,* 441-451.

Weinberger, D.R. (1987). Implications of normal brain development for the pathogenesis of schizophrenia. *Archives of General Psychiatry, 44,* 660-669.

Weinberger, D.R. (1995). From neuropathology to neurodevelopment. *Lancet, 346,* 552-557.

Weinberger, D.R., Berman, K., and Zec, R. (1986). Physiological dysfunction of dorsolateral prefrontal cortex in schizophrenia. *Archives of General Psychiatry, 43,* 114-124.

Wykes, T., Reeder, C., Corner, J., Williams, C., and Everett, R. (1999). The effects of neurocognitive remediation on executive processing inpatients with schizophrenia. *Schizophrenia Bulletin, 25,* 291-307.

Zubin, J. and Spring, B. (1977). Vulnerability: A new view of schizophrenia. *Journal of Abnormal Psychology, 86,* 103-126.

Chapter 11

Anderson, C.M., Reiss, D.J., and Hogarty, G.E. (1986). *Schizophrenia and the family.* New York: Guilford.

Arieti, S. (1962). Hallucinations, delusions, and ideas of reference treated with psychotherapy. *American Journal of Psychotherapy, 16,* 56-60.

Ayllon, T. (1966). Some behavioral problems associated with eating in chronic schizophrenic patients. In L. Krasner and L. Ullman, Eds., *Case studies in behavior modification.* New York: Holt, Rinehart, Winston.

Bateson, G., Jackson, D.D., Haley, J., and Weakland, J. (1956). Toward a theory of schizophrenia. *Behavioral Science, 1,* 251-264.

Beck, A.T. (1952). Successful outpatient psychotherapy of a chronic schizophrenic with a delusion based on borrowed guilt. *Behavior Therapy, 25,* 17-33.

Bellack, A.S. and Hersen, M. (1979). *Research and practice in social skills training.* New York: Plenum Press.

Bellack, A.S., Mueser, K.T., Gingerich, S., and Agresta, J. (1997). *Social skills training for schizophrenia.* New York: Guilford.

Bowlby, J. (1973). *Attachment and loss.* Volume 2: *Separation.* London, UK: Hogarth Press.

Brown, G.W., Birley, J., and Wing, J. (1972). Influence of family life on the course of schizophrenic disorders. *British Journal of Psychiatry, 121,* 241-258.

Brown, G.W. and Rutter, M. (1966). The measurement of family activities and relationships: A methodological study. *Human Relations, 19,* 241-263.

Chadwick, P.D.P. and Birchwood, M. (1994). The omnipotence of voices: A cognitive approach to auditory hallucinations. *British Journal of Psychiatry, 164,* 190-201.

Chadwick, P.D.P. and Lowe, C.F. (1994). A cognitive approach to measuring and modifying delusions. *Behavior Research and Therapy, 32,* 355-367.

Corcoran, R. (2001). Theory of mind and schizophrenia. In P.W. Corrigan and D.L. Penn, Eds., *Social cognition and schizophrenia.* Washington, DC: American Psychological Association Press.

Davidson, L., Lambert, S., and McGlashan, T. (1998). Psychotherapeutic and cognitive-behavioral treatments for schizophrenia. In C. Perris and P.D. McGorry, Eds., *Cognitive psychotherapy of psychotic and personality disorders* (pp. 1-20). New York: John Wiley and Sons.

Drury, V., Birchwood, M., Cochrane, R., and MacMillan, F. (1996a). Cognitive therapy and recovery from acute psychosis: A controlled trial. I. Impact on psychotic symptoms. *British Journal of Psychiatry, 169,* 593-601.

Drury, V., Birchwood, M., Cochrane, R., and MacMillan, F. (1996b). Cognitive therapy and recovery from acute psychosis: II. Impact on recovery time. *British Journal of Psychiatry, 169,* 602-607.

Edwards, J. and McGorry, P.D. (1998). Early intervention in psychotic disorders. In C. Perris and P.D. McGorry, Eds., *Cognitive psychotherapy of psychotic and personality disorders.* New York: Wiley.

Falloon, I.R.H., Boyd, J.L., McGill, C., Williamson, M., Razani, J., Moss, H., Gilderman, A., and Simpson, G. (1985). Family management in the prevention of morbidity of schizophrenia. Clinical outcome of a two-year longitudinal study. *Archives of General Psychiatry, 42,* 887-896.

Fowler, D. (1992). Cognitive behavior therapy in management of patients with schizophrenia: A preliminary study. In A. Werbatt and J. Gullberg, Eds., *Psychotherapy of schizophrenia: Facilitating and obstructive factors.* Oslo, Norway: Scandinavian University Press.

Fowler, D., Garety, P., and Kuipers, E. (1995). *Cognitive behavior therapy for psychosis: Theory and practice.* Chicester, England: Wiley.

Frith, C.D. (1992). *The cognitive neuropsychology of schizophrenia.* Hillsdale, NJ: Erlbaum.

Garety, P.A. (1992). Making sense of delusions. *Psychiatry, 55,* 282-291.

Garety, P.A., Kuipers, E., Fowler, O., Chamberlin, F., and Dunn, G. (1994). Cognitive behavior therapy for drug resistant psychosis. *British Journal of Medical Psychology, 67,* 259-271.

Hogarty, G.E., Kornblith, S., Greenwald, D., DiBarry, A., Cooley, S., Flesher, S., and Leff, J. (1995). Personal therapy: A disorder relevant psychotherapy for schizophrenia. *Schizophrenia Bulletin, 21,* 379-393.

Horowitz, M.J. (1986). Stress-response syndromes: A review of posttraumatic and adjustment disorders. *Hospital and Community Psychiatry, 37,* 341-349.

Jackson, H., McGorry, P., Edwards, J., and Hulbert, C. (1996). Cognitively oriented psychotherapy for early psychosis (COPE). In P. Cotton and H. Jackson, Eds., *Early intervention and prevention in mental health* (pp. 213-227). Melbourne, Australia: Australian Psychological Society.

Jacobs, L. (1980). A cognitive approach to persistent delusions. *American Journal of Psychotherapy, 34,* 556-563.

Kavanaugh, D.J. (1992). Recent developments in expressed emotion and schizophrenia. *British Journal of Psychiatry, 160,* 601-620.

Kazdin, A.E. and Bootzin, R. (1972). The token economy: An evaluative review. *Journal of Applied Behavior Analysis, 5,* 343-372.

Kingdon, D.G. and Turkington, D. (1994). *Cognitive-behavioral therapy of schizophrenia.* New York: Guilford.

Leff, J.P. and Berkowitz, R. (1996). Working with the families of schizophrenic patients. In P.R. Breggin and E.M. Stern, Eds., *Psychosocial approaches to deeply disturbed persons* (pp. 63-85). Binghamton, NY: The Haworth Press.

Leff, J.P., Berkowitz, R., Shavit, N., Strachan, A., Glass, J., and Vaughn, C. (1990). A trial of family therapy vs a relatives' group for schizophrenia: A two year follow-up. *British Journal of Psychiatry, 157,* 571-577.

Leff, J.P. and Vaughn, C. (1981). The role of maintenance therapy and relatives expressed emotions in relapse of schizophrenia: A two-year followup. *British Journal of Psychiatry, 139,* 102-104.

Liberman, R.P., Mueser, K., and Wallace, C. (1986). Social skills training for schizophrenic individuals at risk for relapse. *American Journal of Psychiatry, 141,* 523-526.

Liberman, R.P, Mueser, K., Wallace, C., Jacobes, H., Eckman, T., and Massel, H. (1986). Training skills in the psychiatrically disabled: Learning coping and competence. *Schizophrenia Bulletin, 12,* 631-647.

Lidz, T., Cornelison, A., Fleck, S., and Terry, D. (1957). The intrafamilial environment of the schizophrenic patient. I. *Psychiatry, 20,* 329-342.

Liotti, G. (1988). Attachment and cognition. In C. Perris, I. Blackburn, and H. Perris, Eds., *Cognitive psychotherapy: Theory and practice.* Heidelberg, Germany: Springer.

Maher, B.A. (1974). Delusional thinking and perceptual disorder. *Journal of Individual Psychology, 30,* 98-113.

McCann, L. and Pearlman, L. (1990). *Psychological trauma and the adult survivor: Theory, therapy and transformation.* New York: Brunner/Mazel.

McGorry, P.D., Henry, L., Maude, D., and Phillips, L. (1998). Preventively-orientated psychological interventions in early psychosis. In C. Perris and P.D. McGorry, Eds., *Cognitive psychotherapy of psychotic and personality disorders.* New York: Wiley.

Meichenbaum, D. and Cameron, B. (1973). Training schizophrenics to talk to themselves: A means of developing attentional controls. *Behavior Therapy, 4,* 515-534.

Mueser, K.T. and Glynn, S.M. (1995). *Behavioral family therapy for psychiatric disorders.* Needham Heights, MA: Allyn and Bacon.

Perris, C. (1989). *Cognitive therapy with schizophrenic disorders.* New York: Guilford.

Raphael, B. (1986). *When disaster strikes: How individuals and communities cope with catastrophe.* New York: Basic Books.

Roberts, G. (1992). The origins of delusion. *British Journal of Psychiatry, 161,* 298-308.

Schaub, A. (1998). Cognitive-behavioral coping-orientated therapy for schizophrenia: A new treatment model for clinical service and research. In C. Perris and P.D. McGorry, Eds., *Cognitive therapy of psychotic and personality disorders.* New York: Wiley.

Schaub, A., Andres, K., Brenner, H., and Donzel, G. (1997). Developing a novel coping orientated treatment programme for schizophrenic patients. In H.D. Brenner, W. Hoker, and R. Genner, Eds., *Integrative therapy of schizophrenia.* (pp. 228-251). Bern, Switzerland: Huber.

Schooler, N.R., Levine, J., Serene, J., Brauyer, B., Dimocia, A., Klerman, G., and Tuason, V. (1980). Prevention of relapse in schizophrenia: An evaluation of fluphenazine decanoate. *Archives of General Psychiatry, 37,* 16-24.

Skinner, B.F. (1971). *Beyond freedom and dignity.* New York: A.A. Knopf.

Strachan, A.M., Leff, J.P., Goldstein, M., Doane, J., and Burtt, C. (1986). Emotional attitudes and direct communication in the families of schizophrenics: A cross-national replication. *British Journal of Psychiatry, 149,* 279-287.

Strauss, J.S. (1991). The person with delusions. *British Journal of Psychiatry, 159,* 57-61.

Taylor, S. (1983). Adjustment to threatening events: A theory of cognitive adaptation of paranoia. *American Psychologist, 38,* 1161-1173.

Vaughan, C. and Leff, J. (1976a). The influence of family and social factors on the course of psychiatric illness: A comparison of schizophrenic and depressed neurotic patients. *British Journal of Psychiatry, 129,* 125-137.

Vaughan, C. and Leff, J. (1976b). The measurement of expressed emotion in families of psychiatric patients. *British Journal of Social and Clinical Psychology, 15,* 15-165.

Wing, J.K. (1987). Psychosocial factors affecting the long-term course of schizophrenia. In J. Strauss, W. Boker, and H. Brenner, Eds., *Psychoscial treatment of schizophrenia.* Toronto, Canada: Hans-Huber Publishers.

Wing, J.K. and Brown, G.W. (1970). *Institutionalism and schizophrenia: A comparative study of three mental hospitals, 1960-1968.* Cambridge, UK: Cambridge University Press.

Yung, A.R., McGorry, P.D., McFarlane, C., Jackson, H., Patton, G., and Rakkar, A. (1996). Monitoring and care of young people at incipient risk of psychosis. *Schizophrenia Bulletin, 22,* 283-303.

Zubin, J. and Spring, B. (1977). Vulnerability: A new view of schizophrenia. *Journal of Abnormal Psychology, 86,* 103-126.

Chapter 12

Arieti, S. (1955). *Interpretation of schizophrenia.* New York: Brunner.

Bateson, G., Jackson, D., Haley, J., and Weakland, J. (1956). Towards a theory of schizophrenia. *Behavioral Science, 1,* 251-264.

Bion, W.R. (1984). *Second thoughts: Selected papers in psychoanalysis.* Northvale, NJ: Jason Aronson.

Bruch, H. (1978). A historical perspective of psychotherapy in schizophrenia. In W.E. Fann, I. Karacan, A. Pokorny, and R. Williams, Eds., *Phenomenology and treatment of schizophrenia* (pp. 311-324). New York: Spectrum.

Coursey, R.D. (1989). Psychotherapy with persons suffering from schizophrenia: The need for a new agenda. *Schizophrenia Bulletin, 15,* 349-353.

Freedman, A. (1991). American viewpoints on classification. *Integrative Psychiatry, 7,* 11-15.

Freud, S. (1924). The loss of reality in neurosis and psychosis. *Collected Papers, 2,* 277-282.

Fromm-Reichmann, F. (1954). Psychotherapy of schizophrenia. *American Journal of Psychology, 111,* 412-423.

Glass, J.M. (1985). *Delusion: Inner dimensions of political life.* Chicago, IL: University of Chicago Press.

Glass, J.M. (1995). *Psychosis and power.* Ithaca, NY: Cornell University Press.

Goldstein, M.J. (1985). Family factors that antedate the onset of schizophrenia and related disorders: The results of a fifteen year prospective longitudinal study. *Acta Psychiatrica Scandinavica, 71,* 7-18.

Grinspoon, L. (1969). The utility of psychotherapy with schizophrenia. *International Journal of Psychiatry, 8,* 727-729.

Gunderson, J. (1975). Introduction. In J. Gunderson and L. Mosher, Eds., *Psychotherapy of schizophrenia* (pp. 3-22). New York: Jason Aronson.

Holzman, P. (1975). Problems of psychoanalytic theories. In J. Gunderson and L. Mosher, Eds., *Psychotherapy of schizophrenia* (pp. 209-222). New York: Jason Aronson.

Iacono, W.G. (1993). Smooth pursuit oculomotor dysfunction as an index of schizophrenia. In R. L. Cromwell and C. R. Snyder, Eds., *Schizophrenia: Origins, processes, treatment, and outcome* (pp. 76-97). New York: Oxford University Press.

Karon, B.P. and VandenBos, G. (1970). Experience, medication, and the effectiveness of psychotherapy with schizophrenics. *British Journal of Psychiatry, 116,* 427-428.

Klein, M. (1946). Notes on Some Schizoid Mechanisms. *International Journal of Psychoanlaysis, 27,* 99-110.

Kringlen, E. (1987). Contributions of genetic studies on schizophrenia. In H. Hafner, W. Gattaz, and W. Janzarik, Eds., *Search for the causes of schizophrenia* (pp. 123-142). Berlin,Germany: Springer-Verlag.

Lewin, R. and Schulz, C. (1992). *Losing and fusing: Borderline transitional object and self relations.* Northvale, NJ: Aronson.

Lidz, T. (1973). *The origin and treatment of schizophrenic disorders.* New York: Basic Books.

Lidz, T. and Fleck, S. (1965). *Schizophrenia and the family.* New York: International Universities Press.

Mahler, M., Pine, F., and Bergman, A. (1975). *The psychological birth of the human infant: Symbiosis and individuation.* New York: Basic Books.

Mahler, M.S. (1978). *On human symbiosis and the vissicitudes of individuation.* New York: International Universities Press.

McGlashan, T.H. (1984). The Chestnut Lodge follow-up Study II: Long-term outcome of schizophrenia and the affective disorders. *Archives of General Psychiatry, 41,* 585-601.

Mirsky, A.F., Lochhead, S., Jones, B., Kugelmass, S., Walsh, D., and Kendler, K. (1992). On familial factors in the attentional deficit in schizophrenia: A review and report of two new subjects samples. *Journal of Psychiatric Research, 26,* 383-403.

Nuechterlein, K.H., Dawson, M., Gitlin, M., Ventura, J., Goldstein, M.J., Snyder, K., Yee, C., D., and Mintz, J. (1992). Developmental processes in schizophrenic disorders: Longitudinal studies of vulnerability and stress. *Schizophrenia Bulletin, 18,* 387-425.

Reich, W. (1973). Pathologic forms of self-esteem regulation. In T. Graeler, Ed., *Psychoanalytic contributions* (pp. 218-236). New York: International Universities Press.

Robbins, M. (1993). *Experiences of schizophrenia: An integration of the personal, scientific, and therapeutic.* New York: Guilford.

Rogers, C.R., Gendlin, E., Kiesler, D., and Truax, C. (1967). *The therapeutic relationship and its impact: A study of psychotherapy with schizophrenics.* Madison, WI: University of Wisconsin Press.

Schulz, G.G. and Kilgalen, R. (1967). *Case studies in schizophrenia.* New York: Basic Books.

Stone, M. (1986). Exploratory psychotherapy in schizophrenia-spectrum patients: A re-evaluation in light of long term follow-up. *Bulletin of the Menninger Clinic, 50,* 287-306.

Sullivan, H.S. (1931). The modified psychoanalytic treatment of schizophrenia. *American Journal of Psychiatry, 3,* 519-532.

Sullivan, H.S. (1938). Psychiatry: Introduction to the study of interpersonal relations. *Psychiatry, 1,* 121-134.

Sullivan, H.S. (1953). *The interpersonal theory of psychiatry.* New York: W.W. Norton.

Suomi, S. (1997). Long-term effects of different early rearing experiences on social, emotional, and physiological development in non human primates. In M. Keshavan and R. Murray, Eds., *Neurodevelopment and adult psychopathology* (pp. 104-116). New York: Cambridge University Press.

Tienari, P., Wynne, L., Moring, J., Lahti, I., Naarala, M., Sorri, A., Wahlberg, K., Saarento, O., Seitamaa, M., Kaleva, M., et al. (1994). The Finnish adoptive family study of schizophrenia. *British Journal of Psychiatry, 164* (Supplement 23), 20-26.

Winnicott, D.W. (1965). *The maturational processes and the facilitating environment: Studies in the theory of emotional development.* New York: International Universities Press.

Winnicott, D.W. (1975). *Collected papers.* New York: Basic Books.

Wynne, L. and Singer, M. (1963). Thought disorder and family relations of schizophrenics. I. A research strategy. II. A classification of forms of thinking. *Archives of General Psychiatry, 9,* 191-206.

Chapter 13

Alpert, M. (1985). The signs and symptoms of schizophrenia. *Comprehensive Psychiatry, 26,* 103-112.

Binswanger, L. (1960). Existential analysis of schizophrenia. *Journal of Existential Psychiatry, 1,* 157-165.

Blankenburg, W. (1969). Zur psychopathologie des ich-erlebens schizophrener (On the psychopathology of the I-experience of schizophrenics). In M. Spitzer, F. Uehlein, and G. Oepen, Eds., *Psychopathology and philosophy* (pp. 184-197). Berlin, Germany: Springer.

Boss, M. (1963). *Psychoanalysis and daseinsanalysis.* New York: Basic Books.

Bovet, P. and Parnas, J. (1993). Schizophrenic delusions: A phenomenological approach. *Schizophrenia Bulletin, 19,* 579-597.

Conrad, K. (1958). *Die beginnende Schizophrenia. Versuch einer Gestaltanalyse des Wahns* (The beginnings of schizophrenia. An attempt at a gestalt analysis of madness). Stuttgart, Germany: Theeme.

Edgar, D. (1984). *Mary Barnes: Two accounts of a journey through madness.* London, UK: Methuen.

Heidegger, M. (1975). *The basic problems of phenomenology.* Translated by A. Hofstadter. Bloomington, IN: Indiana University Press.

Jaspers, K. (1923). *Allemeine psychopathologi* (General psychopathology), Third edition. Berlin, Germany: Springer-Verlag.

Kepinski, A. (1974). *Schizofrenia.* Warsaw, Poland: Zaklad Wyddawnictw Lekarskich.

Laing, R.D. (1967). *The politics of experience.* New York: Pantheon.

Maturana, H. R. and Varela, F. (1988). *The tree of knowledge. The biological roots of human understanding.* Boston, MA: Shambala.

Merleau-Ponty, M. ([1945] 1962). *Phenomenology of perception.* Translated by C. Smith. London, UK: Routledge and Kegan Paul.

Mosher, L.R. (1995). The Soteria Project: The first-generation American alternatives to psychiatric hospitalization. In R. Warner, Ed., *Alternatives to the hospital for acute psychiatric treatment* (pp. 111-151). Washington, DC: American Psychiatric Press.

Parnas, J. (1995). Epistomological issues in psychiatric research. *Comprehensive Psychiatry, 36,* 167-181.

Parnas, J. and Jorgensen, A. (1989). A premorbid psychopathology in schizophrenia spectrum. *British Journal of Psychiatry, 155,* 623-627.

Tatossian, A. (1979). *Phenomenology of psychoses.* Paris, France: Masson.

Chapter 14

Alanen, Y. (1997). *Schizophrenia: Its origins and need adapted treatment.* London, UK: Karnak Books.

Asarnow, J.R., Lewis, J., Doane, J., Goldstein, M.J., and Rodnick, E.H. (1982). Family interaction and the course of adolescent psychopathology: An analysis of adolescent and parent effects. *Journal of Abnormal Child Psychology, 10,* 427-442.

Bateson, G. (1978). The double-bind theory—Misunderstood? *Psychiatric News,* April 21, p. 40.

Bateson, G., Jackson, D., Haley, J., and Weakland, J. (1956). Toward a theory of schizophrenia. *Behavioral Science, 1,* 251-264.

Bateson, G., Jackson, D., Haley, J., and Weakland, J. (1963). A note on the double-bind 1962. *Family Process, 2,* 154-161.

Bowen, M. (1960). A family concept of schizophrenia. In D. Jackson, Ed., *The etiology of schizophrenia* (pp. 364-372). New York: Basic Books.

Bowen, M., Dysinger, R., and Basamania, B. (1959). The role of the father in families with a schizophrenic patient. *American Journal of Psychiatry, 115,* 1017-1020.

Doane, J.A., West, K., and Goldstein, M.J. (1981). Parental communication deviance and affective style: Predictors of subsequent spectrum disorders in vulnerable adolescents. *Archives of General Psychiatry, 38,* 679-685.

Esterson, A. (1970). *The leaves of spring.* London, UK: Pelican.

Fromm-Reichmann, F. (1948). Notes on the development of treatment of schizophrenics by psychoanalytic psychotherapy. *Psychiatry, 11,* 263-273.

Goldstein, M.J. (1985). Family factors that antedate the onset of schizophrenia and related disorders: The results of a fifteen year prospective longitudinal study. *Acta Psychiatrica Scandinavica, 71,* 7-18.

Goldstein, M.J. and Rodnick, E. (1975). The family's contribution to the etiology of schizophrenia: Current status. *Schizophrenia Bulletin, 14,* 48-63.

Goldstein, M.J., Rodnick, E.H., Jones, J., McPherson, S., and West, K. (1978). Familial precursors of schizophrenia spectrum disorders. In L.C. Wynne, R.L. Cromwell, and S. Matthysse, Eds., *The nature of schizophrenia* (pp. 487-498). New York: Wiley.

Haley, J. (1959). An interactional description of schizophrenia. *Psychiatry, 22,* 321-332.

Hirsch, S. and Leff, J. (1975). *Abnormalities in parents of schizophrenics.* Oxford, UK: Oxford University Press.

Howells, J.G. (1968). Family psychopathology and schizophrenia. In J.G. Howells, Ed., *Modern perspectives in world psychiatry* (pp. 317-337). Edinburgh, Scotland: Oliver and Body.

Laing, R.D. and Esterson, A. (1964). *Sanity, Madness, and the Family.* New York: Basic Books.

Lidz, R. and Lidz, T. (1949). The family environment of schizophrenic patients. *American Journal of Psychiatry, 106,* 332-345.

Lidz, T. (1973). *The origin and treatment of schizophrenic disorders.* New York: Basic Books.

Lidz, T. (1978). Egocentric cognitive regression and the family setting of schizophrenic disorders. In L.Wynne, R. Cromwell, and S. Matthysse, Eds., *The nature of schizophrenia* (pp. 526-533). New York: Wiley.

Lidz, T., Singer, M., Schafer, S., and Fleck, S. (1965). The mothers of schizophrenic patients. In T. Lidz, S. Fleck, and A. Cornelison, Eds., *Schizophrenia and the family* (pp. 290-335). New York: International Universities Press.

Madanes, C. (1981). Strategic family therapy. In A. Gurman and D. Kniskern, Eds., *Handbook of Family Therapy,* Volume 2 (pp. 396-416). New York: Aldine.

Mahler, M. (1952). On child psychosis and schizophrenia: Autistic and symbiotic infantile psychoses. *Psychoanalytic Study of the Child, 7,* 286-305.

Meehl, P.E. (1962). Schizotaxia, schizotypy, schizophrenia. *American Psychologist, 17,* 827-838.

Mishler, E. and Waxler, N. (1968). *Interaction in families: An experimental study of family process and schizophrenia.* New York: Wiley.

Parsons, T. and Bales, R. (1955). *Family socialization and interaction process.* Glencoe, IL: Free Press.

Ringuette, E. and Kennedy, T. (1966). An experimental study of the double bind hypothesis. *Journal of Abnormal Psychology, 71,* 136-141.

Rolf, J.D. and Knight, R. (1981). Family characteristics, childhood symptoms and adult outcome in schizophrenia. *Journal of Abnormal Psychology, 90,* 510-520.

Sanislow, C.A. and Carson, R.C. (2001). Schizophrenia: A critical examination. In P. B. Sutker and H. Adams, Eds., *Comprehensive handbook of psychopathology* (pp. 403-441). New York: Kluwer/Plenum.

Singer, M.T. and Wynne, L.C. (1963). Differentiating characteristics of parents of childhood schizophrenics, childhood neurotics and young adult schizophrenics. *American Journal of Psychiatry, 120,* 234-243.

Singer, M.T. and Wynne, L.C. (1965). Thoughts disorder and family relations of schizophrenics: IV. Results and implications. *Archives of General Psychiatry, 13,* 471-476.

Singer, M.T., Wynne, L.C., and Toohey, M.L. (1978) In L.C. Wynne, R.L. Cromwell, and S. Matthysse, Eds., *The nature of schizophrenia* (pp. 499-511). New York: Wiley.

Slater, E. and Roth, M. (1969). *Clinical psychiatry.* London, UK: Baillere, Tindall and Cassell.

Tienari, P., Wynne, L., Moring, J., Lahti, I., Naarala, M., Sorri, A., Wahlberg, K., Saarento, O., Seitamaa, M., Kaleva, M., et al. (1994). The Finnish adoptive family study of schizophrenia. *British Journal of Psychiatry, 164* (Supplement 23), 20-26.

Whitehead, A.N. and Russell, B. (1910). *Principia mathematica.* Cambridge, UK: Cambridge University Press.

Wynne, L.C. (1977). Schizophrenics and their families: Research on parental communication. In J.M. Tanner, Ed., *Developments in psychiatric research* (pp. 254-286). London, UK: Hodder and Stroughton.

Chapter 15

Baum, A.S. and Burns, D. (1993). *A nation in denial: The truth about homelessness.* Boulder, CO: Westview.

Beard, J., Propst, R., and Malamud, T. (1982). The Fountain House model of psychiatric rehabilitation. *Psychosocial Rehabilitation Journal, 5,* 47-59.

Bockoven, J. (1963). *Treatment in American psychiatry.* New York: Springer.

Bond, G.R., Witheridge, T., Dincin, J., Wasmer, D., and Pollack, P. (1990). Assertive community treatment for frequent users of psychiatric hospitals in a large city: A controlled study. *American Journal of Community Psychology, 18,* 865-891.

Brown, G.W. and Birley, J. (1968). Crisis and life changes and the onset of schizophrenia. *Journal of Health and Social Behavior, 9,* 203-214.

Ciompi, L. (1997). The Soteria-concept. Theoretical bases and practical 13-year experience with a milieu-therapeutic approach of acute schizophrenia. *Psychiatria et neurologia Japonica, 99,* 634-650.

Consumer Health Sciences (1997). *The schizophrenia patient project: Brief summary of results—September, 1997,* Princeton, NJ: Consumer Health Sciences.

Fairweather, G.W., Sanders, D., Maynard, H., Cressler, D.L. (1969). *Community life for the mentally ill.* Chicago, IL: Aldine.

Franklin, J.S., Kornblith, S., Greenwald, D., DiBarry, A., Cooley, S., and Flesher, S. (1987). An evaluation of case management. *American Journal of Public Health, 77,* 674-678.

Fromm-Reichmann, F. (1948). Notes on the development of treatment of schizophrenia by psychoanalytic psychotherapy. *Psychiatry, 11,* 263-273.

Glass, J.M. (1989). *Private terror/public life.* Ithaca, NY: Cornell University Press.

Hogarty, G.E., Kornblith, S., Greenwald, D., DiBarry, A., Cooley, S., Flesher, S., and Leff, J. (1995). Personal therapy: A disorder relevant psychotherapy for schizophrenia. *Schizophrenia Bulletin, 21,* 379-393.

Jablensky, A., Satorius, N., Ernberg, G., and Harrow, M. (1992). Schizophrenia manifestations, incidence and course in different cultures: A World Health Organization ten-country study. *Psychological Medicine, 51,* supplement 20, 133-184.

Jacobs, H.E., Wissusik, D., and Collier, R. (1992). Correlations between psychiatric disabilities and vocational outcome. *Hospital and Community Psychiatry, 43,* 365-369.

Kane, J.M. and Marder, S. (1993). Pharmacologic treatment of schizophrenia. *Schizophrenia Bulletin, 19,* 287-302.

Laing, R.D. (1967). *The Politics of Experience.* London, UK: Penguin.

Lamb, H.R. (1997). The new state mental hospitals in the community. *Psychiatric Services, 48,* 1307-1310.

Lamb, H.R. (1998). Deinstitutionalization at the beginning of the new millennium. *Harvard Review of Psychiatry* (May/June), 1-10.

Levine, I.S., Lezak, A., and Goldman, H. (1986). Community support systems for the homeless mentally ill. In E.L. Bassuk, Ed., *The mental health needs of homeless persons.* San Francisco, CA: Jossey-Bass.

Menninger, K. (1959). Psychiatric diagnosis. *Bulletin of the Menninger clinic, 23,* 226-240.

Morse, G.A., Calsyn, R., Allen, G., Tempelhoff, B., Ashbury, H., and Howerton, J. (1992). Experimental comparison of the effects of three treatment programs for homeless mentally ill people. *Hospital and Community Psychiatry, 43,* 1005-1010.

Mosher, L. (1995). The first-generation American alternatives to psychiatric hospitalization. In R. Warner (Ed.), *Alternatives to the Hospital for Acute Psychiatric Treatment* (pp. 111-129). Washington, DC: American Psychiatric Press.

Redlick, R.W., Witkin, M., Atay, J., and Manderscheid, R. (1994). Highlights of organized mental health services in 1990 and major national and state trends. In

R. Manderscheid and R. Somnenschein, M., Eds., *Mental health, United States.* 1994. DHHS Publication No. (SMA) 94-3000. Rockville, MD: U.S. Department of Health and Human Services.

Richardson, J. (1987). A road to somewhere: Fountain House and transitional employment. In Breggin, Ed., *Psychosocial approaches to the treatment of schizophrenia* (pp. 215-226). New York: St. Martin's Press.

Stein, L.I. (1992). Innovating against the current. In L.I. Stein, Ed., *Innovative community health programs* (New Directions for Mental Health Services, 62) (pp. 48-67). San Francisco, CA: Jossey-Bass.

Stein, L.I. and Test, M.A. (1980). Alternative to mental hospital treatment. I. Conceptual model, treatment program, and clinical evaluation. *Archives of General Psychiatry, 37,* 392-397.

Sullivan, H.S. (1952). *Schizophrenia as a human process.* New York: W. W. Norton.

Szasz, T. (1970). *Ideology and Insanity: Essays on the Psychiatric Dehumanization of Man.* New York: Doubleday.

Test, M.A. (1992). The training in community living model. In R.P. Liberman, Ed., *Handbook of Psychiatric Rehabilitation* (pp. 153-170). New York: Macmillan.

Test, M.A., Knoedler, W., Allness, D., Burke, S., and Wallisch, L. (1991). Long-term community care through an assertive continuous treatment team. In C.A. Tamminga and S. Schulz, Eds., *Advances in neuropsychiatry and psychopharmacology,* Volume I: *Schizophrenia research* (pp. 239-246). New York: Raven Press.

Torrey, E.F. (1997). *Out of the shadows: Confronting America's mental illness crisis.* New York: Wiley.

Warner, R. (1994). *Recovery from schizophrenia: Psychiatry and the political economy,* Second edition. New York: Routledge.

Warner, R. (2000). *The environment of schizophrenia: Innovations in policy and communications.* London, UK: Brunner-Routledge.

Warner, R. and Polak, P. (1995). The economic advancement of the mentally ill in the community: Economic opportunities. *Community Mental Health Journal, 31,* 381-396.

Weisbrod, B.A., Test, M.A., and Stein, L. (1980). Alternative to mental hospital treatment: III. Economic benefit-cost analysis. *Archives of General Psychiatry, 37,* 400-405.

Wing, J.K. and Brown, G.W. (1970). *Institutionalism and schizophrenia: A comparative study of three mental hospitals, 1960-1968.* Cambridge, UK: Cambridge University Press.

Chapter 16

Alanen, Y.O. (1997). *Schizophrenia: Its origins and need-adapted treatment.* London, UK: Karnac Books.

Andreasen, N.C., O'Leary, D., Cizadlo, T., Arndt, S., Rezai, K., Ponto, L.L., Watkins, G.L., and Hichwa, R.D. (1996). Schizophrenia and cognitive dysmetria: A positron emission tomography study of dysfunctional prefrontal-thalamic-cerebellar circuitry. *Proceedings of the National Academy of Sciences of the USA, 93*, 9985-9990.

Bentall, R. (1990). *Reconstructing schizophrenia.* London, UK: Routledge.

Chapman, L.J., Chapman, J.P., Kwapil, T., Eckblad, M., and Zinser, M. (1994). Putatively psychosis-prone subjects 10 years later. *Journal of Abnormal Psychology, 103*, 171-183.

Claridge, G. (1990). Can a disease model of schizophrenia survive? In G. Bentall, Ed., *Reconstructing schizophrenia* (pp. 157-183). London, UK: Routledge.

Glass, J.M. (1985). *Delusion.* Chicago, IL: University of Chicago Press.

Goldstein, M.J. (1985). Family factors that antedate the onset of schizophrenia and related disorders: The results of a fifteen year prospective longitudinal study. *Acta Psychiatrica Scandinavica, 71*, 7-18.

Gottesman, I.I. and Shields, J. (1982). *Schizophrenia: The epigenetic puzzle.* Cambridge, UK: Cambridge University Press.

Green, M.F. (1998). *Schizophrenia from a neurocognitive perspective: Probing the impenetrable darkness.* Boston, MA: Allyn and Bacon.

Kerr, A. and Snaith, P. (1986). *Contemporary issues in schizophrenia.* London, UK: Gaskell.

Leff, J.P. and Vaughn, C. (1981). The role of maintenance therapy and relatives expressed emotions in relapse of schizophrenia: A two-year followup. *British Journal of Psychiatry, 139*, 102-104.

Meehl, P.E. (1962). Schizotaxia, schizotypy, schizophrenia. *American Psychologist, 17*, 827-838.

Mesulam, M. (1990). Schizophrenia and the brain. *New England Journal of Medicine, 311*, 842-845.

Nuechterlein, K.H. and Dawson, M.E. (1984). Information processing and attentional functioning in the developmental course of schizophrenic disorders. *Schizophrenia Bulletin, 10*, 160-203.

Pilgrim, D. (1990). Competing histories of madness. In R. Bentall, Ed., *Reconstructing schizophrenia* (pp. 211-233). London, UK: Routledge.

Scheflen, A. (1981). *Levels of schizophrenia.* New York: Brunner/Mazel.

Suomi, S. (1997). Long-term effects of different early rearing experiences on social, emotional, and physiological development in non human primates. In M. Keshavan and R. Murray, Eds., *Neurodevelopment and adult psychopathology* (pp. 104-116). New York: Cambridge University Press.

Tienari, P., Wynne, L., Moring, J., Lahti, I., Naarala, M., Sorri, A., Wahlberg, K., Saarento, O., Seitamaa, M., Kaleva, M., et al. (1994). The Finnish adoptive family study of schizophrenia. *British Journal of Psychiatry, 164* (Supplement 23), 20-26.

Warner, R. (1994). *Recovery from schizophrenia: Psychiatry and political economy,* Second edition. London, UK: Routledge and Kegan Paul.

Watt, N.F. (1984). "In a nutshell": The first two decades of high-risk research on schizophrenia. In N.F. Watt, J. Anthony, L. Wynne, and J. Rolf, Eds., *Children at risk for schizophrenia: A longitudinal perspective* (pp. 145-172). Cambridge: UK: Cambridge University Press.

Widiger, T. (1997). Mental disorders as discrete clinical conditions: Dimensional versus categorical classification. In S.M. Turner and M. Hersen, Eds., *Adult psychopathology and diagnosis* (pp. 3-23). New York: Wiley.

Index

Abulia, 177
Accessory symptoms, 15, 18
Adaptive equilibration, 228
Adoptee as proband method, 108
Adoption studies, 108
Affective psychoses, 4
Affective regulation, 88
Agranulocytosis, 142
Akathesia, 142
Akil, M., 126, 134
Alanen, Y.O., 251, 290
Alpert, M., 233
American Psychiatric Association, 23, 25, 26, 30, 32, 34
Amygdala, 127
Anderson, C.M., 182
Andreasen, N.C., 10, 15, 34, 44, 63, 128, 140, 132, 136, 290
Angermeyer, M., 43
Anhedonia, 87
Antipsychotic medications, 139-148
Applied behavioral analysis, 165
Arieti, S., 170, 199
Arndt, S., 44, 63
Asarnow, R.F., 157, 261
Asperger's disorder, 35, 176
Association studies, 117-118
Associational weakness, 19-20
Astrup, C., 42
Atypical antipsychotic medications, 144-147
Autism, 35
Aversive drift, 87, 223
Avicenna, 5
Ayllon, T., 166

Baron, M., 35

Barondes, S.H., 116
Barr, C., 121
Bates, C.E., 39
Bateson, G., 181, 227, 253
Baum, K.M., 158
Beard, J., 272
Beasley, C.M., 146
Beck, A., 168
Behavior modification, 165-167
Behaviorism, 165
Belcher, J.R., 53
Bellack, A.S., 190
Benjamin, L.A., 110
Bentall, R.P., 58, 74
Beratis, S., 42
Bergson, C., 148
Berman, K.F., 137
Berner, P., 23
Bion, W., 206, 208, 210
Binswanger, L., 238, 242
Bland, R.C., 45
Blankenburg, W., 237
Bleuler, E., 14, 17, 20, 22, 58
Bleuler, M., 45, 47, 106
Bloom, F.E., 137
Bogerts, B., 126, 131
Bond, G.R., 276
Boss, M., 242
Bovet, P., 59, 234, 236
Bowen, M., 245
Bowlby, J., 195
Bradbury, T.N., 43
Brain abnormalities in schizophrenia, 128-130
Bray, N.J., 116, 137, 158
Breier, A., 49
Brenner, H., 160

Brockington, I.F., 36, 74
Broen, W.E., 155
Brown, R., 57
Bruch, H., 199
Buchanan, R.W., 51, 123
Buschbaum, M.S., 132

Cadenhead, K.S., 105
Calev, V., 155
Campbell, R.J., 79
Cancro, R., 103
Cannon, T.P., 80
Carlsson, A., 148, 151
Carlsson, M., 131, 142, 148
Carone, B., 49
Carpenter, W.T., 30, 125
Casanova, M., 128
Cassou, B., 107, 111
Castle, D.J., 42, 43
Catecholamines, 142
Cerebellum, 132
Chadwick, P.D.P., 173, 175
Chaotic families, 25
Chapman, L., 81, 209
Charcot, J., 8
Chestnut Lodge, 49
Chromosomal abnormalities, 118-119
Ciompi, L., 46, 280
Claridge, G., 287, 290
Cleghorn, J.M., 132
Cognitive dysmetria, 130-132
Cognitive enhancement therapy, 152
Cognitive slippage, 87, 223
Cognitive therapy, 168-173
Cognitively orientated therapy, 180-
    182
Communication deviance, 253-254,
    257
Comorbidity, 52-53
Computerized tomography (CAT), 126
Concordance, 106-107
Conrad, K., 237
Consanguinity studies, 104
Consumer Health Sciences, 280

Cooper, J.E., 26
Copernican revolution, 5
Copernicus, 5
Corcoran, R., 177
Cornblatt, B.A., 87, 162
Corrigan, P.W., 160
Cortical-evoked potentials, 119-120
Course of schizophrenia, 41-46
Coursey, R.D., 230
Creese, I., 144
Crocetti, G.J., 39
Cross-fostering method, 110
Crow, T.J., 50
Csernansky, J.G., 127
Cuesta, M.J., 63
Cytogenetic studies, 118-119

Daniel, D.G., 123, 137
Danish-American adoption studies, 35,
    110-113
Darwin, C., 6
Daseinsanalysis, 238-242
Davidson, L., 173, 195
Davis, J.M., 140
Daviss, S.R., 126
Dawson, M.E., 155
Defective rationality, 249
Defendorf, A.R., 10
Deficit symptoms, 51-52
Deinstitutionalization, 268
DeLisi, L.E., 126
Delusions, 58, 173-175
    basic, 58
    cognitive deficits, 61-63
    elaborations, 58
    formation, 236-238
    meaning structures, 236
    myths, 60
Dementia, 12
Dementia praecox, 9-13
Dereistic thinking, 9-13
Deutch, A.Y., 145
Diagnostic and Statistical Manuals
    I-IV, 23-34
Diathesis stress, 87-92

Disorganization symptoms, 63-66
Dixon, L., 53
Doane, J.A., 261
Dohan, F.C., 39
Dopamine, 134
    pathways, 143
    receptors, 143-144
Double-bind theory, 253-256
Drury, V., 174
Dual diagnoses, 53

Early signs of psychosis, 178
Eaton, W.W., 39
Edgar, D., 242
Edwards, J., 177
Egocentric overinclusion, 169
Egocentricity, 250
Einheitspsychose, 7
Electroencephalographic activity, 105
Endicott, J., 24
Engel, G.L., 94
Engulfment, 219
Environment mother, 211
Epistemology, 93
Erlenmeyer-Kimling, L., 90
Esquirol, J.E., 6
Esterson, A., 263
Evoked potentials, 119
Expressed emotion, 86-88
Extrapyramidal symptoms, 141
Eye tracking deficits, 156
Eysenck, H.J., 84

Fahy, T., 148
Fairweather, G., 281
Falloon, I.R.H., 182
False-self system, 260
Family
    communication, 253-256
    Danish research, 110-113
    Finnish adoption studies, 113-115,
        262
    theories, 243-263
    UCLA longitudinal study, 260

Family consanguinity research, 104
Farde, L., 148
Feighner, J.P., 30
Feinberg, J., 158
Fenton, W.S., 44, 52
Fisher, M., 103
Flor-Henry, P., 43
Fountain House program, 271-274
Fowler, D., 174
Fowles, D.C., 79
Freedman, R., 118, 200
Freud, S., 19, 201
Frith, C.D., 129
Fromm-Reichmann, F., 202
Functional psychosis, 4
Fundamental symptoms, 15

Gainullin, R.G., 39
Galen, 5
Galvani, L., 6
Gamma-aminobutyric acid (GABA),
        142
Gao, W.J., 148
Garety, P.A., 174
Gender, 42-43
General systems theory, 93-96
Genetic studies, 101-121
    adoption studies, 108
    concordance, 103
    linkage, 113
    penetrance, 103
    twin studies, 106-108
Genotype, 103
Geodon, 145
Gheel, Belgium, 281
Glass, J.M., 208, 218, 268, 270
Glutamate, 147-151
Goff, D.C., 148
Goldberg, T.E., 123
Goldstein, J., 43
Goldstein, M.J., 244, 289
Gottesman, I.I., 23, 79, 90, 94, 102, 106
Grace, A.A., 147
Green, A., 120
Green, M.F., 155, 288

Griesinger, W., 7
Grinspoon, L., 231
Gruszecka, A., 60
Gunderson, J., 230
Gunne, L.M., 142
Gur, R.E., 43
Gurling, H.M.D., 120
Guze, S.B., 37, 80

Haas, G., 43
Hafner, H., 43
Haley, J., 253, 255
Harding, C., 48, 152
Harrow, M., 33, 36
Heaton, R.K., 156
Hegarty, J.D., 45, 49, 152
Heidegger, M., 234
Heinroth, J.C., 6
Heston, L.L., 109
Hierarchical systems models, 221-231
Hippocampus, 127
Hippocrates, 5
Hirsch, S., 260
Hoffman, B.F., 45
Hogarty, G., 161, 182, 188
Hollingshead, A., 41
Holzman, P.S., 156, 200, 229
Horowitz, M.J., 180
Howells, J.G., 246
Hyperkinetic movements, 159
Hypokrisia, 88

Iacono, W.G., 80
Incidence, 40
Index cases, 109
Insanitas, 3
Insanity, 3
Integrated psychological therapy,
        160-161
International Pilot Study
        of Schizophrenia (IPSS), 40,
        53-54, 269

Jablensky, A., 40, 45, 269
Jackson, H., 106, 178
Jackson, J.H., 50
Jacobs, L., 170
Janet, P., 8
Jaspers, K., 29, 59, 234
Jibson, M.D., 145
Jones, P., 121
Joseph, J., 106, 110, 112, 115
Judgment, 105
Jung, C., 14

Kahlbaum, K.L., 8
Kane, J.M., 141, 285
Karlsson, J.L., 103
Kapur, S., 147
Karon, B.P., 231
Kashner, T.M., 53
Kavanaugh, D.J., 183
Kay, S.R., 50
Kazdin, A.E., 167
Kendell, R.E., 26, 32
Kendler, K.S., 35, 105
Kepinski, A., 238
Kerr, A., 287
Keshavan, M.S., 163
Kety, S.S., 35, 102, 108, 110
Kingdon, D.G., 173
Kingsley Hall, 277
Kirkpatrick, B., 124
Klein, M., 205
Kleinman, A., 94
Kling, A.S., 137
Kohn, M.L., 41
Kraepelin, E., 8, 10, 13, 37, 40, 42, 44
Kringlen, E., 101, 106
Kuipers, L., 86

Laing, R.D., 241, 260
Lamb, R., 281
Langfeldt, G., 27
Language, 57-59
Lansky, M.R., 59

Leff, J.P., 86, 182, 289
Lenzenweger, M.G., 63, 105
Levi-Strauss, C., 60
Levy, D., 124
Levine, I.S., 270
Lewin, P., 207
Lewine, R., 42
Lewis, S.W., 42
Lewontin, D., 107
Liberman, R.P., 171
Liddle, P., 63, 126, 129
Lidz, R., 92
Lidz, T., 181, 243, 251, 260
Linkage studies, 119-120
Liotti, G., 172

Madanes, C., 256
Magaro, P., 34
Magnetic resonance imaging (MRI)
    studies, 126-127
Maher, B.A., 57, 61, 137
Matthysse, S., 160
Maturana, H.R., 234
McCann, L., 180
McCarley, R.W., 128
McGlashan, T.H., 35, 45, 49, 83
McGorry, P.D., 177
McGuffin, P., 86, 101, 120
McGuire, P.K., 130
Mednick, S.A., 81
Meehl, P.E., 35, 86, 94, 102
Meichenbaum, D., 171
Meltzer, H., 144, 289
Menninger, K., 277
Merleau-Ponty, M., 233
Mesulam, M., 289
Metathinking, 129-130
Meyer, A.F., 13
Mirsky, A.F., 105, 157
Mishler, E., 257, 260
Modular disjunction, 132-134
Moldin, S.O., 120
Monozygotic twins, 106-107
Morel, B., 8

Morse, G.A., 276
Mosher, L.R., 242, 277
Mueser, K.T., 157, 171, 184
Murray, R., 62, 121

Narcissism, 209
Nasrallah, H.A., 156
Neale, J., 110
Negative symptoms, 50-52, 72-74
    hypofrontality, 136
Neill, J., 90
Neumann, C.S., 158
Neurobiology, 123
    modular systems, 128-134
Neurochemistry, 131-135
Neurocognition, 156, 288
Neurodevelopment, 158-160
Neuroleptic syndrome, 139
Neuroleptics, 139
Nihilism, 70
Nodes of dysfunction, 131
Norman, R.M., 85
Nucleus accumbens, 127-129
Nuechterlein, K.H., 80, 86, 156, 288

O'Donnell, P., 127, 134, 136
O'Driscoll, G.A., 105
Olanzapine, 145
Ott, J., 120
Outcome studies, 46-50
Owens, D.G., 140

Pakkenberg, B., 126
Palha, A.P., 5
Palmer, B., 157
Palo Alto research group, 253-254
Pam, A., 107
Paradiso, A., 128
Paraphrenia, 10
Parent as proband method, 109
Parkinsonian symptoms, 143
Parnas, J., 233, 236

Parsons, T., 247
Penetrance, 103
Penn, D.L., 157
Pennartz, C.M., 135
Perris, C., 169, 172
Personal therapy, 191-195
Phencyclidine (PCP), 148
Phenomenology, 233
Phenothiazine medications, 141-143
Phenotype, 103
Photosensitivity, 142
Physicalism, 165
Pilgrim, D., 291
Pinel, P., 7
Positive symptoms, 50-52
Predicative thinking, 169
Prefrontal cortex, 131-132
Premorbid symptoms, 52
Prenatal factors, 160
Prodromal phase, 43
Program of Assertive Community
    Treatment (PACT), 274-276
Psychodyamic therapy, 199-227
Psychoeducational therapy, 181-188
Psychosis, 3
Psychotic conditions, 4-5
Psychoticism, 66-72

Quarrelsome characteristics, 63, 87

Rabkin, J., 92
Rado, S., 87
Ram, R., 49
Rao, M.L., 136
Raven Progressive Matrices, 83
Reality testing, 57
Redlick, R.W., 267
Regier, D.A., 53
Reich, W., 219
Reider, R.O., 11, 21
Reliability of diagnosis, 36
Rennie, T.A., 46
Research diagnostic criteria, 30

Richardson, J., 272
Ringuette, E., 256
Risch, N., 87, 121
Risk-vulnerability model, 84-85
Risperdal, 145
Risperidone, 145
Robbins, M., 94, 96, 200, 221, 230
Roberts, G.W., 128, 169
Rochester research group, 257
Rogers, C.R., 203
Rolf, J.D., 260
Rose, S., 107
Rosenthal, D., 104, 106, 110

Saccadic eye movements, 105, 156
Sanislow, C.A., 83, 244
Satir, V., 253
Satorius, N., 40, 53
Schaub, A., 189, 191
Scheflen, A., 289
Schizmatic, 249
Schizophrenia, 14
    accessory symptoms, 15-17
    fundamental symptoms, 15-17
    group of, 14-15
    season of birth, 43, 81-83
    spectrum disorders, 34, 102-103
    subtypes, 34
    symptoms, 63-65
Schizotaxia, 35, 87
Schizotypal, 81
Schizotypy, 87-88
Schneider, F., 108, 121
Schneider, K., 28
Schooler, N.R., 182
Schulz, G.G., 221
Searles, H., 61
Seeman, P., 134
Semon, R.W., 19
Separation-individuation, 217
Seroquel, 145
Serotonin, 146
Servan-Schreiber, D., 157
Siever, L.J., 35, 157
Siirala, M., 61

Silbersweig, D.A., 130
Silverton, L., 41
Singer, M.T., 257, 261
Single photon emission computed
    tomography (SPECT), 131
Skewed families, 249
Skinner, B.F., 165
Slater, E., 103
Snyder, S.H., 110
Social cognition, 175-176
Social skills training, 171, 184-185
Spaulding, W.D., 153, 161
Spitzer, M., 135
Spitzer, R., 7, 62
Stein, L.I., 52
Stevens, J.R., 127
Stierlin, H., 19
Stone, M., 204
Stoof, J.C., 144
Storch, A., 60
Strachan, A.M., 182
Straub, R.E., 117
Strauss, J.S., 45, 58, 168
Stress, 85
Stress-vulnerability, 85-86
Suddath, R.L., 126, 134
Sullivan, H.S., 61, 202, 205
Suomi, S., 231, 291
Symptoms, 63-64
Szasz, T., 26

Tallent, R.A., 105
Tamminga, C.A., 63
Tardive dyskinesia, 141
Task groups, 281
Tatossian, A., 234
Taylor, S., 179
Test, M.A., 274
Thaker, G.K., 120
Thalamus, 132
Tienari, P., 103, 113, 231, 261, 263
Token economy programs, 166
Toomey, R., 162

Torrey, E.F., 39, 40, 108
Transitional experiences, 213
    objects, 214
Tuma, A.H., 140
Turner, R.J., 41
Twin studies, 106-108
Two-hit model, 81-82
Typical antipsychotic medications,
    140-142

UCLA family research studies, 260-261
Ulas, J., 134
US/UK Diagostic Project, 26

Vailant, G.F., 45
Validity of diagnosis, 36
Valone, K., 86
Vaughan, C.E., 86
Vermont outcome study, 49
von Bertanlanffy, L., 95
Vulnerability, 83

Walker, E.F., 158
Warner, R., 39, 43, 54, 152, 271, 291
Wasylenki, D., 52
Watt, N.F., 288
Watzlawick, P., 253
Weakland, J., 253, 255
Weinberger, D.R., 126, 156
Weisbrod, B.A., 285
Wender, P.H., 110
Whitehead, A.N., 253
Wible, C.G., 129
Widiger, T., 289
Wiersma, D., 52
Wing, J.K., 30, 45, 167, 183, 268
Winnicott, D.W., 210, 216
Winters, K., 33
Wisconsin Card Sort Test, 156
Wolkin, A., 126, 129

World Health Organization (WHO),
40, 45
International Pilot Study
of Schizophrenia, 53-55
Wrobel, J., 3, 59
Wundt, W., 8
Wykes, T., 161
Wynne, L.C., 111, 227, 257, 260

Zyprexa, 145